ALAIN BADIOU

SUNY series, Intersections: Philosophy and Critical Theory

Rodolphe Gasché, editor

ALAIN BADIOU

Philosophy and Its Conditions

Edited by
Gabriel Riera

State University of New York Press

Published by
State University of New York Press, Albany

© 2005 State University of New York

All rights reserved

Printed in the United States of America

No part of this book may be used or reproduced in any manner whatsoever without written permission. No part of this book may be stored in a retrieval system or transmitted in any form or by any means including electronic, electrostatic, magnetic tape, mechanical, photocopying, recording, or otherwise without the prior permission in writing of the publisher.

For information, address State University of New York Press,
90 State Street, Suite 700, Albany, NY 12207

Production by Judith Block
Marketing by Susan Petrie

Library of Congress Cataloging-in-Publication Data

Alain Badiou : philosophy and its conditions / edited by Gabriel Riera.
     p. cm — (SUNY series, Intersections : Philosophy and Critical Theory)
  Includes bibliographical references and index.
  ISBN 0-7914-6503-9 (hardcover / alk. paper) — ISBN 0-7914-6504-7 (pbk. : alk. paper)
  1. Badiou, Alain.　I. Riera, Gabriel.　II. Series: Intersections (Albany, N.Y.)

B2430.B274A63 2005
194—dc22
                          2004018837

10 9 8 7 6 5 4 3 2 1

Contents

Acknowledgments	vii
Abbreviations	ix
Introduction. Alain Badiou: The Event of Thinking Gabriel Riera	1
PART ONE. MATHEMATICS = ONTOLOGY	**21**
1. On Alain Badiou's Treatment of Category Theory in View of a Transitory Ontology Norman Madarasz	23
2. The Ontological Dispute: Badiou, Heidegger, and Deleuze Miguel de Beistegui	45
PART TWO. THE POEM	**59**
3. For an "Ethics of Mystery": Philosophy and the Poem Gabriel Riera	61
4. Unbreakable B's: From Beckett and Badiou to the Bitter End of Affirmative Ethics Jean-Michel Rabaté	87
5. The Mallarmé of Alain Badiou Pierre Macherey	109
PART THREE. LOVE (Philosophy and Psychoanalysis)	**117**
6. Gai Savoir Sera: The Science of Love and the Insolence of Chance Joan Copjec	119
7. Alain Badiou: Philosophical Outlaw Juliet Flower MacCannell	137

8. Feminine Love and the Pauline Universal ... 185
   Tracy McNulty

PART FOUR. POLITICS AND ETHICS ... 213

9. On the Ethics of Alain Badiou ... 215
   Simon Critchley

10. Can Change Be Thought?: A Dialogue with Alain Badiou ... 237
    Bruno Bosteels

Bibliography ... 263

Contributors ... 269

Index ... 273

Acknowledgments

I wish to thank Rodolphe Gasché, the editor of the SUNY series Intersections: Philosophy and Critical Theory, who was enthusiastic about the project from the start, as well as James Peltz, my editor at SUNY, who steered the book to completion. I am also grateful to Juliet Flower MacCannell and Joan Copjec for their enthusiasm, support, and extraordinary intellectual range. Charles Ramond of the Université Michel de Montaigne Bordeaux 3 and Patrice Vermeren from L'Harmattan generously authorized the translation of Pierre Macherey's chapter, which was originally published in *Alain Badiou, Penser le Multiple*. I would also like to thank Tracy McNulty and the Department of Romance Languages at Cornell University, which provided a venue for presenting part of my work on Badiou. Finally, thanks to Marilyn Gaddis Rose and Ray Brassier for their help with various translations.

Abbreviations

AMP	*Abrégé de métapolitique* (Paris: Editions du Seuil, 1998).
AP	"L'Âge de Poètes," in *La Politique des poètes: Pourquoi des poètes en temps de détresse?* ed. Jacques Rancière (Paris: Bibliothéque du Col‑lége International de Philosophie, Rue Descartes, 1992).
B	*Beckett: L'increvable désir* (Paris: Hachette, 1995).
BE	*Being and Event*, in *Umbr(a)* 1 (1996): 13-53.
C	*Conditions* (Paris: Editions du Seuil, 1992).
CP	*Catégories pour philosophes* (Unpublished, 1992).
CTOT	*Court traité d'ontologie transitoire* (Paris: Editions du Seuil, 1998).
D	*Deleuze: "La clameur de l'être"* (Paris: Hachette, 1997).
E	*L'Éthique: Essai sur la conscience du Mal* (Paris: Hatier, 1983). Trans‑lated by Peter Hallward as *Ethics: An Essay on the Understanding of Evil* (London: Verso, 2001).
EE	*L'être et l'événement* (Paris: Editions du Seuil, 1998).
L&P	"Logic and Philosophy" (lecture, University of California-Irvine, April 2002, handout).
MPh	*Manifesto for Philosophy*, trans. Norman Madarasz (Albany: State University of New York Press, 1999).
MPP	*Manifeste pour la philosophie* (Paris: Editions du Seuil, 1989).
NN	*Le nombre et les nombres* (Paris: Editions du Seuil, 1990).

ODT	"One Divides into Two," trans. Alberto Toscano, in *Lacanian Ink* 21 (2003): 245–53.
P&P	"Politics and Philosophy: An Interview with Alain Badiou," *Angelaki* 3, no. 3 (1998).
PI	"Poèsie au point de l' innomable," *Po&sie* 64 (1994).
PMI	*Petit Manuel d'inesthétique* (Paris: Seuil, 1988).
PPP	*Peut-on penser la politique?* (Paris: Seuil, 1982).
Psy & Ph	"Psycho-analysis and Philosophy" (lecture, University of California-Irvine, April 2002, handout).
QP	"Qu'est-ce qu'un poème et qu'en pense la philosophie?" in *Petit Manuel d'inesthétique* (Paris, Seuil, 1998).
QPP	"Que pense le poème?" in *L'art est-il une connaissance?* (Paris: Le Monde Editions, 1993).
QQA	"Qu'est-ce que l'amour?" in *Conditions* (Paris: Seuil, 1992).
RPP	"Le Recours philosophique au poème," in *Conditions* (Paris: Seuil, 1992).
SD	*La Scène du Deux*, in *De l'Amour*, sous la direction de l'École de la Cause Freudienne (Paris: Champs Flammarion, 1999).
SP	*Saint Paul: La Fondation de l'universalisme* (Paris: PUF, 1997).
TS	*Théorie du sujet* (Paris: Seuil, 1982).
WL	"What Is Love?" trans. Justin Clemens, in *Umbr(a)* 1 (1996).
WTTC	"What Do You Think of the Twentieth Century?" (lecture, University of California-Irvine, April 2002, handout).

Introduction
Alain Badiou: The Event of Thinking

Gabriel Riera

There is little doubt that Alain Badiou is one of the most challenging and controversial contemporary philosophical figures. Published over the course of three decades, his numerous and extensive texts include several books on ontology, mathematics, aesthetics, literature, politics, ethics, and sexual difference. Yet Badiou is a thinker whose exact place in the intellectual landscape of our time is difficult to determine. He approaches philosophy with the recalcitrant rigor of a mathematician and the economy of means of a modern poet, but also with the passion of a militant of truth. Knotting together philosophical and mathematical discourses, his writing renews their traditional alliance and asks fundamental questions of each, while also dramatizing the incommensurability that sets the two discourses apart. In his writing, then, Badiou transforms the terms in which it is henceforth possible to think about the question of philosophy, of its possibility and future, and also to think, beyond the double constraint of the One and of Totality, about the immanent multiplicity in which we are immersed.

Badiou's contributions bring a new perspective to some of the most pressing issues currently being debated in philosophy and the social sciences. Among them are the conditions of political intervention, the possibility of philosophy, the ethics of sexual difference, and the formulation of a subject who is at the same time singular and universal and an ensuing critique of cultural relativism. A serious assessment of Badiou's philosophy forces us to reevaluate these topics, as well as to reexamine some of the tenets of contemporary philosophy.

Alain Badiou (b. 1937) belongs to the generation of philosophers who entered the École Normale at the end of 1950s. Like Etienne Balibar, Pierre Macherey, and Jacques Rancière, he was attracted to Marxism, as well as to psychoanalysis, logic, the history of science, and structuralism. He is professor of philosophy at the University of Paris VIII, editor of the prestigious collection "L'Ordre Philosophique" at Les Éditions du Seuil, and program director at the College International de Philosophie.

Badiou was influenced by Jean-Paul Sartre early in his career, but in the 1960s was drawn to the work of Luis Althusser, Jacques Lacan, George Canguilhem, and Jean Hyppolite. As a student at the École Normale, Badiou attended Jacques Lacan's seminars and took part in the activities of the Epistemological Circle responsible for the publication of *Cahiers pour l'Analyse*. The research conducted by the Epistemological Circle incorporated developments in logic, mathematics, topology, and linguistics. The names Jean Cavaillés and Albert Lautmann are also important points of reference in Badiou's formation since they represent an important tradition of mathematical philosophy in France.

It is not by accident, therefore, that Badiou's work crosses a wide range of disciplines, including ontology, mathematics, topology, modern poetry, theater, film, psychoanalysis, and politics. His is a systematic philosophy that can be situated in the rational tradition inaugurated by Descartes and that responds to Plato's decision of "interrupting the poem," that is, of founding philosophy in mathematical conceptuality and reestablishing a free circulation between the nonphilosophical conditions: science, poetry, politics, and love. However, Badiou pushes this tradition to its limits, since he aims to link what exceeds the means of rational presentation, the *event*, to what is singular par excellence, the *subject*, and therefore to articulate the *generic procedures* through which universal *truths* are produced.

Badiou's philosophy is difficult to classify among the currents that have dominated the second half of the twentieth century. In spite of his conceptual innovations and its unique style of presentation, as well as its attunement to the signs of the time in the fields of art, mathematics, politics, and psychoanalysis (love), there is something untimely in Badiou's philosophy: his systematic drive. The grafting of post-Marxist (Althusserian, Maoist) philosophy to Lacanian topological insights and the combinatory rules of set theory and, more recently, category theory, as well as Mallarmé's poetic writing give Badiou's philosophy a rather unique appearance.[1] Badiou's marginality in the academic curriculum is not only due in part to his public image as a militant philosopher who still believes in the possibility of forms of the collective that defy neoliberal market logic. His nondialectical understanding of the universal as "the trajectory of a distance with regard to a particularity that subtends" (WL 21) generates resistance within a context dominated by cultural relativism. But, most importantly, Badiou's marginality lies in the complexity of its ontology, grounded as it is in the axioms derived from post-Cantorean mathematical set theory.

Philosophy is neither a constructive nor a deconstructive practice for Badiou but the site where thinking seizes the *truths* or *generic procedures* of an epoch. These truths constitute the *conditions* that enable philosophy to accomplish its act: to provide those truths with an articulation to exhibit their *compossibility* (C 65, 79). Philosophy thus disposes the generic procedures of an epoch in a unique configuration and, for this reason, does not constitute itself as the Truth of such procedures, but rather as "incomplete [*lacunaire*] thinking" (C 47) of the multiple coming after its conditions. As a configuration of thought, philosophy derives a series of directives with which to approach the teeming of things, and it does so by means of an analytic procedure that equates mathematics with ontology. Badiou develops his systematic ontology in *L'être et l'événement*, where being refers to the order of the presentation of the pure multiple and event to the dimension of non-being: the real that becomes possible when forced by means of a "discipline of time" and a "fidelity" to its incalculable irruption. The crux of Badiou's philosophy is to propose an ethics of the event whose main prescription is a nondogmatic imperative: "Decide from the point of view of what is undecidable"; a decision whose final goal is to stipulate the effects that the new brings upon a given structure.

Badiou's is a pure multiplicity composed of multiple elements. Contemporary mathematics, especially post-Cantorean set theory, provides for Badiou the only rigorous articulation of such a pure multiplicity. All beings in their being are infinite by prescription—infinite in the secularized sense introduced by Cantor's revolution. The *axiom of infinity* constitutes Badiou's point of departure; it asserts a radical infinity beyond all possible proofs of construction. Inasmuch as it is not a number that one can arrive at by counting, the infinite is unattainable. However, in its secularized version, infinity ceases to be the limit of human finitude in order to become the very medium of existence. The *axiom of the void* also plays a crucial role in Badiou's ontology. The void is a universally included set that belongs to no one in particular. Although ontology presents the multiple, the being of this presentation is empty and subtracts itself from the dialectic of the one and the multiple (*EE* 71). The void is "that from which there is presentation" (*EE* 68) but without being included (counted or represented) in it.

Badiou calls situation any multiplicity structured by a particular count or by a particular criteria of belonging and inclusion (two founding relations of the multiple). The result of counting is a metastructure that designates the situation as One, or as the *state of a situation*. Badiou plays with the political connotation of the word *state*, since it is the principle that intervenes to control excess, to establish the set of the parts or subsets of a set. Knowledge or the *language of the situation* furnishes virtually infinite ways of arranging a situation's part, but cannot provide a global, enabling unity to these arrangements. The state (of the situation) prohibits the presentation of the void, which is the fundamental element for any particularization. The objective order that the state of the situation thus guarantees accomplishes a violent inclusion whose effect is "the disjunction between presentation and representation," between "structure and meta-structure" (*EE* 149). Ontology must describe the conditions that will allow moving beyond the state of a presentation toward a situation of pure presentation.

It is the contingent, unpredictable dimension of the event that interrupts the order of knowledge by attaching itself to the void of every situation. The event called "French Revolution" is, for example, the occurrence that allows us to read the inconsistencies of the ancien régime. It is the truth of the ancien régime, but a truth that cannot be named by the state of the situation called "ancien régime." An event is not a fact; it is a nonempirical, ephemeral, and insubstantial passage that cannot be assigned to any stable element of the situation in which it takes place. The event is the supernumerary excess of the order of being that makes possible the production of a truth. Further, it demands an act of nomination ("Christ's Resurrection," in the case of Saint Paul; "October Revolution," for Marxist–Leninist revolutionaries) from its operator or belated supplement: the subject. It is through the intervention of a subject (a subject who is the aftereffect of the event) on behalf of this truth that an event can be discerned and named as such.

Clearly, for Badiou a truth is neither the correspondence between a subject and an object (*homôiosis, adæquatio*), the (un)veiling of Being (*alêtheia*), nor the result of different productions of practices and discourses at a given time in history (Foucault). A truth is produced by the excessive irruption of an event of whose passage only a name remains. A truth is what results from the subjective process once the name of the event is put into circulation in a given situation. What must be stressed here is that the subject does not preexist the event but, rather, that the event is what makes possible a process of subjectivization. The latter consists in seizing the name of the event in order to make it intervene in a given situation. It is through this intervention that consensual and validated knowledge can encounter the real of a given situation. Because the event is always fleeting, an operator able to establish an effective mechanism of connection must exist. And since the truth of the event is indiscernible from within a given situation (for classical music, "atonal music" is a series of chaotic sounds; for the Greek philosopher, "Christ's Resurrection" is a fable) the language of the situation is unable to name it. In other words, a truth emerges as the outcome of a process in which a "generic subset" of a situation coalesces and is then sustained by a subjective *fidelity to the event*. Further, there is no subject in general, but only a subject of each of the generic procedures or conditions.

A PHILOSOPHY TO COME:
BADIOU AND THE "END OF PHILOSOPHY"

Badiou responds to an age dominated by cultural relativism and skepticism by positing the existence of universal truths. Against the partisans of philosophy's demise Badiou argues that philosophy is possible and necessary. In fact, Badiou emphatically contests all affirmations concerning the "end of philosophy" and instead declares that philosophy operates in terms of the concepts of 'truth,' 'event,' and 'subjectivity' (MPh). He specifically rejects the two inflections that the end of philosophy has taken in contemporary discourses: the Heideggerian version regarding the exhaustion and finalization of metaphysics, as well as the "vulgar" positivist version that sees philosophy superseded by the developments in the natural and human sciences. Faced with this situation, Badiou responds by stressing a classical aspect of philosophy: its systematicness. He establishes a new relation between discourse and mathematical deduction by equating ontology and mathematics as the thinking that operates in the proximity of the disseminated nature of Being. For Badiou there is no One, but a multiplicity of multiples of which the One is the aftereffect of an operation: counting.

Nevertheless, Badiou's arguments against the Sophist and Postmodern partisans of the end of philosophy merits closer inspection, since they evince a more complex series of moves and decisions than the agonistic scenario he puts into play especially in *Manifesto for Philosophy* (1989). What dispute does Badiou's persona, the Philosopher, have with the Sophists? The very possibility of philosophy that he sees endangered by the privilege they grant to language and language-games (there are Sophists, of course, on both sides of the Atlantic). However, within this vast territory, Badiou targets Heidegger's "way to language," and its effects in France. In this particular articulation of the end of philosophy, Badiou takes Heidegger to task for his "suturing" of philosophy to the poem. For Badiou, this operation evinces not only a metaphysical nostalgia for a lost origin (Heidegger's understanding of metaphysics as the forgetting of being signaled by Plato's philosophy), but also a narrow comprehension of technology that condemns mathematical rationality to a matter of "logistics." Badiou proposes a de-suturing of philosophy from the poem in the guise of a "return to Plato" that would both secure a redistribution of *lógos* and the matheme and reestablish a free circulation between philosophy and its conditions (mathematics, poetry, love, and politics).

This configuration explicitly refers to a certain "reactive" version of the end of philosophy, one that would cancel out any inventive possibility. We could even use the expression *defeat of thinking* to characterize this position regarding philosophy's fate, given that it is the one subscribed to by the not so "*nouevaux philosophes*" who are among the targets of Badiou's critique. But it also inscribes the graphics of the "closure (*clôture*) of metaphysics" within a space not totally alien to deconstruction.[2] The second aspect of Badiou's reopening of the question of "the end" thus merits closer inspection. Inasmuch as Badiou's ontology attempts to free thought from the yoke of unicity and transcendence, his project is not alien to the general axiomatic of a deconstruction of the ontotheological motifs of metaphysics. For Badiou, both the One and Totality are belated fictions that block the path to a truth ontology whose goal is the immanence of pure multiplicity. However, in spite of the family resemblance between an ontology of the multiple pure and deconstruction, Badiou parts ways with the latter by taking a different point of departure. It is no longer a question of thinking along the lines of Nietzsche and Heidegger (although Badiou's relation with the latter is complex) but rather of an untimely "return to Plato" or "reversal of the reversal of Platonism." It is in Plato (in *Parmenides*) where Badiou finds all the resources for an immanent ontology.

However, if one fails to recognize this strategic dimension of Badiou's thinking, his return to Plato runs the risk of being interpreted as a no less nostalgic gesture than Heidegger's "return to the Pre-Socratics." It is true that this dimension is often obscured by his own belligerent rhetoric and the schematic approach of some of his commentators who wish to pit him against deconstruction and thus privilege a voluntaristic ethics blind to the undecidable dimension of any encounter with the real. That Badiou's thinking operates on the hither side of the closure of metaphysics is nowhere more evident that in the infinitist bent of his thinking. Badiou's basic axiom (that the One is not) subtends a theory of multiplicities according to which the One will not be the figure of Being as a Totality. The knot that ties together discourse and mathematical writing can only operate on the hither side of the disseminated multiplicity. In a sense, and in spite of Badiou's reversal of Nietzsche's reversal of Plato, the fact that the "One is not" means that the essential possibilities of metaphysics are exhausted. The event is the undecidable excess that makes any form of totalization impossible. And this undecidable excess can only be thought once the figures of metaphysics (God, substance, and transcendental subject) are exhausted.

The return to Plato produces a de-suturing of philosophy from the dominion of one of its conditions, the poem, and thus entails a confrontation with Heidegger's understanding of philosophy. Badiou takes issue with Heidegger's "linguistic turn" where the poem becomes the condition for thinking as such. It is only once the closure of metaphysics is accomplished and the reign of technology is supreme that for Heidegger a handful of poets (Hölderlin being the most prominent) are able to articulate Being and provide us with directives with which to overturn this situation. What Badiou calls the "age of poets" corresponds to the severing of thought's link to its mathematical origin in Plato. By interpreting truth and being as Idea, Heidegger tells us, Plato put thought onto the path of representation and mathematical objectification. While for Heidegger Plato's path signals the erasure of the poem and its ontological potential in favor of a purely instrumental conception of thought, for Badiou ontology must be torn from philosophical and poetic thought, and returned to its genuine mathematical origin, as Plato anticipated. The poem has a place in Badiou's philosophy, but the place of ontology is not in the poem. The latter is incapable of thinking pure multiplicity as such.

By suturing thought to the poem, Heidegger also subordinates it to the divine and thus to the time of the promise. The age of poets is the time of the God (or gods) of the poets: "that on the basis of which there is for the poet an enchantment of the world, the loss of which exposes us to futility" (CTOT 19). But of this god one can only say, "it has *withdrawn*, exposing the world to disenchantment" (CTOT 19). Badiou wants to break with this configuration and carry poetry beyond the motifs of a philosophy of finitude. Today, the imperative of the poem consists in having finished with the figure of the promise, the return of the gods, and the reenchantment of the world. Philosophy, according to Badiou, must rid itself of all nostalgia; it cannot suspend its vocation in the hope of a return of the gods.

BADIOU'S DECISION: "MATHEMATICS = ONTOLOGY"

The return to Plato allows Badiou to wrest ontology from the hold of poetic language and place it back within the context of mathematics. This "mathematical turn" contests the primacy of the "linguistic turn" in twentieth-century philosophy (Wittgenstein) and its most recent postmodern rearticulation in Lyotard's *The Differend*, where philosophy's role is to safeguard the irreducible heterogeneity of different regimen of phrases. In *L'être et l'événement* (*Being and Event*) Badiou demonstrates the constitutive power of mathematical axioms with respect to philosophy's logic. What mathematics offers Badiou is the possibility of manipulating the pure multiple in its quasi inconsistency. Here lies the reason for equating mathematics with ontology. Badiou's ontology deals with the concept of being-as-being and it does so in terms of pure multiplicity; the presentation of this pure multiple that is envisioned as a set and, from the viewpoint of set theory, as a multiple without one. The axiomatic point of departure in Badiou's ontology is the claim according to which "l'un n'est pas" (the One is not) and that therefore "il y a de l'Un" (there is [some] one). This statement asserts the derivative nature of the one; its being the result of an operation ("the counting-as-one") that gives consistency to the swarming of multiples. Second, that the one occupies a place within being, albeit an errant one as evinced by the French pronoun y.

Book 1 of *L'être et l'événement*, "Being: The Multiple and the Void: Plato/Cantor," provides a genealogy of ontology and proves that the reciprocal relation between the one and the multiple is a retroactive fiction. Inasmuch as the theory of sets determines being as having no metaphysical properties, Badiou's *science* of being concerns itself with the presentation of being: not the *what* of being, but the being of its own presentation. Therefore, Badiou is neither interested in representation nor in a philosophy of deferred presence, as in Heidegger's fundamental ontology where being is cut off from its source due to philosophy's oblivion and the collapsing of the ontological difference it entails.

For Badiou, the donation of being can only be presented as multiplicity or as a pure presentation thanks to which being subtracts itself from any relation. The multiplicity of the multiple presents itself under two guises: as inconsistent (without one, without being structured by a particular count) or as consistent (the composition of ones). A *situation* is thus a presentation of multiples counted-as-one and brought to the form of a unity. The presentative character of a situation lies in the fact that in it a multiple is counted, discerned, or named. For example, if one takes the French Revolution as a situation, the multiples that present this situation are individuals, utterances, and places. However, the only thing one can affirm regarding all these multiples is that they *belong* to this situation called "French Revolution," which means that all the multiples presented by a situation belong to this situation.

A situation thus designates the set of counted terms or likely to be counted by an operation of discernment that is proper to it. Nevertheless, the law-of-counting that is at the origin of a presentation cannot differentiate itself insofar as it is the unaccounted term of the counting-as-one that it performs. Badiou deduces from this that a presentation cannot be presented by itself but only thanks to the existence of a different structure whose function is to provide the representation of presentation. The state (of a situation) deals with the situation's parts and is a procedure of discernment and classification.

MATHEMATICS' UNTHOUGHT: THE EVENT

Although mathematics makes it possible to approach the pure multiple and thus mobilizes the dimension of the event, it cannot explicitly think the event. It is here that philosophy must intervene and operate as a metaontology. Badiou's philosophy is a creature of its time and thus responds to the centrality of the event in contemporary thinking by articulating a theory of the event that differs from Heidegger's and Deleuze's, two of the main references in Badiou's conceptualization.

In *Being and Time* Heidegger conceives "the eternity" of the eternal return, the event par excellence, as the Moment (*der Augenblick*) of decision and insight proper to a *Dasein* that temporalizes time by a resolute anticipation of its possibilities. These possibilities are set forth in the horizon of death: by anticipating death, Dasein projects itself in advance into the possibility that Dasein is itself. By existing, by taking over its own facticity, Dasein alone makes possible its own possibilities. Further, Dasein's ecstatic temporality delimits the scope of its presence to itself and to the world inasmuch as it opens, from the direction of the anticipation of its Being-for-death, the different ecstasis of time by which entities can appear as "having been," "present," or "to come." However, the ecstasis of time articulating Dasein's being "'outside-of-itself' in and for itself"[3] and its transcendence in the direction of Being can only give access to a series of represented "to comes" and "pasts." These series refer only to this self-present futurity that Dasein deploys throughout time since Care (*Sorge*) is the unifying structure of being-in-the-world. Because in Heidegger the event is that through which Being is always tied to the destiny of man and man to that of Being, its force is cushioned by the structure of Care. Heidegger integrates the event-character of the Moment to the framework of representation and thus gathers together the Moment as a totalization of time in the *Augenblick* of the instant. This gathering is the property of Dasein.

This is not the case for Deleuze for whom the event is what is always repeated and never exhausted in Being's differing from itself. It is the event of a repetition that repeats only by inscribing difference. There is a common understanding of the event at play in Heidegger and Deleuze: Being is that same which always returns, but returns only to differ itself, or always returns as difference. However, for Deleuze, the event is not what takes place *in* time but, rather, the *instant* as a transcendental synthesis that distributes the before and after on both sides of a static caesura. The event is the affirmation of the virtual and intensive multiplicity of time that marks a break between a virtual past and the present of an action. This means that for Deleuze the event cannot be seized as such and unfolds under two temporal modalities, Chronos and Aîon.[4]

While Heidegger's analytic of Dasein fails to do justice to the event, other phenomenological approaches appear to be more attuned to its altering irruption. Henry Maldiney claims that "the event affects us by shattering both the world's ground where we have our anchoring and the world's horizon under which we find signification."[5] The feature that best defines the event is, for Maldiney, its irreducible character, its not taking place in the world. Likewise, by opposing events to facts, Claude Romano stresses the former's irreducible nature. While facts always take place within the horizon of meaning a world supposes, the event transcends its own effectuation as fact and "appears" as something irreducible to its own context. The temporality of the event is inaugural, retrospective, and prospective, while the fact's temporality is an opening, always past and future. If facts suppose a chronological temporality, the temporalization of the event is not a process; it is more accurate to refer to it, with Romano, as dramaturgy (*dramatique*): in it, nothing changes in the present, but everything has already changed. This change becomes accessible as such only belatedly. The event is at the same time absolutely to come, coming from a future inaccessible to the horizon of waiting, and always already past or without any possible contemporaneity: the event puts into motion a present in perpetual delay with itself.[6] Phenomenology reinscribes this irreducible dimension of the event within the context of the world. For this reason, the event becomes the possibility of an adventure of meaning.

With Heidegger, Badiou shares a common way of "recognizing" the event through a process of fidelity. While in the former it is by means of a resolute anticipation evincing a fidelity to existence itself,[7] for Badiou it is by means of an intervention that refers the event to a previous one. At first sight, Badiou shares with phenomenological approaches, the putting into circulation of the event within the horizon of the world. However, while for phenomenology the event marks the beginning of a hermeneutical adventure, for Badiou it marks a suspension of meaning: it is not a question of recomposing a context but of renouncing meaning and sustaining the event's undecidable character.

The interpretive intervention declares whether a given event is presented in a situation; it maintains the event's undecidability and decides whether the event belongs to a situation by forcing a name out of the unpresented element of the site. The Revolution of 1789, for example, is "French," but France neither gave birth to it nor named the event-character of the Revolution. The historical situation one calls "France" can only be envisioned from the event called "Revolution." The event's name is extracted from out of the void on which the presentation hangs. And because the intervention touches the void, it subtracts itself from the counting-as-one that rules the situation. Inasmuch as the act of nomination does not conform to any law of representation, it is illegal and interrupts the law of representation. From the point of view of the state (of a situation), the event arrives as something enigmatic and, although it occurs on the surface of a situation, it "appears" as an excessive element that is out of place, lacks authority and is thus aleatory. But Badiou's event does not come ex nihilo or, at least, he aims to break with what he calls a "speculative Leftist" conception that dreams of an absolute beginning or a total break with a preexisting totality. If in Heidegger the irruption of the event is totalized by the self-present futurity that Dasein deploys throughout time, in Badiou it is the future anterior, a future having retroactive effects that accomplishes the temporal synthesis between two moments of which the event is an interval.

Badiou's typology of being reveals the existence of a type of multiplicity that transgresses the laws of the axiomatic that were set to formalize it and is thus indiscernible from this very axiomatic. The axiomatic of set theory isolates two types of relations among multiplicities: belonging and inclusion; it is from the latter that the excessive type of multiples originate. Therefore, in Badiou the axiomatic of set theory defines the site of the inexistence that produces truths—the event. The event is an exceptional multiple that is added to a given situation by tracing the passage of an interruption. It produces a caesura because it opens a perspective from which to discern what a situation cannot know or grasp: that which is left unaccounted for by the situation's metastructure. The event, therefore, points to the void or inconsistency out of which a situation holds together.

The event is destined to a given situation and it confers a local extension to it (*EE* 196). Badiou calls evental site (*site événémentiel*) the singular multiple whose elements do not present themselves in a situation. The state of the situation cannot count the terms that make up this singular and abnormal multiple (for example, a family of illegal immigrants whose members are unregistered and thus lack public status) and therefore they lack existence. A site is thus always in the position of internal exclusion in regard to the situation within which it is presented insofar as the site belongs to the situation without being included in it. What is excessive regarding the classes the state counts is neither one (the retroactive result of a structural operation) nor consistent: it is a nothing (*rien*). A site is thus unclassifiable since its excess overflows what the state designates as being a legitimate part of a situation. Moreover, a site is precarious and ephemeral and although it is a requisite for an event to arrive, it is not the event's cause but its idiosyncratic condition.

Because of its intrinsic feature, Badiou defines the event as an "extraordinary multiple"; it is, at the same time, the situation of the multiples of its own site and its own situation, which means that the defining feature of the event is its self-belonging. The event then is an unfounded and autonomous set or situation that subtracts itself from the axiom of foundation (*CTOT* 58). Ultimately, the event is unfounded and autonomous in terms of the situation within which it arrives. The crux of the subject is to inscribe the event within a situation to which it does not belong, given that the event only belongs to itself.

The event's modality of manifestation is that of the eclipse: it is a fading and fragile appearing that produces the dispersion of the site's elements. However, given that the event belongs to itself, its dazzling passage leaves a remainder: a name, the only element by means of which it can survive its own disappearance. The name forbids that the event's disappearance give way to a discourse whose grammar and syntax is grounded in the encyclopedic and classifying language of the state.

Badiou's theory of the event contests the postmodern position that claims nothing like an event ever takes place, as well as relativist positions that posit the existence of a multiplicity of events. Although fragile, for Badiou it is possible to localize an event: it is the truth of a specific situation that, once declared and maintained by a subjective fidelity, has universal scope. Although for both Badiou and Deleuze the event makes something happen and overturns a given state of affairs, for the latter it belongs to a site of virtual conditions of existence for the actual entity. Deleuze locates the event's site in the virtual horizon of preindividual singularities that puts processes of individuation or becoming into motion. Badiou rejects the distinction of virtual and real; its ontology deals with multiplicities as actualities or entities.

SUBJECTIVE INTERVENTION (POLITICS AND ETHICS)

Badiou calls intervention the recognition from which the event testifies to its unexpected and incalculable arrival. The intervention unleashes a "discipline of time" that controls the putting into circulation of the paradoxical multiple of the event (*EE* 232). It is important not to confuse this intervening fidelity with Althusser's interpellation or with its avatar in the statist compulsion for identity politics. In Badiou there is no way of knowing beforehand whether an individual is connected to a given event. Fidelity thus names a process that separates and discerns "the becoming legal of chance" (*EE* 257). A truth is thus what results from a subjective process once the subject puts the event's name into circulation. In Badiou subject refers neither to a network of representations grounded in experience nor to the transcendental constitution of any possible object of experience. Instead it refers to the linkage that brings together the event and fidelity, or the relation between subjectivization and the subjective process (*EE* 264). By the latter Badiou understands the subject's seizure by the caesura of the event, as well as the act by which the subject gets hold of the event's name in order to make it intervene in a given situation. The subject does not preexist the event since she only becomes subject thanks to the interrupting force and the arresting power of the event (*E* 48). For Badiou, Saint Paul is the example of a subject whose fidelity to the event of Christ's Resurrection puts this singular occurrence into circulation and renders it into a universal truth. In both Saint Paul and Pascal, and beyond Christianity, Badiou isolates the militant apparatus (*dispositif*) of truth (*EE* 244–45). In Saint Paul's work, Badiou sees a singular connection between a conception of a subject without identity and a law lacking any formal support that nonetheless makes possible the positing of a universal truth (*SP* 6). Paul's truth that "Jesus Resurrected" cannot be referred to any objective network of knowledge.

The subject is not substance, universal essence, or origin, but the local operator of the production of a truth. Badiou's decentering of the subject has Lacan's theory as its referent in that the subject is the empty scrap of which the unconscious is the truth and Cause (the very place of the void).[8] Badiou rejects this characterization and instead transforms the subject into the productive point of a relation to the being of the void that supplements truth in an innovative fashion. Although Deleuze too treats the subject as a local occurrence that produces a self-giving idea of the self (*soi*), there are some crucial differences between his conception of the subject and Badiou's. For the latter, the subject is rare, while for the former, it is abundant and fulfilled by what she retrieves from each of her relations with the world. Badiou restricts the impact of the event on the subject to the procedures of the situation: to the militant fidelity to a cause. This restriction distances him from Deleuze's conception of the subject as a particular case (being) of the impersonal transcendental field (*virtualité*).

THINKING THROUGH BADIOU: PHILOSOPHY UNDER CONDITIONS

Owing not only to Badiou's broad intellectual range but also to his way of conceiving philosophy, an analysis of his work requires and demands a transdisciplinary perspective. For Badiou,

> the specific role of philosophy is to propose a unified conceptual space in which naming takes place of events that serve as a point of departure for truth procedures. . . . Philosophy's operation always aims to think "together," to configure within a unique exercise of thought the epochal disposition of the matheme, poem, political intervention and love (or the event status of the Two). In this sense, philosophy's sole question is indeed that of the truth. Not that it produces any, but because it offers a mode of access to the unity of a moment of truths, a conceptual site in which the generic procedures are thought of as compossible. (MPh 37)

That philosophy is conditioned by the generic procedures of its time (EE 375) points in two related directions: that philosophy maintains a free circulation among them and that philosophy depends on them for its own existence. By forbidding that one of the procedures becomes the only conditioning discourse, philosophy avoids the obstruction of the condition's free circulation. The obstruction is what Badiou calls "suture," a situation in which philosophy delegates its functions to only one of its conditions. Badiou identifies three types of sutures prevalent in the last two centuries: scientific (positivism and its doctrine of progress), political (revolutionary philosophy and the hybrid represented by "scientific socialism" that juxtaposes a science of History and a voluntaristic form of politics), and poetic represented by the age of poets (AP 22). Philosophy depends on the free circulation of its conditions because of their inventive capacity and their production of truths.

The chapters in this volume assess the scope of a "philosophy under conditions" by investigating the implications of Badiou's philosophical system as well as by analyzing how the different conditions communicate their truths to philosophy and how philosophy in turn reads them. The first section is devoted to the mathematical condition and questions the implications of Badiou's axiomatic identification of mathematics and ontology. Because Badiou breaks with epistemological, grammatical, and logical approaches to mathematics (Frege and Wittgenstein), its specific treatment merits close scrutiny.

As I showed earlier, Badiou's ontology is shaped according to the axioms of set theory presented in L'être et l'événement. In a seminal essay on Badiou, Jean-Toussaint

Desanti observed how Badiou's system is in fact no more than a combination of axioms derived from set theory. By its very adhesion to the set-theoretic axioms that prescribe a universe of absolute, albeit open, proportions, Badiou's identification thesis seems to set the One at the very crux of a philosophical perception intended to destitute it from such primacy. Desanti thus recommended safeguarding the project of intrinsic ontology, that is, one equating inconsistent multiplicities with non-Being and the event, while at the same time arguing for the mathematics of *category theory* in order to develop the thesis on Being.[9]

In an effort to respond to Desanti's recommendation, throughout the 1990s there was a shift from set theory to category theory in Badiou. Norman Madarasz focuses on how Badiou posits the identity of mathematics and ontology in the *Court traité d'ontologie transitoire* (1998). Badiou introduces category theory here as the foundational theory of logic—prescribed ontologically instead of linguistically, as in a universal grammar—while set theory remains that of mathematics. Madarasz examines how Badiou's set theory axiomatic confronts category theory and claims that the principles of Badiou's "transitory ontology" risks becoming a set-theoretic interpretation of the categorical orientation. Badiou's construction, Madarasz claims, performs a double movement that favors set theory: regarding the identity thesis, there is a set-theoretic co-opting of category theory, while with the notion of transitory ontology, he legitimates the demotion of category theory as a foundation for logic. This double movement bears important implications for the status of the One in his immanent ontology of the multiple.

From a more ontological perspective, Miguel de Beistegui interrogates the articulations of Badiou's theory of the event through a comparison with those of Heidegger and Deleuze. The focus of the chapter is Badiou's position regarding the question of ontological difference. According to de Beistegui, for Badiou the ontological difference sooner or later reintroduces transcendence either in terms of poetic language (Heidegger), or in those of the concept of the virtual (Deleuze). Through an examination of Badiou's critique of both Heidegger's and Deleuzes's ontologies in relation to univocity and difference, de Beistegui posits that a "complete failure of communication" took place between these thinkers. The common ground underlying the dispute is, for de Beistegui, the concept of ontological difference that, in his view, Badiou brushes off too quickly.

That the question of ontological difference has a bearing on Badiou's attempts to posit a post-Heideggerian relation between philosophy and the poem is clear from Gabriel Riera's chapter that opens the section on the poem. Taking Badiou's critique of Heidegger's decision to make the poem the condition of thinking as his point of departure, Riera follows Badiou's attempts to articulate a new relation between philosophy and the poem. He examines three articulations of that relation proposed by Badiou and shows how traces of traditional philosophical aesthetics survive in his thinking. To explain this situation, he adduces a slippage in the trope's regulative assignation, or a tension between the postsignifying demands of "being-faithful-to-the-event" of the modern poem and the classical philosophical signifying schema of conceptualization. Finally, Riera asks whether it is possible for Badiou to articulate the call "for an ethics of mystery" with the imperative of its "becoming prose" (Lacoue-Labarthe) that Badiou situates as the final effect of the de-suturing of philosophy from the poem of the age of poets.

Jean-Michel Rabaté reads the portrayal of an "ethical Beckett" in Badiou's *Beckett: L'incrévable désir* (1995). This is a Beckett whose writing has decisive implications for an understanding of desire, language, and human existence. Beckett's *Watt*, especially the interplay between the Law and the "incident" or symptomatic "occurrence," allows Rabaté to examine Badiou's thesis on the link between the event, its meaning, and the new role ascribed to the subject. Following Badiou, Rabaté claims that when they address the locus of the Law, Beckett's texts must confront a radical unnamability. This is a linguistic experience that combines both Sade's and Kant's ethical systems and whose main coordinates are beauty and truth.

Although *Beckett: L'incrévable désir* is the only book Badiou ever devoted to a writer, Mallarmé is a constant point of reference for Badiou's thinking. Mallarmé occupies a central place in both *Théorie du sujet* (1982) and *L'être et l'événement*, but becomes more prominent in *Petit Manuel d'inesthétique* (1998), where Badiou claims that "I wanted philosophy to be finally contemporary with Mallarmé's poetic operations" (PMI 61). Of course, Badiou is not the only contemporary French philosopher to write extensively on Mallarmé and to make use of his insights. For this reason, Pierre Macherey asks "which Mallarmé" is Badiou's? Macherey observes that Mallarmé is not simply an object of thought for Badiou since what interests the latter is to encounter the poem in its operative dimension (where it "does what it says" [TS 99]) and thus utters a truth. In other words, for Badiou it is a question of approaching Mallarmé as an event of thinking while preserving the singularity of his poetic procedures. By means of such a reflection, subtracted as it is from the purview of aesthetics, philosophy and poetry dialogue as equals. Macherey further claims that Badiou presents Mallarmé as the bearer of a "method" and even a "logic"; a "subtractive method" that makes the poem "a negative machinery that utters the being or idea at the very point where the object makes itself vanish." However, it would be a mistake to assimilate this negativity to the nothing opposed to being. The poem's negative force consists in producing a fragment of truth.

Badiou comes close to psychoanalytic theory in that he finds subjective truth where only a void seems apparent. Although Lacan's texts are "event-making for philosophy" and thus an unavoidable point of reference for Badiou's thinking, there are some crucial differences between the two thinkers. The three chapters that comprise the section Love (Philosophy and Psychoanalysis) consider these differences at length. In Badiou love is a condition for thinking and thus a "truth procedure" in which each position, from the vantage point of its particular experience and knowledge, welcomes a truth that addresses humanity in its universality. By positing love as a generic procedure, Badiou contests mystical and romantic conceptions of love that depend on an ecstatic experience where lovers fuse into One. He also subtracts *Éros* from any dialectic of the Other and, finally, rejects the moralistic notion according to which love is simply the "ornamental semblance through which the real of sex passes" (C 268). By focusing on "La Scène du deux," Badiou's commentary of Lacan's theory of love in the *Encore* seminar, Joan Copjec shows the centrality that the theories of love and of sexual difference have in his project. It is in love that Copjec finds the possibility of preserving a form of universality that does not sacrifice difference. By staging a confrontation between Bersani's and Badiou's theories of love, Copjec foregrounds Badiou's use of the concept as a model for the social bond. If for Bersani love is a false lure that sabotages social connectedness, Badiou instead refers to the "successful" sexual relation as an event that announces the truth of sexual difference: that there is a difference and therefore a sexual other. Copjec's focus is the concept of 'suppleance' through which Badiou rewrites Lacan's formulae of sexuation.

It is regarding this last point that Badiou disputes Lacan's use of the infinite in his articulation of the formulae of sexuation. In Badiou's view, Lacan does not bring into play a Cantorean notion of the infinite and, therefore, his formalization of sexuation appears to be grounded in an intuitionist logic. For this reason, Badiou claims that "the infinite is not a set but, rather, a virtual point subtracted from the action of what is finite. This explains why [in Lacan] feminine *jouissance* has the structure of a fiction: the fiction of what is inaccessible" (C 295). When rewriting Lacan's formulae of sexuation, Badiou replaces the universal phallic function (Φ) for an operator of universal Humanity (Hx) and thus displaces the problem of love and sexuation from a dialectics of desire. This move makes it possible to rewrite the ethics of psychoanalysis not in terms of desire but rather in those of the subject's fidelity "to remain suspended between the event's undecidability and the truth's indiscernibility" (C 326). Badiou claims that Lacanian psychoanalysis still operates within a dimension of knowledge (*savoir*) and, therefore, cannot approach the dimension of truth-processes in a positive way. This is a claim open to dispute, as the chapters by Juliet Flower MacCannell and Tracy McNulty make clear.

The location of the concept of the void is where Badiou parts ways with Lacan. While psychoanalysis locates the void in discourse as a symptom of lost jouissance (object *a*), Badiou places it in the formal universality of signification. This topological distinction is not a mere technical distinction but, as MacCannell's analysis shows, has decisive implications for Badiou's understanding of the subject and his conception of politics. For Badiou the void is a real effect of the event and not a by-product of language.

MacCannell's chapter explores Badiou's conception of love and its limits (limits of the Law and language) and claims that Badiou's goal is to reach a field of jouissance beyond words and "for the sake of a dawning composite subject (the Two, the 'we')." MacCannell focuses on several important common areas to both psychoanalysis and Badiou in order to highlight how the latter differs from psychoanalytic discourse in spite of some conceptual overlapping. MacCannell further situates Badiou's subject "at the dreamed-of scene of destruction," and claims that his thinking is characterized by an "aesthetic passion." Finally, she argues that woman is not located in the field of operation of the subject's "creationist sublimation." While for Lacan love is a "creationist sublimation" whose words promise the impossible possibility of a love outside the limits of the Law through its address to the Feminine Thing, Badiou, MacCannell claims, places love "outside the limits of the law," where woman ceases to be its cause.

Tracy McNulty's chapter addresses the implications of Badiou's rewriting of the formulae of sexuation for an ethics of sexual difference and for the feminine position. McNulty locates a structural homology in the function Badiou assigns to the feminine position in "Qu'est-ce que l'amour?" (C) and in *Saint Paul: La Fondation de l'universalisme*. She claims that in both texts feminine love is the necessary support for a nonphallic universalism. For this reason, he is able to rotate Lacan's formulae of sexuation and restore to women the universal qualifier (in *Encore* Lacan defines the feminine position as "not-all" in terms of the phallic function). At stake for McNulty is the relation between the feminine love that supports the humanity function (Hx) and the Christian love that supports the universal by both fulfilling and eradicating the law. However, the elevation of feminine love to the status of support for the universal totality, McNulty argues, neutralizes the very difference that love seems to guarantee.

By bringing together *Beckett: L'increvable désir* and *Saint Paul: La Fondation de l'universalisme*, Simon Critchley addresses Badiou's conception of the relation between event and subject from a different perspective, that of "Politics and Ethics," and its consequences for an ethics of truth. Critchley elucidates the nature of ethical experience for Badiou and claims that, although Badiou's critique of current discourses on ethics in France is justified, his ethics are ultimately formalistic. While positing a grammar of ethical experience, Badiou fails to present a positive determination of the good, says Critchley, and points to the normative connotations of Badiou's theory of the subject for this failure. Since for Critchley Badiou's theory of the subject relies on a voluntaristic power of decision, he claims that it is possible to detect some residues of a heroic theory of great politics.

The volume closes with "Can Change Be Thought?"—a dialogue between Alain Badiou and Bruno Bosteels. By referring to the Pauline metaphor of the "road to Damascus," Bosteels establishes a continuity between Badiou's early texts (*Le Concept de Modèle* and *Théorie du sujet*) and his most recent ones. Badiou's turning point, Bosteels claims, happens in May 1968 and his thinking maintains a loyalty to this event as well as to its lasting effects. Bosteels also proposes a genealogy of Badiou's philosophy by framing it within the context of French Maoism, Althusserian Marxism, and Lacanian psychoanalysis. This, in turn, allows Badiou to discuss how his thinking differed from most orthodox Marxist positions officially sanctioned by the French Communist Party, from Sartre's philosophy of freedom, and from Althusser's structuralist brand of Marxism. Badiou states that Maoism was the knot that made it possible for him to articulate a rigorous formalism with a radical subjectivism.

Badiou also adds important clarifications on how he situates himself in the field of contemporary philosophy. Against more schematic critical assessments of Badiou's thinking that tend to set him against deconstruction, Badiou asserts that he shares with Jean-Luc Nancy and Philippe Lacoue-Labarthe the conviction that a heroic form of politics is over. His goal, however, is to pass through the motif of the end of philosophy to reopen the question of the political toward new possibilities in politics of emancipation.

This interview also allows Badiou to respond to criticism leveled against him by Ernesto Laclau and Slavoj Žižek regarding his dogmatism and absolutism and to make his own understanding of the notion of the event more precise. For Badiou, what matters in the arrival of an event is what unfolds as a system of consequences: a truth. Consequently, the real philosophical question for him becomes "Can we think that there is something new in the situation?" that, in turn, explains why he polemicizes against Michel Foucault's understanding of history in which the event vanishes in the heterogeneous articulations of knowledge and power.

Finally, given the importance that Foucault has had for cultural studies, Badiou also distinguishes his understanding of the relationship between philosophy and its conditions (their linkage) from the "mixture" that, at present, cultural studies articulates. Instead, he posits the need to develop a theory of the "networking" or the "tying together" of truth procedures that would make it possible to reconstruct a formalized concept of culture. This allows us to catch a glimpse of Badiou's work in progress. Not unlike his most influential master "antiphilosopher," Lacan, transmission becomes a key preoccupation of Badiou's teaching. For him it is not simply a question of transmitting very dense and well-articulated philosophical constructions by means of a transparent and unambiguous mathematical notation (matheme), but also to transmit the experience that made such a trajectory and articulation possible. For this reason Badiou has embarked on a discussion of the figures of the present as a way of communicating the "experimental adherences of the very concept itself."[10] His soon-to-be-published *Logics of Worlds* proposes a new articulation of the event and the subject by revising his theory of configurations (*Théorie du sujet*) and the distinction between event and simulacrum (*Ethics*).

NOTES

1. For Badiou's Maoist period, see Jean-Jacques Lecercle, "Cantor, Lacan, Mao, Beckett, *même Combat*: The Philosophy of Alain Badiou, *Radical Philosophy* 93 (1999): 6–13; and Bruno Bosteels, "Alain Badiou's Theory of the Subject: The Recommencement of Dialectical Materialism?" *Pli* 12 (2001): 200–29 and 13 (2002): 173–208. See also Jason Barker, *Alain Badiou: A Critical Introduction* (London: Pluto Press, 2002), 13–38.

2. For a detailed analysis of the question of the closure of metaphysics and philosophical writing, see Simon Critchley, *The Ethics of Deconstruction: Derrida and Levinas* (London: Blackwell, 1992). See also Jean-Luc Nancy's "Philosophie sans conditions" (in *Alain Badiou: Penser le multiple*, Charles Ramond, ed. [Paris: L'Harmattan, 2002], 66–79) in which he claims that Badiou's philosophy is in solidarity with deconstruction's overall project. On Badiou's most recent assessment of the end of philosophy, see "Can Change Be Thought?: A Dialogue with Alain Badiou" (chapter 10 in this volume).

3. Martin Heidegger, *Being and Time*, trans. J. Macquarrie and E. Robinson (San Francisco: Harper, 1962), ¶ 65, 370–80.

4. Gilles Deleuze, *Logic of Sense*, trans. Mark Lester (New York: Columbia University Press, 1990), 122, and *Difference and Repetition*, trans. Paul Patton (New York: Columbia University Press, 1994), 120.

5. Henry Maldiney, "L' Irreductible, " *Epokhè* 3 (1993): 11–49.

6. Claude Romano, *L'événement et le temps* (Paris: PUF, 1999).

7. Heidegger, *Being and Time*, ¶ 75, 439–49.

8. Jacques Lacan, *Television: A Challenge to the Psychoanalytic Establishment*, trans. D. Hollier, R. Krauss, and A. Michelson (New York: Norton, 1990), 9.

9. Jean-Toussaint Desanti, "L'Ontologie intrinsèque d'Alain Badiou," *Les Temps Modernes* 526 (May 1990): 61–71.

10. Badiou's lectures at the Collège International de Philosophie have been published as *Circonstances*.

PART ONE

MATHEMATICS = ONTOLOGY

ONE

On Alain Badiou's Treatment of Category Theory in View of a Transitory Ontology

Norman Madarasz

Of the many philosophical ideas in vogue during the twentieth century, that of "reduction" has fallen into uncertain disuse. After all, does reduction not imply the eminently dubitable feature of transcendent and positivist philosophies that, save for phenomenology, aim to crush the singular through a tendency toward the general? Is it not supposed to carry this out by means of a speculative gesture whose overarching grasp determines its aim and scope? This is at least one way that reduction has come to represent the worst type of formalism in thought. It has also worked at eliminating metaphorical expansion from philosophical analysis. Propelled by the critical weight of certain (social) constructivist views, by which method was made clear and simple, these acts finally seemed to capsize against the arbitrariness of their own omitted dependencies on fictional techniques and writing.

Whether one agrees with the doubts cast upon the notion of reduction or not, the fact remains that it is by no means condemned to twist the real beyond repair and recognition—provided one knows how to rationally discern a component of reality prior to the method of its explanation. Reductions could therefore easily be deemed accurate and even shown to be methodologically necessary or beautiful. In fact, the idea of a beautiful reduction seems perfectly appropriate to describe Alain Badiou's philosophical system. By no means should *reduction* be confused with *exclusion, simplification beyond repair, dehumanization,* or any other term typical of ideological opinion or dogmatic scientific doctrines. As Badiou seldom uses the term *reduction,* let it be spoken softly as a memory to crumbled empires and the élan of revolutionary science. What the term does stand for is how accurately it describes Badiou's refined structural analysis of philosophy in relation to its conditions and to its own historical montage.

Historically, the full sense of the term may have best lived up to its promise only when linked to the premises of description. Reduction would thus signify the careful parting of waters away from judgment and explanation and toward the clarity of receiving what there is to be grasped. At bottom, reduction would be a way of preparing what is given to methodological inquiry. It might handle what is in question without succumbing to ideological conflict regarding how this inquiry relates to the real. And such a fuller, more evolved idea of interaction between the real and the inquiries aimed at deciphering it would require concepts as mobile as 'event' and 'subject,' for example. By linking these strands, we end up with the conception of reduction introduced by and belonging to Badiou's cardinal thesis. The thesis reads simply: ontology *is* mathematics. Or, reversing the formula, mathematics is what of the science of being qua being can be inscribed and written as *lógos*. What this means in simple terms is that whatever falls outside the scope of the Letter (being, event, non-being, void) can still be thought without producing incoherence. By lógos, we mean the instrument and organ of language, of course, but also that of discourse, inscription, notation, and meaningful signs, both descriptive and communicational elements, as well as the explanatory models used to make sense of them.

Unpacking this thesis in a refined and consistent manner forces us to respond to at least two questions: what aspect of mathematics? and which conception of ontology? I will comment on Badiou's radical methodological decision that lies at the heart of his understanding of philosophy. Until then, let us bear in mind that we are sliding right into a historical fresco or, more accurately, a montage that has lent necessity to the relation between the One and the Infinite. First-generation German Romantics elucidated this relation according to which "ontology" ought to be taken as the critical and revised continuation of metaphysics. French philosophy has entirely absorbed this legacy and brought it to new expressions. Admittedly, throughout the twentieth-century, metaphysics has rarely fared better than reduction in trying to survive as a viable category to be thought. It is useful therefore to draw the parameters around the use of the term here. As the critical legacy of its recession, metaphysics refers to a body of knowledge that has been linked to Heidegger's fundamental critique of its own ontotheological past. And as a body of knowledge, metaphysics has not only returned to the principles of Aristotle's unaccomplished science of being qua being, proposed in *Metaphysics*, it has also rejected the universal significance of the modern turn to linguistics put forth by analytic philosophy.

From this vantage point, when a thinker such as John Searle uses the term *ontology* to speak of the "intentionality" that drives our understanding, he limits ontological inquiry merely to ontical questions: to the empirical facts of language acts. That this is the sole extent to which he believes it might be applied is not our concern here. The question of Being and the shortcomings to which both our empirical and rationalist models are bound when striving to develop this question activate ontology in the Heideggerian tradition.

Badiou's thinking belongs to a tradition that includes ontical inquiry, since it also and especially asks about the nature of being qua being. We get nowhere by sweeping the ontical aside then. Badiou situates philosophical inquiry in any one of philosophy's "conditions," the four background conditions of knowledge according to which philosophy can emerge as an autonomous activity of thought: the poem, the matheme, political invention, and love. Philosophy is conditioned by them, but in turn and in its best moments, it also strives to grasp their operations as a whole. Moreover, Badiou has asserted on numerous occasions that philosophy's commitment to thought is precisely to transgress the silence by fiat of Wittgenstein's *Tractatus* 7.0. This means that whereof one cannot speak, one ought to bring it to speech—be it through the silence of Samuel Beckett, Mark Rothko, or Morton Feldman's repetitive patterns whispered from the edge of the void, or from the selvage of that primordial science of the void, mathematics. After working on infinitesimal calculus and model theory, Badiou settled on set theory as what should stand as "mathematics" in its totalized expression. One must recall that set theory itself grew out of number theory, as mathematicians sought to improve their understanding of what numbers are—or, at least, of what "number" is—by defining the operations of succession in integers. The transformation of such entities along a sequential chain produced definitions that relied on an idea best exemplified by Giuseppe Peano in his postulates or principles of mathematical induction. For the set of all positive integers, these postulates state that:

1. 0 is a natural number,
2. every natural number has one successor, which is also a natural number,
3. no natural number has 0 as its successor,
4. different natural numbers have different successors,
5. if 0 has some property, and if when a number has that property then its successor also does, then all natural numbers have that property.

Also known as "recursivity," what this induction globally postulates is the possibility of infusing a temporal fundament to a step-based sequence, although to be fair the temporal variant is here still rudimentary at best. We would have to wait and deal with Real numbers instead of merely the natural series to even get close to time. What is important here is that Peano set out to show how prior to these axioms nothing is demonstrable. This axiomatic commitment is, of course, a key notion for set theory, one that has significantly fulfilled its program of providing mathematics with a foundational theory. So as we count, we recursively schematize both the repetitive drive of the number chain as well as the reformulation of its predecessor an incremental step ahead. These propositions cannot themselves be demonstrated as logical theorems, meaning they stand as axioms. Their terms, as Peano himself wrote, "cannot be reduced further, it is not possible to define the ideas they express by ideas postulated as previously known."[1] Peano's smart formalization led to an attempt in the sciences to reduce mathematics to logic. Badiou proposes a reversal of that project to the benefit of an altogether emancipatory idea of reduction, and thus sets himself at a remote angle to the field known as "philosophy of mathematics." This is largely owing to two key domains that interact in his system: mathematics and, uncharacteristically for set theory, ontology.

Badiou identified ontology's paradigm in set theory. However, he has also had to confront category theory, which has vied for foundational status within the field of mathematics. Albeit in schematic form, in what follows we will attempt a philosophical reconstruction of this ontology to confront it with the notion of category. Badiou's work in the 1990s, which has still not been published in definitive form in English, dealt with how to situate category theory within his thesis on ontology. If with Jacques Rancière one may characterize Badiou's work as a massive critique of the notion of the One, then how to arrange two suitors to the sole unified position of fundament becomes a delicate, although capital, task to establish.

The work of positioning the two options builds up what Badiou calls a "transitory ontology." It deals specifically with the phenomenon of "appearing" as a possible and incomplete formulation of this arrangement between two foundational theories of mathematics and the thesis of mathematics as ontology. To that extent, it is primarily a program put forth in view of relating categories to sets. Yet just as we must contrast the tension in Badiou's thought between being and language, as related to the consensus of a linguistic turn, we must also observe that the philosophical principles of a transitory ontology risk spilling over into what turns out to be a set-theoretic interpretation of the categorical orientation. To what degree is this a problem? Is it a problem for mathematics that sets are refined by knowledge of categories? Is it a problem to find that life is not always what it seems and that the rule of the excluded middle, endemic to set theory but relative to only some constructions in category theory, does not have absolute currency in the real? At any rate such is only one of the intuitionist consequences of equating category theory with a general foundational theory of logic.

Still, Badiou builds his system upon the basis of the set as the most adequate concept by which to handle the idea of the pure multiple. A potentially disturbing spillover of self-contradictory mathematical foundations would have a detrimental effect, at least on the idea that ontology is mathematics if only in its bivalent identity. If categories were irreducible to sets, would ontology and Being themselves be multiplied to such an extent that their contours would dissipate into the very inconsistency to which sets are minimal marker-limits? This chapter will examine this central question.

ON SET AND CATEGORY THEORY AS COMPETING PARADIGMS FOR BADIOU'S THESIS ON MATHEMATICAL/ONTOLOGICAL IDENTIFICATION

In *L'être et l'événement*, Badiou seeks to restore set theory to its ontological ascendancy and develops an "intrinsic" ontology that takes the idea of the "pure multiple" as the basis for the science of being qua being, insofar as it agrees with the axioms of set theory in a massive attack against the One.[2] In this view, there is no One, but only what presupposes it. Its history descends from the Greeks and is taken up by the Arabs as the undefined primary element; its essence is an operation instead of an entity. Badiou names this as "counting-as-One," referring to the abstract operation from which every conception of the One is recurrently inferred. Were the One to be, it would only be discerned by the operation of a movement surging forward, a type of fulguration, or, better, an event. Were we to aspire to locate the conditions of possibility of the One, we would have to opt for an operator immanent to its act instead of indexing one conceptually to what is only presupposed as a starting point.

In this way Badiou aims at a radical realism in which sets, manifolds, or multiples (all synonymous here) are the elementary presentable patterns from which process and consistency emerge. It is a realism in which physics itself would fall short, since it has to assume the effect of the observer, instruments, and mathematics on how the quantum "objects" or particles are grasped (P&P 127). When physics is concerned, it is to the physical, indeed material, dimension of corresponding multiples posited as real. By contrast, Badiou's realist theory of the manifold seeks to capture the inconsistent extensions: the basic preconditions integrated to a certain minimal sense of order that end up granting the idea of the manifold a semiautonomous existence from any individual observer. The being of an inconsistent multiple is not so dispersed as to refuse being pegged by a name—which is precisely what Badiou emphasizes as the intricate crux of mathematics and ontology. Regarding this name, why not settle on the void as the starting point to any counting-as-One, as the logicians did in the wake of the innovations brought about by Arabic algebra?

As the empty set became the central operator to set theory in both ZFC (Zermelo-Frankel with Axiom of Choice) and von Neumann's formalization, its referent—upon philosophical inspection, though Cantor had already had an intuition of it—has proved to be none other than being qua being. Badiou's system supplements this set-theoretic evolution by commanding a strong commitment to a philosophy of the event whose task is to inscribe the process immanent to the *es gibt* (*there is* or *it gives*) of Being, such as the latter stands upon the basic observation that events erupt into and organize worlds. It is only through the event that Being *is*. In Badiou's view Being-in-the-world is the consistent point from which ontology proceeds and thus ought to lend itself to accurate inquiry by means of a method of immanence, one "intrinsic" to its basis as pure multiple.

Jean-Toussaint Desanti initially introduced the term *intrinsic ontology* in consideration of Badiou's work. Despite acknowledging the accuracy of his ontology, Desanti observed how Badiou's system nonetheless was still reduced to a combinatorial instrumentality. By the very fact of its adhesion to the set-theoretic axioms that prescribe a universe of absolute, albeit open, proportion, Badiou's identification thesis would be setting the One at the very crux of a philosophical perception intended to destitute it from such primacy. Desanti consequently recommended safeguarding the project of intrinsic ontology (equating inconsistent multiplicities with non-Being and the event) while at the same time he advised choosing the mathematics of category theory to develop the thesis on Being.[3] Contrary to set theory, category theory allows for the transcription of the mathematical structures and logical operators found as the formative basis of the notion of object. In its attention to structures, and to the relations by which they are constituted, category theory lifts the constraints by which the concept of universe had been limited to univocity. Category theory examines how objects are nothing prior to the relations through which they are constituted. Inasmuch as "object" relations, or more specifically "functors," are fundamental, the actual notion of category is an auxiliary one.[4] Indeed, categories provide the domain and range to functors or relations. As a result, a universe begins to take shape only through the configuration of increasingly complex structures or "diagrams" and, significantly, through their interactions. Such a view smashes representation theories and relativizes philosophies, making each one local to a set framework or perspective. Readers familiar with Deleuze's work from the 1970s will not fail to see the similarities with category theorist J. Bell, here describing the elementary scope explored by category theory: "With the relinquishing of the absolute universe of sets, mathematical concepts will in general no longer possess absolute meaning, nor mathematical assertions absolute truth values, but will instead possess such meanings or truth values only *locally*, i.e., *relative*, to local frameworks."[5]

While in Deleuze's thought the question led to speculating on a bootstrap model of self-engenderment, by which the early term of simulacrum based in Platonic exegesis obtains, in Badiou's philosophy it has led to an altogether different inquiry. Namely, whether by focusing on relations and objects we still deal with ontology as understood in the Heideggerian sense, which means the Parmenidian sense. This is certainly one of the central problems to which Badiou has devoted his work since the end of the 1970s, though it first begins to appear in his work of the 1960s. In 1998 Badiou's research led to a provisional solution, published in *Court traité d'ontologie transitoire*.[6] Whatever the correct course may be, the radical difference between set-theoretic and category-theoretic orientations suffices to destabilize the intrinsic property of ontology, as does the notion of "mathematical foundations" particular to the philosophy of mathematics.

Why do sets and categories differ so radically then? In basic terms, a set is something whose properties can be isolated from its internal components according to the operator "being a member of . . ." and by deduction, "being a subset of . . ." By contrast, the formulation of mathematics provided by category theory is element free. The properties of a category are given only from the arrows (or "morphisms") that trace a relation between at least two "objects" that are merely points here: "The main point of categorical thinking is to let arrows reveal structure."[7] Take the identity morphism, for example: one of the conditions of every category is that an arrow curve about a point, acting simultaneously as "source" and "target." This stands as the object's identity, though clearly the object is nothing but this arrow. From this point, by taking two points or letters, each with their identity morphisms, we get a category, provided that in addition to identity and the arrow between these two points a third letter is added with its arrow(s) to create what is called a "composition" of their morphisms. For this composition to consist, their morphisms must be associative. The elementary objective then becomes to trace morphism compositions according to increasing aggregate complexity and to spot in these subsequent compositions or "diagrams" the acts and conduct of the algebraic equations by which a structure emerges. The end result of these elementary steps is a proof with respect to the "limits" emerging in the given diagram. Such limits may apply to the categorical object as a whole, or to its "subobjects," that is, the categorical equivalent of subsets. Yet this is just a step in one direction, for fundamental to category theory is the idea that relations are reversible and that a diagram of a certain type, when its morphisms are reversed into their adjunct form, underscores the mathematical association of a similar diagram type, for example, intersection is the adjunct of (set-theoretic) implication.

The difference between set and category is significant regarding the idea of object and relation. It becomes fully instructive when considering how the difference between objects is established. In set theory, if one can postulate that sets "contain" members and subsets, then one can prove whether they are identical by comparing two sets. For any set A and for any set B, if *a* belongs to A and *b* belongs to B, and *a* is equal to *b*, then it stands to reason that A is equal to B, at least in terms of set theory. Indeed, one of set theory's virtues is its ability to prove that identity of manifolds is a function of the equality of their internal properties, and consequently so is difference. The import of this sentence has been enshrined in set theory as the axiom of extensionality.

For category theory, identity is not at all a function of equality. Identity is a case of "isomorphism": two structures are identical if they have the same arrow compositions, the same aggregate of relations. In this case the structures are said to be identical, defined "up to one isomorphism." Giving more depth to the central notion of category theory, a relation is drawn between two points prior to which there is no antecedence to the arrow. Indeed, the existence of the arrow is merely a matter of space-time convention. Nonetheless, within that convention, isomorphism stands as the absolutely minimal arrow prior to which there is nothing, but only from which there can be objects or movement, or in its own terminology "commuting" categories.

As structures grow more complex, they acquire elasticity with respect to various limits in feedback to which a notion of "universe" slowly begins to take shape. Yet, such a universe is only relative to the various compositions and diagrams organizing it. These statements acquire general characteristics for that local universe as a whole. This is why a significant idea of category thinking consists in defining not one but a plurality of possible universes, structures, or, in mathematical parlance, "opposes." The theoretical project goes on to determine what actions are possible in a given universe. In fact, one of the essential features of a topos is to be composed of truth-value morphisms. Not that a topos includes such morphisms; it is composed of them as a complex category. The feature of such truth-value morphisms, moreover, underlies the apparently greater stage of completion of category theory regarding its operations, for within its structural mapping every topos displays its own logic—whether classic (bivalent) or intuitionist.

By contrast, sets lie in a single "open" universe wherein the notion of limit may only be imposed as a local property consequent to a set's internal contents and components. Otherwise we get into the dilemma of having to determine whether a very large set is a member of itself. It remains strictly impossible in set theory to attribute a qualifier (either existential or universal) to the idea of absolute set, or set of all sets. Were this attempted, it would entail, as it already has, a series of paradoxes all caulked onto the infamous antinomy that Russell deciphered in Frege's symbolic axiomatization, itself a precursor to set theory. As in ZFC, adhering to the impossibility of a set of all sets is what has brought set theory its power, up to the limit of the idea of one universe, at least. By contrast, not only is such a large universe possible in category theory, but the existential and universal qualifiers are themselves morphisms relative to a certain topos or toposes.

I would surmise that at this point we begin to perceive how set theory may be reduced to category theory, though not vice versa. What ultimately shifts in this reduction of set theory to category theory remains our understanding of the notion of object. As stated, an "object" is only determined by its morphism(s), or arrow(s). In other words, an object is neither determined internally nor independently from these morphisms. This makes category theory, in the words of Jean-Pierre Marquis, "a generalized mathematical theory of structures. One of its goals is to reveal the universal properties of structures of a given kind via their relationships with one another."[8] If morphisms are factors of convention, that is, an object is but a letter or point, then we are shuttled back philosophically to the question of literality and lógos as what stands at the edge of what there is. And mathematical literality, in the categorical stream, does not only point to an extrinsic or externalist model of manifolds; it establishes relations as prior to elements or to sets themselves. It construes Being from Relations. The problem that emerges from within Badiou's system should now be self-evident. How can the thesis by which mathematics is identified with ontology sustain two versions of the sciences of being-qua-being, and, moreover, two concurrent ones, if we are to trust the opinion of mathematicians themselves?

To settle this question, Badiou proposes what he calls a "transitory" ontology. Its underlying strategy is to deal less with being than with appearing. Insofar as category theory lays special emphasis on synoptically illustrating algebraic equations through the painstaking construction of categories and toposes, it would be fair to say that in Badiou's option what underlies the categorical orientation's object-theory, regardless of its complexity, is how categories are drawn out into formal operativity, synoptically conditioned. This last point leads us to conclude that Badiou uses philosophy in order to satisfy the stakes posed by the category-theoretic orientation in its ties to the *visible*, ontically understood.

Transitory ontology therefore has a special function. It must deal with the relation between Being and the Visible insofar as these manifestations are subordinate to the real, construed as unrepresentable. The latter ultimately stands as a process-background regulating the formation of structures in general. But as the notion of relation is key to this commitment, how does it fare within set theory? What is the extension of the idea of relation in set theory and does it differ dramatically from category theory? The very idea of an identity relation between ontology and mathematics depends on a clear elaboration of this problem.

THE INFINITE AND THE APPEARING

The ontological decision at the origin of Badiou's system strikes a blow at the ancestral relationship between the infinite and the One. Set theory asserts that the infinite is the inscription of a letter. Furthermore, this letter declares a fundamental subtraction of the multiple-infinite with respect to a totalization by the

One because one cannot posit the existence of a class of all classes, a set of all sets, without entailing a series of contradictions liable to compromise the whole theory. This is why Badiou goes beyond the formula 1/infinite = Being, with three theorems: (1) without-One = operation of multiples, (2) Being = in-consistent multiples, and (3) Void = (proper) name of Being. This has an immediate upshot for the finite, which signals the existence of the infinite as merely one phenomena-type of being finite, namely *in-finite* being. An element of a set is both identical to itself (an element or individual member) and it is also other than itself (part of its collective being or a subset). The quantity of these subsets cannot be limited by forcing a number of adhesions, a quantity of agglomerations, or effusion of agencies. This means that not only is the finite conceived along the lines of interiority, its structure is fundamentally split between its elementary-being and the partitive-being that exceeds it. The disconnected phenomenon between these two modes of being holds the stability of the *dansein*, to repeat Badiou's neologism; it determines the finite and not the infinite as the place of complexity.[9]

A major objection raised against Badiou's ontological thesis is that in his system the radical identity with mathematics would be transhistorical. To be sure, the notion of relation, the interest with which it has been renewed by category theory, is not a contemporary invention. Yet, if it is integrally postulated as one of the accidents or properties of substance, according to the paradigm of Aristotelian reason, it becomes painstaking to have to argue in favor of its transhistorical character. After all, relation, as with the Platonic notion of simulacrum, is now disconnected from the paradigm that had dominated Western and Eastern thought for over two thousand years. The contemporary idea of category implies its own reduction, always with respect to its arrows, and never in subordinate mode as an "accident" to universal substance, as in Aristotle's *Categories*. In this contemporary sense, category is hypostatized by no substance, nor does it hypostatize itself into substance.

Badiou nonetheless locates this historical affiliation of category in the Aristotelian heritage, and one wonders if there is no accident involved here. In Badiou's view set theory, with its intrinsic ontology, axiomatic approach and rooting in ontology, stems from Platonism. However, in the argumentative virtuosity Badiou displays, this coordination between Aristotle and Plato comes close to philosophical self-interest at best, or, at worst, to Sophistry. Badiou needs Plato. The work of the Academy's founder most clearly exhibits the emergence and process of philosophy. Aristotle and Kant, on the other hand, appear in Badiou's reading to deter philosophy from its greater potential, notwithstanding the vast and innovative range of the sciences created by Aristotle and Kant, especially in their relativizing mathematics and the matheme to logic. Even more, Kant literally banished the interest of logic in the *Critique of Pure Reason*, and mathematics in its wake, for failing to show great potential in formalizing pure and practical reason and judgment. In what should no longer surprise us, Kant had in fact based his own method on a categorical approach.

The Aristotelian thesis that "Being is said in multiple ways" undergoes an interpretative correction in Badiou's work. Perfectly in line with contemporary Aristotle scholars, he transforms the thesis into "the *being* is said in multiple ways." Ontology becomes transitory insofar as its deals with beings or existents (*seiendes*). Briefly put, integration of the notion of category into Badiou's system leans on this translational interpretation of Aristotle. The latter undergoes a philological correction regarding the notion of *on ê on* (Being qua Being) successfully argued by French philosophers Michel Narcy and Barbara Cassin. And in terms similar to the interpretive element added to this translation, it is imperative to point out that beings are beings-there, as in Heideggerian terminology, insofar as they are what incorporate the very essence of appearing. Appearing "is as such what links or connects the being to its site. The essence of appearing is the relation" (*CTOT* 192).

There is a transitional aspect within Aristotle that moves from ontology to logic, or from mathematics to logic. In this regard, Being, expressed at the heart of Book Gamma of Aristotle's *Metaphysics*, expresses mediation. It takes shape as a *pros hen* or directionality. This is the sole condition by which the science of Being qua Being consists. Aristotle strictly rules out any further conceptualizing of "beings" as supervened by Being. Moreover, the idea of directionality, or sense broadly construed, holds to the fact that Aristotle declared this science to exist. Admittedly, to Being qua Being one cannot grant existence without granting in the same stroke existence to the set of all sets. For this reason, in reference to Aristotle Badiou writes that "it will be demanded from whomever declares the existence of a science of Being qua Being that they explicate the formal axioms of every transmissible discourse" (*CTOT* 184). Needless to say, Aristotle himself fell short of the task, leaving the science of Being qua Being as an unfulfilled suggestion while refusing to allot mathematics its Pythagorean–Platonist extension as a universal science of eternity.

Still, the pure and empty multiple, subtracted from the One, can be attributed as a property of Being. In a mode faithful to Platonism, this allows Badiou to assert that "ontology" is a science of *Being*-qua-Being, a science of the void of which multiples are woven in their infinite development. By contrast, "logic," here taken as the logic or logics of ontology, or "ontologic," is a science of *being*-qua-being—or of what appears—a science of the for-itself whose field deals with the multiple ways by which *being* is said, meaning the multiple ways in which it is lived. Badiou insists on the moment of decision with respect to ontological commitment. Nonetheless, he does everything to limit its possibilities to a single ontology. The importance of his affiliation to Plato holds to the transhistorical continuity of the philosophical concepts of truth, eternity, and the Idea. This commitment counters the historical currency of the vision expressed by Aristotle, particularly the one made possible by later medieval scholasticism's devotion to the reduction of mathematics to logic. One need not dig very deep to get a sense of the modern inspiration emerging from this tradition, mounted against the univocal character of universal Being through the refined discourse of increasingly pragmatic, cultural, and relativist philosophies.

In Badiou's perspective, Platonism better describes philosophy as being under condition of an event in thought. Platonism attests to the surfacing of the infinite through the finite world, as it were. "Plato's fundamental concern is to declare the immanent identity and co-membership of the known and the knowing mind, their essential ontological commensurability. Were there one point on which he is Parmenides' son asserting 'the Same is both Thought and Being,' it is on that point" (CTOT 96). That the infinite is ontology, that is, mathematics, attests to the fact that its projects have fundamentally been to relate to the One. But Platonism has always been devoted to the multiple of the multiple, or the other of the Other (a possibility well established in *The Sophist*) and not to the proliferation of difference between possible universes.

In keeping with Platonism, Badiou adheres to the basis laid down by the Greek master. Plato wrote with the conviction that human beings dispose of the power to understand the interaction between the sensible and the intelligible as expressed in the Idea, that is, of what is thought insofar as it is thought. But Badiou has pierced Plato's dogmatic affiliation to the One and the Good in a Spinozian act by replacing these with the latter's peculiar commitment to the infinite, though with one major exception. Spinoza used the *more geometrico* as the means by which Being could be warranted as infinite. But when defining the infinite as sub specie aeternitatis, Spinoza went a step further: the concepts used to understand Being were suddenly sealed from temporal analyses, indeed cut off from any indentification with time itself.

From this insight, Badiou goes on to maintain his conviction in the limits of category theory, as a way to approach the turbulent terrain whereby the Relation precedes Being. For whatever is manifest in the dispersion of multiple possible universes, to be part of the real one must also be connected in some way, were it through the loosest idea of relation. This is a question that turns philosophy back to how the infinite is linked to the finite through an organization of pure multiplicities. As such, Badiou's conviction, in contrast to Lavendhomme's, is that set-multiplicities have greater currency in relation to the immanent expression of the real.[10] Immanence proves to be the methodological gambit most faithful to draw out this configuration.

Mathematics is therefore Being's thought in a finite, localized expression. Plato knew this and it is in his philosophy of mind rooted in metempsychosis. Badiou's commitment to mathematics and the subject has led to his affiliation with a recast Platonism: "Platonism is the recognition of mathematics as a thought that is intransitive to sensible and linguistic experience, dependent on a decision that makes space for the undecidable, and assumes that all of what is consistent exists" (*CTOT* 98). As a paradigm for ontological choice that lends Platonism a primordial role and in its goal to inquire into the mysteries lying beyond what language may construe, set theory continues to stand as fuller and richer in promise than category theory.

However, even in its most ambitious manifestation, category theory attempts to show that this disposition itself is but one modality of its possibilities. Badiou is skeptical on this option. And I would like to argue that this is so due to the recurring trace of what the One lends itself to believe: that only *it* can offer a universal safeguard to the relativist expansion of categories. Yet it is obvious that to adhere to such recurrence is to weaken the idea of pure multiplicity. By contrast, it is also what appears as binding the pure multiple to a vastly stretched One through a dialectic so loose as to be a nonrelation. We now must turn to deepening Badiou's struggle with this dialectic. In the process, we will examine some interpretations formulated by category theorists regarding the foundational aspirations of the theory.

CATEGORY AND TRANSITORY ONTOLOGY

Up to now I have described Badiou's claim that category theory is actually the foundational theory of logic, of ontologic, while set theory remains that of mathematics. This is a position he established in the course of the 1990s based on a critical suggestion by Desanti regarding *L'être et l'événement*. Admittedly, Badiou's position has not been constant, and its current version is tentative at best. Within the scope of mathematics itself there is awareness, indeed even accusations, that set theory has based itself on the innovations introduced by category theory. For the sake of homology with mathematics, it is important to notice how Badiou performs a double move, both of which favor set theory. Regarding the identity thesis, there is a set-theoretic co-opting of category theory, while regarding the argument leading to the notion of "transitory ontology," there has been a legitimate demotion of category theory in his philosophical system. As convenient as it has been thus far, its tentativeness suggests that Badiou's identity thesis has not sufficiently debunked the One from its ontological throne. The project would require replacing the One with an immanent manifold theory on philosophical self-generation in relation to Being and the Event. In fact, his thesis remains torn by the prospect of two ontological versions at the heart of mathematics.

I would also maintain that Badiou has not convincingly shown that the notion of Relation, or non-Relation, does not in fact stand prior to philosophical inference broadly understood: prior to three fundamental notions of set theory. These are all related to the Platonic vocation and its central operators are difference (the axiom of extensionality), the primitive name of Being (the axiom of the empty set), and the undecidable (the state in which the continuum hypothesis stands regarding the broadest orientation in thought on the proliferation of infinites in the "generic orientation in thought"). Nonetheless, the conception of these axioms relies fundamentally on the notion of Relation, above and beyond Being. However, the wild card here, ontologically speaking, remains the Event. As non-being, the event sustains and justifies the notion of process as that from which Being arises, and as such it is the Event that should stand prior to the Relation. The question is whether in set theory the Event truly stands autonomously in relation to its ontological objectives.

What grants interiority to the ontological perspective is the capacity to determine the identity of a set from the property-features of its members and subsets. But category theory takes shape from the notion of difference. To shelter his thesis from objections, it is therefore of capital importance for Badiou to localize the notion of difference in all of its varieties as derived from logic, and not as a fluctuating manifold. Because as a fluctuating and irreducible manifold, if difference were to condition ontology, the ontological decision would entail two legitimate versions (two absolute and competitive universes). Where there are at least two ontologies, the manifold would then lend itself to an anarchic violence whose consequence would perhaps prove Heidegger right regarding his declaration that only a God can save us. Badiou may well be a playwright, what he is not is a tragedian. Set theory thus remains the paradigm of ontology *tout court*.

I do not wish to take leave of these questions or this state of incompletion, which is perhaps structural, without returning to what nonetheless remains the optimistic tone of Desanti's text. Where Badiou opposes extrinsic and intrinsic ontology, Desanti keeps the hope of an intrinsic ontology very much alive, all the while expressing himself at a distance from set theory. His devotion to the latter, as with Badiou's, is linked to the idea that were ontology to exist, it would not be able to prescribe Platonic realism without respecting the exigencies of the intrinsic. The challenge then is not to yield on the interpretation of the categories, while ordering them necessarily to the side of a relativism by the sole fact of the multiplication of universes. This said, it does not seem implausible that the course of these decisions will depend in turn, on the elaborations in the mathematical theories and prescriptive arguments developed and crafted by category theorists themselves.

It is therefore instructive to consider what these theorists already have to say on this debate between relation and membership. Namely, is it possible that the idea of "relation" is presupposed to a deeper extent than that of intrinsic membership, and is therefore the true regulative principle to the real? Surely not if the notion of relation cannot be shown to be independent of a class. Then again, such dependency merely reinforces the definition of category as first elaborated by Eilenberg and MacLane, and recalled above by Bell.[11] At the cost of keeping set theory as ontology, Badiou risks not fully debunking the Heideggerian montage of the historicality of Being to the benefit of the intricate congenital bond that has historically conditioned mathematics and philosophy. Moreover, the strength of his intuition has held firm as both a sufficient and necessary condition for a paradigm shift within French thought toward mathematics and away from the poem and mysticism.

However, this idea of bond as an original condition of ontology seems best conceptualized in the concept of Relation, only after which Being becomes its subject of inquiry. The question is whether outside of Being there is identity between the event, or non-being, and the relation, or whether there is also an order of antecedence. To settle the question in favor of the former, it would surely be helpful to find a notion of the event within categorical thought. This does not seem to be possible. Yet the strong antecedence of foundational connectedness, however loosely construed, does seem to favor category theory in its foundational pretensions far more than set theory. In the early 1990s, Badiou flirted with the categorical orientation as another possible version of ontology.[12] At least he expressed this himself in response to Desanti's remark. But the place rendered to the categorical orientation is located clearly in a logic of possible universes whose merit is also to have released logic from its reduction to linguistic syntax, despite the inventive wealth of the latter. Furthermore, to what extent is the question modulated when we provide a deeper analysis of the meaning of *foundational*?

For starters, many category theorists no longer accept a single definition given to the term *foundational*. Bell, for instance, cites two senses of foundational: strong and weak. The strong sense would allow all mathematical operations, as well as the current logico-metatheoretical framework for mathematics—proof theory—to be reducible to category theory. Given that such a reduction involves both a combinatorial component, regarding the inscriptional properties of the formal language, and a semantic component, regarding the interpretation and truth of the expressions of that language, Bell considers category theory to be unable to achieve its foundational ends. This would be owing to the fact that it cannot make any claims to providing a specifically categorical definition of a set or class. As mentioned before, even its key notion, functor or relation, requires a class domain: a category within which a transformation may occur. In his view, "in order to understand what a category is, you first have to know what a class is."[13]

Conversely, Lavendhomme adheres to the plausibility of category theory fulfilling its program of supplying mathematics with a foundational theory. But, he adds, it would still be too early to say so for sure. Even were the set concept to play a fundamental role in mathematics, "the description of mathematical concepts—algebraic ones, for example—is done both more profoundly and more operationally in a categorical formulation than in a usual logico-set theoretic one."[14] It seems that from the perspective of mathematics, and of mathematicians, everything depends on how the idea of set—an intrinsic manifold—is transformed within category theory.

Such progression depends on one of the most remarkable discoveries to have emerged within category theory: the notion of topos. But it also relies on the degree to which one is willing to grant pertinence to the unorthodox history of topos theory offered by McLarty. Before coming to McLarty's view, let us look further at this idea of topos. Let an elementary topos be defined as a category with finite limits and power objects (i.e., parts and whole). This immediately involves, among other things, the subobject truth-value classifier "Omega." In set-theoretic logic, one could say that Omega is the class of {true, false}; but in categorical logic, that is, as what applies in toposes, there is neither necessity to a bivalent logic nor to a single class of truth-values per topos. One can easily encounter "time-dependent" toposes in which at time t1, Omega = {true, false}, and at time t2, Omega = {false, false}, with the resulting topos being ({true, false}, {false, false}). Simply put, a topos is a logically complete construction of a universe made solely of morphisms.

Now, regarding the foundational potential of category theory based on the power of such a structure, the orthodox view is as follows: "The paramount achievement of topos theory is to have identified the basic core of set theory in such a way that the set concept becomes manifest in contexts (such as algebraic geometry or constructive mathematics) where before its presence was at most tacit."[15] To which McLarty argues outright, in what was then an unorthodox idea, that "the view that toposes originated as generalized set theory is a figment of set theoretically educated common sense."[16] The task of choosing between these two reasons comes down to what Badiou terms an "ontological decision" (CTOT 198).

To be sure, Badiou would never merely claim to be demoting category theory to philosophical relativism or to the terms used to reverse theoretical relativism in general. The interpretation of category theory as logic may proceed from a linguistic prescription, or from an ontological one. Just as he establishes the identity thesis between mathematics and ontology as organized by set theory, so also does he ensure that the foundational theory of logic is also mathematically prescribed when defining logic as follows: "logic is, within mathematics, the movement of thought by which justice is brought to the being of appearing, i.e. by what affects Being insofar as it is Being-there" (CTOT 194).

Yet to what extent do we still face a hierarchical paradigm here, and does the pure multiple not have a more generic, because far less constrained and certain a configuration, when rendered into the relationless condition whereby the different possible universes of topos theory obtain? McLarty argues that it is common in philosophical comments on categorical foundations to find the sort of incomprehension "allowing the *object theory* to be categorical set theory but assuming it requires membership based set theory as *metatheory*. In fact categorical set theory (i.e. the description of set theory axioms in a topos) can stand with no metatheory at all, as ZF [Zermelo-Frankel] is often taken to do."[17] To his credit, Badiou does not reduce elementary topos theory as a generalization of set theory. McLarty argues primarily against the commonsense view held within mathematics that leads to reading set theory into any mathematics one meets. The drawback of such thinking is that it often leads to focusing on isolated categories. But McLarty does insist that "in fact category theory arose from studying relations between categories."[18] So it would not be specific to set theory, to mathematics or ontology, to consider, as does Badiou, that categories and toposes hold together as if they were modalities of a univocal universe. As previously pointed out, categories are less important in the overall theory than are relations, functors, and adjunct (or dual) functors. As for the question of univocity within category theory, there is still no consensus on a category of categories rich enough to handle all of mathematics as effectively as a foundational theory should.

As for spreading ambiguity over the very term of *foundation*, it is undeniable that from a philosophical perspective it is a required step to make. Marquis carries out a lateral deconstruction of the term into six senses (logical, cognitive, epistemological, semantic, ontological, methodological, or pragmatic), clearly refusing any priority to the notion of set.[19] He accurately and pointedly shows that most ordinary mathematical objects may be encoded in set theory. Which is why in its broader pretensions category theory would have to be foundational in the cognitive sense as well. Is this feasible without reactivating the conception of universal grammar, or psychologism? It seems evident that were category theory to provide such a foundational theory it would have to account for the drawbacks of analytic philosophy, and integrate the latter's current search through phenomenology for answers related to its cognitive dilemmas.

However, Marquis's lateral breakdown succeeds not least because his stated objective is to show how category theory justifiably has foundational pretensions. Yet to carry out his "philosophical" analysis, he completely presupposes a reduction of ontic principles to ontological ones. This claim is made evident in the fifth sense of foundation he proposes: "OntFound (S, T): S is an (relative) *ontological* foundation for T." For Marquis states explicitly that the two concepts underlying this interpretation of ontology are membership and existence—the two leading principles of ontic determination par excellence. I have sufficiently pointed out that using the term *ontology* in reference to essentially ontic principles is a by-product of the history of analytic philosophy and its decision to perform a methodological cut whereby Being in its Parmenidian dimension is excluded. Clearly, this sense of foundation does not warrant as thorough a breakdown as Marquis proposes. Badiou's thesis does not so much as include and order these diverse senses, something that Marquis considers as specific to a philosophy of mathematics, as it maintains its totalizing, universal, and univocal sense.

By contrast, Marquis does isolate a statement from Lawvere in which the sense of foundation corresponds to Badiou's. In 1966 Lawvere speculated on whether category theory could provide a foundation for mathematics, with foundation understood as "a single system of first-order axioms in which all usual mathematical objects can be defined and all their usual properties proved."[20] Now this sense of foundation, as Marquis shows, has actually become specific, though not even the cognitive sense can do without presupposing the notions of "collection and operation" as quite typical of a set-theoretic approach. Is this not confirmation of Badiou's reading that category theory is ontologically prescribed?

Returning to Lawvere's statement, let us consider a fundamental tension between possibility and the real: "in the mathematical development of recent decades one sees clearly the rise of the conviction that the relevant properties of mathematical objects are those which can be stated in terms of their abstract structure rather than in terms of the elements which the objects were thought to be made of."[21] In the perspective of relating category theory to set theory, a sticking point remains the impossibility by the latter to absorb very large categories, such as the category of categories. Yet there is an expression of possibility in category theory that must be philosophically borne in mind. For the relationship between different toposes does not fall short of being compossible; they do not cancel each other out by the radical opposition between the logical structures and interpretations among them. Paradox does not hinder category theory. Yet it may very well impede the idea of what is real. Which is why it should be borne in mind that category theory is the production of *possible* universes. Or rather the sense of "possible foundation" remains category theory's greatest challenge to draw out, as the subsequent question of "possible in terms of what"?

Still, if I am led to the observation that there is a set-theoretic interpretation of category theory organizing Badiou's ontological thesis, it is for a specific reason. It is from the point of the "there is" (*il y a* or *es gibt*), hence of Being's idea of operativity in a univocal universe, that the judgment of the dynamic character of the arrows of a category or more complex structures is determined. In line with the philosophical inquiry here developed, there is a significant distinction between Being and possible universes. Regarding possibility, one requires a local, indeed localizable, class of propositions. Enter topos theory, "allowing one to understand in depth how logical variability is marked, which is also the contingent variability of appearing with respect to the strict and necessary univocity of being-multiple" (*CTOT* 199). We have now come full circle—Badiou's ordering depends on a radical choice in favor of an intrinsic ontology.

What is an ontological decision in the language of a mathematician? Bell gives a perfect example. On the nature of "universe" in set theory, Bell notes how Paul Cohen's discovery of the independence—or undecidability—of Cantor's continuum hypothesis had led to uncertainty about the real universe of sets. Faced with such undecidability, the question of radical, ontological choice immediately confronts us as to what we might do with this uncertainty and where we might like to proceed with the set concept.[22] We have the possibility of abandoning the notion of absolute universe of sets, thereby making the continuum hypothesis into a variable model relative to ZFC and best formalized in a topos. Or we may choose, like Badiou, to see in the unbridgeable gap of Cantor's continuum hypothesis two infinite sizes represented in the real line—between the power (or number) of set members and the power of subsets—as the real "wandering" (*errance*) proliferation of sets in a universe which, while absolute and unique, is even more importantly open, boundless, or the very expression of the non-Relation.

Category theory has only been around since the 1940s. Everything would seem to suggest that it is going to continue to develop whether in its foundational aspirations or not. The main complaint issued by its practitioners is that in order to clarify the very notion of multiple, manifold, or set, set theorists draw from categorical resources all the while omitting to emphasize that these notions should only exist or have a referent in relation to the arrows tracing them. Doubtless, the difficult foundational question remains as the ground from which passions are set to soar the highest. By emphasizing this tie between category theory, logic, and possibility, Badiou's reductive Platonism turns out to be no reduction at all. He, rather, draws out the process presupposed for reaching the most viable thought of the real. And no matter how many ways there may be of possibly expressing the real, there is only one way of saying "there (it) is." This is part of the beauty of being committed to ontology. In it there is a refusal to allow the semantic to rule over the deontic. This is a disposition to faith as process and event if ever there was one. In the act of taking on mathematics through this broad scope wherein the *forclusion* of Being becomes the first object shed from the field of mathematics—and vice versa—Alain Badiou's contribution to shifting French philosophy away from its Heideggerian montage is well on its way toward being accomplished.

Yet just as accomplishment is a retroactive category, so is the notion that a category's philosophical truth will be settled in the future perfect. This element is integral to Badiou's theory of truth as dual and incomplete, relying on homology with the generic orientation of the nature of the real's undecidability. And as what regulates the relation between the part(s) and the whole(s) of the real, it is still set theory's commitment to adjourning any desire for final conclusions that makes this paradigm the legitimate source of Badiou's devotion. Thus understood, it is ultimately this "generic orientation" that remains key to the structure of mathematical–ontological–discovery in Badiou's perspective.

NOTES

1. G. Peano, Preface to *Arithmetices principia novo methodo exposita* (Torino, 1889).

2. A. Badiou, *L'être et l'événement* (Paris: Les Editions du Seuil, 1986).

3. J.-T. Desanti, "L'Ontologie intrinsèque d'Alain Badiou," *Les Temps Modernes* 526 (May 1990): 61–71.

4. J. Bell, "Category Theory and the Foundations of Mathematics," *British Journal for the Philosophy of Science* 32 (1981): 349–58.

5. J. Bell, "From Absolute to Local Mathematics," *Synthese* 69 (1986): 409–26.

6. The translation of this book is forthcoming from Harvard University Press.

7. C. McLarty, "Uses and Abuses of the History of Topos Theory," *British Journal for the Philosophy of Science* 41 (1990): 351–75.

8. J.-P. Marquis, "Category Theory," *Stanford Encyclopedia of Philosophy* (1996–97), online edition.

9. *Dansein* is, of course, a play on *Dasein*, with the accent placed on the French *dans*, a spatial preposition equivalent to the English *in*. The result produces a neologism of the type, *insein*, though the English term clearly loses the pun.

10. R. Lavendhomme, *Lieux du sujet: Psychanalyse et mathématique* (Paris: Editions du Seuil, 2001).

11. Bell, "From Absolute to Local Mathematics," 411.

12. "It was Jean-Toussaint Desanti who first made me notice that an ontology exclusively founded on set theory—what he would call an 'intrinsic ontology'—failed to recognize the contribution, a capital one in his view, of a mathematical conception based on the sole datum of morphisms, or regulated correlations between structures. I can say that it was by placing philosophy under condition of *topos* theory that I managed, after a long period of wandering or abstention, to at least partially resolve my problem" (A. Badiou, *Court traité d'ontologie transitoire* [Paris: Editions du Seuil, 1998], 125).

13. Bell, "Category Theory."

14. Lavendhomme, *Lieux du sujet*.

15. Bell, "Category Theory."

16. McLarty, "Uses and Abuses of the History of Topos Theory."

17. Ibid.

18. Ibid.

19. Marquis, "Category Theory."

20. W. Lawvere, "The Category of Categories as a Foundation for Mathematics," *Proceedings of La Jolla Conference on Categorical Algebra* (New York: Springer, 1966), 1–20, quoted by Marquis in "Category Theory."

21. Quoted in Marquis, "Category Theory."

22. Bell, "From Absolute to Local Mathematics."

TWO

The Ontological Dispute
Badiou, Heidegger, and Deleuze

Miguel de Beistegui
(Translated by Ray Brassier)

Alain Badiou's philosophical project can be succinctly summarized. It consists in a genuinely metaphysical attempt to free thought from the double horizon of unicity (whereby it posits itself as ontology) and transcendence (whereby it is theology). It is to the extent that for such thought "the norm for what is thinkable consists in the unification of the singular entity beneath the power of the one" (*CTOT* 25) that the latter continues to be superimposed onto the entity and immanent being superimposed onto that transcendence. To think being without resorting to the one, which is to say, as pure multiplicity, this would be the hallmark of a genuine ontology, one that would finally put thought onto the path of immanence. To overcome metaphysics as ontotheology means to undo "the commandeering of being by the one" (*CTOT* 26). Accordingly, Badiou summarizes his project thus: "to invent a contemporary fidelity to that which has never been subject to the historial constraint of onto-theology or the commanding power of the one, such has been, and remains, my aim" (*CTOT* 28).

This would seem to be consonant with a certain strain of thought that, from Nietzsche to Heidegger and Deleuze, will have left its imprint on our century. But this is also the point at which any similarity with the Nietzscheo-Deleuzean and Nietzscheo-Heideggerian projects ceases. For on the one hand, this overcoming is in no way posited as a purely deconstructive gesture, and refuses the identification of ontotheology with metaphysics as such. Thus, all ruminations concerning the putative "end" or "closure" of "Metaphysics" remain entirely foreign to it. And on the other hand, Badiou refuses the identification of ontotheology with that which, since Nietzsche, has been designated as "Platonism." Why? For the simple reason that it is in Plato himself that Badiou locates the possibility of exiting from this metaphysical impasse. It is the Platonic text itself that furnishes the key for metaphysics of immanence, which is to say, for a thought of being as without-oneness. For, contrary to Aristotle, for whom mathematical entities, *mathematika*, have merely a pseudo-being or the being of a rigorous fiction, it is in fact Plato who is the first to acknowledge the ontological dignity of mathematics: for Plato, mathematical entities truly *are*. And it has to be admitted that Badiou's reading of Plato—which goes against the grain of the last century's most influential interpretations, all of which can be traced back to Nietzsche—is as startling as it is fascinating insofar as it uncovers a Plato who proves to be the intractable opponent of all Platonism.

In complete contrast to the dominant interpretation, Badiou maintains that Plato must be credited with having put thought on the path of ontology *sensu stricto*. But this is achieved at an apparently exorbitant price for philosophy itself, insofar as the ontological task now falls to mathematics rather than philosophy. In other words, the overcoming or exit out of ontotheology in the name of a genuine ontology necessitates relocating the ontological realm as such from philosophy to mathematics:

> What is rationally sayable of being as being, of being as devoid of any quality or predicate other than that its exposure to thought as that which is, is said or rather written as pure mathematics. And the effective history of ontology coincides exactly with the history of mathematics. (*CTOT* 188)

Thus, the solution proposed by Badiou is apparently paradoxical in that it does not hesitate to divest philosophy of the very task with which so many thinkers—Heidegger foremost among them—had identified it. Hence the paradoxical character of this discourse which affirms that ontology has always been nothing other than mathematics, even if it is only since Cantor that it has genuinely "rejoined" its conditions. Badiou invites us to perform a radical, one could even say counterhistorical, conversion: once thought has fastened onto being as being (or being-without-oneness), once it has turned itself into a thought of pure multiplicity, it necessarily assumes the form of the mathematical axiomatic; more specifically, of set theory. Only the latter is capable of thinking the multiple (in other words, that which is) without having to go by way of the combinatorial legislation of the One. With Cantor, "we move from a restricted ontology, in which the multiple is still tied to the metaphysical theme of the representation of objects, numbers, and figures, to a general ontology, in which the cornerstone and goal of all mathematics becomes thought's free apprehension of multiplicity as such" (*CTOT* 35).

Let us grant that this divestment has occurred. Let us grant, for the time being, that mathematics, in the form of set theory, has supplanted the work of the philosophical concept in its attempt to think being-without-oneness, or pure multiplicity. Let us grant that mathematics is that thought. What is there left for philosophy? What can it be now that it is no longer ontology? Is it still anything at all? Or does it purely and simply disappear in the wake of what is henceforth a mathematical thinking of being as being, a thinking that until then, and notably under the influence of Heidegger, had been envisaged as the originary terrain of philosophy as such, the ultimate stronghold behind which it should take refuge? In the final analysis, and in spite of Badiou's reservations and even aversion to all diagnoses of this kind, should one not admit that philosophy is dead, that it has been progressively divested of all its territories, shorn of all its metaphysically rooted branches: physics, cosmology, biology, psychology, politics, and so forth? With Badiou, philosophy loses its grip on the roots themselves, which is to say, ontology, thereby signing its own death warrant or rather death certificate: having "divested or unburdened itself of physics, cosmology, politics, and many other things" (*CTOT* 35), it is now incumbent on philosophy to "divest itself of ontology *stricto sensu*" (*CTOT* 55–56). Does this mean that there is nothing left for philosophy but the memory of its past glory, the memory of a life that is now over? Does this mean that philosophy has now entered into a period of mourning and that nostalgia is the only mode of existence available to it? We shall see that such is not the case. We shall even see that this gradual divestment, this slow agony, is in reality the sign of philosophy's coming realization.

It is in fact notable that, in the eyes of Badiou, this deposing of philosophy's ontological grandeur is inscribed in a history that, far from being regrettable, indexes the possibility of its advance: "In fact, the movement whereby, in identifying its conditions, philosophy purges itself of everything foreign to it, spans the entire history of philosophy" (*CTOT* 55–56). This gradual divestment of philosophy's territorial authority is interpreted entirely positively: we have to see in it the very possibility of philosophy as such, the realization of something Badiou characterizes neither as an essence nor a destiny but as nevertheless pertaining to a singular historical possibility. Philosophy is still to come, in two senses.

First, it is incumbent upon it to identify the ontological vocation of mathematics. Aside from its moments of so-called crisis, mathematics effectively thinks being "but is not the thought of the thought that it is" (*CTOT* 55). To think the thought that mathematics is, philosophical thought is required. It is incumbent upon philosophy to state and legitimate the equation: mathematics = ontology. Thus, philosophy is like that supplement of thought required by mathematics itself, which for the most part thinks being as being without deploying its own thinking dimension. Nevertheless, we should not forget that in this very gesture philosophy defers to mathematics and "unburdens itself of what seems to be its highest task" (*CTOT* 55).

Apart from this reflexive traversal of real mathematics—which is carried out in an exemplary and detailed fashion in *L'être et l'événement*—it is also incumbent upon philosophy to grasp that which "subtracts itself" from ontological determination, that which is not being as being. But that which subtracts itself from being in this way, that which interrupts it and upon which mathematics stumbles or falters, is the event. Thus, philosophy is just as much a general theory of the event or of non-being as it is the identification of genuine ontology. As thought of the event, philosophy is theory of that which subtracts itself from the ontological subtraction (that of being-without-oneness). How are we to understand this? Let us begin by obviating two misunderstandings. First, the event's subtraction from being in no way constitutes a return to the one. There is no question of a return to the one by means of the event, and the event does not come to take the place of the one. Second—and this second point is tied to the first—this subtraction is not complete: as we shall see in a moment, the event is not out-of-being, it remains linked to it, but according to a modality that is peculiar to it. But then it may be asked: Why the need for a theory of the event? Why does Badiou feel the need for such a concept? And why can he only envisage it as an interruption, a subtraction, rather than, for example, a supplement, or more radically still, being itself? This is the point at which there emerges a profound disagreement with those two dominant instances of contemporary thought that Badiou's own thought continuously challenges: Heidegger and Deleuze. Both think being as event, whether it be the event through which being is always tied to the destiny of man, and man to the destiny of being, as is the case with Heidegger, or the event as that which is always repeated and never exhausted in being's differing from itself, the event of a repetition that repeats only by inscribing difference, as is the case with Deleuze.

Yet in the eyes of Badiou, the event is a point of rupture with regard to being, and pertains to a structure that he characterizes as one of "trans-being." To think such an event, to think it in its being, need one invoke, as Deleuze believes, a theory of multiplicity that is heterogeneous to the purely mathematical one that accounts for the entity as (actual) entity? For Deleuze, such a theory—heir to Bergson's—is that of intensive or qualitative multiplicities, and must be rigorously distinguished from extensive or quantitative multiplicities, which pertain only to actual entities. For Deleuze, a distinction must be made; or, rather, *the difference must be made*—an entirely productive or genetic difference—between being understood as virtual horizon of preindividual singularities, and the entity understood as process of individuation for the aforementioned singularities. Strictly speaking, the *evental* site is that of the virtual conditions of existence for the actual entity. And philosophy is the science of virtual multiplicities. But Badiou refuses to grant the virtual the status of reality, which Deleuze bestows upon it: there is only the actual, and multiplicities are actualities or entities. Number itself, for example, is a multiplicity: it is "a form of multiple-being," "a movement in being," and even "the site of being as being" (*CTOT* 149)—a status that neither Deleuze nor obviously Heidegger are willing to attribute to it. As a result, the science of being as being is the science of the entity as entity: being a multiplicity, a reality-without-oneness, is the essence (or being-ness) of the entity. And it is precisely insofar as the entity is defined as a multiple, or set, that the question of the being of that entity, understood in terms of a multiple of all multiples or set of all sets, is inconceivable. Thought, Badiou tells us, "cannot maintain the assumption that a multiple, hence an entity, recapitulates all entities without collapsing into inconsistency" (*CTOT* 190). Thus, there is no set that recapitulates all that is, no category subsuming the totality of what is, considered as multiple being. It follows from the very fact that the entity is multiple that there cannot be a term unifying that multiplicity as such:

> It is impossible for thought to grasp as an entity a multiple composed of all entities . . . *it is an essential characteristic of the entity as entity that there cannot be a totality of all entities, once it is thought exclusively on the basis of its entity-ness* [*étantité*]. (*CTOT* 190)

Since the entity-ness of the entity is its multiplicity, there is no way of going on to identify a multiplicity of that very multiplicity, a set of all sets. A multiple of all multiples would be nothing other than the One-All. This is precisely the ontotheological temptation that Badiou discerns ultimately even in Heidegger and Deleuze. This is why there cannot be a genuine difference between being and the entity, and why *being* must be understood to mean "entity-ness." It is also the reason why the Deleuzean thesis of the univocity of being remains doomed from the outset: almost in spite of itself, it tries to constitute being as set of all sets (*D* 78–81). Better to stick with the equivocity of the entity. And better to confine oneself to a purely local conception of multiplicity. Because the entity-ness of the entity cannot mean its totality (*pace* Heidegger, for whom metaphysics is the thought of *das Seiende im Ganzen* [being-as-totality]), the ontology of the multiple can only be locally circumscribed. In spite of all that separates them, Deleuze's thought maintains an affinity with that of Heidegger in that it remains a thought of ontological difference, which it continues and reinvents, and the univocity of being merely reinscribes the "meaning" (*Sinn*) of being.

From Badiou's point of view, the thought of ontological difference sooner or later entails the reinscription of a horizon of transcendence, whether it be that of language, in Heidegger's poetic sense, or of the virtual, in the Deleuzeo–Bergsonian sense. That is why in order to think the being of the event, which means the event in its immanence, there is no alternative but that of positing a single, axiomatically homogenous theory of multiplicities. Even though it constitutes a rupture relative to the law of extensive multiplicities, the event remains homogeneous with it. In fact, an event is nothing but or nothing more than a set or multiple, but one whose very upsurge, whose being as event, is peculiar in that it subtracts itself from one of the axioms of multiplicity: the axiom of foundation. In Badiou's vocabulary, an event is an unfounded multiple. Thus, the event does not subtract itself from the law of multiplicity as such; it is not just outside-being (which would be meaningless). It is a suddenly emerging, unexpected multiplicity, and hence one that is unfounded. Only by postulating this category of unfounding (which should be carefully distinguished, as Badiou invites us to, from the movement whereby the actual is ungrounded by the virtual in Deleuze) is it possible to account for what is as novelty, as that which overtakes and overturns a state of affairs.

One can say that, regardless of their origin or the domain in which they arise, these events make something happen. This is to say that they overturn a given state of things (political, poetic, scientific, philosophical, etc.), that they mark it in a way which is irrecusable for it, and in such a way that it becomes entirely natural to say in its wake that things will never be the same. To postulate any sort of heterogeneity, as Heidegger and Deleuze both do in their own way, between being and entity, or in Badiou's vocabulary, between being and event, will always ultimately entail the reinscription of a dualism, a Two, and consequently the manacling of thought once more to the counting-as-one. It will always ultimately entail confirming ontotheology's grip on the thinking of being envisaged as philosophy. If there is a Badiouan ontology, there is no room for ontological difference in it. Yet must we rid ourselves quite so abruptly of ontological difference considered as philosophical problematic? Have we not moved too quickly beyond the question of being as question of the difference between being and the entity? Does the latter really and necessarily condemn us to a dualism and to the commandeering of being by the one? Have we not been too hasty in reducing ontology to mathematics? All these questions will ultimately have to be dealt with.

But not before we have first provided a broad outline of Badiou's interpretation of the century's most significant ontological conceptions, which I have already mentioned, that is, those of Heidegger and Deleuze. The former deserves credit for having reopened thought's ontological dimension and providing the twentieth century with being as a matter for thought: "There is no doubt that we are indebted to Heidegger for yoking philosophy to the question of being once more" (*CTOT* 25). Or again: "As far as philosophy is concerned, it seems reasonable to say that our era will have been marked, or stamped, by the question of Being. This is why it is dominated by Heidegger" (*D* 31). The second deserves credit for reformulating the question of being, pursuing it in a direction very different from Heidegger's, while nevertheless continuing to identify it with philosophy as such, beyond both the analytical tradition "whose grammatical or logical reductions he execrates" and the phenomenological current "whose reduction of living actualizations into mere correlates of intentional consciousness he severely criticizes" (D 32). Nevertheless, Badiou continues, it has to be recognized that the Heideggerian attempt runs aground on a historial conception of truth whose destiny remains tied "to the unfounded promise of a salutary reversal" (D 26), and hence to a poetic motif that only serves to consolidate philosophy's "linguistic turn." And in the case of Deleuze, to whom Badiou devotes a remarkable little essay, it is a question of saluting his metaphysical adventure, his systematic and continually renewed attempt to construct a thought that is tangential to all ruminations on the end of metaphysics, to all fetishization of language (whether of the logico-grammatical or poetic sort); all the while noting his inability to develop a theory of multiplicities that are entirely independent of the One: for Badiou, the theory of virtual multiplicities, which coincides with the philosophical gesture as such, is constantly threatened by the thesis of the univocity of being, and this thesis is itself maintained only at the cost of reintroducing the Two or the Double. Like Heideggerian ontology, Deleuzean ontology indexes an impasse that only mathematics can avoid. Before retracing Badiou's footsteps, before embarking with him upon this new ontology, which he considers to be the only possible one because it is the only thinkable one, we will ask ourselves whether Heidegger and Deleuze do in fact fail according to the terms laid down by Badiou, or whether there is still something to be said for continuing to frequent them. But first we must provide a more precise account of this double critique.

In the case of Heidegger, this critique seems to be coordinated around a double axis. On the one hand, there is the critique of what Badiou calls the "linguistic turn," and which, in its Heideggerian version—which it is important to distinguish from its logico-analytical version—has poetic saying serving as the condition for thought as such. In this era of the accomplishment or closure of metaphysics, signaled in our own time by the untrammeled reign of technological objectification as destiny of truth, it is a question of recognizing that only a handful of poets have managed to articulate Being, or at least the conditions for a turning in thought away from the will to power and mastery as fulfillment of the history of subjectivity, toward the disclosure of the Open understood as what withdraws—and hence keeps itself in reserve—from this very history. Thus, it is a question of recognizing the extent to which the distress of our era, as well as the possibility of overturning it in favor of what remains buried and forgotten, finds a voice in the utterances of a handful of poets, first among whom is Hölderlin. It is in this way that thought finds itself "placed under condition of the poets" (MPh 30), to take up Badiou's expression. But this overturning or turning delineated by poetry corresponds precisely to the severing of thought's link to its mathematical origin in Plato. By interpreting truth and being as Idea, Heidegger tells us, Plato put thought onto the path of representation and mathematical objectification. By interrupting the metaphorical and poetical narrative—a claim that, in my eyes, is only partly true and needs to be at least nuanced—through the "ideal paradigmatic of the matheme" (*MPh* 31), Plato decisively steered the destiny of being toward the forgetting of its disclosure.

From Heidegger's point of view, the installing of the matheme signals the erasure of the poem and its ontological potential in favor of a purely instrumental conception of thought. We can expect nothing from mathematics, unless it be an ever more effective and efficient instrument for measuring and hence manipulating the world.[1] But certainly not thought, and still less a thought of being as such. It would be difficult to imagine a starker contrast than the one between Heidegger's verdict and Badiou's. Badiou's conception of the matheme, of the way in which philosophy relates to it and his reading of Plato with regard to mathematics are the polar opposite of Heidegger's. For Badiou, as we have seen, ontology must be torn from philosophic and poetic thought, torn from language itself, and returned to its genuine mathematical origin, as anticipated by Plato. The poem has its place in Badiou's philosophy—one that I cannot hope to elucidate here. But the place of ontology is not in the poem. The latter is incapable of thinking pure multiplicity as such.

But thought does not just depend on the poem. It also depends on what is announced in the poem, and in the utterances of Hölderlin in particular, which is to say, the promise of a return of those gods who, as a result of their flight, have left the world to the abandonment of its own disenchantment. By rendering thought dependent upon the poem, Heidegger also renders it dependent upon the divine. Not the divinity of ontotheology, the God of faith and grace, or God as Supreme Being, granted, but the God (or gods) of the poets nevertheless. Neither living subject of religion, nor metaphysical Principle, the god of the poets is "that on the basis of which there is for the poet an enchantment of the world, the loss of which exposes us to futility" (*CTOT* 19). Of this God, as Badiou rightly points out, one can "neither say that it is dead nor alive," but only that "it has *withdrawn*, exposing the world to disenchantment" (*CTOT* 19).

The question of the poem then coincides with that of the retreat of the gods. And as such, the question is neither philosophical nor theological. The space of the poem is that of man in the face of this flight, and its fundamental tone is entirely nostalgic. From the depths of this nostalgia, the poem envisages "the chances of a re-enchantment of the world brought about through the improbable return of the gods" (*CTOT* 19). Throughout his life, Heidegger will have declared the necessity of enduring the end of ontotheology and of experiencing the death of God even as we await the salvation of another divine event, thereby leashing thought to the possibility of this promise. This is his "aporia." In the final analysis, Heidegger will have merely shifted territory from the Christian God to the God of the poets. Is this not just to swap one transcendence for another? In the name of his "contemporary atheism," Badiou wants to break with this arrangement and carry poetry still further. Today, the imperative of the poem consists in winning the right to its own atheism, in having done with the figure of the promise, the return of the gods, and the reenchantment of the world. Philosophy must rid itself of all nostalgia, and cannot suspend its destiny to the promise of an event to come.

What can one say about this critique, this irrecusable leave-taking with regard to Heidegger's thought, other than that it seems to me as lucid as it is imperative? What is there to say, other than, yes, Heidegger will have invested too much of Western history in a poetic gesture that renders our present dependent upon the departure of the gods and their eventual return? What can one say, other than, yes, Heidegger's suspicion not only with regard to mathematics but to the sciences of nature seems to me unwarranted and in need of its own critique? Yet this is not where I would situate what is essential in Heidegger's thought. And it is only from this other site, which Badiou acknowledges without ever really acknowledging, that I would hope to take up the dispute. But not without having first examined Badiou's critique of Deleuze. For ultimately it is the same question, the same site, that I would hope to identify in Heidegger and in Deleuze, in what will constitute my own reservation with regard to Badiou's thought. In the final analysis, the dispute will bear on the relation between univocity and difference.

In the case of Deleuze, Badiou's critique is at once more lengthy and more precisely defined. Nevertheless, it can be summarized in a few words: ultimately, the fundamental thesis of Deleuzean thought, that of the univocity of being, remains incompatible with the theory of multiplicities, the thought of difference, and the drive toward immanence. This is why, for Badiou, it must be abandoned in favor of a mathematical ontology of sets. It is this threefold incompatibility that I will now try to unpack as succinctly as possible.

Badiou is right to insist on the fact that everything in Deleuze's thought brings us back to the univocity of Being, with which philosophy completely coincides.[2] No doubt, it has to be admitted that there exist many forms of Being, within each of which "individuating differences," which could be called "entities," are given. But the essential thing is that Being is the same for all entities, it is univocal, and hence is said of all entities in one and the same sense, so that the multiplicity of meanings, the equivocity of entities, has no real status.

But, Badiou warns us, the price for stringently maintaining the thesis of univocity is high, not to say exorbitant. For as Deleuze himself explains, ultimately, it is necessary that multiplicity (entities, meanings) be of the order of the simulacrum, it being understood that the numerical difference through which it is deployed in the universe is purely formal as far as the form of being to which it refers back is concerned (thought, extension, time), and its individuation purely modal. In the Deleuzean universe, the realm of entities is the stage for the simulacra of Being.

But for Badiou, in spite of the fact that Deleuze, in a gesture that is supposed to free thought from Platonism, sets out to "make simulacra rise to the surface" and to "affirm their rights,"[3] this is completely unacceptable. Why? Because the real becomes at least partially dissociated from the actual, and the actual envisaged as only partially real, because in order to think the actual as such, it is necessary to suspend it to something else, which alone is capable of accounting for it. But to do this is to (re)open the door to transcendence. The introduction of a virtual dimension into thought is the sign of this inability to think the intrinsic multiplicity of the actual. The One can be affirmed only on condition of being maintained outside of actuality, and of the real being envisaged as a multiplicity that is primarily virtual. For Badiou, on the contrary, immanence excludes the All (the set of all sets) and the only envisageable point of rest for multiplicity, which is always a multiple of multiples (or a set made up of other sets), is the empty set, or the multiple of nothing.

If Being is said in a single sense, what is this sense? What is the name of Being, the one through which its single sense is said? I believe it is a single name, which characterizes the thought of Heidegger as well as that of Deleuze, a name that, for structural reasons to which I will come back, always invokes others. In any case, it is a name that Badiou fails to mention in the list of names of Being he compiles in his little book on Deleuze. This name is that of "difference." For Deleuze as well as for Heidegger, it is a question of thinking Being *as* difference. But difference is always in-between. It is in its very nature to designate something other than itself, to double itself. And if, as I believe is the case for both Heidegger and Deleuze, this difference is a primary or originary difference, so that it never presupposes the terms between which it is situated but on the contrary engenders them, then it is a difference grasped in the movement of its own alterity, in its becoming *other*. Badiou, for his part, asks himself: Why does Deleuze always require two names in order to say that being has one only sense? Why is there a (finite) multiplicity of names for Being? What are these names? Badiou lists some of them: the virtual and the actual, time and truth, chance and eternal recurrence, the fold and the outside. Leaving aside the question whether all these names and all these pairs do effectively function as names for Being in Deleuze, I will restrict myself to the first, which in any case Badiou correctly acknowledges to be the most fundamental.

What does he say about it? That although Being is said of the difference between virtual and actual, one of these terms, that is, the virtual, seems to designate Being as such (by way of contrast to the actual entity). Thus, one of the terms seems to be endowed with greater weight, or a position of ontological priority. Which is as much as to say that the virtual is envisaged as ground, even if the concept of 'grounding' is reconceptualized as an 'un-grounding,' or as that into which the actual is dissolved, and even if it is distinguished from the whole notion of mimesis, from the notion of original and image, of model and copy, which Deleuze believes to be at work in Plato. The virtual functions as ground according to a double determination:

> It is determined as a problem, as virtuality for an invented solution. But it is also determined by the circulation of the multiplicity of problems throughout the virtual, because every virtuality communicates with all the others, just as a problem is only constituted as a problematic site, in the vicinity of other problems. . . . The virtual is the ground of the actual, as being of the virtuality that the actual actualizes. But the virtual is also ground of itself, because it is the being of virtualities, insofar as it differentiates or problematizes them. (D 76)

As ground of the actual, the virtual must not be thought outside of the object itself. For if the virtual was in fact separated from the actual object, univocity would be shattered: Being would be said in two senses, according to objective actuality and according to in-objective virtuality. Thus, it is the object itself that must be double: actual–virtual. How can we not see in this doubling of the object a failure of the thought of being as univocity? What lesson can we draw from the fact that "with regard to the thought of the actual object, inevitably determined as an image, the price of the most magnificent contemporary attempt to restore the power of the One is an extremely precarious theory of the Double" (D 79)? In the final analysis, the virtual as ground cannot be harmonized with the univocity of Being-one. The price of univocity is the pernicious reinscription of a horizon of transcendence: even as un-grounding, the virtual participates in a logic of grounding that is ultimately incompatible with the univocity of Being-one.

Why? Because the virtual ceaselessly doubles itself, or doubles its object into a virtual aspect and an actual aspect, thereby reintroducing analogy and the Two precisely at the moment when it was supposed to leave them behind. Deleuze can think the One (the virtual) only by doubling it (every object has its virtual as well as its actual aspect, its pure past as well as its present). In this regard, Deleuze remains resolutely Bergsonian. So that Badiou can ask himself whether the basic problem with Bergson, and therefore with Deleuze who follows in his wake, may not reside in the fact that "the creative power of life, which is the name of the One, continuously engenders doubles, and we can never be sure that these do not ultimately constitute categories, or an equivocal parceling out of Being" (*D* 79–80). Far from dispensing with analogy and its procession of categories, which correspond to so many territories of Being wherein entities are distributed, univocity would seem to end up reinforcing it. The heroic attempt cannot succeed and the "song of the virtual" is ultimately the swan song of univocity. The "realization" of the virtual is accomplished through the "irrealization" of the actual, pure and simple: "the more Deleuze tries to tear [the virtual] from its irreality, its indetermination, its in-objectivity, the more it is the actual or the entity that becomes irrealized, indeterminate, and ultimately in-objective insofar as it is subjected to a ghostly doubling. In this trajectory of thought, the Two installs itself in place of the One" (*D* 81). What is the point? What is the point of bringing out the virtual as ground if it is only to turn the actual entity into an unreal, ghostly entity? What is the use of widening the bounds of the real if it is only to narrow those of the actual? In the final analysis, Badiou does not see why he should compromise actuality on behalf of a shadowy virtuality, why he should give up his actual multiplicities, and what he willingly acknowledges as his equivocity of being, his empty grounding, for a univocity and a grounding that can only be maintained at the cost of insurmountable aporias.

Perhaps this is the reason why Badiou's thought is not a thought of difference. Although it is a thought of being as multiplicity, it does not envisage the latter as difference. Difference is not multiple enough: by privileging one term and irrealizing the other, by reinscribing height and hierarchy, it invariably reintroduces a Two and consequently a form of transcendence at the very point where multiplicity disperses and disseminates. In which regard Badiou would agree with Derrida. But ultimately—and this is not something I can hope to show here—if Derrida's thought is also, and perhaps above all, a thought of difference, this may not be a coincidence.

With regard to the relationship between difference and Being, I need to say at least the following, which holds as much for Heidegger as for Deleuze. Heidegger's thought is not a thought of multiplicity. It is well and truly a thought of difference. But difference is not so much envisaged as the difference between two unities (or two entities) as the difference between the entity as *one* and the being of that entity, which is neither one nor multiple, since the multiple is merely the *without*-one, or the negation of the one. Granted, being is that single term on the basis of which beings as a whole are illuminated: it is the *pros hen* sought by Aristotle, on the basis of which the science of being would finally become possible. But Being is not the category, still less the genus, on the basis of which entities as a whole can be thought. Being is not the All. If Heideggerian ontology is a *subtractive* ontology, if being does in fact subtract itself from the one, it is from the one as *koinon* (as what is common to beings as a whole); this is an ontology that subtracts itself from the thought of the entity-ness of the entity. But that whereby being subtracts itself from the entity-ness of the entity, envisaged as that which is common to beings as a whole, is difference, not multiplicity.

Here we come back to a determination that is as valid for Deleuze as it is for Heidegger. For Heidegger, who says nothing about the status of multiplicity, the latter could pertain only to the entity considered in its present actuality or entity-ness—something which Badiou, as we have already seen, quite openly acknowledges, since he refuses to envisage a dimension of the real added onto actuality, and consequently treats being and entity-ness as entirely equivalent. But I would say that for Heidegger (as well as for Deleuze) ontology begins with difference, and that the "question" of being is entirely that of its difference from the entity, or of being *as* difference. Being is the movement of difference as such, the spatiotemporalizing movement or operation through which "there are" entities. Whether this movement be envisaged, from a Heideggerian point of view, as epiphany of being in its historial unfolding, or from a Deleuzean point of view, as process of individuation (physical, biological, artistic, etc.), changes nothing.

For Heidegger as well as for Deleuze, being is that Same which always returns, but returns only to differentiate itself, or always returns *as* difference. It is being as event. In the final analysis, there is only a single name for being: difference. But since it is of the very essence of difference to differentiate itself, difference is always given or apprehended in the very space that it differentiates, trailing in its wake that other which it itself is: the entity. Yes, for Deleuze, the virtual is in fact the name of Being. But as pure difference, the virtual is so constituted that it always produces the actual. Yes, the actual is in fact what is, but as the end result of a preindividual engendering, an ontological process that is decided on the near side of the individuated entity. Deleuzean ontology is an ontology of the preindividual real, a thought of being in the process of individuation. And if, as Deleuze himself says, the individuated entity is of the order of the simulacrum, it is insofar as it gives itself as constituted, as finished, but only on the basis of a horizon of gestation, of a differentiating genesis, which it is the task of thought to reconstitute. Only by envisaging the One as a difference-without-identity is it possible to maintain the thesis of the univocity of being. But by identifying being with difference, by making of the latter the very sense of being, one is bound to double it, to inscribe it in a series of the Two: being and time, being and entity, being and man, earth and world, and so forth, for Heidegger; or virtual and actual, difference and repetition, differentiation and *differenciation*, Aîon and Chronos, and so forth, for Deleuze. Because it only is insofar as it differentiates itself, being is always also something other than itself. Never itself as such, never in complete proximity to itself in its pure self-presence, being is only ever in that interval wherein the entity comes to be. Being is that interval, that interstice wherein beings as a whole are played out.

In light of the foregoing, we might be tempted to conclude that there has been a complete failure of communication between Badiou and his opponents. In the final analysis, there would seem to be no common ground underlying this "bone of contention" or dispute. From a Heideggerian and Deleuzean viewpoint, it would seem that, in spite of the radical displacement to which Badiou—in what seems to be an ultimate divestment of philosophy—subjects ontology by shifting it from philosophical discourse to mathematical thought, the result is merely a continuation of traditional ontology; even without-one, Badiou's ontology remains a thought of the entity in its presence (or actuality), and consequently incapable of raising itself to the thought of ontological difference. From Badiou's point of view, whether in its Heideggerian version (the question of being as question bearing on the meaning or truth of being) or its Deleuzean version (being as One-All), the univocity of being leads only to a devaluation of the entity, a reinforcing of thought's horizon of transcendence, as well as a doubling of the One into Two, and consequently to an ontology of the counting-as-one, a pre-Cantorian thought of multiple being. Thus, there would seem to be no solution. Not that there is any undecidability here. On the contrary, it is precisely here that one has to choose, to decide. In the end, it would seem to come down to a matter of taste, as Deleuze wrote to Badiou. But before reaching this point, I would contend that Badiou's critique of Heideggerian and Deleuzean ontologies passes too quickly over the meaning and importance of the ontological difference, and that aspect of it whereby the "merit" of Heidegger, as well as of Deleuze, lies not so much in having put ontology back onto the philosophical agenda, but in having tied it to the concept of '*difference*'.

NOTES

1. In this regard, Heidegger would seem merely to be perpetuating a long-standing suspicion that philosophy has always harbored about mathematics: thus, for Badiou, philosophy is "partly responsible for the reduction of mathematics to the status of mere calculation or technique, a ruinous image to which it is reduced by current opinion" (*CTOT* 38).

2. "There has only ever been one ontological proposition: Being is univocal" (*Difference et Repetition* [Paris: PUF, 1969], 52); "Philosophy is indistinguishable from ontology" (*Logique du Sens* [Paris: Minuit, 1969], 210).

3. Gilles Deleuze, *Logiques du sens* (Paris: Minuit, 1969), 302.

PART TWO
THE POEM

THREE

For an "Ethics of Mystery"
Philosophy and the Poem

Gabriel Riera

Adding a prefix to the imposing but discredited concept of 'aesthetics' has been a commonplace for some time now. In the last two decades, we have come across the *anti-*aesthetics and the *para-*aesthetics, as if its fortunes and misfortunes could only become legible through the inflections left by a linguistic particle.[1] Whether a massive refusal of idealistic aesthetics or a turning of aesthetics against itself, it is always the case of a negative inflection whose modalities may very well indicate that if aesthetics can be considered a thing of the past, art still returns as a decisive *condition for thinking.* It is precisely this issue that is at stake for Alain Badiou and that will be the focus of this chapter.

Badiou's *Petit Manuel d' Inesthétique* is an example of a negatively inflected aesthetics. By "*inesthétique*" Badiou understands "a relation of philosophy to art which, by positing that art is in itself producer of truths, does not pretend in any manner to make of it an object of philosophy. Against aesthetic speculation, an 'inesthétique' describes the strictly intra-philosophical effects produced by the independent existence of some works of art."[2] On the one hand, Badiou's "inesthétique" is an antiaesthetics: the opposite of a speculative aesthetics or a philosophical understanding of art according to which the latter is endowed with the task of furnishing an ontological presentation of a speculative metaphysics. On the other hand, three positive features define it. First, the crucial statement, according to which art is in itself a producer of truths. This is a decisive thesis for Badiou's project of rearticulating the relation between philosophy and poetry. Second, the truths of art are both "immanent" and "singular." And last, the inesthétique limits itself to describe the "intraphilosophical effects" that the independent existence of *some* works of art produce. Although it aims to describe the truths of art, the inesthétique is not a philosophy of art, since it does not conceive of the work of art as the ground of truth;

that is, it does not share the foundational scope of Heidegger's ontology of art. Further, an inesthétique description is doubly restricted: it is concerned only with intraphilosophical effects as they apply solely to *some* works of art. In this sense, Badiou's inesthétique is also a para-aesthetics, albeit a restrictive and selective one: it can be characterized as "a critical approach to aesthetics for which art is a question not a given."[3]

However, the positive values of the prefix *para-* ("by the side of," "alongside of") do not fully render the topological interlacing of philosophy and the poem Badiou seeks to articulate. This has to do with the status of the intraphilosophical character of the truths of the poem: the adjective *philosophical* indicates that although they *belong* to the work of art, the poem's truths are nonetheless *included* within philosophy. The belonging that immanence stipulates must yield to the inclusion of the intraphilosophical in such a way as to assure a circulation between the poem's operations and those of a philosophical description. The tension between belonging and inclusion seals the avatars of the negative, as well as the fortune and misfortune of Badiou's inesthétique. The reason lies in the fact that Badiou ciphers in the prefix *intra-* not only the challenge of thinking the negativity of art in a positive manner, but also his attempts to posit a new type of relation between philosophy and the poem. This oscillation has to be tackled from the viewpoint of the concept and the matheme, as well as from that of art and the poem. It remains to be seen whether the declension of the prefix *intra-* does justice to the double demand of the immanent and singular nature of poetic truths, or if their inclusion in the philosophical field do not leave traces of a more conventional type of philosophical aesthetics.

The positing of a new relation between philosophy and art organizes the *Petit Manuel d'inesthétique*'s overall architecture, as well as its internal scansions. Badiou wants to delineate a relation between philosophy and art that is neither didactic (Plato), classic (Aristotle), nor romantic (Hegel). These three types of relations, according to Badiou, are prevalent in contemporary articulations such as Marxism (Brecht), Romantic hermeneutics (Heidegger), and Freudianism (Lacan). Contrary to the new relation between philosophy and art that Badiou proposes, these three articulations do not posit that the truths of the work of art are simultaneously immanent and singular.

To establish a new rapport between philosophy and the poem, Badiou engages Heidegger's thinking. For this reason, my reading will be guided by Badiou's crucial deployment of the concept of the 'age of poets' (*Manifesto for Philosophy* and "L'Âge des poètes"), since it allows him to challenge Heidegger's notion of the "end of philosophy" and to call for a "return to Plato." I will concentrate on whether Badiou succeeds in articulating a space where the poem is exposed and, at the same time, exposes an alterity or trans-being (event). From this space, a series of inherent truths to the poem's operations are derived that have a bearing on philosophy itself. This would allow the poem to be finally liberated from the hierarchical relation to which it has been submitted and subjected since Plato, and in which it would no longer be endowed with a metaphysical burden.

In summary, this chapter examines three articulations of the relation between philosophy and the poem proposed by Badiou. First, the notion of the age of poets: a philosophical category able to cut loose philosophical discourse from the "Siren's song" of the poem. The question of the end is crucial here, as well as the articulation of the "negative" operations of the poem that the end brings into play. Second, the philosophical use of the poem, such as Badiou deploys it in "Le recours philosophique au poème" in *Conditions*, in which he argues against Heidegger's own articulation of the relation between thinking and poetizing in view of articulating a different relation or unrelation (*dé-rapport*) between philosophy and the poem. This new articulation also provides the philosopher with guidelines for philosophically *using* the poem's truths. I show that it is here that some traces of a more traditional philosophical aesthetics survives in Badiou's thinking and that this is due to a slippage in the trope's regulative assignation. Regarding tropes, everything happens between knowledge and truth, which means that there is a tension between the postsignifying demands of "being-faithful-to-the-event" of the modern poem and the classical philosophical signifying schema of conceptualization. I claim that this tension presents problems for Badiou's schema of compossibility (the relationship between philosophy and the non-philosophical fields). The "return to Plato" commands a deployment of the economy of use, illustration, and example that contains the excessive errancy of poetic truth that Badiou conveys in terms of the poem's inesthétique operations.

Badiou presents the third and final articulation I examine under the heading of an "ethics of mystery," which calls for a deposition of philosophy's magisterial attributes and an acknowledgment of its exposure to unfounded regimes of truth (poetry being the unfounded par excellence). This exposure does not leave the scope of Badiou's foundational project intact, since the impact that the unfounded conditions impress upon philosophy supposes a redefinition of the graphics of compossibility, as well as of its temporality. Philosophy is now defined as the incomplete (*lacunaire*) thinking of the multiple coming after its conditions.

It is important to stress that the final formulation of the relationship between philosophy and the poem allows for an opaque point around which to tie together the knot of compossibility. The figure this knot composes makes it necessary to ask whether this ethics of mystery enables the alterity of the poem to convey the simultaneously immanent and singular truths that Badiou's inesthétique strives for. Finally, I examine whether it is possible to articulate the call for an ethics of mystery with the imperative of its "becoming prose" (Lacoue-Labarthe) that in *Court traité d'ontologie transitoire* Badiou situates as the final effect of the de-suturing of philosophy from the poem of the age of poets.

PHILOSOPHY UNDER CONDITIONS: THE COLDNESS OF THE MATHEME, THE HEAT OF RHETORIC

Before engaging in a close reading of Badiou's positing of a new relation between philosophy and the poem, it is essential to contextualize this problematic within the frame of his philosophical system. In the absence of a complete translation of *L'être et l'événement*, the reader who approaches Badiou for the first time and by way of the *Manifesto for Philosophy* may be doubly surprised not only by Badiou's belligerent rhetoric, but also by his passionate appeal to philosophical truth. She could also be misled in her appreciation of Badiou's philosophical style since no other contemporary French philosopher seems to be as far removed from rhetoric and linguistic experimentation as Badiou. In fact, Badiou's thinking does not lead us into the paralogisms of language-games, but instead into the cold discipline of the matheme, as the almost intractable *L'être et l'événement* makes evident. With Badiou a cold discipline once again founds philosophy and carries on the unfinished "Cartesian meditation" that the Nietzcheo–Heideggerian "reversal of Platonism" interrupted.

The *Manifesto*, however, does not begin with the matheme but with rhetoric, even if for Badiou language is not a transcendental ground. Its rhetoric does not imply counting, as in *L'être et l'événement*, but calculating.[4] In *L'être et l'événement*, Badiou states,

> Conceptually the experience will be that of a deductive invention, one in which the result would be entirely transmissible through knowledge; language, finally, refusing the poem, will be under the authority of that which Frege called an *ideography*. The whole will oppose to the temptation of presence the rigor of the subtractive, in which being can only be said inasmuch as it is un-supposing [*unsupposable*] to all presence and all experience. (*EE* 35, emphasis added)[5]

If there is invention, it does not occur at a conceptual level, but on a deductive one. Badiou's ontology revolves around the notion of the event: the presentation of the void. But this presentation can only emerge by an act of nomination: "the event—inasmuch as it is the exclusive destiny of the void's presencing [*présentification*]—emerges in the paradox of being only named in the disappearance of that to which it refers" (*EE* 245). An event can only be named at the moment when it vanishes or disappears, given that its key operation is subtraction.[6] This "ideographic invention" does not "add" a new entity; it is not a question here of inventing new concepts in an effort to describe in a singular fashion the different occurrences of the virtual field (Deleuze). It is also not the case of letting the other come into language (*invenire*) while deconstructing the ontotheological apparatus (*dispositif*) of invention (Derrida).[7]

Although the *Manifesto for Philosophy* is an accessible point of entry to Badiou's thinking, one wonders if its rhetoric does not come too late to dispel the effects of a supposed "end" and to put the "Sophists" in their place. It is a text in which the very question of philosophy's presentation is enacted without any explicit interrogation. Which genre or mode does the *Manifesto* belong to? This question is legitimate inasmuch as Badiou legislates limits and establishes borders between philosophy and the poem which, once reestablished, are used in a diatribe against the Sophists.

The nineteenth and twentieth centuries have been prolific in the production of manifestos, a programmatic form of writing characteristic of artistic and political movements, whose most distinguishing feature is its militant tone. Strangely, the tone of this refounded, "cold" philosophy is that of the passionate militant. It could be said that the genre or mode of the manifesto is that of a certain type of welding that takes the form "x *as* y": art *as* politics (Futurist and Surrealist manifestos) or art *as* positivist science (Zola), and politics *as* messianic eschatology (*The Communist Manifesto*). The manifesto is the discursive space of articulation and of suturing that is produced around the concept of 'the end,' which is crucial not only for Badiou's project of de-suturing philosophy from its dependency on nonphilosophical configurations, but also for the *Manifesto for Philosophy*'s rhetoric.

However, have the so-called Sophists announced the end of philosophy? We need to return to Heidegger to examine why this notion generates such misunderstanding: "what is meant by the talk about the end of philosophy [*Ende der Philosophie*]? We understand the end of something all too easily in the negative sense as a mere stopping, as the lack of a continuation, perhaps even as decline and impotence. In contrast, what we say about the end of philosophy means the completion of metaphysics [*die Vollendung der Metaphysik*]."[8] For Heidegger the "end of philosophy" does not mean that philosophy is finished. He rejects the notions of stopping, decline, and impotence that are crucial not only for Badiou's rhetoric but also for his historical schema. Rather than an apocalyptic end, Heidegger points to a notion of completion, an indication of the exhaustion of the possibilities of metaphysics, which demands that the very concept of the end be interrogated.

No ironic use of the discourse of the end exists in Badiou, and even if he mentions or quotes other discourses of or on the end, he inhabits and uses them to proclaim another end.[9] It could be argued that Badiou is interpreting the end of philosophy from an apocalyptic perspective while at the same time retaining some of Heidegger's directives regarding "the completion of metaphysics." For Badiou the suturing of philosophy to nonphilosophical fields produces "disasters"; that is, in Heidegger's terms, it repeats a metaphysically dominated way of thinking and therefore, entails a prolongation of the danger (*Gefahr*). But while Heidegger and some contemporary thinkers submit the concept of the end to a radical displacement and reinscription, Badiou seems to take it at face value. The *Manifesto for Philosophy* therefore does not seem to be very different from any other type of manifesto: it takes its "style of presentation" from a militant tradition, posits a program, and denounces in block those against which it is attempting to clear a space of reflection.

In the presentation of its program, the militant ghosts of a noninventive politics haunt the *Manifesto* since, according to Badiou, Marxism has become an academic discipline unable to produce events. This programmatic presentation is also shaped by two of the four generic procedures or conditions: art and politics. The rhetoric of the *Manifesto* is sutured and the stitches take the particular configuration of the "aesthetic-political avant-garde."

Under the heat of its militant rhetoric, truth, philosophy's "invariant," suffers. The *Manifesto*'s presentation makes evident that Badiou's rhetoric is the venerable rhetoric *of* philosophy. In the *Manifesto*, rhetoric is deployed in an attempt to "translate"—or one should say "transliterate"—the unfolding of the eventual truth-production of the four generic procedures or conditions achieved in *L'être et l'événement*. This systematic "transliteration" takes place by way of a "deductive invention" whose language is that of an "ideography" (Frege). Within the frame of a limited repertoire of conceptual personae (the Philosopher and the Sophist) and topoi (possibility, the end, the conditions, the suture, the event, etc.), this "ideographic" writing is rendered into communicable and transmissible knowledge.

The cold, disorienting, objectless truth of the matheme becomes the warm and reassuring knowledge of the militant's rhetoric. But should it not be this way, should one not expect an orchestrated, calculated repetition of philosophy's constitutive diatribe against the Sophists? Is it possible to posit a return to Plato, as Badiou does, without redeploying the opposition between the conceptual personae of the Philosopher and the Sophist? In other words, if there is calculation (rhetoric *as* calculation) in Badiou, would this not be the only localizable example, a *punctual use*, as it were? I will show how Badiou, to a large extent, operates within a classical philosophical determination of rhetoric and that this occurs at strategic moments: first, when Badiou attempts to secure the de-suturing of philosophy from the poem (an operation on which the possibility of philosophy depends); that is, when he attempts to clear a new space to posit a post-Heideggerian articulation of the relation between philosophy and the poem; and second, when he makes the protocols under which philosophy may have recourse to the poem explicit. It is here that tropes are understood as either an illustration or an instrument in view of a determined finality, and that this understanding takes place within the context of a philosophical suture of the poem to rhetoric, to rhetoric as philosophy. For a philosophy that seeks to formulate a new relation between philosophy and the poem and to stipulate the negative—postsignifying—operations of the poem in a positive way, this may very well be the sign of a relapse into a traditional philosophical formulation.

Badiou's return to Plato (although inflected by a post-Cantorian mathematics) remains faithful to a classic determination of rhetoric. His philosophical decision—"Plato's" matheme against "Wittgenstein's" language-games—closes off any possible type of reflection on language since, according to the *Manifesto*'s rhetoric, it would fall under the jurisdiction of the Sophist, that is, of Rhetoric. But, as we will see below, in Badiou's rhetoric there is a slippage in the trope's regulative assignation. Regarding tropes everything happens, between knowledge and truth. Or in other words, there is a tension between the postsignifying demands of the being-faithful-to-the-event of the poem (its inesthétique effects) and the classical philosophical signifying schema of conceptualization. It is this very tension, I claim, that threatens Badiou's schema of compossibility and compromises his call for an ethics of mystery.

Badiou's project does not explicitly reflect on language; the rigor and coldness of the matheme precludes that possibility. Nevertheless, what is most striking about this project is that its cold splendor is a legacy of the modern poem, of the poem of the age of poets. Everything takes place within the scope of the letter that obligates philosophy (it is "la lettre de l'être"), since it puts philosophy under condition. But, at the same time, it is a question here of a letter that seems to enjoy a certain exteriority, a certain margin of unconditionality. This is a strange conditioning and at the same time unconditioned type of letter. I will follow here some of the avatars of this strange letter particularly when it is involved in the rearticulation of the relationship between philosophy and poetry.

Badiou's repositioning of philosophy, including his own philosophical project, is not achieved at once, since the very notion of end is left unthematized in the *Manifesto for Philosophy* and will only be fully thought in *Conditions*. Badiou's philosophical decision concerns the very question of possibility and the possible. But it also depends on the question of grounding, since an assertion of possibility that does not confront the tenets of the end of philosophy would have been untenable for Badiou. He must therefore confront Heidegger's narrative of the end of metaphysics and its basic corollary of the forgetting of Being, as well as the Heideggerian form of the dialogue between thinking and poetizing. This confrontation aims at wresting the philosophical saying from the proximity to the poem and, in so doing, activate the old and venerable "discord between philosophy and poetry" that constitutes Plato's legacy. What is remarkable in Badiou's repetition of this by now common scene in contemporary philosophy is his call for a return to Plato. From Nietzsche to Heidegger and beyond, this century has been anti-Platonic, according to Badiou, and the only way to refound philosophy is through a repetition of the Platonic gesture.

The twist and turns of this return to Plato are manifold and its consequences are diverse. On the one hand, it aims to liberate what philosophical modernity has repressed—the matheme—although the scope of this repressive philosophical modernity is limited to a post-Nietzschean configuration. On the other hand, it must account for an articulation in which none of the nonphilosophical fields will have dominion on the others. There are two competing versions of the return to Plato in Badiou. The first deploys the figure of the circle in which the return to the philosophically proper assures an integral founding. In this version, the matheme is privileged over the poem. The second version takes the figure of an ellipsis that interrupts any return to a proper ground: philosophy cannot be integrally founded. In this version, the matheme and the poem are conceived neither under the logic of opposition nor of compatibility: compossibility is thus pushed to the limits of nomination.

The "return" is accomplished in terms of an axiomatic derived from Cantor and post-Cantorian mathematics through which it is possible to deal with being qua being, pure multiplicity, since for Badiou the axiomatic of mathematics has a constitutive power with respect to philosophical logic. This privileging of mathematics lies in the matheme's proximity to the disseminated nature of the pure multiple. Mathematics is the thinking of the multiple pure as ontology. Moreover, the return seeks to establish a new topology of the four generic procedures and to secure a place for philosophy as the guarantor of the "truths of the time." In this sense, philosophy is endowed with the power to unfold what is left unthought by mathematics. Philosophy is possible only if the "free play" of the four generic procedures is operative and its key element is the de-suturing of philosophy from any generic procedure (nonphilosophical fields) asserting dominion on the others. The suturing to one of its conditions entails the obstruction of truth's circulation for philosophy and then impedes compossibility: the impossibility of reading the historical situation. No meaning derives from this reading, since philosophy's task is not to offer a positive incarnation of truth but rather the empty "figure" of those truths produced in nonphilosophical fields. Through the turns and detours of the "return to Plato," the differend between the poem and the matheme is revisited.

POETIC SUTURE

In the *Manifesto for Philosophy*, Badiou introduces the age of poets as a key philosophical category that indicates the moment when philosophy sutures itself to only one of its conditions. By *suture* Badiou understands an interruption of philosophy's ability to assure the compossibility (*compossibilité*) of the truths produced by the four generic procedures. *Compossibility* is a term that indicates the quality of being compossible; a classic philosophical concept that refers to one thing's possibility of existing alongside others at the same time. In Leibniz, the term expresses a relation in which two possible terms or events can coexist without the opposition of one of the terms entailing the suppression of the other. Badiou deploys this concept in order to explain the way in which philosophy relates to the nonphilosophical fields: the possibility of philosophy's existence is posited alongside the simultaneous coexistence of science, politics, love, and poetry.

The moment indicated by the expression the *age of poets* is not a historical moment decreed from the viewpoint of the totality of an accomplished system to be transcended and transformed into a higher ground of knowledge. "Philosophy under conditions" names a situation in which the former is no longer a field of knowledge, since in it philosophy deals with truths it does not produce—it operates under the effects of these truths. The conditionality of philosophy in Badiou names the possibility for thinking in the aftermath of Heidegger, or once philosophy is disentangled from the poem and a new type of relation is established between philosophy and the poem:[10]

> If philosophy is, as I claim it to be, the configuration of the fact that its four generic conditions (the poem, the matheme, the political and love) are compossible in the eventual [*événémentiel*] form prescribing the truths of the time, a suspension of philosophy can result from the restriction or blockage of the free play required in order to define a regime of passage, or of intellectual circulation between the truth procedures conditioning philosophy. The most frequent cause of such a blockage is that instead of constructing a space of compossibility through which the thinking of time is practiced, philosophy delegates its functions to one or another of its conditions, handing over the whole of thought to one generic procedure. *Philosophy is then carried out in the element of its own suppression to the great benefit of that procedure.* (MPh 61, emphasis added)

This suturing of philosophy to the poem produces a decisive effect: philosophy abandons operations proper to thinking that the poem then comes to occupy. Badiou's formulation unfolds a series of issues that demand closer examination.

The syntagm age of poets names, from the viewpoint of philosophy and in philosophical terms, something that concerns thinking and not poetizing:

> In spite of the word "poets," the category "age of poets" is not immanent to poetry. It is not the poets who have declared that this age is theirs. . . . In spite

of the word "age," it is not a historical category. It does not pretend to periodize poetry according to its own scansions.... Finally, it is not a question of an aesthetic category, or of a judgment of taste. The age of poets is a philosophical category. It organizes a particular way of thinking the knot between the poem and philosophy, such as this knot becomes visible from philosophy's perspective. "Age" refers to an epochal situation of philosophy. And "poets" refers to the poem as a condition of philosophy. I call "age of poets" this moment proper to philosophy's history when the latter is sutured, that is, handed over or submitted to only one of its conditions. (AP 21–22)

We are dealing here with philosophical categories and protocols that are employed in order to apprehend (in the sense both of understanding and of encompassing) the poem. This suture of thinking to the poem is evaluated by a double set of criteria. On the one hand, it is experienced as a negative phenomenon from the very interior of philosophy: "in a situation in which philosophy is sutured either to science or to politics, certain poets, or rather certain poems, come to occupy the place where, ordinarily, are declared strategies of thinking that are properly [*proprement*] philosophical" (AP 22). Philosophy relinquishes something that belongs to its own jurisdiction and the poem, which was expatriated by Plato and later repatriated and regulated by Aristotle, takes charge of operations deemed proper to philosophy. Badiou describes the scene of suturing as a true theater of operations.

To be able to speak of the poem in philosophical terms and to gain "poetic truths"—directives for thinking—philosophy must declare the *end* of the age of poets. If in the *Manifesto*, Badiou's narrative denounced the end (of philosophy), here he announces another end, that of the "age of *the* poets":

I can read in Celan that, yes, the poem demands to be relieved from the poem..., or rather that the poem-thinking once it comes to the shattering of its material support, its song, demands to be re-opened to the pure dimension of its sense. Which could also mean: the age of poets is closed. (AP 29)

In both cases, however, he interrogates neither the notion of end nor the eschatological dimension it brings into play. There is a good end, the one declared by the "Philosophers" and a bad end, the one announced by the "Sophists." In other words, Badiou's rhetoric yields here to the passion of the militant, which is always a passion of the end, for the end, in view of an end. One wonders if the return to Plato, which calls for repeating the poet's proscription, can simply be sustained by a rhetorical sleight of hand, one that does not sufficiently engage the end of the end. Is it simply by relocating the notion of end that the outcome of de-suturing will succeed in articulating a new relation between philosophy and the poem?[11]

The evaluation of poetic suturing provides us with another insight: poetry's occupation of "philosophy's originary vocation"—"to think the epoch as the site of compossibility of the different truth-procedures" (*MPh* 37)—entails that the poem itself take a stand on the question "What is thinking?" In other words, poetry's occupation of operations proper to philosophy revolves around a pivotal point: "the poems of the age of poets are those in which the poetic saying is not only a thinking which informs a truth, but is also compelled to *think this thinking*" (AP 23). Nevertheless, the negative criterion becomes a positive one: the (intrapoetic) thinking of this (poetic) thought—a nonself-reflective thinking, since it is always a set of operations unfolding in the poem, *as* poem—is not something that is excessive regarding philosophical operations. Rather, it is a legacy: "the age of poets bequeaths us, in order to liberate philosophy, the imperative of a clarification without totality, of a thought of that which is at the same time dispersed and inseparated, of a non-convivial reason, *cold for having neither object nor orientation*" (AP 36, emphasis added). Poetry's occupation of philosophy's theater of operations is, in the end, a beneficial one; it produces a truth about the time and a law to be followed: "cold reason."

Badiou's first attempt to rearticulate the dialogue between thinking and poetizing is highly problematic. The conditioning effects of poetry on philosophy appear to be forceful enough to provide philosophy with truths, but not compelling enough to rearticulate the philosophical determination of poetry. Therefore, they do not lead to a formulation of a new type of relation, one in which the philosopher does not have the upper hand. If the de-suturing of philosophy from the poem has taken place, one cannot see a new relation being established, but rather the reactivation of a classical hierarchy, even if a complicated interplay is at stake between the "figures" of the poem and the "maxims" of thinking.

This impasse is due to two reasons. First, inasmuch as the poem occupies operations left vacant by thinking, its maxims condition philosophy even when the poem is understood as the space of intrapoetic operations (*mise en œuvre*) belonging to maxims of thinking. The immanent truths of the poem are negatively connoted by an usurping characteristic that allows the Philosopher to deploy a defensive line in order to then annex them as part of its territory. Second, because philosophy reverses the sign of the prefix *intra-*, it can read the poetic event in terms of maxims of thinking and treat them as a legacy: The poem's intraphilosophical truths thus become extrapoetic or at best parapoetic. The passage from an intraphilosphical poetical operation into a proper philosophical one thus remains muddled. It is hard to tell where inclusion ends and belonging begins. In other words, the philosopher who operates under the de-sutured condition of the poem appropriates the poetic maxims and uses them as a model for thinking precisely because philosophy's "propriety" remains unquestioned. We will see below that the question of *use* is not an accidental one; the return to Plato demands the deployment of the economy of use, illustration, and example. We will also see that this economy of use supposes a logic of the border and the frame able to contain the excessive errancy of poetic truth. A logic of localization thus awaits us in the very text of philosophy.

In his attempt to redraw the graphics of the dialogue between thinking and poetizing, Badiou's own language produces a displacement of predicates. The poem is spoken in terms of "maxims" and "operations"; it becomes a fiction of method and provides figures for what is unpresentable to thinking. The operations of the age of poets (coldness, disorientation, de-objectivation) are such that they can be expressed in the "rigorous" language of deductive thinking, whose unconditioned condition is the matheme (AP 29-38). It is in this philosophical decision to name these operations as such that we can locate the first seeds of what will become Badiou's inesthétique.

The philosopher, operating under condition, appeals to the poem in a space in which philosophy and poetry have been de-sutured. However, the de-suturing does not change the classical hierarchy between philosophy and poetry. What gesture is constituted in this philosophical recourse to the poem? How can the matheme, the poem's classical rival, come to provide philosophy with a matrix and language that, although producing the de-suturing of philosophy from the poem, does not, in its turn, reproduce the classical philosophical determination of "literature" (that is, a suturing of the poem to the concept)?

Badiou's first attempt to rearticulate the dialogue between thinking and poetizing reveals a critical tension. The "reversal of the reversal of Platonism" goes hand in hand with the reversal of the motif of the end: the end of philosophy proclaimed by the Sophists is disqualified in terms of a de-suturing, which authorizes the Philosopher to declare the end of the age of poets. However, the motif of the end remains unthought by Badiou and the reversal can only be attributed to the *Manifesto*'s militant rhetoric. Also a classical economy of use stipulates how to philosophically employ the immanent truths of the poem and thus risks securing their singularity. What does this use of the poem imply?

ON WOUNDS, SUTURES, AND STITCHES (*POINTS*): "A RELATION OF THE FOURTH TYPE"?

The return to Plato, the proclamation of the end of the age of poets, and the de-suturing of philosophy from the poem call for a new dispute with Heidegger's own articulation of the relation between thinking and poetizing. This time "to rethink that which joins and disjoins the poem to philosophical discourse is an imperative which Heidegger compels us to submit ourselves to" (RPP 94). It is through this dispute that the possibility of establishing a different relation or non-relation between philosophy and the poem may allow for a more rigorous articulation. This new articulation could also provide the philosopher with guidelines for philosophically using the poem's truths. It remains to be seen if both exigencies can be satisfied in a single stroke; that is, if the response to these two heterogeneous exigencies can satisfy the demand of the pure multiple.

Badiou's critique is axiomatic: it contests Heidegger's type of compossibility, his claim of the cobelonging of *lógos* and the poetic, but it must also proceed in such a way as to not fall back into the space of speculative aesthetics. Badiou's task, in Heidegger's aftermath is to think the poem's provenance, as well as to think thinking (*la pensée*) in its operative distance vis-à-vis the poem.

To achieve this goal, Badiou distinguishes between what must be either preserved or rejected in Heidegger. He retains three insights: the autonomous function of the thought of the poem (*la pensée du poème*); the determination of the common destiny shared by the poet and the thinker; and, finally, the risky exposure of philosophy to the poem. What he finds imperative to reject in Heidegger's is the reactivation of the sacred since the German philosopher endows the poetic saying with a foundational function. This last point invites two comments that can only unfold from the viewpoint of the risky exposure of philosophy to the poem.

First, we saw that, although he changes grounds, Badiou remains within the scope of a foundational project. Why is the matheme then endowed with the privilege to dislodge an ontopoetics? In his evaluation of Heidegger's effect in the French context and regarding the figure of the philosopher-poet, Badiou offers two examples. René Char is dismissed as someone who assumes a posture and embodies a "*prétension présocratique*," while Michel Déguy is evoked as an example whose poetic project is still dependent on the suture of the age of poets.[12] Be that as it may, Badiou never raises the possibility of a forceful interruption of Heidegger's ontopoetics from the perspective of the poem.

(A brief aside is in order here. There is a revealing omission when Badiou reviews the so-called Heidegger-effect in France: Maurice Blanchot.[13] Although Blanchot is not a poet in the narrow sense of the term, as early as the 1940s he exposed Heideggers's ontopoetics to a rigorous critique, for example, in "La parole 'sacrée' de Hölderlin."[14] Blanchot's "*rapport du troisième genre*" and his "*parole plurielle*" are decisive in any rearticulation of the relation between philosophy and the poem. Are Blanchot's *récits* not responsive enough to the risky exposure of philosophy to the poem, to the excessive errancy of the poem and to the pure multiple? Although outside the scope of the present study, Badiou's silence on Blanchot deserves a careful analysis.[15] This aside is meant to suggest that the privileges of the matheme should be taken neither at face value nor as the unique generic procedure able to undermine a "metaphysics of presence" and an ontopoetics. There is also a common hinge between Blanchot and Badiou: Mallarmé. Later in this chapter, I will show how Badiou's final formulation of the "relation of the fourth type" echoes Blanchot's formulation of "The Gaze of Orpheus." It is revealing that someone like Badiou, who has radically contested contemporary debates on ethics, should articulate an ethics of mystery in terms that are very close to those of Blanchot. Finally, it is in Blanchot's reflections on writing that it is possible to locate a break with the Romantic determination of literature and with the "God of the poets" that takes writing to a space where the promise of an eventual return of God is no longer operative. It should be recalled that for Badiou these are the two imperatives for the poem: "to conquer its own atheism and therefore to destroy the phraseology of nostalgia, the posture of the promise or the prophetic destination of the Open from within the power of language" [CTOT 21]).

Coming back to Badiou's assessment of Heidegger's directives on the poem, it is necessary to add that for the former it is imperative to contest the German philosopher's modality of suturing the end of philosophy to the nonargumentative authority of the poem. But it is equally necessary not to relapse into traditional pre-Heideggerian ways of conceiving the relation between philosophy and the poem. The idea is that this relation of the fourth type cannot be articulated within a space belonging to aesthetics—identifying rivalry (Parmenides), argumentative distance (Plato), and aesthetic regionality (Aristotle).

Badiou's is a twofold strategy. First, it points to those elements of the poem in which the rivalry with philosophy will be dissolved: poetry is the thinking of the presence of the present (Mallarmé) and not of the compossibility of time, philosophy's proper thought. Moreover, poetry is the naming of the event in the void of meaning (Celan): these two thoughts belong to the poem. Second, these two thoughts cannot challenge the grasp of the concept because philosophy is on the hither side of meaning: it deals only with what produces a hole in meaning—truth. For Badiou truth does not consist in either adequacy or disclosure and does not pertain to knowledge because it is an empty concept. Truth is not what knowledge produces but rather what, in a given situation, exceeds the sets of knowledge (*savoirs*) available. Truth is what escapes knowledge, what knowledge cannot name: the result of an event that "makes one-multiple on the one hand from all the multiples that belong to its site, on the other from the event itself" (*EE* 200). But then why is it that there is a constitutive rivalry between philosophy and the poem, one that produces anxiety, stress, pain, and painful memories to the former?

> What causes philosophy's constitutive displeasure regarding its conditions, the poem as well as the others, is having to depose, together with meaning, that which is determined as enjoyment, precisely at the point where a truth comes to make a hole in the forms of knowledge that produce meaning. (RPP 102)

Badiou's terminology (*déplaisir*, *déposition*) indicates that the new relation he seeks to establish impresses its effects upon an old wound, leaving a mark and the memory of a wound (*blessure*) on a sensitive stitch. If the stitching of philosophy to the poem is a painful event for the former, its de-suturing is no less so. In his critique of Heidegger's poetic suture, Badiou also responds to those he calls "postmodern" thinkers for whom "art would always challenge the concept, and it is in terms of this challenge, of this wound, that it would be necessary to interpret the Platonic gesture according to which one could only establish the royalty of the philosopher by the proscription of the poets" (RPP 101). The Platonic gesture, Badiou seems to imply, is not a defensive one because the articulation we are dealing with is not classically Platonic. It is no longer a question of the rivalry between the intelligible and the sensible (the concept and the figure). There is a change involved here, since philosophy does not aim to interpret truth but rather to found a proper site in which to utter why and how a truth is not a meaning:

> But "philosophy" begins when this component shows its inconsistency. When it is no longer a question of interpreting the real procedures on which truth lies, but of founding a proper place where, under the contemporary conditions of these procedures, it is possible to state how and why a truth is not a meaning but, rather, that it is a hole in meaning. This "how" and this "why," founders of a place of thinking under conditions, can only be practiced in the displeasure produced by a refusal of donation and of hermeneutics. They demand the primordial desertion of the donation of meaning, the ab-sense, an ab-negation regarding meaning [*la défection primordiale de la donation de sens, l'ab-sens, l'abnégation quant au sens*]. Or even an impropriety. They demand that the truth-procedures be subtracted from the eventful singularity which weaves them in the real, and which ties them to meaning in the mode of its traversing. (C 102)

By deposing meaning, the philosopher under conditions finds himself, as does the poet, facing the risky exposure to the event. Everything seems to indicate that, in his attempt to secure a post-Heideggerian articulation, Badiou's reflection manages to posit a new relation in which philosophy and the poem expose themselves to the event, according to their respective truth-producing regimes and no longer as part of a hierarchical structure dependent on the subordination of poetry to philosophy. But suddenly, it is the painful stitch that commands the repetition of the Platonic gesture. In spite of the rearticulation of the terms, the philosophical program reserved for figurative language is one that has always been reserved for it from the perspective of the concept. We are faced with an even stranger double movement, one that divides within itself and enacts an overdetermined disavowal. If philosophy and the poem expose themselves in different ways to the same outside, to what is unnamable or indiscernible, how does the philosopher deal with the poem?

Badiou recognizes that the link between philosophy and the poem is a narrow one, since the former is "an effect of language." Nevertheless, he claims that "philosophy determines the literary as fiction, as comparison, image or rhythm, and as story. Deposition takes here the figure of a placement" (RPP 104). Badiou must therefore make a concession, an avowal that he states as if it were a circumstantial fact: philosophy is an "effect of language" and not simply the end product of a "deductive invention" (EE). Moreover, the disturbing deposition of meaning that a philosophy under conditions entails is assigned to a still conceptual economy of placement:

> In the texture of its exposition philosophy undoubtedly *makes use* of fictive incarnations. . . . Philosophy *makes use* of the image, of the comparison, of rhythm. The image of the sun serves to expose in the light of presence that there is something essentially *withdrawn* in the idea of the Good. . . . Finally, philosophy makes use of the story, of the fable, and of the parable. (RPP 104, emphasis added)

What at first appeared to be a new relation (one in which the common destiny of the poet and the thinker were established on a common abyssal ground and therefore one in which the dominance of the latter upon the former was dissolved) finally reverses itself into a symmetrical, hierarchical relation. The double exigency, the reopening of the "Cartesian meditation" and the remaining faithful to the poem, cannot be answered in a single stroke. The scheme of *use* reintroduces the most classical and unfaithful philosophical type of response to the poem. Philosophy de-sutures itself from the poem, but once again stitches the poem to a philosophical—rhetorical—suture, perhaps one whose form does not fully correspond to the de-sutured space of philosophy Badiou is advocating. The rhetorical stitching of the poem to philosophy indicates the relapse into a pre-Heideggerian determination of poetic language. The return to Plato activates the philosophical purging of rhetoric; one is not far from Plato's distinction between a "good (philosophical) rhetoric" and a nonphilosophical one, as it was the case in the *Phaedrus*. But this return to Plato confirms and affirms one of the most insidious philosophical gestures: the determination of rhetoric as philosophy's subordinate other (*Republic*, Book VI).

How has philosophy traditionally dealt with figures or tropes? One approach affirms an original figurativeness and recounts the story of its effacement or forgetting. It supposes the effacement of the figure as the origin of philosophical concepts and, therefore, a sensible origin of conceptual abstraction. In this type of discourse, figures are affirmed at the expense of the concept (Rousseau and Nietzsche, albeit differently). There is, however, a second type of discourse, one that axiomatically chooses what is univocal as a philosophical ideal. Its calculated purpose is to separate figuration from what is sensible to arrive at the pure abstraction of the concept. In this discourse, a metaphor is a detour with regard to a proper reference that must be preserved at all cost. This reference brings a surplus of polysemy to language underwritten by propriety and universality; a surplus of meaning that philosophy may very well evacuate in delimiting the domain of proper meaning. Derrida refers to this way of dealing (without dealing) with metaphor as "la relève métaphysique de la métaphore dans le sens propre de l'être."[16] What is important about this movement is that it follows a metaphorical movement, inasmuch as *metaphor* is defined as the "elevation" of a sensible referent into an ideal signification.

Can Badiou's way of treating metaphors be included in any of these two discourses? Yes and no. Yes because he appeals to the most traditional philosophical modality of dealing with literature: that of a localized figurality, a controlled type of use of tropes regulated through a logic of localization:

> Nevertheless, these literary occurrences as such are placed under the jurisdiction of a principle of thinking that they do not constitute. They are *localized* in points where, in order to finish establishing a place from which to utter why and how a truth makes a hole in meaning and escapes interpretation, it is necessary, by a paradox in the exposition, to propose a fable, an image or a fiction to interpretation. (RPP 105, emphasis added)

The poem produces a truth, but the poetic—"literary"—element is not turned into a concept, as one would expect in the classical determination of metaphor. Instead, metaphor comes "au point de l'imprésentable"; it is placed where no concept can be invoked: around the hole produced by truth. Nevertheless, this localization is regulated from an implicit economy of truth that supposes a proper—philosophical—use of the figure or poem. In this sense, Badiou's schema is classical. However, as I indicated above, Badiou's treatment of tropes cannot be fully included in a classical schema since he attempts to accommodate a new element to the classical schema.

For Badiou truth results from an eventful procedure. It is always a situational truth linked to the event's site. A truth cannot provide an exact designation of the event since its way of relating to conceptual knowledge is one of subtraction. In a situation, a truth is therefore the production of a nondiscernible multiplicity: "une vérité est cette consistance minimale (une partie, une immanence sans concept) qui avère dans la situation l'inconsistance qui en fait l' être" (MP 90). In other words, a truth bears witness to the "wandering excess" of being.

Nevertheless, Badiou's theory of the philosophical use of metaphor is commanded by an implicit philosophical determination grounded in a notion of truth as adequacy (*adæquatio*). There is a conceptual determination (*savoir*) of metaphor, even if figurative language is mobilized in terms of what exceeds knowledge. Is it by chance that Badiou's example of the localized use of metaphors is that of the sun, "*the image of the sun* that is used to bring to the light of presence something essentially *withdrawn* in the idea of the Good"?

There seems to be a montage of the ruling metaphor (that of the sun) upon an articulation that does not fully accommodate it. The sun, as is well-known, is the very example of the sensible. In the tradition inaugurated by Greek philosophy, the sun is at the center of rhetorical theories that understand metaphor as the transport of the sensible into the nonsensible, or of the familiar into what is unknown. However, Badiou's reference to the metaphor of the sun cannot be taken at face value, given that the schema he deploys supposes a rearticulation of the figurative dimension of language not to the sensible nor to the concept, but to the unpresentable dimension of truth. Yet, the metaphor of the sensible, the figure determining the classical economy of signification, is invoked and inscribed into a postsignifying articulation. In other words, the classical Platonic–Aristotelian montage of metaphor is incommensurable when deployed not to illustrate but to name that which belongs to the subtractive dimension of the event. This incommensurability lies in the nature of the regime of truth. The presupposition underlying the classical deployment of the metaphor of the sun is that there is adequacy between the improper sensible presentation and the proper intelligible concept. Badiou thus accuses the Sophists through an argument that is too dependent on a premodern schema of signification, for which the deposition of meaning is not compelling enough. In other words, Badiou "Platonizes" against the postsignifying regime of the modern poem.

"AU *POINT* DE L'INNOMABLE," OR FOR AN "ETHICS OF MYSTERY"

The positing of a relation of the fourth type between poetry and philosophy or poem and matheme, does not seem to materialize in Badiou. This is due to the grafting of a classical economy of signification on to a space in which it is no longer a question of the sensible presentation of the concept but, rather, one of the unpresentable dimension of truth as event. In other words, the return to Plato cannot secure a new type of relation without rearticulating the terms of that relation in a different space.

The Platonic opposition between the matheme and the poem must be reactivated this time in terms of both post-Cantorian mathematics and modern poetry. Badiou has to reopen the space of the modern poem, even as he declares the end of the age of poets. This reactivation and the new articulation it will yield are presented under the classical philosophical question "What is a poem?" It is under the syntax of the *ti esti* that the Platonic metaphor of the sun will be deployed again, but this time onto a different orbit, one whose scope puts the very form of the *ti esti* in disarray. Let's follow Badiou's new formulation in the *Petit Manuel d'inesthétique*:

> Nevertheless, this opposition in language of the matheme's transparency and the poem's metaphorical obscurity presents formidable problems for us moderns. Plato cannot sustain the maxim promoting the matheme and banishing the poem. He cannot do so because he himself explores the limits of *dianoia*, of discursive thinking. When it is a question of the supreme principle, of the One, or of the Good, Plato must agree that we are there *epékeina tês ousías*, beyond substance, and consequently outside of everything that is exposed to the grasp of the Idea. He must acknowledge that the donation in thinking of Being beyond beings does not let itself be traversed by any *dianoia*. *He himself must have recourse to images, as that of the sun, to metaphors.* . . . In short: where what is at stake is the opening of thinking to the principle of what is thinkable, when thinking must become absorbed in the grasping of that which institutes it as thinking, Plato *submits language to the power of the poetic saying*. (QP 36, emphasis added)

Through Plato it is necessary to acknowledge (*il faut avouer*) that an effect of language constitutes philosophy. In other words, philosophy is no longer simply and incidentally under the effect of language, as was the case earlier: language now begins to acquire a constitutive scope. Moreover, the opposition between the metaphor's obscurity and the matheme's transparency is located "in language." Therefore, it is necessary to admit (*il faut avouer*), again through Plato, that what puts philosophy into motion and opens thinking to "its" own principle (the gift of thinking) escapes the grasp of discursive thinking (*dianoia*). Philosophy's principle is not "its own," or at least not fully, since it comes from an anarchic "origin" that not only forces Plato to "submit" language to the power (*puissance*) of the poem, but also compels Badiou to submit the return to Plato to an excessive trace or point. The circular appropriating movement of the "return" will be interrupted in a point and by a point.

After these two far-from-compelling avowals, the heliotropic metaphor is again invoked to bear witness to this scene, but this time in a new montage whose frame is no longer that of the page of a philosophy book. Rather, it is displaced from the traditional rhetorical context to signal the very opening of philosophy's intelligibility. Therefore, the metaphor of the sun is invoked not only to bear witness but also to provide us with an example of its powerlessness. It should not be forgotten that the sun is also the rule for the imperfect metaphor, the best example of the failure of its property in terms of adequacy. It is this failure, however, that always renews the interval or difference that philosophical discourse attempts to reduce when proposing a theory of the philosophical use of metaphor. In other words, the metaphor of the sun is not an example among others, but the example that, by structuring the metaphorical space of philosophy, also indicates that a reference to a proper origin is missing—"at its very origin."[17] The metaphor of the sun, therefore, points to an excessive trace, a point that will not be fully accounted for and that calls for an ethics of mystery.

Everything revolves around this point now, whose effects will be decisive because "we moderns endure the linguistic interval of both the poem and the matheme in a totally different fashion from the Greeks" (QP 36). This endurance will not only provide "us moderns" with a rearticulation of the relation between the matheme and the poem, but will also affect the scope of Badiou's foundational project.

Compossibility, it should be remembered, is the form that knots together philosophy to the four generic procedures. Within the context of this articulation, the "linguistic" interval between the poem and the matheme can be neither that of opposition nor of compatibility. The possibility of composing the knot must face the impossible; compossibility must face impossibility, and "Platonizing" against the modern poem will consequently be of no avail.

A new articulation must be posited diagonally to the founding Platonic opposition between the poem and the matheme, which depended on the poet's proscription. What is at stake now is that "when examined from philosophy's perspective, poem and matheme are inscribed within the general form of a truth-procedure" (QP 39). The terms of the discussion are modified in order to respond rigorously to the initial determination of a philosophy under conditions. If in the first articulation the matheme was endowed with the power to protect philosophy from the Siren's song of the poem, both the matheme and the poem are now approached in view of their common feature: the general form of a truth-procedure.

However, what still must be determined is their respective regimes of truth-production. This determination unfolds by situating philosophy under the double condition of the matheme and the poem and in view of a general theory of being and the event, inasmuch as they are knotted together by truth, in truth. Within this frame, the determination of both the poem's and the matheme's truth are conducted in terms of the ways in which poetic and mathematical languages deal with nomination and, above all, with what exceeds it. In terms then of a dialectic of power/powerlessness (*puissance/inpuissance*) when faced with the event, "for a truth is the work in the proximity of being of a vanished event whose only remains is the name" (QP 46). What are the mathematical and the poetic regimes of truth? How do mathematics and poetry deal with nomination? Both mathematics and poetry, inasmuch as generic procedures, produce truths out of the pure multiple. For Badiou, any truth is a power: from a new theorem one gathers directives to reorient thinking; from a new poetics one derives a new program for thinking.

Let's first examine mathematical nomination:

> Mathematics produces truth out of the pure multiple as the primordial inconsistency of being in so far [sic] as being. Poetry makes truth out of the pure multiple as a presence coming to the limits of language. Or, the song of language as the capacity to present the pure notion of "there is" in the very effacement of its empirical objectivity. (QP 39–40)

The language of mathematics, characterized by a "deductive fidelity," faces the challenge of consistency. But consistency, after Gödel, is its excessive point and mathematics cannot name it. The power of producing mathematical truths is intertwined with a constitutive powerlessness. The fidelity to the event, which is shaped upon a mathematical paradigm ruled by consistency, comes face to face with a point that escapes the possibility of an integral foundation.

What is the situation with poetic language?

> The poem's power of revelation folds around an enigma so that the verification of this enigma should make all the real of powerlessness out of the power of what is true. In this sense, "the mystery in literature" is a true imperative. When Mallarmé claims that "there must always be an enigma in poetry," he is founding an *ethics of mystery* that is the respect, through the power of a truth, of its point of powerlessness. The mystery lies in the fact that any poetics leaves in its center what it cannot bring into presence. [*Le mystère est proprement que toute poétique laisse en son centre ce qu'elle n'a pas le pouvoir de faire venir à la présence*]. (QP 41, emphasis added)

One cannot sublate the interplay between power and powerlessness in a dialectical way. Poetic revelation is intertwined with an anarchic enigma or, rather, poetic revelation is the intertwining of the enigma. This enigma traverses the poetic saying with an excessive trace and requires an ethical approach: a response to an impossible demand, or a demand for the impossible. Poetic mystery lies in the fact that there is a point at its very center that cannot be named.

Badiou's formulation resembles that of another reader of Mallarmé: Maurice Blanchot. It should be remembered that in the Orphic adventure that Blanchot refers to in *L'espace littéraire*, Eurydice is a figure that dissimulates both "the profoundly dark point towards which art, desire, death, and the night all seem to lead," as well as "the instant in which the essence of the night approaches as the *other* night." Orpheus's task is "to bring the point into the daylight and in the daylight give it form, figure, and reality" not by direct optical contact, but by a "detour." However, we know that in Blanchot's reading of this myth, Orpheus forgets "the ultimate requirement of its impulse [*l'exigence ultime de son mouvement*]." This exigency is not the fact of having a work, but that "someone should stand and face this point [*quelqu' un se tienne en face de ce point*]," Eurydice. But she is not all that is there to be "seen"; Orpheus is also faced with "ce qui dissimule la nuit, *l'autre* nuit, *la dissimulation qui apparaît*."[18] This dissimulation that appears by disappearing can only be named by a forcing (*forçage*) of language. It is this impossible forcing that Blanchot's *récits* produce when they approach the unnamable point indicated by "Viens."[19]

For Badiou, any naming of the event is also of a poetic nature, since it is able to fix what disappears. The power of poetic language lies in its fixing what disappears (presence), although it is this very power that poetry cannot name. Orpheus, in his descent into Hades in search of Eurydice, comes into contact with what is unnamable ("ce dont une vérité ne peut forcer la nomination" [QP 42]), a point where the power of language is condensed and Orpheus cannot name. For Badiou, Mallarmé's "Sonnet in ptyx" produces a naming: "no doubt the *ptyx* would be the name for that which the poem is capable of: to produce out of language a coming into presence previously impossible. Except that precisely that name is not a name, that name does not name" (QP 45). Through Mallarmé both Blanchot and Badiou reach the threshold of language.

Mathematics and poetry are exposed to a point that subtracts itself from their respective power of nomination. They are both interrupted and open to an excess that calls for an ethics of mystery. But they also submit philosophy to operating under condition:

> Between the matheme's consistency and the poem's power, between these two unnamable points, philosophy renounces establishing the names clogging what subtracts itself. In this sense, philosophy is, *after* the poem and *after* the matheme, and *under* their thinking condition, the incomplete thinking of the multiple of thoughts. (QP 46–47, emphasis added)

The final articulation of the relation of the fourth type between philosophy and the poem demands a deposition of philosophy's magisterial attributes and an acknowledgment of its exposure to unfounded regimes of truth (the poem being the unfounded par excellence). This exposure to the unfounded does not leave the scope of Badiou's foundational project intact. The graphics of compossibility supposes a redefinition of the impact that the unfounded conditions impress upon philosophy itself, as well as of compossibility's temporality. Philosophy is now defined as the incomplete thinking of the multiple coming after its conditions.

It is important to stress that the final formulation of the relationship between philosophy and the poem allows for a point of opacity around which the knot of compossibility may be tied together. Nevertheless, for Badiou's graphics of compossibility to work and for the unfounded dimension of the poem not to disrupt the possibility of composing the knot, he must assign the poem the power to fix what, by definition, cannot be fixed. In other words, it is as if the passage from powerlessness to power were still preserving traces of a dialectical schema.

I would like to close by coming back to the two prefixes (*intra-* and *in-*) with which I opened this chapter. A philosophy operating under conditions seems to restore the immanence and singularity of the truths that nonphilosophical fields produce. However, does this ethics of mystery do justice to the inesthétique's demand of thinking the negative in a positive way? What characterizes the intraphilosophical poetic operations of the poem for Badiou is the ability to give a proper name to negation (to give a nonfigurative name to the operations proper to the poem: what in "L'Âge des poètes" he refers to as coldness, disorientation, etc.). In the *Petit Manuel d'inesthétique*, the nonfigurative names of negation are *le dissolu* or *désobjectivé* in Mallarmé, *l'intotalisable* in Pessoa, *le delié* or *inconsistant* in Celan, and *l'empirer* or *le mal dit* in Beckett. These names indicate poetry's break with the promise of a possible "return of the gods"; they are the names of what Lacoue-Labarthe calls the "becoming prose of the poem."

What is at stake in Badiou's borrowing of Lacoue-Labarthe's expression, one that the latter has coined in order to take issue with Badiou's understanding of philosophy's suture to the poem? Badiou first employs Lacoue-Labarthe's expression in the preface to the *Court traité d'ontologie transitoire*. The expression thus appears within the context of a reflection on the question of the "Death of God" and of its legacy for thinking in Hölderlin, Nietzsche, and Heidegger. Badiou's active appropriation of Lacoue-Labarthe's expression may point to his realization that what threatens the suture's operative value is what this prefatory essay rejects: the nostalgia of the promise. If this is the case, then once the imperative of the poem is its "becoming prose," the stipulation of an ethics of mystery that seemed to secure a new relation between philosophy and the poem becomes harder to sustain: "the poem cannot be the melancholic guardian of finitude, the yoke of a mystic of silence, nor the mastering of an improbable threshold" (*CTOT* 21). What an inesthétique approach to the poem brings to philosophy is a set of disembodied, neuter (neither melancholic nor nostalgic) directives concerning our situation such as the poem utters it: "here nothing is promised to us but the power to remain true to what comes to us" (*CTOT* 23). If ending with the motif of finitude is the only way in which philosophy can expose itself to the multiple without one, a negatively inflected aesthetics makes the poem pay a high price for its "becoming prose."

NOTES

A first version of this chapter was presented at the Symposium of the California Psychoanalytic Circle (San Francisco, April 1999) and subsequently appeared as "*Don du Poème*: Alain Badiou after the 'Age of Poets'" in *(a): The Journal of Culture and the Unconscious* 1 (Fall 2000): 10–33. A second version was presented as "For an Ethics of Mystery: Badiou's *Inésthetique*," in the Department of Romance Languages, Cornell University, November 2001.

    1. I am referring here to Hal Foster, ed., *The Anti-Aesthetic: Essays on Postmodern Culture* (Port Townsend, WA: Bay Press, 1983) and to David Carroll, *Paresthetics: Foucault, Lyotard and Derrida* (New York: Methuen, 1987). For a critique of idealist aesthetics, see Peter Bürger, *Zur Kritik der idealistischen Ästhetik* (Frankfurt am Main: Shurkamp Verlag, 1983); Jean-Marie Schaeffer, *L'Art de l'âge moderne* (Paris: Gallimard, 1992) and *Adieu à l'esthétique* (Paris: PUF, 2000); Gérard Genette, *L'Œuvre de l'art: Immanence et transcendance* (Paris: Seuil, 1994) and *L'Œuvre de l'art: La rélation esthétique* (Paris: Seuil, 1997); and Peter Osborne, ed., *From an Aesthetic Point of View: Philosophy, Art and the Senses* (London: Serpent's Tail, 2000).

    2. Alain Badiou, *Petit Manuel d'inesthétique* (Paris: Seuil, 1998), i.

    3. Carroll, *Paraesthetics*, xiv.

    4. "The one is not, there is only the counting-as-one [*compte-pour-un*]; the counting-as-one is nothing but the system of conditions through which the multiple allows itself to be recognized as multiple" (*EE* Méditation 1). Although I use the word *calculation* here, I distinguish the way Badiou deploys rhetoric from Derrida's and Levinas's. Badiou's approach differs substantially from the calculated language-games that Derrida engages in order to think the entanglement of transcendence and empirical configurations, or that Levinas performs in order to let the other of discourse come into discourse.

    5. Except for the passages from *Manifesto for Philosophy*, all translations are mine. All references to Alain Badiou's works will be given parenthetically in the body of the text.

    6. "La passe par le matheme autorise les vérités à dire quelque chose sur l'être; elle autorise les vérités à dire l'excés errant de l'être, où s'avére une fois son caractère soustractif" (Françoise Whal, "Le Soustractif," preface to *Conditions* [Paris: Editions du Seuil, 1992]).

7. See Gilles Deleuze, *What is Philosophy?* trans. Hugh Tomlinson and G. Burchall (New York: Columbia University Press, 1994); and Jacques Derrida, "Psyché: L'invention de l'autre," in *Psyché: Inventions de l'autre* (Paris: Galilée, 1987) 11-61.

8. Martin Heidegger, *The End of Philosophy* (New York: Harper and Row, 1973), 84.

9. On this topic and the differences between apocalyptic and eschatological discourses, see Jacques Derrida, *D'un ton apocalyptique adopté naguère en philosophie* (Paris: Galilée, 1982).

10. Alain Badiou, "Le récours philosophique au poème," in *Conditions* (Paris: Seuil, 1992).

11. Lacoue-Labarthe points out that although the concept of 'suture' is operative, the welding of philosophy to the poem is not the crucial one. It is rather the welding of philosophy to myth (to a mythology) by means of the poem that determines the political effects of poetic suturing. I claim that the *Manifesto*'s rhetoric is underwritten in part by the effects of this philosophically (Platonic) constitutive archipolitics of the end. See Philippe Lacoue-Labarthe, *Heidegger: La politique du poème* (Paris: Galilée, 2002), 43-77.

12. For Michel Déguy's response to Badiou, see his *La raison poètique* (Paris: Galilée, 2000).

13. In the *Manifesto*, Blanchot falls under the category of a "fetishism of literature" (60).

14. Maurice Blanchot, "La parole 'sacrée' de Hölderlin," in *La Part du Feu* (Paris: Gallimard, 1949). The essay was originally published in *Critique* in 1946.

15. This reading will link Badiou and Blanchot on several common issues: the refusal of the One and the writing of the multiple; the excessive errancy of the multiple; the critique of a "religious" ethics; the critique of hermeneutic reason and of *Ereignis*; the welcoming of the event; the thinking of an inventive politics; the poem as an outside escaping the jurisdiction of philosophical knowledge; an objectless "subject" (passivity).

16. Jacques Derrida, *Marges—de la Philosophie* (Paris: Minuit, 1972), 320.

17. See Jacques Derrida, "White Mythology," in *Margins—of Philosophy*, trans. Alan Bass (Chicago: University of Chicago Press, 1982), 207-72; and "Le Re-trait de la métaphore," in *Psychè*.

18. Maurice Blanchot, "Le Régard d'Orphé," in *L'espace littéraire* (Paris: Gallimard, 1955).

19. In my *Intrigues of the Other: Ethics and Literary Writing in Levinas and Blanchot* (forthcoming), I approach the question of an ethics of writing that, in Blanchot's case, leaves behind "the time of the promise."

FOUR

Unbreakable B's
From Beckett and Badiou to the Bitter End of Affirmative Ethics

Jean-Michel Rabaté

Alain Badiou's slim essay on Beckett is perhaps the first book one should open to get acquainted quickly with both authors. A beginner wishing to find his way through Beckett's tangle of texts would no doubt be greatly helped by this neat pedagogical guide that ends with a suitably original selection of prose passages. And a philosopher eager to find a shortcut through Badiou's often difficult and specialized books could do worse than use this book as pleasurable pretext leading to elegant and provocative theoretical discussions.

The Beckett book is conveniently short, with barely seventy pages of text, as if to imitate Beckett's own drift toward minimalism, and prove that one can write mercifully condensed philosophical essays. It is also partly autobiographical: Badiou reminisces about his Sartrean beginnings, his first encounter with Beckett's oeuvre in the mid-1950s, and then expatiates on the follies and promises of youth. It is also obliquely self-referential, since a number of these short chapters cover the same ground as the more demanding essay "L'écriture du générique: Samuel Beckett" (first published independently in 1989, then taken up as the last text collected of *Conditions*). All this, along with the untranslatable riddle posed by the adjective *increvable* associated with *desire*,[1] testifies to the long-standing importance of Beckett's work for Badiou, a body of texts to which he has kept returning, along with Mallarmé and Rimbaud, to identify a number of crucial issues better broached by poets and novelists than philosophers. It is also the only book Badiou has devoted to a literary figure. However, let us not be mistaken, more than a poetological reading of the Irish writer, it is a mostly philosophical reading that is provided here. Badiou takes his bearings in two main traditions, phenomenology and scientific rationalism, with key references to Descartes, Husserl, and Kant, although he never forgets the "letter" of Beckett's text and its varied and cunning rhetorical strategies.

There is very little nostalgia in the autobiographical opening of the book, however: there Badiou sums up his earlier response to Beckett, a response that is taken to be emblematic of two common misreadings. As he says, youth is that rare moment when one is both deeply impressed by new encounters leaving permanent marks on one's subjectivity, the blessed moment when the "new" impacts and leaves fruitful experiences to which one can decide or not to remain true, but it is also a moment when one is deeply although unwittingly determined by invisible waves of fashion. The dominant fashion in 1956 was to read Beckett as a nihilist, a pessimist absurdist, a dark comedian who staged metaphysical clowns wandering under an empty sky so as to ruminate on an absent god and express as wittily as possible the despair inherent to man's estate. On the other hand, he was also seen as one of the "moderns," haunted by the question of pure writing, the endless restating of language's opacity and intransitivity, in short through the lens of Blanchot's post-Hegelian ontology of a reflexive language speaking by itself and of itself. Badiou even describes himself as a "young cretin" (B 8) caught up between Sartre and Blanchot and possessed by the brilliant idea of bridging the gap between a Sartrean ethics of freedom and negativity and a Blanchotian meditation on language as language. His youthful endeavor would have consisted in "completing the Sartrean theory of freedom through a careful investigation of the opacities of the signifier" (B 7). What even today does not look like such a bad project if one thinks of writing a thesis on Beckett was, according to him, not the way. No, Badiou is definitive: that would have been a misstep, missing what is essential in Beckett's trajectory. Indeed, Beckett seems to offer an unforeseen confirmation of Aristotle's dictum that philosophy is made for (and by) older men and women!

BADIOU'S READING PROGRAM

Badiou remembers how he would memorize and regularly quote Beckett's most cynical, most desperate sentences, often missing their irony and their specific energy. His favorite book was *The Unnamable*, and it took him time to realize that for Beckett himself this book had constituted a dead end for which he had paid dearly by being plunged into almost ten years of silence. As Badiou explains, it took him many years to undo the cliché of an anxious nihilist and also to refuse the direct opposite view, which was then offered soon after, of a "thin Rabelais" (B 9) only interested by wholesale derision, stressing the farce of everything, sending off literature in a postmodern massacre of all values. "Neither existentialism nor modern baroque. Beckett's lesson is a lesson of measure, exactness and courage. This is what I would like to establish in these few pages" (B 9). In fact, it is an ethical

Beckett that Badiou aims at portraying, a writer who can teach us something useful and true about desire, language, and our limited human life. One might almost say that it is a Lacanian Beckett who is suggested by Badiou's program, a writer who shows why it is essential to never yield on one's desire even in the face of wholesale perversion and impotence. In fact, what Badiou finds in Beckett is a lesson in affirmation, a lesson made more poignant and powerful as one has multiplied all the reasons that show how impossible any affirmation is.

Badiou is aware of a chronological divide in Beckett's career—there are the works leading to the first trilogy that culminates with *The Unnamable*, then the moment of quasi silence between *Texts for Nothing* (1950) and *How It Is* (1960). Then comes a new departure, with experiments in different media such as film, television, and very short plays leading to unclassifiable short texts culminating once more with the second trilogy of *Nohow On*. Battling against objectified meanings, Badiou refuses the ready-made stereotypes that treat Beckett's oeuvre either as a single block (no doubt fallen from an obscure disaster, to quote Mallarmé) or as a linear progression toward formal minimalism wrapping up a cynical or nihilistic philosophical project (B 11). On the contrary, if Beckett's works are punctuated by hesitations and caesuras, they nevertheless oscillate between rigorous philosophical abstraction aiming at positing some sort of phenomenological reduction by other means and series of affirmative poetic variation on essential themes. While Beckett relentlessly refuses to inscribe himself in any given genre, blurring the distinction between novel and short story, theatrical play and performance, it is oriented by the positive answers it provides to Kant's three fundamental questions: "Where would I go if I could go?" "What would I be if I could be?" and "What would I say if I had a voice?" (B 12). After the ten-year hiatus, he adds a fourth question: "What am I if the other exists?" (B 12).

Badiou's main insight is that these four questions do not remain aporetic, that they do find an answer and a positive one at that: "Finally, all the genius of Beckett tends toward affirmation in nearly aggressive fashion. The form of the maxim is not unknown to him, and it always brings along a principle of strenuously forward-going attrition (*un principe d'acharnement et d'avancée*)" (B 13). Thus, he logically refuses to take Beckett at his word when he would stress a negative compulsion to write. For instance, shortly before his death, Beckett answered a questionnaire sent by the daily newspaper *Libération* with the question: "Why do you write?" the most condensed statement possible: "Bon qu'à ça!" ("Only good for that" would be an equivalent). Badiou contradicts him firmly: "Not totally, Beckett, not totally! Only good for that, but not totally!" (B 13). Badiou is thus following a fundamental rhetorical trope that is to be found in many pages of Beckett, the so-called epanorthosis, or the qualifying modification that often transforms the meaning radically.[2] A passage of *Ill Seen Ill Said* quoted by Badiou will provide a simple example:

> Was it ever over and done with questions? Dead the whole brood no sooner hatched. Long before. In the egg. Over and done with answering? With not being able. With not being able no to want to know. With not being able. No. Never. A dream. Question answered.[3]

Even if it seems that the passage concludes that there are no answers, it nevertheless answers, precisely in the verbal energy that heaps precisions, qualifications, rectifications, double negatives, and tangled contradictions. No, indeed, "it" will never end or reach an absolute period. This is the paradoxical space of Beckett's later prose, a space that Badiou starts describing in terms of a few basic devices like so many "operations" (B 17). Rather than just enumerate tropes and figures, Badiou concludes that the specific beauty of the work forces us to be responsible to it. We are responsible to the "letter of beauty" (B 17).

How is this letter constituted? Badiou shows how Beckett's operations duplicate a "methodical askesis" and go back to Descartes and Husserl in their wish to "suspend" everything that is inessential in order to reach the real and the true. This is why all the trappings of the clownish humor and the elements of despair and anxiety already described are to be taken as the substance of the text itself. Beckett is unsurpassable in the way he reduces bodies to paralyzed cripples, even mere ectoplasms or shapes in a jar, fitting Winnie in a hole in *Happy Days* and imagining himself occasionally as an egglike sphere with a few apertures. This is, in fact, his way of returning to a Husserlian *epoché* (B 19) that will finally expose what is generic in man. Beckett initiates in fact a serious investigation on "thinking humanity" (B 19); if he proceeds by way of systematic destruction, it is in order to discover what resists, what remains indestructible. Such a fundamental indestructibility will then yield a new foundation for ethics. Before, it will have questioned the role of the event, of its meaning and the links between infinity, truth, and the void. As I too wish to remain as close as possible to the letter of Beckett's texts, I will analyze more at length the first text in which all of these issues are brought together, *Watt*. Indeed, *Watt* can be taken as a point of departure to verify Badiou's thesis about the links between the event, its meaning, and the new role ascribed to the subject.

Badiou takes *Watt* as a sounding board when he wishes to explain how Beckett has moved from a Cartesian universe (so dominant in *Murphy*) to a world in which the principle of the absurd does not rule out calculation but on the contrary starkly opposes the infinity of serial proliferation to the unique occurrence of an incomprehensible event. In a crucial chapter entitled "The event and its name," Badiou sets the foundations for what is, according to him, Beckett's aim, the investigation of the minimal condition of freedom (B 40). This entails examining *Watt*, a novel in which "the prose oscillates between the grasp of an indifferent being and the torture of a reflection without any effect" (B 40). He continues:

In *Watt*, the place of being is absolutely closed, it validates a strict principle of identity. It is a complete, self-sufficient and eternal space. . . . Knowledge is deprived of any freedom, it is reduced to questions about the laws of the place. The thing is to try, always in vain, to understand the impenetrable designs of Mr. Knott. Where is he now? In the garden? Upstairs? What is he preparing? Whom does he love? Facing these obscure laws—this is the Kafkian dimension of this book—thought irritates itself and tires itself out. (B 40–41)

What saves thought from this aporetic dead end is the emergence of a few "events" coming outside the law; events called "incidents" by Beckett. The first of these is the arrival at one point of two piano tuners, the Galls. They exchange a few perfunctory remarks and go about their business. We never know why this event is selected among so many others, yet it provides a conceptual riddle that has to be solved:

The incident of the Galls . . . ceased so rapidly to have even the significance of two men, come to tune a piano, and tuning it, and exchanging a few words, as men will do, and going, that this seemed rather to belong to some story heard long before, and instant in the life of another, ill-told, ill-heard, and more than half-forgotten. So Watt did not know what had happened. He did not care, to do him justice, what had happened. But he felt the need to think that such and such a thing had happened then, the need to be able to say, when the scene began to unroll its consequences, Yes, I remember, that is what happened then.[4]

This commentary can be taken as one of the best statements about Badiou's own ethics of the event. In order to be an event, the "incident" or symptomatic "occurrence" has not only to be deployed outside the Law but also to afford a radical questioning of the law. As Badiou writes, these events are "paradoxical supplements" (B 41) defined, to quote Beckett, by "great formal brilliance and indeterminate purport" (W 71). Let us attempt to probe deeper their structure and function.

THE LAW AND THE "PARADOXICAL SUPPLEMENT" OF THE EVENT

I will illustrate Badiou's insight into the event with one example: this is a scene in which the eponymous hero is seen trying to enter the room of another servant in Mr. Knott's house. Watt believes that an examination of Erskine's room will disclose the secret of their master's mysterious calls, of his regular rings from a bell heard from within that very room. Unhappily for him, the door of Erskine's room is locked all the time. Not only is it locked, the lock is a complex one, and the key never out of its owner's pocket more than a few seconds. After several pages of speculations as to why Watt cannot steal the key or pick the lock, a further factor is added when we learn that Erskine has sewn the pocket in which he keeps the key to the front of his underhose. The narrator wonders how he could be expected to have known such a trifling detail and then heaps on new impossibilities:

> and so always, when the impossibility of my knowing, of Watt's having known, what I know, what they knew, seems absolute, it could be shown that I know, because Watt told me, and that Watt knew, because someone told him, or because he found out for himself. For I know nothing, nothing, on this subject, but what Watt told me. And Watt knew nothing, on this subject; but what he was told; or found out for himself, in one way or another. (W 125–26)

The main conclusion to be drawn is that it is totally impossible to enter this particular room under these circumstances. Radical means are then considered:

> Watt might have broken the door down, with an axe, or a crow[bar], or a small charge of explosive, but this might have aroused Erskine's suspicion, and Watt did not want that.
> So that what with one thing and another, and with Watt's not wishing this, and Watt's not wanting that, it seemed that Watt, as he was then, could never go into Erskine's room, never never get into Erskine's room, as they were then, Watt would have to be another man, or Erskine's room another room.
> And yet, without Watt's ceasing to be what he was, and without the room's ceasing to be what it was, Watt did get into the room, and there learned what he wished to know. (W 126)

We will never know more than this, except that Watt got in by some "ruse" about which nothing is told. We will not be spared anything about the contents of this room, which includes a painting with a circle and a dot, but no "key" is ever given to the reader. However, it is the description of the painting that provides a solution by proxy ("by ruse") to the riddle of how Watt could enter into a locked room. In the abstract painting, a circumference is interrupted at its base, and the dot seems to be floating in the air on a parallel plane so one cannot tell which plane comes first in front of the viewer:

And he wondered what the artist had intended to represent (Watt knew nothing about painting), a circle and its centre in search of each other, or a circle and its centre in search of a centre and a circle respectively, or a circle and its centre in search of a centre and its circle respectively, or a circle and a centre not its centre in search of a centre and its circle respectively, or a circle and a centre not its centre in search of a centre and a circle respectively, or a circle and a centre not its centre in search of its centre and a circle respectively, or a circle and a centre not its centre in search of a centre and its circle respectively, in boundless space, in endless time (Watt knew nothing about physics), and at the thought that it was perhaps this, a circle and a centre not its centre in search of a centre and its circle respectively, in boundless space, in endless time, then Watt's eyes filled with tears that he could not stem, and they flowed down his fluted cheeks unchecked, in a steady flow, refreshing him greatly. (W 126)

Here is a text that, once read literally, makes one feel dizzy so as to convey a feeling that is not far from the sublime. Its mimetic value lies in its being able to suggest infinity by textual means. Besides, the incident of such a lawless or impossible event calls up a famous allegorical situation, since it inverts Kafka's positioning of the Law in *The Trial* as a door that can be entered by only one person, a Law whose guardian manages to dissuade the only legitimate investigator from pursuing his quest. In Kafka's allegory of "Before the Law," the famous door remains open while not rendering entrance any easier. It is only when it is too late and the man from the countryside is going to die that the doorkeeper (who remains outside, just like his listener) tells him that the door by whose side they have waited was meant for no other person: now that the he is about to die, the keeper will shut it: "The door keeper perceives that the man is nearing his end and his hearing is failing, so he bellows in his ear: 'No one but you could gain admittance through this door, since the door was intended for you. I am now going to shut it.'"[5]

What becomes painfully clear is that if there had been no guardian, the man from the country would have gone through the door. Does the doorkeeper deceive the quester? No, at least if we accept the argument put forward by the priest, who rebukes K. for entertaining such a thought: according to him, K. does not pay enough respect for the written word and imagines a contradiction where there is none (*The Trial* 215). If we accept the structural homology leading to an inverse parallelism, the main difference between Watt as a character and Kafka's man from the country is that Watt plays the role of "guardian" or *Türhüter* in Mr. Knott's house, even if we are privy to his arrival and then later departure. Although already inside, he is in fact within the interiority of a Law without understanding anything of its rules and reasons. At most, he can exert a ruse as we have seen—even though readers are not told how he can achieve it: the ruse is clearly textual, it is, in fact, the text or, more precisely, the textual condition that can suspend belief and disbelief.

Badiou notes slightly disapprovingly that *Watt* still tends to the religious sphere, with a hero who is obsessed by the need to provide meaning when there is none (B 42). However, the point here is that being inside the Law provides no illumination, does absolutely not help. Here, Beckett and Kafka agree: this is what the discussion between K. and the priest conveys in *The Trial*. At least, there is no need to blame the guardian, since he is not a persecutor but as much a victim as the dying man. The law's main source of power consists in endless deferrals and infinite combinatory calculations. While Beckett and Kafka both acknowledge the Law's domineering power, Kafka shows the massive impenetrability of a Law that condones injustice and abuse, whereas Beckett shows its reversible nature and the multiplication of subsequent logical ramifications devoid of purpose. Beckett also suggests proximity to Lacan's Law when he makes it clear that its representative on earth is a Mr. Knott, who as "No" or "Not" ties up the knot giving access to the symptom. Beckett's law is serial and additive, and its layered and splintered logic regulate *das fruchtbare Bathos der Erfahrung*—"the fruitful bathos of experience" (W 254).

Following Badiou, one can assert that Beckett's texts, whenever they address the locus of the Law, all end up measuring themselves with a radical unnamability. When they attempt to approach it, they inevitably encounter a certain limit or foreclosure of their language. *Watt*'s foreclosure and disclosure of this Law will then postulate a "sadistic" system of ethics that it is necessary to explore. It comes from the "torture" generated by the constant struggle of thought against itself: there a Cartesian cogito turned against itself meets the perversion of the Kantian law. One of Badiou's most often repeated comments about Beckett is that he stages the "torture of the cogito" (B 32, 36-38, 70).

THE TORTURE OF THE COGITO

What might provide a first insight into Beckett's concept of torture in the context of *Watt* is geography. *Watt* was written as Beckett was hiding from the Gestapo between 1942 and 1945 in Roussillon, within eyesight of the neighboring village of La Coste—a mere fifteen miles away in fact. Sade's castle, at least the haughty ruins that remain, is visible from the top of the little ridge from which Roussillon faces the slightly higher Lubéron chain of mountains. What would Beckett have thought of this proximity, at a time when history seemed to show the possibility of a renewal of wholesale sadism with all its attendant torture chambers, and when, as Passolini tried to demonstrate with Salo, Sade's fantasies seemed to come to life with a vengeance? This question derives also from that fact that in the 1930s, Beckett had accepted to translate into English Sade's *The 120 Days of Sodom* for Jack Kahane who had founded the Obelisk Press. Knowlson's biography provides a few details, explains that Beckett wanted to publish an anonymous translation, as he feared that the association of his name with Sade's would even more damage his already compromised reputation in Ireland. Beckett's comments are revealing:

> The obscenity of surface is indescribable. Nothing could be less pornographical. It fills me with a kind of metaphysical ecstasy. The composition is extraordinary, as rigorous as Dante's. If the dispassionate statement of 600 "passions" is Puritan and a complete absence of satire juvenalesque, then it is, as you say, puritanical and juvenalesque.[6]

Beckett's comparison with Dante is illuminating and the remark on Sade's Puritanism quite groundbreaking, it anticipates theses later developed by Klossowki and Blanchot about Sade. Beckett hits on a nerve in Sade's writing when he speaks of a "surface obscenity" that is not pornographic. Sade is *the* writer intent upon showing what exceeds the stage while never really seducing the reader by his eroticism.

An approach to Beckett's sadism should take *Watt* as a focus for a second reason. At the time Beckett was looking for a publisher for this very experimental novel in Paris, he was briefly associated with a group of English and American writers among whom was Austryn Wainhouse, the first translator of Sade's "Philosophy in the Bedroom." When *Watt* was finally published in Paris by Maurice Girodias, the publicity poster he distributed announced the novel along with Henry Miller's *Tropics*, Apollinaire's erotic tales, and Sade's *Justine*. Such a coincidence indeed follows the serial logic of Badiou's events.

Sadism erupts for the first time in Beckett's fiction (if we set aside the curiously aggressive behavior of Mr. Endon facing the other inmates of the mental hospital in one passage in *Murphy*) in the third chapter of *Watt*. There we find ourselves in a strange asylum where the inmates comprise "Sam," who looks very much like the author, and Watt, who has by that time left Mr. Knott's house. This is how we learn via Sam of Watt's adventures at Mr. Knott's, as we have seen with the story of Erskine's room. One of their favorite pastimes during their long discussions is to play with rats living by the river. The scene looks deceptively idyllic and pastoral at first but is soon tinged with horror:

> But our particular friends were the rats that dwelt by the stream. They were long and black. We brought them tidbits from our ordinary as rinds of cheese, and morsels of gristle, and we brought them also birds' eggs, and frogs, and fledglings. Sensible of these attentions, they would come flocking

round us at our approach, with every sign of confidence and affection, and glide up our trouserlegs, and hang upon our breasts. And then we would sit down in the midst of them, and give them to eat, out of our hands, of a nice fat frog, or a baby thrush, or seizing suddenly a plump young rat, resting in our bosom after its repast, we would feed it to its mother, or its father, or its sister, or to some less fortunate relative.

It was on these occasions, we agreed, after an exchange of views, that we came nearest to God. (W 153)

One finds here all the main characteristics of Sadean mischief and perversity. The pastoral Rousseauism evoked earlier is immediately turned upside down. Watt and Sam frolic in lush meadows with all the blandishments of a peaceful Mother Nature. Sade never forgets his conflicted relationship to Mother Nature by ceaselessly demonstrating that its most basic law is murder. Moreover, the object of the transgressive gesture is parenthood. Roland Barthes liked quoting Sade's sentence that seemed to condense the Sadean fantasy and endow it with a specific grammar: "To bring together incest, adultery, sodomy, and sacrilege, he buggers his married daughter with a host."[7] Like Sade, Beckett's animus aims at subverting the foundational notion of the family as the site of an older morality (as one sees in *Antigone*). Not unlike the Libertine's endless exactions and tortures, Sam and Watt's gesture shifts vertiginously from a sham goodness for animals to utter cruelty, surprising the poor creatures who had believed in their benevolence. And like the Sadean garrulous torturers, the two friends "reason" upon their actions and elaborate a discourse leading to the heights of a parodic antitheology. They aspire to emulate an absolutely evil God of Evil, the "supreme Being in wickedness" as Lacan said in his seminar on *Ethics*.

Another passage in the same chapter links such Sadism with the evil brought into the world by the Nazis. The institution in which Watt and Sam meet is not just a mental hospital but also a concentration camp: "This garden was surrounded by a high barbed wire fence, greatly in need of repair, of new wire, of fresh barbs" (W 154). Each garden surrounds a little house, all the houses being connected by a dense network of hedges. Whoever wants to pass from one to the other risks being caught in wire. Their fate is called up in the language of ludic seriality:

while persons at once broad-shouldered and big-bellied, or broad-basined and big-bottomed, or broad-basined and big-bellied, or broad-shouldered and big-bottomed, or big-bosomed and broad-basined, would on no account, if they were in their right sense, commit themselves to this treacherous channel, but turn about, and retrace their steps, unless they wished to be impaled, at various points at once, ands perhaps bleed to death, or be eaten alive by the rats, or perish from exposure, long before their cries were heard; and still longer before the rescuers appeared, running, with the scissors, the brandy and the iodine. (W 155)

In this case, some rats, it seems, are allowed to take their revenge.

OF RATS, MEN, AND TERMITES

For Beckett as for Sade, the foundation of the cruel fantasy is an inverted theology as Klossowski and Lacan demonstrate. The Libertines have such a hatred of religion that in *The 120 Days of Sodom*, the most severely punished violation is to merely mention God. This point had not been missed by Beckett, who rewrites Pascal's maxim about man who wants to be an angel or god but who ends up being a beast; in *Watt* man is not even able to a rat, but rats are these curious theological creatures who happen once in a while to eat a consecrated host. As Mr. Spiro lectures to Watt in a train, here is the problem (which had been, by the way, mailed to him from Lourdes):

> A rat, or other small animal, eats of a consecrated wafer.
> 1. Does he ingest the Real Body, or does he not?
> 2. If he does not, what has become of it?
> 3. If he does, what is to be done with him? (W 26–27)

Again, the exposure of the problem and its partial solution generates the kind of sublimely serial textuality I have described earlier:

> Mr. Spiro now replied to these questions, that is to say he replied to question one and he replied to question three. He did so at length, quoting from Saint Bonaventura, Peter Lombard, Alexander of Hales, Sanchez, Suarez, Henno, Soto, Diana, Concina and Dens, for he was a man of leisure. But Watt heard nothing of this, because of other voices, singing, crying, stating, and murmuring things unintelligible, in his ear. With these, he was not familiar, he was not unfamiliar either. So he was not alarmed, unduly. Now these voices, sometimes they sang only, and sometimes they cried only, and sometimes they stated only, and sometimes they murmured only, and sometimes they sang and cried, and sometimes they sang and stated, and sometimes they sang and murmured, and sometimes they cried and stated, and sometimes they cried and murmured, and sometimes they stated and murmured, and sometimes they sang and cried and stated. (W 27)

Such lists of verbal permutations make *Watt* easily recognizable, and their idiomatic signature launches the whole writing into a purely serial exhaustivity. Semantic vertigo parallels the absurdly rational knowledge of theologians. Logical exhaustion leads to a hollowing out of meaning. No doubt Watt understands almost nothing in Spiro's verbiage, and while he shuts off his mind, he announces the perverse couples of later plays, as when Lucky is forced to "think" on command in *Waiting for Godot*. This passage is followed by a paragraph in which appears for the first time in the novel a device that will recur systematically, the mimetic rendering of a lacuna: "the racecourse now appearing, with its beautiful white railing, in the fleeing lights, warned Watt that he was drawing near, and that when the train stopped next, then he must leave it. He could not see the stands, the grand, the members', the people's, so? when empty with their white and red, for they were too far off" (W 27). Syntax has given up, the non sequitur of the perceiving subject's perspectivism has been replaced by a network of gaps and silences that signals a deviant textuality.

The metaphorical isotopy of the rat can serve as red thread through these complex devices. It is not a total coincidence if the "Ratman" treated by Freud looks so often like a Beckettian character! If man cannot even aspire to the dignity of a rat, according to Beckett, it is that he is not much raised above that of the termite:

> For the only way one can speak of nothing is to speak of it as though it were something, just as the only way one can speak of God is to speak of him as though he were a man, which to be sure he was, in a sense, for a time, and as the only way one can speak of man, even our anthropologists have realized that, is to speak of him as though he were a termite. (W 74)

A philosophy of the "as if" is the only access to a true definition of man. Given the limits of language previously sketched, one can say that if man is not a metaphor, man can be "man" only by catachresis.

The idea recurs when Watt tries out names on things as if they were so many old rags found in an attic. "Not that Watt was in the habit of affirming things of himself, for he was not, but he found it a help, from time to time, to be able to say, with some appearance of reason, Watt is a man, all the same, Watt is a man, or, Watt is in the street, with thousands of fellow-creatures, within call" (W 79). Troubled, Watt can no more say of a pot that it is a "pot" than of a man that it is a "man":

> and Watt's need of semantic succour was at times so great that he would set to trying names on things, and on himself, almost as a woman hats. . . . As for himself, though he could no longer call it a man, as he has used to do, with the intuition that he was perhaps not talking nonsense, yet he could

not imagine what else to call it, if not a man. But Watt's imagination had never been a lively one. So he continued to think of himself as a man, as his mother had taught him, when she said, There's a good little man, or There's a bonny little man, or There's a clever little man. But for all the relief that this afforded him, he might just as well have thought of himself as a box, or an urn. (W 79-80)

By a curious slippage, this linguistic dereliction calling up the crisis of language experienced by Lord Chandos (in Hugo von Hofmannsthal's famous 1902 "Letter") produces in Watt a feeling of despair that nevertheless inverts itself in ultimate relief. There is nothing more to do; all is really lost, even the rats have abandoned the ship:

Not that Watt longed at all times for this restoration, of things, of himself, to their comparative innocuousness, for he did not. For there were times when he felt a feeling closely resembling the feeling of satisfaction, at his being so abandoned, by the last rats. For after these there would be no more rats, not a rat left, and there were times when Watt almost welcomed this prospect, of being rid of his last rats, at last. It would be lonely, to be sure, at first, and silent, after the gnawing, the scurrying, the little cries. (W 81)

The rat traverses all the layers of pseudohumanity we think we inhabit, from a voracious greed for godlike transcendence to the lonely panic of the animal in the midst of death throes. The rat is thus more human than men, which may explain why we have this vignette of a Beckett who was shocked by the violence of his friends in Roussillon. "Josette Hayden could remember one occasion being with Beckett on the farm when the Audes discovered a rat and were about to kill it. Beckett rushed to intervene, picking the rat up and running across a field to let it run free into a ditch."[8] We are quite far from Sam and Watt's cruel games. Yet, it is in this tension between an unnamable humanity and a mediation on the worst perversions that an ethics is nevertheless possible.

POST-SADEAN OR POST-KANTIAN ETHICS?

Given its insistence on the issue of the conditions of possibility and impossibility, *Watt* can clearly be described as "Kantian"—a thesis to which Badiou subscribes, since he points out how often Beckett alludes to Kant (B 80). Such is, for instance, P. J. Murphy's opinion in "Beckett and the Philosophers": "Watt is a Kantian novel."[9] Following Badiou's lead, I want to add that this is as Kantian as it is Sadean, and that both systems of ethics are linked. A textual confirmation could be brought by the famous "Addenda" at the end of the book (from which one always quotes:

"No symbols where none intended," a sentence read by Murphy as another proof of *Watt*'s Kantian structure), which looks like a direct borrowing from the Addenda left by Sade at the end of *The 120 Days of Sodom*. It is in such supernumerary pages (673 and 674) that Sade invents the Ratman's torture as a last frenzied afterthought. If indeed Knott calls up Kant—the moral law is, after all, a way of formalizing what one "can't do"—my main contention, however, is that Beckett's project is comparable to Adorno's and Horkheimer's in *Dialectic of Enlightenment*—a book coincidentally written at the same time as *Watt* by two exiles from Nazi Germany. Like the refugees from the Frankfurt School, Beckett aims at a radical questioning of the "madness of Reason," as he explained in an interview with Michael Haerdter:

> The crisis started with the end of the 17th century, after Galileo. The 18th century has been called the century of reason, *le siècle de la Raison*. I've never understood that; they're all mad, *ils sont tous fous, ils déraisonnent!* They give reason a responsibility which it simply can't bear, it's too weak. The Encyclopedists wanted to know everything. . . . But that direct relation between the self and—as the Italians say—*lo scibile*, the knowable, was already broken.[10]

One could extrapolate from this sweeping critique by stating that Beckett's sadism hides a quest for an ultimate religious or transcendent Law behind or beneath the human. This would not be far from the main thesis of *The Dialectic of Enlightenment*.[11] For Adorno and Horkheimer, Kantian reason leads ineluctably to the calculating rationality of a totalitarian order. Its counterpart is the systematic mechanization of pleasures in Sade's perverse utopias. Kant's *Critique of Practical Reason* stresses the autonomy and self-determination of the moral subject, and defines thereby the pure form of ethical action. In Kant, the philosophy of Enlightenment meets global capitalism with a vengeance: any human concern has to be ruled out, what matters is merely the conformity of Reason with its own laws, a Reason that must then appear abstract and devoid of any object. All "human" affects are pushed further away from an independent and all-powerful Reason. Juliette is thus more logical than Kant when she draws the conclusions that Kant denies: the bourgeois order of society justifies crime, provided crime be regulated by a rationality that controls all activities and pleasures. The famous Sadean "apathy" functions thus like a good equivalent to Kantian "disinterestedness," both being underpinned by the "brutal efficiency" of the bourgeois conquest of the world. The "right to enjoyment" includes logically an absolute extension of its field—up to my right to enjoy the bodies of others, and to do with them as I like. The counterpart of this globalized rationality is the systematic mechanization of perverse pleasures in the Sadean orgy. Barthes had noted how the orgy was to function as a perfectly oiled mechanism, in which everyone has a part to play since nobody can be left idle.[12]

This image should send us on a new track with respect to *Watt*. We know how overdetermined the eponymous hero's name is, but may note that its particular spelling does not just call up the first metaphysical question ("What is x?" or more simply: "What?"), but points to the name of the most famous of Watts, namely, the inventor of the steam engine. By a curious coincidence, James Watt (1736-1819) was a contemporary of Immanuel Kant (1724-1804) and of the Marquis de Sade (1740-1814). Watt's name is synonymous with the inception of the industrial revolution in Europe. His main invention was based on a simple interaction of pistons, rods, and cylinders transforming energy into work. It is not such a stretch to see this as a sexual mechanism as well: the steam will easily emblematize bodies whose enjoyment is to be produced in a number or repetitive performances. While calling up the idea of the conquest of the whole world by modern technology, a real "rape" of Nature in fact, the libidinal engine sends us closer to Alfred Jarry and Marcel Duchamp. Their "bachelor machines" metaphorize the social production of desire. From Sade's orgies to the "Bride laid bare by her bachelors, even," a single continuum limns an ideology of erotico-technological relationships and posits as a utopian good the new *perpetuum mobile* of desire. From the Sadean orgy organized as a montage chain in an automated plant to the eternal masturbators of the nine "malic moulds" gazing at the vaporous bride beckoning from above in Duchamp's "Glass," the machine materializes a certain type of mechanical reproducibility. Watt's name thus condenses the "whatness" of technology, an "essence" that, as Heidegger notes in his writings on technology, has by itself nothing technological, and the name of one of the inventors who paved the way to today's technological revolution. The Law is a sadistic bachelor machine that nevertheless transforms us into "human" subjects.

In his *Critique of Practical Reason*, Kant showed that the moral subject's autonomy implied a rigid formalism: the law is the law only if it is devoid of content. Any other human consideration must be excluded, what matters is the simple conformity of practical reason to maxims that become as many general axioms. Juliette is thus more logical than Kant when she draws consequences neglected by the philosopher: the order of society can justify crime if crime is accomplished in accordance with universal maxims. The law should regulate over all actions and include all sorts of pleasures and transgressions. One can therefore understand the pedagogical function of the prologue in *Watt*. It introduces a Mr. Hackett whose Puritanism is such that he is upset when he sees lovers kissing on a bench. A hyperrealistic description presents their embrace:

> for the lady held the gentleman by the ears, and the gentleman's hand was on the lady's thigh, and the lady's tongue was in the gentleman's mouth. Tired of waiting for the tram, said Mr. Hackett, they strike up an acquaintance. . . .

Taking a pace forward, to satisfy himself that the gentleman's other hand was not going to waste, Mr. Hackett was shocked to find it limply dangling over the back of the seat, with between its fingers the spent three-quarters of a cigarette. I see no indecency, said the policeman. We arrive too late, said Mr. Hackett. What a shame. (W 6)

In this exemplary narrative ellipsis, Beckett makes fun both of Hackett's puritan voyeurism and of his reliance on bourgeois property rights. Hackett makes the logical mistake of considering that his right to enjoy a rest on a bench includes the right to own it. However, he is aware that his desire is only kept alive if the object remains forbidden: "This seat, the property very likely of the municipality, or of the public, was of course not his, but he thought of it as his. This was Mr. Hackett's attitude towards things that pleased him. He knew they were not his, but he thought of them as his. He knew were not his, because they pleased him" (W 5). Through an exemplary concision, Beckett sums up in two lines the paradoxes of desire staged earlier in *Murphy*.

The general law is that the desiring subject can only wish for what he has lost or will never have. One moves from *Verneinung* of the kind: "I know that this is not mine, but nevertheless . . ." to a logical deduction: "I know that this does not belong to me, otherwise I would not be able to enjoy it. But my *jouissance* entails that I have claims to its continuous possession." As in Sade's works, Beckett's serial games with language always derive from a maternal origin both possessed and lost, a locus that hesitates between the status of logical "matrix" sending us on a asymptotic recuperation almost achieved through permutations and that of a primal "matter" to be reshaped or distorted by discourse. This painful hesitation often triggers an outburst of a matricidal rage that aims at dismembering the mother's body. Another passage can posit this moment in more precisely anatomical terms. It is when Hetty calls up in front of Mr. Hackett the birth of her first child, and remembers how she had had to cut the umbilical cord with her own teeth:

> That is a thing I often wondered, said Mr. Hackett, what it feels like to have the string cut.
> For the mother or the child? said Goff.
> For the mother, said Mr. Hackett, I was not found under a cabbage, I believe.
> For the mother, said Tetty, the feeling is one of relief, of great relief, as when the guests depart. (W 12)

Is this the same mixture of relief and despair that seizes the captain after the rats have left his sinking ship? What counts here is the ironical implication of Mr.

Hackett's jibe: as he was not born under a cabbage (one may remember the vitriolic aside in *The Unnamable*: "Enough of acting the infant who has been told so often how he was found under a cabbage that in the end he remembers the exact spot in the garden and the kind of life he led there before joining the family circle"[13]) and as he has been a "newborn" too, he has not forgotten that first cut but simply never knew how the feminine side might perceive the "cut."

TRUTH AND JOUISSANCE

If one may recognize in Mr. Hackett's position the seeds of a Sadean meditation on castration as the limit of jouissance, one should not forget how this term sends us both to erotic ecstasies and to legal possession. "Proclaiming the law of jouissance as the foundation of some ideally utopian social system, Sade expresses himself in italics . . . : 'Lend me the part of your body that will give me a moment of satisfaction and, if you care to, use for your own pleasure (*et jouissez, si cela vous plaît, de celle du mien*) that part of my body which appeals to you.'"[14] In a lecture devoted to the "other side (*l'envers*) of the subject" of his seminar on Anxiety, Lacan quoted the acme reached by a Libertine who, engaged in the torture of a woman, roared: "I had her by the skin of the cunt!"[15] Lacan sees in this climactic ejaculation the expression of a fantasy that wishes to turn the subject inside out, as a glove. Only then can the subject of the fantasy come close to what he or she imagines to be the jouissance of God, a God seen as the *Dio boia* mentioned by Joyce in *Ulysses*, that is a "hangman god," a God who is unsurpassable in evil.

It is from the point of view of such a negative theology, an antitheology as it were, that Beckett, just like Sade and Lacan, articulates his "reversion" of the subject in the name of the Other. Pierre Klossowski was the first to underline the kinship between Sade's thought and the heresiarchs of gnostic descent: a similar hatred for the body linked with a mystical cult of the orgasm underpins a fantasy of a lost original light, a light that has been out of reach since the beginning of the world. Lacan will insist later on the central concept of an "other jouissance" (closer to femininity as an exception) in a movement that would not be in debt to the jouissance of the Other, since this is this Other whom the Sadean Libertine tries vainly to emulate in exhausting rounds of tortures and orgies. Klossowski demonstrates very cogently the links between this negative theology of jouissance and another jouissance of writing. This is equally because this complex intermeshing of concepts is articulated by the Law that we need another kind of writing, a writing of excess.

In his book, Klossowski stresses that Sade was not just a "pervert" or a monster but above all a writer. A boring and repetitive writer, for sure, but whose writings allow us to understand the crucial link between fantasy, the perverse imagination, and the Law understood as the jouissance of the Other:

> The parallelism between the apathetic reiteration of acts and Sade's descriptive reiteration again establishes that the image of the act to be done is re-presented each time not only as though it had never been performed but also as though it had never been described. This reversibility of the same process inscribes the presence of nonlanguage in language; it inscribes a foreclosure of language by language.[16]

Sade's symptom is thus not sadism, it is writing, a writing that hesitates between the repetitive fantasy of an outrage to a Mother Nature and a reiterated questioning of the Other's jouissance.

The foreclosed language of Sade's fictions opens up the space of the outside in a curious and ironical pragmatism of fantasy. Sade's well-known irony, so visible in his letters from the Bastille to his wife, ultimately questions the position of the superego in any type of value system. His writings cannot be reduced to fantasies since they examine how fantasy is determined from the Outside by the Law. In a book that comes very close to Badiou's reading of Kant, Lacan, and Saint Paul, Monique David-Ménard examines Lacan's confrontation of Kant with Sade critically, and shows how Lacan could misread key elements in Kant's philosophy, erasing for instance the difference between knowledge and thought that is central to his *Critiques*.[17] Lacan appears too Hegelian when he conflates Kant's notion of the Thing-in-itself with Respect for the Law just because both are unthinkable entities. Like Klossowski, David-Ménard suggests that Sade's works are not just a blueprint for male fantasy (the neurotic imagining himself as a pervert). Sade cunningly points out the dark side of humanitarian ethics when he posits the issue of man's universality in his relation to the unconditionality of the Law (even through a caricature of the Law). Respect or blasphemy both address the same underpinning of fantasy by the Law of Desire seen negatively as the obscene jouissance of the Other. But whereas the transgressive principle so well described by Lacan, Adorno, and Horkheimer does not necessarily imply a detour via writing, what Sade, Beckett, and Klossowski demonstrate is that a transgression that questions the limits of humanity and the law presiding over limits will postulate the need for writing, at least an *other* writing. Thus, the serial writing deployed so systematically in *Watt* transforms infantile rage facing the mother's body into the bland serenity of pseudo-rationality. It allows writing to take its bearing in function of the Name as "No" and "knot" that is Mr. Knott's first version of what Lacan will later identify via Joyce as the *sinthome*'s knot:

> Watt suffered neither from the presence of Mr. Knott, not from his absence. When he was with him, he was content to be with him, and when he was away from him, he was content to be away from him. Never with relief, never with regret, did he leave him at night, or in the morning come to him again.
>
> This ataraxy covered the entire house-room, the pleasure-garden, the vegetable garden, and of course Arthur. (W 207)

Such ataraxy combines the Sadean ideal of impassability in the most extreme enjoyments and the Kantian idea of a regulation of reason by itself. The central question of *Watt* would thus be a Sado–Kantian one: "But what was this pursuit of meaning in this indifference to meaning?" (W 72). If we agree to see *Watt* as a Kantian novel and a Sadean fiction too, staging the torture of thought, it is because rational knowledge is a machine that barely hides relations of domination, fear, or indifference. "Too fearful to assume himself the onus of a decision, said Mr. Hackett, he refers it to the frigid machinery of a time-space relation" (W 19). In their language staging a repetitive foreclosure, Sade and Beckett denounce the darker side of universalistic ethics. If man is defined by the unconditionality of his rapport to the Law, then it is a welcome breath of fresh air to let subversion remind us of the reverse of the subject, its determination from behind as it were. A cruel or simply hilarious parody attacks the reverse of the subject, inverts respect by a blasphemous inversion that sees in the Law the mere projection of the obscene and boundless jouissance of an evil Other.

The risk, never avoided by Sade, is that Libertines will devote their lives to an exacting approximation of a jouissance whose slave the Libertine becomes just as he believes he is its master. Beckett offers a different view of excess, an excess irremediably mediated by semantic serialism. And the new linguistic apathy leads to an ineluctable acknowledgment of the void—something that Sade's world cannot accept. Thus, *Watt* can break into poetry in a paradoxical supplement:

> who may tell the tale
> of the old man?
> weigh absence in a scale?
> mete want with a span?
> the sum assess
> of the world's woes?
> nothingness
> in words enclose? (W 247)

These rhymed lines are to be found in the "Addenda," which as we have seen, correspond to Sade's last "Notes finales" and "Tortures in supplement" added to the *"grande bande"* written between October and November 1785. In this frantic supplement, Sade says "*vous*" to himself and begins by exhorting himself to follow faithfully his own plan, thus positing a veritable Kantian law of textuality as a noteworthy supplement to his text: "under no circumstance deviate from this plan, everything has been worked out, the entirety several times re-examined with the greatest care and thoroughness."[18] Similarly, Beckett hesitates between parading his own inexactitudes and miming a logical pattern of exhausting repetitions. But it is again thanks to Badiou's insights that we can make sense of these lines: they point to the creation of a void that alone provides a safe and stable point of nonmeasure by placing a wedge between infinity and singularity.

Badiou stresses "beauty" and "truth" as the central concerns in Beckett's works. These are not absent from Sade's work either. But beauty is often reduced to a cliché, since it is the shared feature of all victims: beauty is no sooner described with hackneyed adjectives then it has to be relentlessly transgressed, humiliated, tortured. Beauty has to be forcefully subjected to the domination of truth, the truth of transgressive desire. It was Lacan who had seen quite well how this position could make Sade appear as a "martyr" to truth. Lacan develops this insight in the seminar on "The Reverse of Psychoanalysis" when he explains that the Other is this paradoxical being that "has a body but does not exist" (like the *increvable* serial victims of the torturers) and only posits itself by saying "I am who I am."[19] Sade is important in the sense that he deploys all his efforts in order to try to placate this Big Other. Sade agrees to be the slave or hostage of absolute jouissance, as we have seen, but Lacan adds then that this is why Sade remains a "theoretician" (S17 75): he is too much "in love with truth" (S17 76). His excessive love for Truth precipitates a purely symptomatic repetition. Truth appears thus as "the sister of forbidden *jouissance*." Or, to be more precise, Truth is the "sister-in-law" of jouissance; just as Sade seemed to be really in love not with his wife but with his sister-in-law Anne-Prospère de Launay de Montreuil with whom he had fled to the south in 1772 (Lacan suggests that this is not so different from Freud's attachment for his sister-in-law Mina Bernays). Sade was in love with truth, no doubt partly because of a well-named "sister-in-law" who thus embodied the old Law of courtly love: if there is love for beauty, there is no love in marriage (S17 77).

Sade who was quoted by Lacan in Seminar X as a key to the "reverse of the subject" as we have seen, turns in Seminar XVII into an exemplary writer, the symptomatic figure of a hostage to Truth. Lacan had just read Deleuze's book on Sacher-Masoch and like Deleuze he contrasts Sade's humorless, exhausting, and ultimately deluded efforts to accumulate transgression to approach an absolute jouissance but only asymptotically with Sacher-Masoch's contractual humor. A masochist will not need to emulate God, he can be happy just being God's servant (S17 75). Which is, by the way, the solution found by Watt: Watt never tries *being* Mr. Knott, and the undemanding acquiescence of the main character is one of the mainsprings of Beckett's savage humor. Beckett remains the philosopher of the couple, obsessed by all the varied permutations on duality, even "after" Watt has left Mr. Knott's house and is facing "Sam." On the other hand, Sade tends to the One and only, relentlessly. Thus, ultimately, if Sade is so boring, it is less because as Barthes would suggest, his text is a text of jouissance and not pleasure (an argument that might save Philippe Sollers's experimental fiction from unqualified boredom but not Sade's novels, plays, and tracts) than because it remains theoretical. His novels seem stuck in the groove of an all-too-theoretical demonstration in the name of truth. This is his love of truth that led him to become, in his life, a martyr—which is why he has attracted the passionate hagiographies devoted to him by Sadean specialists. Sharing with Sade a real desire to disappear wholly, Beckett has gone one step further and has prevented such adulation (even though quantity of biographies are being written about him). He has done so, as Badiou states in his concluding remarks, by "having fulfilled his task," that is, creating beauty without forgetting truth and ethics thus "composing the poem of the unbreakable (*increvable*) desire to think" (B 79).

NOTES

1. A recent film might suggest "unbreakable," if the term could suggest more than the physical resistance of an "unburstable" tire and keep a hint of "unkillable" allied with "tireless."

2. See Bruno Clément's *L'Œuvre sans qualities: Rhétorique de Samuel Beckett* (Paris: Seuil, 1994) for an excellent analysis of this recurrent trope.

3. Samuel Beckett, *Ill See Ill Said*, in *Nohow On* (London: Calder, 1992), 80.

4. Samuel Beckett, *Watt* (London: Calder, 1976), 7. Hereafter *W* and page number.

5. Franz Kafka, *The Trial*, trans. Willa and Edwin Muir, rev. E. M. Butler (New York: Schocken Books, 1984), 214-15.

6. Quoted by James Knowlson, *Damned to Fame* (New York: Simon and Schuster, 1996), 269.

7. Roland Barthes, *Sade, Fourier, Loyola*, trans. Richard Miller (Berkeley and Los Angeles: University of California Press, 1989), 33.

8. Knowlson, *Damned to Fame*, 307.

9. P. J. Murphy, "Beckett and the Philosophers," in *Cambridge Companion to Beckett*, ed. John Pilling (Cambridge: Cambridge University Press, 1994), 229-45, 229.

10. Quoted by Douglas McMillan and Martha Fehsenfeld, *Beckett in the Theatre* (New York: Riverrun Press, 1988), 231.

11. See Max Horkheimer and Theodor W. Adorno, *Dialektik der Aufklärung* (Frankfurt: Fischer Verlag, 1969).

12. Barthes, *Sade, Fourier, Loyola*, 152–53.

23. Samuel Beckett, *The Unnamable*, in *Three Novels* (New York: Grove Press, 1991), 291–414, 324.

14. Jacques Lacan, *The Ethics of Psychoanalysis*, ed. Jacques-Alain Miller, trans. and annot. Dennis Porter (New York: Norton, 1992), 202.

15. Unpublished Seminar X on "Anxiety," March 6, 1963, 146–47.

16. Pierre Klossowki, *Sade My Neighbor* (Evanston, IL: Northwestern University Press, 1991), 41.

17. Monique David-Ménard, *Les Constructions de l'Universel* (Paris: Presses Universitaires de France, 1997), 22–27.

18. Marquis de Sade, *The 120 Days of Sodom and Other Writings*, trans. Austryn Wainhouse and Richard Seaver (New York: Grove Press 1966), 673.

19. Jacques Lacan, *Séminaire XVII, L'Envers de la Psychanalyse* (Paris: Seuil, 1991), 74. Hereafter S17 followed by page number. Translations are mine.

FIVE

The Mallarmé of Alain Badiou

Pierre Macherey
(Translated by Marilyn Gaddis Rose and Gabriel Riera)

> I wanted philosophy to finally be contemporary with Mallarmé's poetic operations.
> —*Petit Manuel d'inesthétique*
>
> My philosophy accepting the conditions of poetry . . .
> —*Petit Manuel d'inesthétique*

Mallarmé is everywhere in Alain Badiou's work, so much so that one can consider this preoccupation and interest one of its most distinctive features. Especially since Badiou's work establishes a singular link between philosophy and poetry through the intervention of Mallarmé and the reflection—we are almost tempted to say rumination—which he obsessively and obstinately devotes to him. This is a reflection reserved not only to the study of a monographic nature of one or another aspect of Mallarmé's poetic production, but is present as well in both *Théorie du sujet* and *L'être et l'événement*. Here it is associated, mixed, and implied (in forms that nevertheless remain to be elucidated) with a philosophical argument developed on its own ground, where it meets Mallarmé as a protagonist, a "thinker" who must be reckoned with. Consequently, Badiou's reflection does not approach Mallarmé as an object of thought equal to any other, but rather presents itself as a reflection of Mallarmé, where he is simultaneously what is reflected and what reflects itself in an operation that allows that something like a truth be uttered. And by the mediation of such a reflection, philosophy and poetry dialogue as equals; one of the conditions of this dialogue being that poetry is withdrawn from the purview of aesthetics and installed in the order of what Badiou calls "in-aesthetics." By this he means in-aesthetization as a poetic operation: the condition by which poetry has its speculative dimension restored.

It is thus worthwhile to ask which Mallarmé is reflected and reflects himself in the work of the philosopher Alain Badiou; how this reflection functions and why it is Mallarmé, alongside a few others, who is placed at the forefront as a master of truth "emblematic of the relationship between philosophy and poetry" (C 108), and thus constituting the privileged vector of this reflection.

First, which Mallarmé? An essential Mallarmé, let us say, rendered adequate to the vocation proclaimed in a number of his own poetic or theoretical productions; purified and thus transformed into a figure of his work, like the Mallarmé of Mallarmé in some respects. Not, to be sure, someone cut off from his time, to which flutters of a fan, faded furniture, and other dated affectations inexorably reduced him. Rather, detached from it, in the sense of a withdrawal that, by the distance it establishes in relation to them, delivers the quintessence of those things absent to themselves. They are thus transformed into quasi-metaphysical operators of this disappearance, which also organizes their power of revelation. This Mallarmé, let us make no mistake, is the true Mallarmé, not in the historicist sense of an accountable exactitude that would claim to exhaust the details of the thing by stating everything on the subject of Mallarmé as a literary critic or biographer, but rather Mallarmé such as eternity has changed him; having become, in the Mallarméan sense of the term, his own "tomb." Under this condition he releases his pure thought to the scrutiny of a philosophy that, according to an expression often encountered in Badiou, undertakes to place itself at his level, at his height. Essentialized, Mallarmé remains at a vertiginous height, like a constellation of thought whose necessary order, or rather necessary disorder, withdraws itself from direct apprehension and, once any hermeneutical demand has been relinquished, asks for the difficult effort of deciphering that leads beyond the illusions of meaning to the event of truth, to the event that is the emergence of truth.

Restored to its purity and stripped of any anecdotal character, Mallarmé is presented as the bearer of a "method" and even a "logic." A "subtractive method" that transforms the poem into "a negative device that utters the being or idea at the very point where the object disappears." As Badiou puts it, this method "subjects the object to the experience of its lack" (QPP 219). This strategy of elision and lack, which in certain respects could evoke Hegel's negativity of essence, is discussed at length in *Théorie du sujet* (92–128) and in the text on "La méthode de Mallarmé," presented as a counterpart of "La méthode de Rimbaud" in *Conditions* (108–29), which constitutes the purified repetition of those preceding analyses. "What the poem says, it does" (TS 99): this is a performative strategy not content with simply speaking on the subject of this lack of being, the world restored to its essential place, "where there will have taken place but the place." By stating "the lack of the lack," which is quite different from Hegel's salvific and redemptive negativity, it is the poem that brings about this lack: a negativity of incompleteness in which the poem is, paradoxically, the completed, rule-bound and, consequently, rigorously conceived implementation. Having renounced the mirage of imitation in all ways possible, the poem does not reproduce the world in its absence, but rather produces the absence of the world in the space of language that is its site; the poem says literally, it announces the being that has become absent from the world in the future anterior, which is quite different from evoking or suggesting its presence. We could say, in other words, that the poem, dictating its intervention to the poet, is responsible for uttering the unrepresentability of the world, of thus opposing the pretense of representing it by producing the illusory union of the true and the beautiful, such as traditional aesthetics would wish.

Thus understood, Mallarméan poetics appears inseparable from his "project of truth," which proceeds from the dissolution of particular significations, inasmuch as they claim an immediate positivity. Subjected to schemes of isolation and separation, these significations explode, and the machine of the poem has no other function than to produce and immobilize this explosion. "What the poem says, it does": it does not speak of the world's nothingness in the form of a gloss uttering the secret of its presence, but annuls the world concretely, if we may say so, by elevating the poetic word to its maximum power, thus transforming it into an intervention device, an action. This is why Mallarmé's method and logic do not make him a philosopher, a commentator on truths, which nevertheless he can be on occasion in some of his prose pieces and philosophical texts, even the great ones. His poetic action, embodied in the production of poems, offers the philosopher objects to comment on, ideas in a pure state, so to speak, materialized in verbal organizations perfectly closed in upon themselves. These are not, however, segments of meaning to be interpreted, but rather traces left by the poetic action of the de-segmentation of truth, which liberates it from the prison of meaning.

These are the singular characteristics of a poetic action often received as the manifestation of hermeticism. And here still interpretation fails to attain the truth of the thing. Mallarmé is not hermetic, in the sense of a well-hidden secret that ought to be found out; he is only difficult because, as an essential poet, he is a producer of enigmas that elicit thought. Not in order to make a truth, preexisting its decoding, see the light of day, but to insinuate the truth itself in the act by which it occurs and literally produces itself in the form of an enigma and, at the limit, of nonsignification. The secret is, finally, that there is no secret, since all the poem has to say is displayed, scattered, dispersed, properly spaced out, black on white in the constellation that the text is for eternity, once the dice is thrown. In "Mallarmé professeur de morale" (1943), Michel Leiris explained that Mallarmé invented "a language that aims less to describe or recount than to unleash some movements of the mind."[1] These mental movements which the machine of the poem provokes, and here we must use *provocation* to the full extent of its meaning, are the exercises of a thought in action, of a thought freely confronted by the exigencies and constraints that impel it, without for all that obliging it to mold itself to some preestablished program. Given the elocutionary disappearance of the poet or the foreclusion of the poem's subject, the machine of the poem runs by itself; it presents itself, and therein lies its essential nature, that like a machine-to-cause-thinking produces flashes of truth.

How should we read this Mallarmé-rendered essential, who exists as a proposition or occasion for truth? His method calls for a no-less-demanding one, since neither the poem's directions for use are furnished with the poem, nor in his accompanying prose, where the poet delivers bursts of his poetic art. These we can put to use only if we have already entered the dynamic of the mind just discussed, without which the poem is null and void. Badiou states that "it is the poems that light up the prose, and the effectiveness of both the thought-poem of the event and of the undecidable that retroactively authorizes the ambiguous formulation of a program. We go from thought to the thought of thought, and not the other way around" (C 127).

Starting up the machine-to-cause-thinking that is poetry: this is the astonishing manner in which Badiou reads Mallarmé. He takes poems such as "Faun," "Prose for des Esseintes," "Sonnet in yx," or "Hush to the crushing cloud" literally, not to gloss them word for word in order to wrest their hidden meanings, but to work on their bodies and to have them produce the event of truth, given that they are its inciters or triggers, rather than its bearers or vectors. This work passes through the production of a new text, a "first reconstructed state in which the poem is delivered to its latent prose and subtracted from all poetry, in order that philosophy, from prose, may lead it to its own ends" (C 110). This passage through prose functions much like an attempt at a translation that accomplishes a narrative transposition of the poem and teaches, for example, that "A throw of the dice" is the story of a shipwreck, and "Hush to the crushing cloud," a narrative of disappearance: the latter is the theme, or in popular parlance, the subject of the poem. This indispensable preliminary operation brings the reading back to a plane of normally ordered syntactic intelligibility, which constitutes the indirectly legible framework of the poem. Not unlike the text of a dream that gives up details to be sorted out, it must be reconstituted to measure its force of truth. But this operation is only preliminary because in the cases just mentioned the poem obviously does not consist simply of a theme, the catastrophe of a disappearance, but in the formal arrangement it itself produces on the page, uncovered once one retraces the inverse movement. This movement confronts the very text of the poem with its "translation," without making the text appear as a reciprocal retranslation of the first translation, the former having led from the poem to the prose that presents the central theme. What matters therefore is *what* the poem's rigid formal arrangement on the page and *what* its throw of the dice brings about in relation to its theme or latent content, such that the passage through the prose allows for the revelation and novelty that the narrative dullness of this prose is itself powerless to utter. This is what happens with "Hush to the crushing cloud" where the subject is, so to speak, a shipwreck. In the particularly sophisticated reading that Badiou proposes, the poem is neither the narrative nor the evocation of certain aspects or episodes of this shipwreck, but the foregrounding by purely verbal means of the fact that the shipwreck has already taken place and thus is no longer. Therefore, it leaves behind not the negative event it was and is no longer, but rather the evasive trail of its power of nullification that one cannot equate with nothingness as the simple opposite of being. Although simplifying this analysis to the maximum, we can say that the subject of the poem being a shipwreck, what the poem utters about this subject is the shipwreck of the shipwreck. Likewise, the "Sonnet in yx" is not the more or less convoluted and anecdotal evocation of an absence, such as the factual reality of an empty room exhibits, but the attempt to say what is absent in the absence, the absence of absence, the nothingness of nothingness: that is, its force of negation, that by which a fragment of truth happens.

This back and forth movement of poetry to prose and from prose to poetry produces an effect of closure and brings forward what it is properly finished in. In a surprising passage from *Théorie du sujet*, Badiou enacts this operation of closure by adding a supplementary tercet of his own to the four stanzas of "Hush to the crushing cloud." He pursues the shipwreck of the shipwreck dialectically to the point where, as the magic power of the negation of a negation that converts itself into an affirmation, the wrecked object, the vessel, reappears at the surface of the waves (TS 108). Now, Badiou did not write this fifth stanza in order to complete the poem. As it is not included in the constellation of the poem, he ironically conveys that this fifth stanza is deprived of any poetic reality; that it literally does not exist. Therefore, the poem shines in its absence and is thus perfectly closed upon itself, fixed, completed in its enigmatic closure that subtracts it—subtraction being, in Mallarmé, the poetic operation par excellence—from any possibility or perspective of suggestion or evocation. This is why Badiou claims that, although "opaque outside, Mallarmé's poetic machine, nevertheless, possesses only one meaning. We should stop the lazy outlining of obstacles, which makes many say that the power of the enigma is to tolerate one hundred indirect responses. With an absolute dialectician like Mallarmé, there is no 'polysemy'" (TS 92). As the poem ends in its factual interruption, it draws its power of completion from its incompleteness and finitude, identical to the one that contains the constellation resulting from the dice throw. In Badiou's eyes, this is what distinguishes Mallarmé's pure poetry from Beckett's or from the prose poems of Rimbaud, which do not produce a similar effect of closure and therefore give way to the possibility of being continued beyond them. The poem as Mallarmé produces it is such because it is materially closed upon itself, self-sufficient. It is by virtue of this closure that it functions as a poem, on the condition of course that we plug it in and turn it on like a machine to make us think.

Now we can begin to understand why Badiou chooses Mallarmé as an example of the link between poetry and philosophy, such as he conceives it. The introductory page of the recent *Petit Manuel d'inesthétique*, in which Mallarmé's figure appears in several places, makes this evident: "against esthetic speculation, inesthetics describes the strictly intra-philosophical effects that the independent existence of some works of art produce" (PMI 7; TS 92). Faithful to the principle of rarefaction and excellence that guides Mallarméan poetics, Badiou includes only "a few works of art" in the field of his philosophical inesthetics that we may conclude have been carefully chosen: in the field of language, not only Mallarmé, but also Rimbaud, Pessoa, Beckett, and Celan. However, Hugo, Baudelaire, Verlaine, Reverdy, and Aragon are excluded, as well as Vielé-Griffin, Rodenbach, or Verhaeren, no doubt considered too narrative, or too "expressive" to be treated as machines-to-cause-thinking. Badiou's use of this severe principle of selection is obviously meant as a way to escape the trap of a generalized aesthetics that would pose the question of the relation of art to truth in the abstract. From his point of view, it is not art qua art that produces truths, and, indeed, most of the time, it does not produce any, as it adheres to the mission of edification or entertainment, all the forms of seduction that society commonly assigns to it. As for truth, it is only produced in some exceptional cases, which bear witness, by their exceptional qualities, to the will of rupture that defines the poetic event in its essence: Mallarmé being its unique and irreplaceable testimony.

From this point of view, Badiou's project becomes clearer: it draws the narrow limits of an Art-Thought beyond which most artistic products are rejected, since they are possessed by the vertigo of the image and meaning, and offered to an aesthetic consumption that cuts them off from any relation to truth. This is one of the manifestations of what we must label Badiou's Platonism, which, in a very classic manner, amounts to an anti-Aristotelianism. As soon as we affirm this, we also identify the adversary that, in his reading of some poetic texts cited in passing, Badiou attacks from the first: mimesis. The grandeur and exceptional qualities of Mallarmé's poetic strategy and that of a few others consists in knowing how to rescue poetry from the trap of the referent in all its forms, from the mirage of presence. This is what constitutes Poetry restored to its essence, which happens only exceptionally and has nothing to tell us about the world. One could say in oft-repeated words that poetry reflects nothing, "reflection" being the noun that realism, whether it be socialist, has given to ancient mimesis, thus leading back to art's pretension to represent reality in a more or less conforming manner. Now, to represent reality can have the effect only of linking to this reality those who welcome representation and consider it ready money, or, in the final analysis, to alienate them. Thus conceived, inesthetics is the bearer of a latent negative aesthetics, in which art and its controlled vertigo are factors of subservience and alienation.

An inverse option to Badiou's reading of several carefully chosen works of art, in which Mallarmé occupies a privileged place, would be to forgo tracing such lines of demarcation and, as a hypothesis, to exclude the ensemble of artworks from the alienating purview of aesthetics and its hedonist attachments, even when these productions are clothed in mimetic form and display themselves in terms of image and meaning. After all, in his own work as a writer, which we suspect is not entirely cut off from his activities as a philosopher, and as a philosopher reflecting on the poetry of Mallarmé, Badiou has excluded poetry and privileged the novel and theater: narrative and drama, the two genres on which Aristotle built his *Poetics*. To conclude, we must pass over this point very quickly: the image, whether verbal or plastic, is not simply the evocation of a presence, but also, in its other facet, the de-representation of what it represents and therefore produces, projecting it into a mimetic space, a potentially critical distance. As a consequence, the effect of reality that the image produces is not alienating, at least not fatally, but it can function as a means of liberation if we know how to put it to work correctly. If this is understood, we may prefer to that strictly localized and selective inesthetics in which Badiou's reading of Mallarmé is inscribed, the program of a generalized inesthetics, which would not be a new positive aesthetics, but would restore to the whole of art, or at least to most of it, a certain familiarity whose degree ought to be reevaluated with the work of thought in a determined manner each time. In the case of Mallarmé privileged by Badiou, this familiarity becomes palpably evident. But this does not mean that in other cases and in other forms less directly obvious, and thus more difficult to appreciate, works of literature that at first glance are offered only to current consumption may also, when appropriately read, be able to rise or be raised to the height of truth, and thus reflect themselves in thought.

NOTE

1. Michel Leiris, *Brisées* (Paris: Gallimard, 1992), 83.

PART THREE

LOVE
(Philosophy and Psychoanalysis)

SIX

Gai Savoir Sera
The Science of Love and the Insolence of Chance

Joan Copjec

Stretches of parched prose filled with mathematical symbols and irrigated by a militant passion that does not balk at identifying its enemies, the work of Alain Badiou—which also comprises a project antipathetic to the most recognizable forms of feminism—seems an inhospitable environment for a theory of love and sexual difference. The surprise is that one blooms there nevertheless, improbably robust, even—I would argue—central to the project as a whole. Although he writes far less about it, Badiou lists love as one of the four (truth) conditions of philosophy, alongside science (primarily mathematics), politics (uncompromisingly confrontational), and art (in its most austere forms).[1]

No less unexpected (for different reasons) is the sprouting of love in the tutor text of Badiou's theory on the topic: the *Encore* seminar of Jacques Lacan in which the analyst remarks more than once on the incredulity of his audience, which is noticeably stunned to hear him speak of love not as an imaginary lure (designed to disguise the traumatic truth of the principled failure of sexual liaisons), but as a real encounter. More than anything else, it was the publication of *Ethics: An Understanding of Evil* that established the reputation of Badiou in the United States.[2] I want to argue a relation between this work on ethics and that on love and will do so by showing ways in which the two topics are linked in Freud and Lacan. My intention is to try to justify (to use Badiou's fond phrase) "the frequent arrogance of followers of psychoanalysis," who insist on forcing philosophy to confront the Freudian "revolution in thought." I hope, by returning to the psychoanalytic theory that supports his thesis on love, to suggest the importance of the psychoanalytic challenge for the work of Badiou in general.[3]

A critical saturation point seems to have been reached with regard to Lacan's seminar on *Ethics*; all of a sudden one hears rumblings of a revolt against the "Sophoclean" legacy that underpins it. This revolt is, with some justification, antiheroic and antisublime; it wants to deny the exemplary nature of Antigone's act and to focus not on the content of the particular tragedy of *Antigone* analyzed by Lacan but on the Athenian form of tragedy itself in order to locate an ethics in the way that artistic form staged the internal contradictions of social thought that were even then being elaborated and realized in the new political form of the Athenian city-state. I will suggest not only that the content and form of this tragedy are not so easily separable but that, far from being superseded in Lacan's thought, the *Ethics* seminar continued to be generative. Thirteen years later, Lacan dedicated a seminar to sexual difference and feminine sexuality, which he titled "Encore" partly in order to drive home the fact that he was again addressing issues dealt with in *Ethics*. I have elsewhere proposed a number of correspondences between these two seminars, but I want to name another and equally important one here: the particular "internal contradiction of social thought" to which Lacan returns in *Encore* is that between the ethical standards and the "high degree of selflessness" fostered by highly organized and durable groups and their hostility to sexual difference and erotic love. That these last interfere with the formation of artificial groups is both a fact to which Antigone, with her fierce and loving devotion to her brother, bears witness and the major thesis of Freud's *Group Psychology and the Analysis of the Ego*. Lacan draws out the radical implications of this interference in *Encore* while developing the most far-reaching theory of feminine sexuality to date. In the end, this enabled him to theorize woman not negatively, as Hegel did, as "the eternal irony of the community," but, positively, as the scourge of the horde. The difference between the community and the horde is what is at stake here.

Let me summarize briefly Freud's original thesis: group feeling finds its source in envy, which individuals seek to set aside by "identifying themselves with one another by means of a similar love for the same object."[4] Identification with other members of the group is, in other words, secondary, the consequence of a particular "contrivance"—or "quilting point," we could say—which serves to hold the group together. This contrivance is not just the members' love for the same object or leader, but the sense that this love is requited, that is, it is the illusion that the group's leader loves them all equally and that they are all worthy of his love.

Freud appears to argue that this phenomenon of universal love can be exposed as an illusion simply by exposing the leader's selfish character, but he reveals instead a structural problem that depends on the exceptional or exterior position of the leader (that is, on the fact that he cannot be counted as one of the members of the group) and on the constitution of equivalential relations among the members. It is no coincidence that Badiou distinguishes the love relation from relations of equivalency. He defines relations of equivalence as symmetrical. By this he means that the equivalential relation is one in which the terms enter into it identically: "the term **a** has to **b** the same relation as **b** to **a**. In other words, with regard to the same relation, the terms **a** and **b** have no singularity of position. Moreover, their differences do not enter into the relations conceived as a fixing of places. Conversely, a relation respecting the singularity of the terms it joins would not accept an indifferent symmetry of the places it prescribes." ("Two" 181/45) We can read in Freud an effective confirmation of this conclusion where he denies that the relation of the leader to the members of the group is one of love and implies that it is, rather, a relation of indifference to their differences.

To telegraph the contrast between the leader's bearing toward the members of the group and the bearing of love, Freud quotes this cannily precise, if cynical, aphorism of George Bernard Shaw: "being in love means greatly exaggerating the differences between one woman and another" (SE 17:140). In other words, love knows nothing of the "symmetry of everyone's relation to each other" (to use Rawls's phrase); rather, it operates according to a "logic" of preference.

What captures our attention from the start is the fact that Shaw's aphorism performs in Freud's text a double function by identifying not just the disruption love introduces into relations of equivalency, but also a strong connection between women and love. For, Freud's point is that artificial groups depend not only on the exclusion of erotic love, but on the exclusion of women as well, whether explicitly, as in the case of the Army and the Church, or implicitly in the fraternal order, or regime of brothers, which came into being in the latter half of the eighteenth century, along with emerging nation-states and modern racism.[5] Love, Freud argues, is able to cross every sort of group barrier, "it breaks through the group ties of race, of national divisions, and of the social class system" (SE 17:141). This power of love is not merely a "poetic" function but carries for Freud a political value. "Miscegenation"—in the widest sense of a libidinal crossing of any social barrier whatever—is for him a force of civilization, and this at a time when in almost every other quarter it was feared as the cause of its demise.

I mentioned earlier that Lacan's rereading of *Antigone* differs from Hegel's in that it makes woman a positive force against the stultifying order of the horde or "group spirit" rather than a kind of unfortunate flaw, responsible for the crumbling of every community. Here we see clearly how *Group Psychology* prepares the way for Lacan's position, for Freud, too, presented woman, erotic love, and their corrosive effects on artificial groups as "important factors in civilization" (SE 17:141). Freud was profoundly suspicious of groups, not primarily because of the passions they unleash but because of the passions they outlaw. While group psychologists were busy defining the volatility of emotions as the characteristic problem of groups, Freud maintained, on the contrary, that groups are founded on a fettering of libido. At this point he stopped to point out that *libido* is a term taken from the study of emotion. Certain emotions, or affects, are paralyzed by group identification. Moreover, faced with the argument that group identity allows individuals to go beyond their selfish interests to pursue altruistic aims such as equality and justice for all, Freud contended that these "lofty" aims are invented precisely to protect our selfish interests: "Social justice means that we deny ourselves many things so that others may have to do without them as well or, what is the same thing, may not be able to ask for them" (SE 17:121).

It is with Freud's argument in mind that Lacan confronts the hypothetical proposition Kant invents in the second *Critique*:[6] suppose someone offered you a night with the object of your deepest passion. Could you forgo it if you knew that accepting the offer meant that you would be beheaded the very next morning? Kant brushes past this hypothetical proposition quickly in order to get to the next, properly ethical one, by construing the answer to the first as noncontroversial. Surely anyone would be able to perform the simple calculation and abandon the object of passion under such circumstances. But Lacan questions Kant's haste in dismissing the ethical dimension of this parable, in not seeing that in some cases the proposition would not be a matter of a simple calculation. Like Freud, Lacan argues that the proper domain of ethics is passion, erotic love, not the illusory universal love that contrives to turn us into good soldiers of Christ or of the State. There can, however, be no ethics that does not lay claim to any universal and thus when Lacan returns to the themes of his *Ethics* seminar in *Encore*, it is partly to articulate a relation between love and universality, to oppose the universal love of the leader with a universality specific to erotic love.

The first hurdle to overcome in reading the latter seminar is, no doubt, its infamous pronouncement, "There is no sexual relation" by which audiences pretended to be scandalized and that continues to block comprehension of Lacan's thesis on love even now. Rapport has a scent, the odor of the officially odorless, like airplane air. By saying that there is no sexual relation, or rapport or ratio, Lacan meant to say that there is no science of love, no formula for it, not that love is a false lure, which is what audiences thought he said. If this is what they heard, I am tempted to attribute the error less to the text's baroque style of argumentation than to the audience's own beliefs, their victimization by a peculiarly modern skepticism about sexual love. This skepticism was the precipitate of the wedge that was driven by modern groups between affectionate and sensual feelings. This resulted in part in a new preoccupation with sex, conceived as the core of one's being, one's secret identity, which thereby ensured that sex would end up both promising happiness (now defined as subjective rather than objective, as formerly) and thwarting it in singular fashion. But not only did people begin to look to sex to make them happy,[7] they began seriously to doubt the possibility of a happy outcome to erotic love, which at this point became conceivable as a strategy for deceiving oneself about the impasses of sex. This skeptical position would appear to be the one espoused by *Civilization and Its Discontents*, in which Freud argued that a salient feature of modern neurosis is the sense that civilization itself is at war with sex. This alone would appear to destine sex to become the source of our deepest discontent, yet Freud never ceased believing in the possibility of erotic love.

It is as creatures of the skeptical view, however, that Lacan's audience latched onto his negative pronouncement, "There is no sexual relation (*Il n'y a pas de rapport sexuel*)," while failing sufficiently to notice that it appeared holding hands with its positive twin: "There is (some) One (*Y a d'l'Un*)."[8] With this second statement, Lacan introduced his concept of '*suppleance*,' a term plucked from the obscurity of eighteenth-century French rhetoric where it was used as a synonym for *catachresis*.[9] Suppleance names a term that substitutes itself not (as is the case with other tropes) for another prior term, but for an absence. This recourse to the field of rhetoric is deliberate, a point Lacan underscores by referring to his ethics—in a television interview made at the time of the *Encore* seminar—as one whose imperative was to "speak well of one's desire."[10] Psychoanalysis demands only that we speak eloquently, winningly, movingly, as rhetoricians say, not of one's arguments, one's reasons, but of one's desire. One's duty is not simply to "move one's audience beyond reason," but to move oneself beyond the formulas and ratios that substitute for reason.

Lacan is positing here that the symbolic impasse that confounds every attempt to construct a sexual ratio can be supplemented or "made up for" by this rather odd, supernumerary One, which he refers to as an "obstacle," an obstacle precisely *to* the sexual relation (*SXX* 45). Badiou begins his self-described "commentary" on Lacan by foregrounding the concept of suppleance and directing us to approach it by two paths at once: formally and ontologically (*SD* 177, 42). In formal terms, if the impossibility of constructing a sexual formula attests to a lack in the symbolic, an insufficiency opened up in the human drive in contrast to animal instinct, suppleance introduces an excess that writes this lack in the symbolic. Approaching suppleance ontologically, one is obliged to note that if there is no sexual formula, then love exists only as an aleatory adventure. Love, as we will see, revolves around an affirmation that cannot be justified by the conceptual or symbolic sphere in which it appears.

This supplemental element on which love depends does not in any way repair the symbolic deficit, but maintains it instead. Lacan uses the analogy of the *quark*, the nonsense word invented by James Joyce and appropriated by physicists: when physicists added "quarks" to the universe of atoms in order to "fill out the picture" of the world, to cement the universe as a coherent whole, the addition had the opposite effect of breaking up the universe, dispersing it.

The One forged by suppleance is not some universe or "bower of bliss" that the lovers come to inhabit. They are not bound by a love that embraces them as members of a group are by the supposed love of their leader. Instead, the supplementary One serves, as was said, as an obstacle to this embracing or "fusional" one precisely by designating the latter's absence, the absence of a third term outside the two lovers, which they could thus share as members of a group, share a common ego ideal or cause. The link formed by the supplementary One thus refutes the "humanist" hypothesis of love, which states that lovers come together because they find they have something in common, even if this something is as diffuse as their common humanity. Love is, rather, the "intersection of two substances that have no part in common" (SXX 17).

At the same time, love cannot be a simple addition of two quite separate terms, a one plus one, because the supplementary One designates the impossibility of counting not just the two together as one, but either of the two as one. Neither of the two forms a one, either prior to or as a result of their loving encounter. This refutes, then, the "complementary" hypothesis of love—proposed by Aristophanes's myth of a severed sexual being and more recently by Jerry McGuire—which assumes that the lover finds in the beloved his or her complement. The madness of love consists in this creation of Two where there never was a one and which is not itself one. It is thus wrong to speak of love as building a "nation of two" separate from a nation, or state, or any group whatsoever. Love is antithetical to groups not because it builds smaller, less unwieldy, and more powerful ones, but because love creates an "intersection" or linking of subjects in a fundamentally different way.

While much more needs to be said about the Two of love and the One of suppleance, I will do so by straying for a time from this Lacanian-Badiouan vocabulary in order to approach the problem once again from Freud's theory. If this concept of suppleance is a Lacanian invention, one can nevertheless find in Freud—in *Three Essays on the Theory of Sexuality*, *Jokes and Their Relation to the Unconscious*, and "Creative Writers and Day-Dreaming," particularly—references to a supplemental element, called an "incentive bonus" or "fore-pleasure," which prefigures it.[11] An incentive bonus is defined in the "Creative Writers" essay as a "yield of pleasure" that enables "the release of still greater pleasure." This is an idea worth scratching one's head over. How does this supplement of pleasure, which Freud describes as "purely formal," release more pleasure? While the process remains mysterious at this point, Freud suggests that it somehow allows us to overcome "the feeling of repulsion ... which is undoubtedly connected with the barriers that rise between each single ego and the others" (SE 9:153). It is Freud himself who has taught us, however, that such feelings of repulsion are aroused not by the ego of the other but by the revolting private fantasies that are the concern of this essay, that is, we are often revolted by the other's *jouissance*. Because he knows this, Freud is not at all surprised by the fact that the daydreams and fantasies of others do not give us any pleasure, but leave us cold, at best, and at worst fill us with disgust, what piques his curiosity is the fact that the fantasies, or fictions, of creative writers are such an important source of our delight. The key to explaining this curious fact, Freud speculates, lies in the writer's ability to "soften the character of his egoistical daydreams by altering and disguising it, and . . . [thus to] bribe us by the purely formal . . . yield of pleasure" (*SE* 9:153). Since we are not given much to go on here, we might be tempted to suppose that the skill of the writer consists in deleting obvious personal markers or blurring the outline of his fantasy in order to make it more appealing to a greater number of people, who would thus be able to see themselves in the written fiction. Through this operation, the creative writer's fantasy is able to become the common fantasy of many. But if, as I will suggest, art—like love—is not a matter of sharing something, then we must search for a different way of understanding Freud's tentative explanation. We must note, moreover, that Freud's analysis proceeds not by proposing that an abstraction of features takes place, but on the contrary that something is added to produce the softening, altering effect; it is the incentive bonus, characterized as both a quantum of pleasure and as purely formal, that produces the universalizing effect.

One other point: the transformation of the egoistical into the universalizable fantasy appears, by implication, to be accompanied by the opening up of an aleatory dimension. Freud begins his essay by attributing the pleasure we take in our own daydreams to their ability to assure us that things will remain the same, that the future will bring us a familiar contentment, one patterned on successes and satisfactions experienced in our past. Fantasies hook an uncertain future on to a pleasurably experienced past. The assurance they offer may thus be summarized as the comfortable sense that "Nothing can happen to *me*!" (*SE* 9:150). By contrast, the fantasy of the creative writer, we may surmise, gives us the sense that "Something *can* happen to me!"

In short, we find *in nuce*, in Freud's little essay, the formal and ontological themes we isolated as essential to the concept of suppleance. It is legitimate to read this essay as an early attempt to formulate what would turn out to be a theory of sublimation. This would then allow us to contrast the social link created by suppleance or sublimation with that created by repression (which is the other destiny of the drive). But to do so, one must first confront Foucault's condemnation of psychoanalysis' "repression hypothesis," since this condemnation has interposed itself between Freud's text and its meaning. Scolding Freud for his negative characterization of the relation between society and sex, Foucault offered instead this positive hypothesis: at the end of the eighteenth century, there was a massive incitement to think and talk endlessly about sex, the better to construct it as the secret of the subject's identity. Foucault might have saved his breath, for Freud's theory of repression is a positive hypothesis. It defines repression not as a means of preventing or avoiding satisfaction, but on the contrary as a means of achieving it.[12] This is indeed why Lacan attributes to the superego—the agent of repression—not a prohibition against enjoyment, but an incitement to "Enjoy!" It turns out that the repressive hypothesis Foucault castigates belongs not to Freud but to the sociologists of his time and one can actually watch Freud wrestle to defeat it in *Civilization and Its Discontents*. The gist of the sociological account is that society is the agent of the division between the social and the sexual. Freud's psychoanalytic breakthrough comes when he finally asserts that it is the superego and not society that is the source of repression. This is not to say that the superego is merely an internalization of society's prohibitions. On the contrary, if the superego suddenly grows stronger at the end of the eighteenth century, it is because the law in modern society no longer functions with the same force or effectiveness it once did, no longer serves as a bulwark against jouissance.[13] The task of social law was redefined in the modern period as the prevention of a reemergence of absolute power, only recently demolished, and the promotion of the subject's "squatter sovereignty," only recently sanctioned; law thus ceased at this point to act as a sufficient restraint against the drive. A strengthened, increasingly cruel, and obscene superego begins to act imperiously, as a law unto itself, and commands enjoyment freed from social controls precisely because the social barriers against libido have been weakened. This superegoic insistence on libidinal independence does not curb the libido but, on the contrary, permits it to intensify, to acquire, in Freud's words, an "extraordinary and dangerous strength." Thus, while contemporary sociologists pitted restraint against liberation, Freud observed a more complex relation between the two: the relative freedom from social barriers or "liberation" of libido did not liberate the subject, but shackled him to a new law of jouissance; enjoyment was "imperativized" or transformed into a duty. Foucault was right, then, to observe the rise of a terrible new law at the end of the eighteenth century but wrong about where it came from and how it functioned.

Freud's concept of 'repression' does nevertheless bear some resemblance to its use in common parlance; under repression, libido or drive is still conceived as fettered and it operates, as Freud puts it, "in the dark." Why is this? His thesis states that the distinctive mark of repression is the "vanishing of the idea" or the removal of the ideational representative from consciousness. It is the vanishing of the idea that seems to be responsible for rendering the drive inoperative. It is as if the libido, in ceasing to be submitted to the same level of social restraint, in being promoted as the secret core of the subject's being, had as a consequence lost any stake or representation in the social and thus became completely solipsistic. Unlinked to any social or conscious influence, it could no longer be altered, only intensified. Were it so completely cut off from society, however, there would be no way of knowing there was any such thing as drive and so Freud reasons that some derivative or fragment of the vanished idea must enter consciousness, some partial idea or thing, some fetish, he says, must exist to betray its "intimate connection" to the repressed idea.

Everything depends, I argue, on understanding the relation between the "fragmentary idea," and the "ideational representative." While it may seem that the first is metonymically connected to the second, I will insist not only that the two are distinct, but that their distinction holds the key to the difference between the repression and the sublimation of the drive. Moreover, through this distinction, we will be able to bring the concept of ideational representative closer to that of the incentive bonus or fore-pleasure and to connect it to the operation of suppleance. Significantly, the concept of the 'ideational representative' has been dismissed in a recent history of psychoanalysis as a "catastrophic turn in the Freudian problematic," one that betrays the very concept of drive.[14] The justification for this dismissal is that since drive is "wholly other" to representation and thought, to speak of an ideational representative of the drive is to confound the order of drive with the order of representation and thought and thus to betray drive absolutely. One recognizes in this charge a variation of Leibniz's "Principle of Indiscernibles," reformulated by Wittgenstein in his well-known dictum, "Whereof one cannot speak, one must remain silent." The Leibnizian principle states that their can be no "indiscernibles for thought . . . [no] explicit *concept* [or representation] of what is subtracted from thought" (*MPh* 99). Lacan effectively defends the so-called catastrophic turn in Freud's thought and opposes the Leibnizian principle when, as mentioned earlier, he formulates the ethical imperative of psychoanalysis as "Speak well of your desire!" We are now prepared to offer a preliminary definition of that rhetorical term to which Lacan emphatically links this imperative: suppleance allows us to speak well of our desire not by translating jouissance into language, but by formalizing it in a signifier that does not mean but is, rather, directly enjoyed. This operation supplements the absence in language of a signifier that could translate jouissance with a signifier that marks this absence.

There will be more to say about this operation later, for the moment let us recall that with repression there is no ideational representative (and no suppleance), but only a fragmentary or fetishistic idea. This idea is described by Freud as having an "intimate connection" with the repressed libido. What does this mean? Is it that the fetishistic idea represents this libido, the subject's secret enjoyment? As I have indicated, enjoyment is conceived as "wholly other" to representation and indeed to the social in general. This means that if the idea can be thought to represent the subject his enjoyment, the secret of his being, it can only do so negatively, by announcing its own failed and fragmentary relation to libido. An illustration would be handy and so I turn to a perfect parable of repression, Henry James's

"The Beast in the Jungle."[15] Here we find John Marcher, the story's egotistical hero rigidly clinging to the fetishistic idea that he has been tapped for some great destiny. While he is otherwise indifferent to social life, this idea secures for him a narrow foothold in it. The idea keeps him going but it also prevents him from doing anything other than protect himself from accidents that might befall him, such as love, which places itself fortuitously in his path but which he declines in order to stay true to his idea, the one that holds the secret of his happiness. The problem is that, like all such ideas, it represents this happiness fragmentarily by placing it at a distance from him, in the future: you will one day be fulfilled, it says, if you will put all things aside but me. We are reminded of what Freud says in *Group Psychology* about the effect of putting the leader in the place of one's ego ideal: one becomes hypnotized by the external ideal while losing interest in everything else. And thus does Marcher spend his life waiting, eyes on the prize, blind to the world and to love. Eventually, however, after the woman who waits beside him dies, he comes to the realization, upon seeing a bereaved stranger at the cemetery, that he is indeed different from this man so clearly pained by the recent loss of a great love. Though the reader expects Marcher finally to see that he has wasted his life in waiting, he comes rather to the self-(pre)serving conclusion that this waiting has been his fulfillment. For, he now sees that his destiny was to have been "the man of his time, *the* man, to whom nothing on earth was to have happened" ("Beast" 366). If this is a parable of Freud's positive thesis on repression, it is because Marcher's revelation demonstrates that repression, in its reliance on a fetishistic idea, does not simply alienate the subject from his happiness, but allows him to be happy in this alienation, to enjoy living at a distance from his enjoyment, or to find satisfaction in preventing anything from happening.

The example of Marcher also proves that the repression of drive in modern society does not result in a curtailment of libido but in rendering it solipsistic. Yoked to a fetishistic idea—the ideational representative "vanished"—the drive is cut off from contingent developments. The repressed idea thus persists unaltered and develops only in intensity, eventually taking on the form of a terrible and portentous beast. As with Marcher, the subject maintains a sense of his singularity, yet this singularity is only a particularity that appears to him as an alien idea and is fully compatible with the emergence and durability of artificial groups, which supply their members with their fetishistic ideas.

In turning now to the alternative love represents, it will be instructive to attend to the way Leo Bersani, a psychoanalytic theorist of considerable acumen, remained skeptical about love for so long.[16] His resistance to unburdening himself of this skepticism stemmed, I argue, from the pressure of an error located upstream from his current work, in his reflections on Freud's theory of fore-pleasure in *Three Essays*.[17]

In the midst of his discussion of suppleance, Lacan poses a question, "Is Eros a tension toward the One?" (*SXX* 5). This formulation seems designed to recall the section on fore-pleasure in Freud's essay. Bersani's work effectively (and correctly) answers this question in the negative by staunching the idea that the drive seeks discharge through attachment to a preordained sexual object. He dismantles the teleological picture of the drive and problematizes the idea that libido proceeds toward the "opposite sex," culminating in a taken-for-granted genital sexuality. But Bersani ended up taking his argument too far and proposed initially that drive is in fact indifferent to external objects as such and seeks merely to turn endlessly, solipsistically, around on itself to produce a self-shattering enjoyment. In response to Freud's warning that fore-pleasure poses a danger to sexual life if, failing to function properly as a means of attaining end-pleasure (or discharge), it becomes an end in itself, Bersani countered that far from being a danger to sexuality, fore-pleasure is its very definition. End-pleasure is thus dismissed.

But Freud's text is not so simple; here is what it says and what Bersani's reading neglected to remark: "The danger [posed by the mechanism of fore-pleasure] arises if at any point in the preparatory sexual processes the fore-pleasure turns out to be too great and the element of tension too small" (*SE*, 7:211). From Bersani's argument, one would have expected an intensification of fore-pleasure to be linked to a maintaining of tension at maximum pitch, but here an intense fore-pleasure is accompanied by a decrease in tension. It is necessary to posit then two separate destinies of fore-pleasure. A first fore-pleasure, combined with a lack of tension, results in a diminution of the motor energy necessary for action. This fore-pleasure is compatible with Bersani's solipsistic drive, which turns around itself rather than moving forward toward an external object and with the fettering of the drive characteristic of repression. That leaves a second fore-pleasure, which is combined with tension. Is it necessary to read this part of Freud's argument, as Bersani long ago argued, in a teleological way? It is true that Freud claims that this tension is necessary for "proceeding forward with the sexual process," but—remarkably—he does not marry this process to a predestined goal. He describes this forward push not as an impulsion toward a natural end, but on the contrary as "an impulsion to make a *change* in the . . . situation" (*SE* 7:209, emphasis added). Tension becomes the sign, then, as Lacan said of love, "that one is *changing* discourses" (*SXX* 16), that one is encountering something new, something other. My point is this: the surplus tension added to fore-pleasure is not one that pushes the drive forward toward (fusion with) the One, but something quite different: a tension caused by the One, the One of an "internal inhibition" (as Freud puts it in this essay), or the One of the "obstacle" (as Lacan puts it in *Encore*).

Fore-pleasure of the second sort, like the incentive bonus of the "Creative Writers" essay, seems to be a formalization of jouissance that results in the modification of the drive. This is the conclusion one draws from a careful reading of Freud, but this conclusion might be indirectly confirmed by another source. However slight Freud's little essay appears, one can make out a line of filiation that connects it to Kant's monumental *Critique of Judgment*. This connection is discernible in the persistence of the question regarding the universal validity of aesthetic judgment or the pleasurable availability of the artist's fantasy to others. Kant and Freud both wonder why the work of art does not leave others cold, or worse, overwhelm them with disgust. Kant considered the key to his whole critique of taste to lie in the answer to this question: Does the feeling of pleasure (or aesthetic enjoyment) precede the judgment ("this is beautiful") or does judgment precede the pleasure? He answered that if one were to claim that pleasure in the object came first, pleasure would have only private and not universal validity, for it would in this case "depend directly on the presentation of the object *as given*." That is, the pleasure involved would be "mere agreeableness in the sensation."[18] It must therefore be the case that the universally communicable judgment comes first. But this is not a simple alternative, for since aesthetic judgment involves no cognition, no concept of the object, and has only a subjective determining basis, then the basis of judgment can only be an experience of pleasure. In short, there must be a kind of pleasure that is itself a judgment. Or, before aesthetic pleasure/enjoyment is possible, there must first be a fore-pleasure that is itself a judgment.

With repression, I argue, the antagonistic relation between the social and the sexual manifests itself in an *alienation* of jouissance, of private enjoyment, which seems always to be beyond symbolic or social recuperation. But Kant here opens the door to the conception of a different sort of antagonism, one that results this time not from an *exclusion* of jouissance from the symbolic field, but from its supernumerary *inclusion*. The tension Freud located in the second type of fore-pleasure is, I argue, the effect of the introduction into the interior of the symbolic of a heterogeneous element: pleasure as judgment or, in Freud's strictly homologous terms, a formal pleasure. This tension permits the subject to overcome its indifference to objects—or, to abandon the solipsistic circuit of the drive—and to move toward an encounter with the aesthetic or loved object. And the concept of this tension-filled fore-pleasure allows both Kant and Freud to avoid the problem of teleology without falling into the trap of regarding will or drive as indifferent to objects.

According to the commonplace notion, sublimation involves a change of objects; one substitutes a socially deplorable or useful object or activity for one that is socially valorized. Lacan decimates this notion with a single blow: sublimation, he says, involves not a change of objects, but changing the object. Freud and Kant agree that there can be no criteria for objectively distinguishing loved or beautiful objects from others that are not. A subjective choice is involved in the designation. The beloved or beautiful object differs in no way from other objects, except in the fact that the subject loves it or deems it beautiful. But this single stipulation does not yet get at what Lacan means by "changing the object," as Kant implicitly acknowledges when he observes that if aesthetic judgment came after and simply reported the pleasure we took in an object, the latter would remain unchanged, would remain the object as given. What changes the object is the fore-pleasure, or aesthetic judgment, or incentive bonus. The question now is: how?

If fore-pleasure, the incentive bonus, the ideational representative, and aesthetic judgment are products of suppleance, they function, as was stated earlier, to name not a feature or object, but an obstacle to the formation of one, the one of fusion or unity, or the absence of any foundation. It is the naming of this obstacle or absence that changes the object. For, with this name, the object ceases to be, for the subject, synonymous with its "presentation as given" and becomes lovable precisely in its capacity to be other than it is. But this alteration of the object could not take place if the subject herself were not simultaneously altered. The name or judgment strikes at the heart of the subject of love as well by naming the obstacle that prevents her from coinciding with herself. The lover thus identifies herself with the gap this noncoincidence opens up, that is, with her own capacity to be other than he is or, to put it differently, with the lack of any determining cause of her being or actions.

Now, one might expect that the destruction of both the unitary subject and a unitary object would annihilate the possibility of any operation of conjunction, would result only in a scattering. But this is not what happens, recall, in the scenario Freud presents in *Three Essays*. There we saw that the unfettering or freeing of the drive through tension-filled fore-pleasure was associated with its forward thrust. Toward what? The implication is that the drive pushes toward an object, but Freud also says, as I have noted, toward making a change (I will now add:) in the object. Kant, Freud, and Lacan line up on this issue and all at once it becomes possible to see on what they agree. If all three disavow any teleological dimension to the passionate embrace of the object, this is because the beautiful or beloved object is not external to the drive but internal to it. In short, in order to conceive love or aesthetic pleasure, it is necessary to imagine a topological structure, or an effect of folding, by which the supplementary term or *fore-pleasure* modifies the trajectory of the drive in such a way that it now includes the object.

The lover of the beautiful/beloved object, who identifies with the absence of any external cause of her desire, is free to choose her own motivation, her own object-cause of desire. But if this choice of object is not to be confused with a determination, that choice has to be conceived as an invention or a change of the object, which converts it from an ordinary, found object to one that is—what? A word often used by Freud with reference to the object of love is *overvaluation*; the loved object is one that has a surplus value for the subject. Here is what Lacan has to say about this surplus value: "Analysis demonstrates that love, in its essence, is narcissistic, and reveals that the substance of what is supposedly object-like . . . is in fact that which constitutes a remainder in desire, namely, its cause" (SXX 6). This passage, by associating the surplus value of the loved object with narcissism, may seem to support the thesis that love is merely an illusion designed to flatter the lover's ego or self-image. The lover chooses to love only someone similar or complementary to the image he has of himself. But this reading conflates narcissism with egoism. What is remarkable about Freud's theory of narcissism, however, is that it accords the subject the status not of an imaginary identity, nor even a fixed symbolic one, but of a hypothesis. Freud hypothesizes that a quantum of libido is originally attached to the subject itself, but the only evidence we have of this narcissistic libido is the subject's libidinal attachment to objects in the world, or object-libido. In other words, Freud hypothesizes that an excess or remainder of libido persists beyond that deployed in the cathexis of objects; it is this remainder of libido that accounts for narcissism, for the subject's narcissistic cathexis of itself.

I propose that this theory of narcissism be read against the backdrop of various philosophical speculations about the subject's disappearance in his or her particular thoughts or perceptions. When I am running after a streetcar or absorbed in looking at a portrait (to use Sartre's examples), I drop out of my own consciousness, or am conscious only of the streetcar-having-to-be-caught or the portrait's beauty.[19] From where, then, does self-consciousness arise; how do I become an object of consciousness to myself? Without going into the complexities of this philosophical problem, let us admit that the two examples Sartre gives here are quite different inasmuch as our consciousness of the distance and speed of the streetcar involves an objective judgment, while the contemplation of a portrait involves a judgment of taste, it relies on a feeling of pleasure rather than on conceptual thought. If one reads Freud's theory of narcissism and Kant's theory of aesthetic judgment together, one sees that they are united by the fact that something akin to "self-consciousness" emerges along with the consciousness of pleasure. What distinguishes, for Kant, the merely agreeable from the beautiful object is that while the first gives us only a feeling of pleasure or gratification, in the second, this feeling of pleasure is, as it were, "reflected" or taken as an object such that it becomes possible to say that one feels pleasure in one's feeling of pleasure. In other words, with the agreeable object we have a subjective feeling of pleasure, but no subject, while in relation to the beautiful or loved object, a feeling of narcissism arises, a feeling in which the subject "feels himself" (Kant's phrase). It is important to emphasize that this feeling of self relies on no concept or image of the self, but *is* only a feeling of pleasure.

It is the absence of any reliance on an image that most clearly separates narcissism from egoism. I would argue that the narcissism involved in the "subject's feeling himself," or in "feeling its own state" (as Kant refers to it), the feeling of pleasure taken in the feeling of pleasure, is an indication not of a "state," but of the fact that the subject is, in Lacan's words, "changing discourses," or moving herself beyond herself. In this sense, Freud can be understood to "correct" Kant. The sense of pleasure at stake in the experience of love or beauty is not a sense of a harmony (of the faculties), but of a tension or noncoincidence of the self with itself. On the other hand, Kant may be understood to correct a possible misreading of Freud whereby his position regarding the narcissistic nature of love is taken to mean that what we love in the beloved is simply the pleasure we receive from him or her. This last is a description, Kant makes plain, of our relation to a merely agreeable object, which we like not for itself but for the gratification it provides. The agreeable object is of interest to us or useful in this sense. The same is not true for the beautiful or beloved object; we do not like it because it gives us pleasure, but for itself.

This discussion returns us to the opposition set up by Freud in *Group Psychology* between artificial groups and love, between the overvaluation that takes place in love and the hypnotic experience of collective fascination fostered by groups. I have argued that the members of a group, by identifying with the ego ideal or fragmentary idea that alienates them from their happiness, surrender their freedom and become fettered with regard to love and the invention it implies. In doing so, they become alienated from their happiness or happy only in their unhappiness. This alienation serves to protect them from chance. Focused on the ideal, they reject everything that happens to come along, every opportunity, every satisfaction, because none are not "it," that is, each falls short of the ideal. If love poses a threat to the group, this is because it turns us from our hypnotic fascination with the ideal and thus from our contempt for or dissatisfaction with the contingencies of life. Love brings us not the satisfaction of deferral, of never getting what we want, but the satisfaction of obtainment, of which we can never get enough. This last phrase is meant to explain why Lacan, in his comments on the narcissism of love, continues to speak of a lack of satisfaction: "a remainder in desire . . . sustains desire through its lack of satisfaction" (SXX 6).

The opposite of the alienation of satisfaction is not—one needs to make clear—a satisfaction that would be present to itself. Freud never shied away from the basic fact that sexual pleasure, jouissance, knows no satisfaction, in the sense of respite; the nature of jouissance is that it has to be repeated, again and again, without surcease. One mistakes what this basic claim essentially claims, however, if one one associates, as many do, repetition with failure, that is, if one assumes that the (sex/death) drive repeats itself because it is never quite satisfied. On the contrary, it is only repetition that satisfies the drive. It is only between the first and the second time, or, between any two movements of a repetition, that satisfaction is obtained; and it is only between these two movements that psychoanalysis locates the subject. Thus, the phrase *lack of satisfaction* means something different in reference to love than it does in relation to the ego ideal. In the latter case, the phrase refers to a lack of coincidence between the ideal and everything that falls short of it, while in reference to love it indicates the lack of coincidence of the subject with itself. Here it is a matter not of falling short but of going beyond.

I will add, by way of acknowledging some untied threads, not a few final words but something akin to an opening remark. While in groups the ego ideal performs the universalizing function and universalizes the members it links in a relation of equivalency, in love the subject performs the universalizing function through her declaration/judgment of love/pleasure. What is universalized in this instance is the loved or beautiful object.

NOTES

This chapter is dedicated to the memory of Sam Gillespie, one of the most brilliant and promising thinkers of his generation, a devoted proponent of Badiou's work, and a beloved and esteemed friend.

1. Though Badiou's theory of love is dispersed throughout his texts, just two are devoted exclusively to the topic: "What is Love?" trans. Justin Clemens, in *Umbr(a)* 1 (1996), special Badiou issue, ed. Sam Gillespie and Sigi Jottkandt (from Badiou, *Conditions* [Paris: Seuil, 1988]) and "The Scene of Two," trans. Barbara P. Fulks, *Lacanian Ink* 21 (Spring 2003) (from Badiou, "La scène du deux," in *De L'Amour* [Paris: Flammarion, 1999]). I have written about "What is Love?" in *Imagine There's No Woman* (Cambridge, MA: MIT Press, 2002) and will therefore focus mainly on "The Scene of Two" here.

2. Alain Badiou, *Ethics: An Essay in the Understanding of Evil*, trans. Peter Hallward (New York: Verso, 2001).

3. Alain Badiou, *Manifesto for Philosophy*, ed., trans., and intro., Norman Madarasz (Albany: State University of New York Press, 1999), 82.

4. Sigmund Freud, *Group Psychology and the Analysis of the Ego: The Standard Edition of the Complete Psychological Works of Sigmund Freud*, ed. and trans. James Strachey (London: Hogarth Press, 1953–74) 17:120. Hereafter *SE* followed by volume number and page.

5. The phrase, and a powerful conception of the "regime of the brother," is found in Juliet MacCannell, *The Regime of the Brother* (London: Routledge, 1991).

6. Jacques Lacan, *Book VII: The Ethics of Psychoanalysis*, ed. Jacques-Alain Miller, trans. Denis Porter (New York: Norton, 1992).

7. See Leo Bersani, "Can Sex Make Us Happy?" *Raritan* 21, no. 4 (Spring 2002): 15-30.

8. Jacques Lacan, *Book XX: Encore—On Feminine Sexuality, the Limits of Love and Knowledge*, ed. Jacques-Alain Miller, trans. Bruce Fink (New York: Norton, 1998), 5 (translation modified). Hereafter *SXX* followed by page number.

9. For this historical reference, see Patricia Parker, "Metaphor and Catachresis," in *The Ends of Rhetoric: History, Theory, Practice*, ed. J. Bender and D. E. Wellbery (Stanford, CA: Stanford University Press, 1990), 72-106.

10. Jacques Lacan, *Television: A Challenge to the Psychoanalytic Establishment*, ed. Joan Copjec, trans. Denis Hollier, Rosalind Krauss, and Annette Michelson (New York: Norton, 1990), 39.

11. See Sigmund Freud, *Three Essays on the Theory of Sexuality*, in *SE* 7:208-11; *Jokes and Their Relation to the Unconscious*, in *SE* 8:44; and "Creative Writers and Day-Dreaming," in *SE* 9:143-53.

12. I derive this thesis from the following statement, among others: "It is not easy in theory to deduce the possibility of such a thing as repression. Why should an instinctual impulse undergo a vicissitude like this? A necessary condition of its happening must clearly be that the instinct's attainment of its aim should produce unpleasure instead of pleasure. But we cannot well imagine such a contingency. There are no such instincts: satisfaction of an instinct is always pleasurable" (Freud, "Repression," in *SE* 14:146).

13. This same thesis, articulated in a slightly different way, can also be found in MacCannell, *The Regime of the Brother*.

14. Michel Henry, *The Genealogy of Psychoanalysis*, trans. Douglas Brick (Stanford, CA: Stanford University Press, 1990), 298.

15. Henry James, "The Beast in the Jungle," in *The Turn of the Screw and Other Short Fiction* (New York: Bantam, 1981), 1-104, 325. I recommend Robert B. Pippin's fine reading of this tale in *Henry James and Modern Moral Life* (Cambridge: Cambridge University Press, 2000), not the least of its virtues is that it lends support to my argument here.

16. Leo Bersani, "Sociability and Cruising," in *Umbr(a)* 1 (2002): 12-37.

17. See Leo Bersani, "Sexuality and Esthetics," in *The Freudian Body: Psychoanalysis and Art* (New York: Columbia University Press, 1986), 29-50.

18. Immanuel Kant, *Critique of Judgment*, trans. Werner S. Pluhar (Indianapolis, IN: Hackett, 1987).

19. Jean-Paul Sartre, *Being and Nothingness*, trans. Hazel Barnes (New York: Washington Square Press, 1992), 49.

SEVEN

Alain Badiou
Philosophical Outlaw

Juliet Flower MacCannell

> Love, which it seems to some I have down-graded, can be posited only in that beyond, where, at first, it renounces its object. This also enables us to understand that any shelter in which may be established a viable, temperate relation of one sex to the other necessitates the intervention . . . of the medium known as the paternal metaphor.
> The analyst's desire is not a pure desire. It is a desire to obtain absolute difference, a desire which intervenes when, confronted with the primary signifier, the subject is, for the first time, in a position to subject himself to it. There only may the signification of a limitless love emerge, because it is outside the limits of the law, where alone it may live.
> —Jacques Lacan, *Seminar XI*

PROLOGUE: ON LOVE AND LAW

I first encountered Alain Badiou some years ago in Chicago when we each delivered a plenary address at a conference cosponsored by the Collège Internationale de Philosophie. The morning after my talk on "Love Outside the Limits of the Law,"[1] Professor Badiou sought me out and presented me with a copy of his book *Conditions*, in which he had inscribed: "*à Juliet Flower MacCannell, en souvenir d'un croisement de pensée à Chicago*" (to Juliet Flower MacCannell, in memory of a meeting of thoughts in Chicago). At the time I knew relatively little of Badiou's work, apart from his public debates on philosophy and poetry with Philippe Lacoue-Labarthe. Since then I had occasionally reminded myself of his gift to me, but put off considering in detail how my view of love "crossed" with his: were our thoughts parallel or opposed? As both Badiou and I claim to be inspired by the *Ethics* seminar of Jacques Lacan, I am grateful to Gabriel Riera, editor of the present collection, for the opportunity (and the prompt) to address the question of our "crossing" systematically. My exegesis of Badiou's peculiar conception of Love (and its limits—the limits of law and language) requires a preliminary reflection on the differences between his ideas of language and the unconscious and my own.

If, in the end, I find myself crossing against Badiou's interpretation of Love (I am, for example, unlikely to forgo the sexual difference that grants my word a feminine specificity Badiou would rather see evaporate), the exercise illustrates how Lacan's readers often take his work in very distinctive directions.[2]

Our emphases differ. Both of us derive much from Lacan and from domains such as philosophy and literature. We each use Lacan with social and political aims in mind. While I am inclined to favor the literary-verbal-psychoanalytical, Badiou follows a unique bent that shades his philosophical understanding toward the conceptual-mathematical. It could thus be said that the real or rational explanation for our differences on Love is that Badiou's context is philosophical, while mine betrays echoes of a literary and artistic French civilization that, from the beginning, cast itself in the role of philosophy's dangerous but necessary supplement—as the goad to its social (and sexual) conscience.

But I anticipate. It is more crucial to explore Badiou's avowed consonance with Lacanian psychoanalysis, which requires examining the axioms of his mathematical approach to philosophy. This will show that while Badiou's accent on Love shares much with Lacan's theory and methods—questions of the Subject, Truth, the Unconscious, and Topology—important theoretical and practical distinctions remain, particularly with regard to Woman. In what follows, I try to map the coordinates of Badiou's system to clarify his relation to Freudian-Lacanian psychoanalysis; after that, questions of the Art of Love, Literature, and Woman will prevail.

OF BADIOU'S "TRUTH": BEING BEYOND LANGUAGE

Alain Badiou is an unusually consistent, highly formal thinker. His *L'être et l'événement* cannot be read without the excitement one always feels on encountering anyone—from Hegel to Schreber—who has dedicated themselves so fully to drawing out the implications of their profound personal experience of simple, powerful, and universal Truths. Epoch-making Truths, Truths of an "Evental" nature Badiou will call them (*evental* being a necessarily awkward translation of Badiou's equally odd term *événementiel*). Truths that are a "piercing through" [*transpercement*] (*E* 52),[3] Badiou says that we recognize such Truths by the way we are "seized by" them:

> This seizure manifests itself by unequalled intensities of existence. We can name them: in love, there is happiness; in science there is joy (in Spinoza's sense: intellectual beatitude); in politics, there is enthusiasm; and in art there is pleasure. These "affects of truth" . . . sign the entry of some-one into a subjective composition. (*E* 53)[4]

If this sounds like Christian or other spiritual or political enthusiasms that exalt the experience of Truth (think of seventeenth-century mysticism, Reformation Protestantism, militant movements) Badiou counts on his fierce, uncompromising atheism (E 25), declared anti-Nazism and his aggressive opposition to individual subjectivity to belie such links with his thought. He distances himself as much from organized religion as from organized ("statist") politics, and he gauges their degree of "Evil" by the depth of their misprision regarding the nature of the "Truth." Authentic Truth, for him, is always a "truth in progress" (E 71), and by this measure Badiou views all established religions and political states as equally torpid, simulated truths. Untruths, really, that fail to be universal, objective, and innovative—the inflexible criteria for his definition of Truth.[5] Yet, he admits that Evil is an effect of this same Truth: "Terror, betrayal and disaster are what an ethic of truths, as opposed to the impotent morality of human rights—tries to ward off. . . . But . . . these have become real possibilities only through the truth-process itself" (E 71).

A real Truth for Badiou is one that alters and even destroys the "State" (state of being, political state, state of knowledge) to make room for what he calls a "new situation," defined as a place where thought can begin (again), and where Truth will have transformed the finite space of thought into the transitory situation. "Being there" is no longer a given for Badiou, who denounces the concept of '*il y a*' (Heidegger's and Lacan's alike).[6] In the new landscape for thinking, Being will become a "decision" that forges a "new man" whose condition is indiscernibly yet indelibly marked by the Event that produced it.[7] "Indiscernibly" because the Event is fleeting and unavailable to consciousness ("the event has as its being, disappearing").[8] "Indelibly" because its Truth bears the unmistakable imprint of, well—Truth. Real Truths offer Being ("multiple-being")[9] a fresh situation. (Or should we say a new situationist being?)

Badiou's all-determining Encounter with Truth does have an undeniably subjective, spiritual coloration. But because in his system no truth qualifies as Truth unless it is acknowledged by a "we" (a multiple-being, a "we-subject"), its authenticity is supposed to be guaranteed by its collective character. Badiou, that is, credits the we-subject with being the only entity actually endowed with "subjectivity," simply because its Truth requires a collective acknowledgment. This we-subject exists, however, only because it is a subject of the Truth—whose criterion is that it is recognized (collectively) as Truth by a we-subject (E 55). The circularity of this definition is logical only in a spiritual way, and in fact the Truth of the we is prized by Badiou chiefly because it is that kind of Truth which mentally "sets us free"—free from the lifeless rules that support imitation over creative innovation and tie us down to our present state of being.

Badiou opens *L'être et l'événement*, his major philosophical statement, by listing several of these "subjective truths" and outlining the truth-procedures he used to arrive at them. He rarely fails to recite this list in subsequent work, since it provides the reasoning behind his break with contemporary philosophy. Like his contemporaries, Badiou concurs in the universal nomination of Heidegger as the last comprehensive European philosopher, but he strongly dissents from the near-universal accord granted Heidegger's verdict that philosophy ends/fulfills itself in poetry. According to Heidegger, philosophy's destiny is now an "archi-esthetic" one. Badiou counters that when Heidegger wedded philosophy's fate to poetic destiny (culminating one line of Nietzschean thought), he set it toward "nihilistic closure" (*EE* Introduction)[10] and committed the error responsible for philosophy's current state of stagnation (see *L'être et l'événement* and *MPh* 69-77). Badiou, like some Benjaminian "destructive character" hastening to free us from a slackened body of thought now drained of its originary energy, is almost viscerally impatient to arrive at the far side of Heidegger's conceptual system.[11]

It is in this frame of mind regarding Heidegger that Badiou is seized by the first of his liberatory Truths: philosophy must get beyond its aesthetic turn. His plan of action has two wings: the first, a conservative one, calls for a "return to Plato"; the second, a radical one, has a more fundamental dictate in mind: he says that philosophy must be freed from its captivity by language-rules—rules that become mandatory only because philosophy has been made a local region or province of poetic language.

Badiou seeks liberation from language primarily for the sake of Being. As if in reply to Heidegger's "Why is there something rather than nothing?" Badiou argues that the German philosopher could not have answered his own ontological question because he submitted the thinking of Being so absolutely to language. To Badiou, the capital flaw in Heidegger's system (its "void") is its logocentric twinning of the poetic and philosophical vocations. A valuable void nonetheless, if it can be used to indicate a "way out" of the post-Heideggerian impasse and help reinvigorate philosophic productivity. The way out? Turn, Badiou admonishes philosophy, in an entirely new direction: away from the linguistic and toward the mathematical.[12]

This brings us to a second capital Badiouian Truth: that Being is not One. Language, for Badiou, is indissolubly linked to the thinking of the "One," the "one" that emerges only with and from language. This "one" is what Lacan called the "signifier,"[13] which lays the ground rules for (and the limitations on) the thinking of being. Badiou argues that since Being's real multiplicity cannot be thought from within the confines of language, we truly "think ontologically" only when the thought of Being is freed from the hegemony of a logic (*lógos*, language) that depends on the "One." Mathematics becomes thus the superior ontological tool—albeit not traditional mathematics. Only topology, an innovative formal mathematics, can tackle the problem of Being for it conceptually unmasks the essential falsity of equating Being with "One." To conceive Being as One depends, that is, on the illusion that counting begins with (0) → 1 and then goes on, incrementally, to infinity ∞. Topologically speaking, however, there is no "1": there is only a leap from nothing to all, from (0) → to (an "infinite") 2.

Thus the third major Badiouian "Truth": "Mathematics is the science of being qua being" (P&P 11). Lest we object (with Wittgenstein[14]) that mathematics is a form of logic and therefore falls under the same necessity (and the same laws) that rule language, Badiou invokes topology as a theory that enables us to divorce mathematics from logic. Classical mathematics counts Being from One, which, according to Badiou, reduces it to a branch of accounting, "a calculating disposition where thought no longer thinks . . . the sub[s]traction of thought in favor of a blind and technical potency of the rule."[15] Conversely, topology is a mathematics that does not "count from One" but "from Two." It works by means of graphic functions and algorithms rather than by calculation and measurement. Badiou deems topology superior to ordinary mathematized logic because its unified theory and method touches the heart of ontology: to begin with 0 and reach infinity is the same as finding the infinite potential in what is not (or the Being in non-being)—with the added appeal of overthrowing accepted rules and long-standing notions. As a further bonus, it also frees mathematics from the tasks of measuring and counting (i.e., from the division Descartes thought its very essence) in favor of algorithmic functions and comparative morphisms.[16] Mediation thus becomes unnecessary, as there are no measurable degrees or logical steps between 0 and ∞. Badiou will, indeed, propose to use topology to gauge innovation in politics, creativity in the arts and whatever else serves as a condition of thought (and support for thought is his paramount concern).

Since Badiou situates topology in the void between two modes of being, nothing and infinity, we can see why he believes it opens an entirely new manner of thinking in all domains (L&P 3; *EE* introduction). Topology becomes the exemplar of truth-procedures that have the power to alter states of thought (i.e., these being a priori obstacles to thought), and to transform them into the transitory situations or the discontinuous conditions where alone productive thinking occurs—and (multiple) Being as such emerges.

On the Uses and Abuses of Topology: Badiou, Lacan, and Freudian Psychoanalysis

On one level, Badiou seems to want the same thing Lacanian psychoanalysis does: to find a subjective truth there where only a void is apparent (a gap in discourse, a stumble, a failure). Badiou embraces Lacan as a comrade in arms, and he generously praises Lacan's topologization of verbal logic, which Badiou says opens "the possibility of a modern regime of the true . . . a history of truth finally *totally* disjointed from . . . exactitude, or adequacy" (BE 16).[17] Lacan's genius, according to Badiou, consists in his having been able, through topology, to divorce thought from its function as a measure and model of reality—since reality, for, Badiou lies elsewhere.

The rhetoric of a truth beyond "reality" is always compelling. Yet, doubts linger. For Badiou's "truth" and Lacan's turn out not to be exactly the same thing.

Lacan deployed topology, correctly, to infer what cannot be measured directly, that is, as a way to find the same thing Freud sought when he put to use gaps in his patients' speech: to indicate where something real (*jouissance*) was being left out of a symbolic arrangement. Lacan's algorithms of the paternal metaphor and the maternal metonym mark where the subject's inmost being is "enjoyed," although this enjoyment is radically unavailable for direct inspection—Lacan calls it the "impossible" in every discourse. The hypothesis is that an intangible, covert psychical object (a missing jouissance) is unconsciously held in common by interlocutors, implying thereby that the interlocutors are withholding their inmost "being" from their actual dialogue. But this "inner being" is strangely extimate, for in reality it is produced only by the discourse that takes place between subjects. Lacan marks as *(a)* the unconscious object in play in subjective intercourse (psychically unrepresented and unrepresentable) in his mathemes: object of envy, object of love, half void and half plenitude. The object *(a)* represents, in the unconscious, the subject's impossible fantasmatic enjoyment to itself (its death drive and its life force), while the signifier represents this subject to another signifier.

Devised to guide the analyst toward locating missing jouissance (mentally embodied in the subject's object *a*), Lacan's mathemes are supple and efficient tools for analyzing psychical configurations. But for Lacan the *(a)* is also implicated in sociosymbolic systems as well as in psychical ones, as the excess energy generated by the "turbines" of the signifying process (S17 92). Hence, he elaborates his mathemes into discourses: of the hysteric, the master, the university, and the analyst (and later, of the sadist and the capitalist).[18] In *Seminar* XX (Encore), Lacan terms these discourses "forms of the social tie" evolved to "treat *jouissance*"—to eliminate the excess drive-energy fortuitously sired by the very symbolic agreements designed to contain it.[19] When subjects attempt to drain off the excess effects/affects of the object *a* through speech, they are also inadvertently reproducing them. This by-product is never fully harnessed for social use; hence, the need to dispose of *(a)* energy otherwise: to prevent damage to the social "whole." But how? To deploy speech to resolve the residual (uncontained) energy in discourse inevitably creates yet more excess. Lacan's topology does not solve the problem; it only maps, as mathemes, the discourses that appear and reappear in (and as) familiar political, social, and amorous arrangements, each purporting to provide viable "solutions" to the *(a)* problem yet unable to do so fully.[20] This is perhaps fortunate; for if they do not resolve the excess, this also means that no social "whole" ever really exists. There are only discourses, each claiming to cover the whole while "social wholeness" is only fiction to which (Lacan is sadly aware) millions have been ruthlessly sacrificed.[21]

The *(a)* is thus subjective but also intersubjective for Lacan. The *(a)* of the algorithm mathematically marks its product or remainder; it is the hidden residue or product of relations between figures of the discourses, that is, of the subject and master; the analyst and patient, the teacher and student. Lacan invoked topology, then, chiefly to demonstrate where (and that) something has been "dropped out" of human discourse/intercourse; to describe obliquely how people act when they are responding to an internal, alien, and entirely unconscious element—fantasies of enjoyment that also seem to them (unconsciously) to be their "truth."

Badiou, in comparison, barely seems interested by how people are. He has virtually no stake (not even topological) in describing human foibles the way Lacan does. "How people are," we might even say, is Badiou's least concern, the very thing he is anxious to separate real thinking from. Badiou instead puts topology to speculative, rather than to descriptive-analytic use—in the service of thinking being where it has a future-oriented, creative function. Because topology can, according to Badiou, actually deduce the "indiscernible Truth" dimension of being, he refuses to limit its application to seizing the unavowed edges of an inter/subjective transaction, as Lacan uses it. Badiou deploys topology to think through the void (the nihilism) of everyday life, in search of some far shore where a New Life will begin for Thought—and for the Subject. To get there, quotidian existence (or everyday nihilism) must be burst open by the eruption of a creative void—a process to which topology alone holds the magic key.

To Badiou, rupture is the one thing with the power to move the Subject from the "void of the possible" to the "realization of the impossible." He therefore refuses to regard the void in discourse (Lacan's *a*) as a symptom of lost jouissance. Instead, Badiou's topology seeks to annul in advance any and all discursive resolutions of excess jouissance, in favor of entering directly into the void in and of extant symbolic systems—and putting the jouissance hidden there to productive use. He aims to open a field of jouissance that would not be the by-product of language,[22] and to do so not for some suffering individual's sake (as in a psychoanalysis), but for the sake of the dawning composite subject (the "Two"). The we concealed by its linguistico-logico splitting that only a topologized logic can disclose.

This brings me to the first crucial reservation I have regarding Badiou's special adaptation of psychoanalytic terms for his philosophy of revealed Truth: his desire to get beyond language. He systematically deploys Lacanian terms in an effort to dissuade psychoanalysis from its original objective, that is, to prod it away from the analysis of what *is* and of how people *are* (discovered by listening to what people say and fail to say), and shift its primary method to topology.[23] Likewise, he uses psychoanalysis to persuade philosophy to reorient itself toward unconscious, nonverbal thinking, independent of a verbal model of mathematic/scientific logic. Badiou, instead, counts on "unconscious thinking" to yield subjective truth through mathematically exact truth-procedures: "mathematics is precisely the thinking which has nothing to do with the experiences of consciousness. Thinking which has no relation to *reality*, but which is the knot of *letters* and the *real*" (P&P 10). He thus directs his own thinking toward the (topologically) productive power of the unconscious—productive *of* Truth. What he hopes to gain by entering into the void of conscious thought—without the assistance of language, and without aestheticizing it (as Deleuze, he complains, tends to do), is access to "Truth." He therefore alters considerably the twin concerns of psychoanalysis, the *knowledge* and the *truth* in unconscious thought, to favor more directly reaching a Truth beyond Knowledge.

Freud, let us recall, conceptualized "unconscious thoughts" as unspeakable and unavowable—but these thoughts contain a knowledge, a knowledge the subject conceals from itself, a knowledge of enjoyment. In Freud's "other scene" (the unconscious), jouissance troubles and pains the subject: it is the site of a singular subject's senseless suffering. The Freudian field comes to this unconscious site by way of the symptom and by way of a breach in a patient's discourse. The two, symptom and lapsus, each reveal a subjective Truth (jouissance, Lacan will call it) that insists beyond the reach of speech. But the analyst infers the nature of this Truth only by its manner of manifesting itself: as an organic anomaly in one case (symptom), or by absenting itself from speech in another (failed act or linguistic lapsus). Lacking direct access, the classical Freudian analyst deploys sophisticated rhetorical strategies to "construct" the barred truth, which is, let us be clear here, always the truth of a fantasy.[24] The analyst inverts a patient's narrative to make it state the opposite of what it openly claims, or she or he draws out allusions the patient's speech is unconsciously designed to mask. Freud calls such inferential language-work "constructions" and they form a kind of topological projection that can suggest the links missing in a signifying chain.[25] The Freudian starting point is with words and their failure, not absolute zero, not the absolute void.

Badiou's "unconscious thinking," in contrast, simply exists outside the regime of language and speech. In the void of the language-system, effervescent "affects of truth" well up. Badiou's unconscious, that is, contains nothing to be dreaded, for it is a pure aftermath of a critical Event that is not open to inspection, not susceptible to conscious recall, not dependent on painful traumas, and is reached exclusively through topology. His Subjective Truth (a truth of Being, not of Meaning) appears when and only when a void is inserted, by an Event, into discursive knowledge. For Badiou, the Real/Truth is to be discovered not by Freud's type of sophisticated verbal-rhetorical analysis, but by calibrating the subjective impact of an Event, and then topologically mapping the mental crater it leaves behind. Topology can grasp this Truth, Badiou believes, because methodologically it, too, begins with the void (zero; the philosophico-topological equivalent of the psychoanalytic unconscious): "For me the void, the void-set, is first of all the mathematical mark of being qua being. . . . Philosophy localizes the void as the condition of truth on the side of being *qua* being" (P&P 9).

Somewhat like Deleuze and Guattari, then, Badiou seems primarily concerned with the productive power of the unconscious—productive of Truth. No mere aftereffect of speech (as traumas and primal scenes in Freud and Lacan are), Badiou's Event makes a void in subjective life that is neither phenomenological/existential nor psychoanalytic in character. And this void is not a symptom produced by an inability to say; it is a positive place to begin making Truth count. Badiou insists: his void "*is not* that of consciousness, not Sartre's nothingness," it is a way of "thinking of the *effect of truth* outside conscious and reflexive production" (P&P 10).

While Badiou confers this exceptional privilege on unconscious thinking (P&P 10), he complains that "psychoanalysis localizes the void in the Subject" (P&P 9), making the knowledge of truth it yields too unique and individual. Psychoanalytic truth, the implication is, fails to attain the status of a universal, one of Badiou's cardinal criteria of Truth.[26] Badiou is thus not looking for the same "subjective truth" analysis is; he is looking for the universal truth-value (subjectively, i.e., collectively, acknowledged) of an unconscious thinking accessible only by a precise sequencing of truth-procedures. His mathematized logic thus goes against the grain of psychoanalytic logic, which he must significantly alter to place in the service of universal rather than singular, individual truths. He does not accept the way psychoanalysis deals with the universal through language and its excess.

An ontological comparison with Lacan's approach is now unavoidable. Lacan, too, positions being beyond words: the *parlêtre* is a *manque-à-être* (the speaking being is a want-to-be). For Lacan, however, there is no way back to the being from which language sunders the human animal—except in unconscious fantasy and its representative object (the object *a*). Lacan places the split that the signifier makes in the subject as one that comes between the subject's being and its meaning, that is, between being and the subject formed by language (only words can promise meaning).

Badiou, in contrast, marks the division of being at a different point: the break appears between a being-which-is and a being-in-progress—a being affirmatively not the retroactive effect of a linguistic signifier. The rupture accomplished by the signifier in Lacan becomes, in Badiou, a break achieved solely by the power of Evental Truth (a void in knowledge). "All theory consists of localizing the void which authorizes truth; of placing it, and of making an algebra and a topology of it" (P&P 11).

Badiou, though resonating with the Freudian–Lacanian unconscious, nonetheless gives that unconscious a philosophically positive spin. To the dark energies that brew there for Freud and Lacan, Badiou brings the light of mathematics—and it could even be said that he makes light of them. His unconscious is a source of luminescence without shadows, not a disturbing darkness; it is a genial, even congenial space where joys, "unequalled intensities of existence" (*E* 53), and "real fraternity" rather than individual suffering are at last experienced as truth, not merely as utopian fantasy (WTTC 4). Indeed, the way Badiou depicts Evental truth is reminiscent of Alfred de Vigny's "*Le Christ aux Oliviers*": an advent that cuts time "en deux parts, l'une esclave et l'autre libre" (into two parts, one enslaved, the other free). Truth divides the singularized, half subject (dominated by the One) from the multiple authentic Subject, which is Badiou says, a being-without-one. And it does so, according to Badiou, without resorting to the splitting-and-reconciling figures of language.

If unconscious thought is a "thinking which has no relation to *reality*, but which is the knot of *letters* and the *real*" (P&P 15), for Badiou the contours of this "*real*" (which he equates with Truth[27]) are easy to grasp (topologically) as the subjective truth of being as a "collective-multiple." But exactly why does Badiou choose the term *letter* here? Compare Lacan for whom the letter *(a)*, as the byproduct of the signifier, holds its own kind of "ontological" authority over the unconscious. Lacan's letter makes legible how the Real has impacted a particular human body: the analyst can trace where jouissance (the Real) has returned to the body from which it has been carved away by the signifier by reading its marks. On the body shaped by the signifier, that is, pockets of fantasmatic fullness appear where only symbolic loss had been inscribed. The signifier alters the organic body, substituting a linguistic logic for its original (*organic*) organization. However, the signifier can never fully eradicate "animal jouissance." Or, rather, the abolishing of animal jouissance produces the psychical fantasy that jouissance surreptitiously reenters the body (as "sex drive" and "death drive"). In Lacan, body and mind are coimplicated. Moreover, when Lacan designates the mark of the returned Real a "letter" of the body, it is first because it psychically resembles a mark physically stamped or engraved in a material matrix. But Lacan's letter of the body is also addressed—to an unknown Other (unconsciously).

Here Badiou seriously diverges. He concerns himself neither with the address of the letter nor with the embodied symptom that acts as its *facteur*/postman. Badiou's axiomatic faith in the letter derives less, that is, from Lacan (whose letter is also always "knotted" with the Real) than from his own stake in topologizing ontology, whose letters—not figures or words—form the backbone of the algorithm and the matheme. In Badiou, the letter is a purely formal mental cavity, hollowed out by an Event and now filled with Truth. In Lacan the body's letter is filled with excess jouissance; in Badiou its mental contents are a pure function of the truth: "an *excess beyond myself* induced by the passing through me of a truth," Badiou says (E 49). This excess is not the aftermath of speech, but the consequence of the insertion of a void. Through this void alone, Badiou tells us, do we attain happiness in love, joy in science, enthusiasm in politics, and pleasure in art (E 53).

Badiou's void is thus psychologically filled with excitement, exhilaration, joy; it is a space where the simple absence of signifying logic permits the jouissance/Truth of multiple-being to flower. Truth is a joy, however, that comes only after the Event (E 53). The advent of the void results from the Event's smashing impact on consciousness; the Event is thus supposed not to be an unconscious phantasm produced in an animal body by the rebound effect of the signifier's cutting and pruning. The inexplicable void in the heart of a system of thought, of language, of logic is not interjected *by* the signifier, but *despite* it, for Badiou. The void opens the Truth of that Event, which shatters the false hegemony of the One (God) the signifier brings in its wake—a One that is also the "Other." The reality of the void introduced by the Event, Badiou says, is "indiscernible" precisely because it is a rupture with the One and thus with knowledge. This "immanent" break alone permits thinking to begin (again—Badiou takes a long view; there is an eternal return, he says, to the process).[28] This explains why Badiou is more than eager to meet the void head-on, confident that the topological method will keep it a true void, that is, free of horror and pain (unlike the Freudian unconscious). In his theory, the positive outcome (happiness, joy, pleasure) of confronting the unconscious fully justifies his strict refusal of verbal-logic-as-we-know-it.

Yet, as Badiou makes unconscious thought the zero-point of thinking, he grows more at odds with the psychoanalytic conception of the unconscious as the site of the subject's specific kind of knowing (and even perverse enjoyment in knowing) what it does not want to know. Badiou's Event brings knowledge, but only the knowledge of a truth-in-progress, not of a prior traumatic encounter with a brutal Real. Badiou says: "For Lacan, the void is not on the side of being. I believe this is a crucial point of conflict" (P&P 9), and indeed, he once challenged psychoanalysis to debate with him the question, "Is there a logical subject?" (P&P 12). The Freudian-Lacanian patient, in contrast, is the subject not of "no-knowledge," but of an unconscious knowledge about the painful and guilty enjoyments obtaining in the unconscious, a knowledge she or he simply "does not want to know anything about." The subject of psychoanalysis, that is, is individualized by its peculiar desire not to know what it in fact already knows because in that knowledge lies its unavowable jouissance. The "multiple-Subject" for whose sake Badiou enters the unconscious is therefore the reverse of the classic psychoanalytic one. It arises in the void of thought from which the knowledge of an infinite, nonspecific Truth—the Truth of the Subject's infiniteness—flows. The effect of Badiou's vision recalls spiritual (albeit, as we know, atheistic) conversion.

The Freudian unconscious is indeed the site of a singular, unique knowledge recognized unconsciously by the analysand, but it is wrong to overlook that it is also produced as knowledge only collectively, through the work the patient does with the analyst who witnesses its effects. The knowledge gained in an analysis is a knowledge of the jouissance lodged in the unconscious, a jouissance that is unavowable pleasure and unbearable horror, in equal measure, staged in a fantasy scenario of a fulfillment that is impossible in everyday, social reality. The knowledge gained by "going there"—to the unconscious—comes at the cost of patients' realizing how much they take pleasure in their pain, or their learning that drive satisfaction is never an unalloyed gratification.

Consider this striking Freudian example, the case of Rat Man.[29] Here we can trace where the body and mind of a patient is unified at a single point where unconscious enjoyment defies (and belies) his conscious speech about pain. Freud listens to the Rat Man relate his horrible, tormenting fantasy of being gnawed by rats. While he speaks, however, Freud notices that

> at all the more important moments while he was telling his story his face took on a very strange, composite expression. I could only interpret it as one of *horror at pleasure of his own of which he himself was unaware*. . . . He broke off his story in order to assure me that these thoughts were entirely foreign and repugnant to him.[30]

The immediate sequel to the Rat Man's unwitting revelation of horrific enjoyment confirms the true (unconscious) addressee of his fantasized enjoyment: "'a person who was very dear to me' . . . the lady whom he admired."

Freud's passage demonstrates the way analytic procedures carry words into realms where they cannot really go, or as Lacan put it, the way psychoanalysis aims at finding out why "in the spoken or written word, something stumbles."[31] The reward for such painful work is this: the analysand learns the truth about his subjective truth—that the jouissance tormenting him (with its mixture of "horror at pleasure") is not really his own. It is instead the Jouissance of a tyrannical, cruel, or abusive Other, compelling bloodthirsty sacrifices as commands with which the subject unconsciously yet unfailingly complies. The analysand's fantasized enjoyments seemingly impel his words and acts, but these are in fact not his own enjoyments: they are remote-controlled by the ghostly/ghastly Other. The subject unconsciously addresses this Other (here the "lady"), offering up its own pain, and sacrificing its own pleasures, in elaborate fantasy scenarios of seduction or castration. The subject, that is, "enjoys" not for its own sake, but in order to satisfy the Other's demand for Jouissance.[32] Analysis then goes about deconstructing the patient's "address" to the fantasmatic Other by deploying the signifier, and releasing jouissance-energy for alternative, and hopefully creative uses.

Badiou proposes to deal with unconscious subjective truth in a completely different way, by treating it with shortcuts that dispense with the analytic partnership. He would first alter the reality that sets off suffering by simply abolishing the Other topologically, that is, by refuting the logic of the One. The destruction of the One will then produce an entirely new mode of unconscious (prized by Badiou as the real effect of the Event of a Truth), by freeing it from the meander of the verbal address. Once out from under the illusion of a dominating One, the Badiouan unconscious becomes immune to abusive mystifications about the power of the overwhelming Other. Liberation will come, thus, not at the end of a long analysis, but will arrive automatically with the Subject's birth to presence. The Subject (as a $[-1]$) will be born only through the Event of Truth, the truth of its multiplicity, its nonsingleness.

Topology, providing the mathematical proof that Being is not One, is therefore, in Badiou's opinion, the surest route to rendering the unconscious habitable: it liberates the Subject from unconscious submission to the One (and consequently, to the Other). Bear in mind that the Subject of the unconscious is neither the end point/by-product of discourse, as in Lacan, nor the effect of repression, disavowal, and denegation, as in Freud. The Badiouan Subject is in no way formed by the dynamic tension between the laws of language and logic, speech and the drives. Instead, Badiou quite simply thinks (or tries to think) the Subject outside the laws of logic and language.

For most of us, such a fully outlaw Subject would be unthinkable, wrenching. Badiou nonetheless paints its portrait so genially and enthusiastically as to make it (and the process of reaching it) seem serenely uncomplicated.

In both theory and in practice, Badiou's Event exists less for the sake of the suffering subject than for the sake of philosophy (in the long run, his principal concern). Subduing the unconscious formed by the division of language and of sex (the Freudian unconscious) and replacing it with the void created by the Event of Truth is meant less to cure than to reward the (renewed) Subject with a "next" type of unconscious: a permanent void permitting fresh creation to take place in perpetuity. "Mathematics is the veritable apparatus of localisation of the void," he writes (P&P 11). For the properly formalized (topologized) Subject, Badiou sees the void opening on to a New Age (overtones intended), an age of "fraternity" (L&P 4). By refusing to restrict his truth-procedures to the difficult pathway that psychoanalysis forges through language and its repressed silences, Badiou de facto valorizes the rupture installed Eventally and grasped mathematically as a better way to refresh the Subject and "make room" for new creation.

Philosophic borrowings from the psychoanalytic unconscious are not entirely new to philosophy (think of Will James's *Varieties of Religious Experience*), but the desire to set the unconscious to work in the service of productivity is more commonly found among poets and artists, like the early-twentieth-century Surrealists for whom language (including its other face, the unsayable) was held as common cause. Still, Badiou remains philosophically consistent. His interest in unconscious thinking is fundamentally driven by his scientific desire to place the unconscious fully within the compass of a unified mathematical method (topology) and his philosophical desire to get beyond the limits, the suffering and the guiltiness of language—Heideggerian guilt.[33] To achieve this, the discoveries of Freudian psychoanalysis do not inspire him as they did Lacan. His distinctively antianalytic, militantly heroic style indicates the difference: "Let us posit *our* axioms. There is no God. Which also means: the 'One' is not. The multiple 'without-one' . . . is the law of being" (*E* 25). Another example:

> A truth punches a "hole" in knowledges, it is heterogeneous to them, but it is also the sole known source of new knowledges. We shall say that the truth *forces* knowledges. The verb *to force* indicates that since the power of a truth is that of a break, it is by violating established and circulating knowledges that a truth returns to the immediacy of the situation. . . . If a truth is never communicable as such, it nevertheless implies, at a distance from itself, powerful reshapings of the forms and referents of communication. (*E* 70)

Badiou's upbeat philosopher is primed to confront head-on the challenge the void presents, poised to plunge into it topological apparatus in hand, exploiting its thoughts for the immediacy of Truth. As Buffon knew, style is the man, and Badiou's forceful[34] assertions betray the appreciable distance between him and the gingerly psychoanalyst, delicately working through the imbalance between representations of Words and Things in a patient's unique and singular unconscious.

It should by now be clear, I imagine, that I see no real way to reconcile Badiou's philosophico-mathematical truth procedures with psychoanalytic ones, wherein language is paramount and coming to know an unconsciously acknowledged, but unavowable truth is the aim. Badiou's goals superficially resemble those of psychoanalysis (creating a virtual portal into the experience of jouissance and gaining a unique knowledge of it). However, Badiou's "thinking being unconsciously" is simply not the way of language. Moreover, the jouissance he hopes to find there is an unalloyed joy, unmixed with pain, shame, or fear, as in Freud. One is thus left to ponder how and why he seems so bent on joining the two fields and why he so insistently recalls Freud's "other scene" whenever he conjures up a "new scene of representation" where topology will resolve key human dilemmas.

Of the Freudian Unconscious, and Badiou's

Badiou says that "the void is the destiny of any event" (P&P 9). Like that of the Freudian unconscious, his void is a space where traditional linguistic rules and philosophy no longer hold sway. A site, therefore, of adventure: Badiou takes the terrain of the unconscious as a place to flex his mathematized logic's muscular strength and to sound a call to courageous action. But didn't Freud, too, characterize the unconscious geographically as an unknown country into which he would lead "his people"?[35] Yes, but Freud believed its space was not an empty void. What dwells in this unlit land are hounds from Hell, demons demanding the subject's blood, vampiric guilts from which analysis tries to liberate the patient enslaved by them.[36] In contrast, Badiou's unconscious is strangely luminous; a creative space where the "happiness of love," the "joy of science," the "enthusiasm of politics," and the "pleasure of art" flower (E 53). For him, lunging into the void of thought poses no risk to sanity: if one is armed with topology rather than puny linguistic logic alone, the unconscious can be entered and conquered, and its fruits enjoyed. Despite Badiou's disclaimers as to its indiscernible vacuity, great rewards (happiness, joy, truth-jouissance) seem to be hidden there in the void once it is (topologically) freed from domination by the One (and the Other).

Badiou plays the bold hero, zealously forging ahead into uncharted territory (the void, the unconscious) to map and mine its resources, a hero who can prepare this ground for habitation by the new (multiple) Subject, who will have no need of the talisman of words to protect him from the destruction the unconscious harbors. Its dangers will have been nullified in advance by mathematical "formalization" (WTTC 11),[37] and Badiou's philosopher-mathematician's exertions are intended to realize an "ideal of formalisation [sic]" (P&P 10) that universalizes truths for its subjects, their truth as the "multiple subject," the "subject without one." Formalization can dispense with the psychoanalytic tactic of introducing the organizing principle of a new linguistic signifier to quell unconscious horrors, since the Event neutralizes the horror in advance. For Badiou, then, the stake in entering the void is not the risk of meeting up with abominations; it is, rather, the gamble of figuring out how to think starting from absolute nothing. Or, rather, to restart thinking—which to Badiou is exactly the same thing as thinking. Badiou's bet, not unlike Pascal's wager, turns the void into a positive locus where unnecessary (i.e., linguistic) constraints on the thought and action of a Subject too "logically" defined are purged and stripped away.

Such tabula rasae appear from time to time in the history of philosophy, and more perniciously in human social history as well. They are not, of course, the only way of thinking about the subject, and they are assuredly not the Freudian way. But the infectious enthusiasm now spreading internationally for Badiou's philosophy shows how strongly the dream of "new beginnings" and of effacing the past maintains its attractiveness for our philosophy. We must not, nonetheless, mistake Badiou's rupturing, annihilating Events for those great personal and collective shocks experienced throughout the twentieth century (the Holocaust in particular, but also the nuclear). His shattering Events are never history's horrors; they are merely the key turning points in the chronicles of philosophy—the latest of these being the "event of mathematics" (L&P 1). Although this wrenching, obliterating Event has the same absolute power to disrupt thought and memory for Badiou's we-subject, it is not a trauma in a Freudian sense, where present and past are imbricated. Rather, the value in the Event (to which Badiou ascribes productive and speculative power—the power to restart thought) lies in its ability to break with both the past and with current opinions alike; to disrupt daily routines, and most importantly, to fracture philosophical assumptions and givens. Would disconnecting thought from its painful traumatic determinations and the human tragedies that produced it, have a blessed side? Perhaps that is on Badiou's mind as he seeks to substitute a mathematics that thinks outside conscious and reflexive production for this wretched state of human affairs, a mathematics that he would have automatically demythify consciousness (and the unconscious) formed on the model of the One (or the big Other). A Mathematics that thinks in the unconscious destroys in advance the myth of the Other/One for whose benefit the subject suffers.

How innocent it seems. Yet, Badiou's desire to think "outside conscious and reflexive production" (P&P 10) is certainly open to distressing interpretations (thinking "with the blood," for example), and could readily be construed as a return of irrationalism or mysticism. After all, the dream of thinking unconsciously has a long and unfortunate history in religion, romanticism, and fascism, all of which found it attractive for reasons ranging from the perceived virtues of an extreme spiritualism (opposing dull, ordinary life), to the promise of a final solution to the mind-body split. A similar aura lingers around Badiou, although he would vigorously disavow it. To him, thinking "outside conscious and reflexive production" chiefly betrays his personal and theoretical impatience with mediation—dialectical, verbal, and mathematical: his haste to get to what he calls an "other scene" that follows after the Event. Topological procedures that dispense with the long, wordy process of individual treatment (*cure*) can directly "tear away . . . truth from consciousness" (P&P 10).

It remains difficult to reconcile Badiou's very positive inflection of the unconscious, knowledge, and Truth with his unflagging praise for the great contribution psychoanalysis has made to (his) philosophy, a psychoanalysis that does not view the unconscious so positively.[38] He readily concedes that psychoanalysis is incompatible with his work so long as psychoanalytic theory and practice remain configured as they currently are. But if their common ground is not to cure individuals, nor to offer a method for analyzing the human world taken as it is, where does Badiou see them linked? Even Rousseau, a real revolutionary, felt that in order to reach a new plane of thought he had to "take men as they *are* and the laws as they *might be*." Badiou consistently takes leave of laws (verbal, logical) as they are, in favor of men as they might be.[39] For Badiou, I believe, the important thing is not simply to access the unconscious, but to solve it: to solve once and for all the problem of unconscious suffering (the oppression by the Other-who-is-the-One). And to solve it in the simplest possible way: mathematically.

A closer look at Badiou's "Other Scene," the "new scene of representation" that comes after-the-rupturing Event, is now inescapable. For it should not be forgotten that in *Seminar VII* Lacan calls the region (toward which Badiou with all due diligence speeds) "the space of destruction," the realm where the impossible (the Real, Death, and Death Drive) resides. Badiou is openly inspired by *Seminar VII*, although he envisions his other scene as a promised land of the impossible suddenly become possible, and as a space that permits something new to come into play. He is, indeed, supremely confident that the Subject arriving at this other scene will find no trace of pain, guilt, or torment, for its destructiveness will already be mathematically defused.

Nonetheless, Badiou and psychoanalysis do cross, in the sense of an important encounter rather than being at loggerheads, not in his philosophy but, ironically, in his aesthetic attitude. To assert this is, I realize, completely counterintuitive, given Badiou's acute wish to demolish the aesthetic turn in philosophy. It now remains for me to argue the case more fully.

Destruction: The Scene of the Real—and of Creative Sublimation

Badiou calls his face-off with the void an "encounter with the Real," though he does not use the Real in quite the same way Lacan does. For Lacan, the Real lies outside the limits of the law[40]—the law of the signifier and of the social arrangements that follow in its wake. The Real, Lacan says, "suffers from the signifier" (S7 134) and yet (as he points out in *Seminar VII*), we would have no concept of the 'beyond' (where the Real appears) were it not for the Law: "Is the Law the Thing? Certainly not. Yet I can only know of the Thing by means of the Law. . . . Without the Law the Thing is Dead" (S7 83). The Real that the Subject seems to experience is the real of its drives, which nonetheless are only an afterimage of the Law.[41] Lacan's Real (which he calls the "impossible"—impossible for human consciousness to apprehend) appears thus on the side of blank Nature and Death—on the side, that is, of everything that constitutes a heroic provocation for Badiou. Philosophical mathematics is to be the Event that forces entry into Truth and cuts short the need to struggle with imperfect linguistic-symbolic instruments. It can force the Real to become habitable reality. Thus, where in Freud and Lacan a major lapse in logic and in the law of the signifier surrenders the subject to the force of the drives and leads to dangerous subjective collapse, for Badiou this moment is the prize: supreme Truth value. Badiou believes the Real-as-the-Impossible is precisely what must be compelled to become possible. In other words, Badiou wants to drive what has driven us, seizing its energies for other purposes.

Badiou's fantasy—of reaching the end point of the signifying chain in a minimally threatening way—was already tellingly described by Lacan in *Seminar VII*. Lacan says that wherever a subject dreams about the disappearance of the signifying chain, that is precisely where Death Drive makes its entrance:

> As soon as we have to deal with anything in the world appearing in the form of the signifying chain, there is somewhere, though certainly outside of the natural world, which is the beyond of that chain, the *ex nihilo* on which it is founded and is articulated as such. . . . It is there, too, that destruction is registered, that it enters into the register of experience. (S7 210)

It is no small irony that what Lacan has to say about this drive to end the reign of lógos, of the One, of the signifier and of linguistic logic reveals that Death Drive (the principal architecture of the space of destruction) is ultimately only a "creationist sublimation." The call to destroy everything built by the work of language, Lacan says, is always a ruse, a dissimulated stratagem of creativity, a self-deception that enables one to tap the unbound energies of Drive-as-destruction in the interest of introducing something new into the world.

Ex nihilo: out of the void. The "destructive" wish to nullify the signifying chain and all that is (the result of that chain) is even doubly ironic, for the will to destroy, the willingness to put signification to death, is a will that could never exist without the signifying chain it attacks. Lacan says the Will to Destruction, to radical rupture, to confrontation with the Real (an encounter the subject of language makes every effort to miss) remains a pure "function of the signifier":

> Death drive . . . is the dimension introduced as soon as a historical chain gets isolated, and the history presents itself as something memorable and memorized in the Freudian sense, namely, something that is registered in the signifying chain and dependent on its existence. . . . If everything that is immanent or implicit in the chain of natural events is considered to be subject to the so-called death drive it is only because there is a signifying chain. (S7 212)

By "registered" in the signifying chain Lacan does not refer to what is actively, historically recalled; he is referring to what is remembered only unconsciously: the jouissance lost to that chain and obscured by it. We might say that Death Drive forges an imaginary supplement to a brute Real by denying that it is itself only one more link in the signifying chain, by pretending it is the beyond of signification.

"Will to destruction. Will to make a fresh start. Will for an Other-thing," Lacan says (S7 212).

When Death drive hides its dependence on the signifier, it hides from itself its real purpose, which is to make new production possible rather than impossible. I propose to locate Badiou's Subject here, at the dreamed-of scene of destruction, at the end point to the whole history of language and thought—here where jouissance (Badiou's "affects of truth") get "registered." Lacan again:

> *Jouissance* presents itself as buried at the center of a field that has the characteristics of inaccessibility, obscurity and opacity; moreover the field is surrounded by a barrier which makes access to it difficult for the subject to the point of inaccessibility because *jouissance* appears not purely and simply as the satisfaction of a need but as the satisfaction of a drive.... It is there, too, that destruction is registered, that it enters into the register of experience. (S7 210)

Yet one more irony: Lacan tells us that the aim of reaching the plane of Death Drive is not even really to unearth the jouissance buried by the signifier. It is actually to "introduce into the natural world the organization of the signifier" (S7 214). To make new art, new poetry. For Lacan, at the heart of all modern ethics and aesthetics lies a ruse of the creative impulse, which always claims to overthrow the regime of the signifier, the word, and the One to secure a jouissance barred by them, but that only succeeds in adding new signifiers to the chains that bind. Death Drive, then, only seems to banish reflection and differential thinking, for all the while it is in fact dissimulating the (re)introduction of thought into the world—a "thought" that is "actualized" in the world "in the intervals introduced by the signifier" (S7 214).

Intervals, divisions, distinctions, categorizations, cuts: everything the differential structure of the signifier requires. These logical divisions and linguistic rulings have evoked the chief ethical and aesthetic reactive responses of modern thought. Transgressing what is becomes necessarily a ride aboard Death Drive, a risk undertaken solely for the sake of new creation (S7 109). A cardinal feature of creative/destructive Death Drive, Lacan tells us, is its persuading the Subject that there is no given being, no "*il y a*."[42] It promotes the illusion that the slate can be wiped entirely clean of whatever already "exists," the illusion that one can begin afresh from zero and not from One. In art, Lacan finds examples plentiful, and takes his first illustration from the caves at Altamira, where successive layers of paintings by various artists of different epochs all depict the same thing—each drawn over the last: "Every appearance of this way of proceeding consists in overthrowing the illusory operation [of historicity] so as to return to the original end" (S7 139). For the artist, this "original end" is the testing of his individual power to render aesthetically his encounter with the Thing: "It's as if," Lacan says, "in a consecrated spot it represented, for each subject capable of undertaking such an exercise, the opportunity to draw or project afresh what he needed to bear witness to, and to do so moreover over what had already been done before" (S7 139). The artistic impulse is thus a creative contradiction: to begin again is also to destroy. Badiou's inspiration in Lacan grows somewhat clearer.

Lacan updates his Paleolithic example of the aesthetic impulse by combining it with an ethical impulse visible in the troubadours of courtly love poetry and in the writings of Sade. The courtly love poet, wishing at all costs to start afresh, provisionally deprives himself of language (the usual poetic words, the common symbolic weapons ordinarily at his disposal) by falling in Love. To express this Love, the old words are useless; he must forge new symbols. Why? to murder the Thing, for the symbol is the murder of the Thing. Is the Thing his Lady? No, not really. He must aim toward her, at what lies beyond her, in the field of the Real; he must confront the Thing She (the Lady) both represents and dissimulates. She serves to blind him to his own true aim, which is precisely to miss his aim, to avoid encountering the Thing. Thus is new (love) poetry born.

Located in the heart of the field of Destruction, Woman is the "Thing" that shows itself as the beyond of the regime of the signifier—and yet she is also the object defined by the signifier even in its apparent absence: an "object," Lacan says, that is "raised to the dignity of the Thing." Hers is a "beauty" that, even in the experimental voiding of the signifier, still functions like the signifier. It is a barrier against the horror of the Thing and against the desire to go directly to Destruction: "Beauty disarms desire" (S7 238).

Lacan analyzes Sade's ethics in the light of his esthetics. Sade, for his part, attempts the opposite of the courtly poet, that is, to exercise his powers on behalf of the Thing. Bent toward "destruction," Sade openly condemns the signifier for what it is: a "creationist" cover, an artificial device for mastering the Thing, and a theological ruse of the One. Sade, who is opposed to mastery and curses the idea of God, valorizes the Natural cycle of destruction (followed by new creation) over the signifier. Sade even calls for Natural Laws to overthrow merely human ones. Yet, bizarrely enough, Lacan notes that even Sade did not dispense entirely with the device of the beautiful Lady—his victims are always exquisite, unblemished.

But when Badiou hastens to the site where the One is to meet its demise, the other scene, we find something else. Here, no logical signifier—and no Lady—materialize to inspire or limit the process of "creative destruction." For Badiou the destruction suffices in itself to prepare a rich New Life for the Subject, as entering the void of thought (voided of the linguistic rule of the One) permits contact with creative powers capable of destroying whatever is in favor of thinking what might be. Purest revolution without a history, only a future. Badiou urges "the invention of a *possibility*" (P&P 6), naming the truth-process he champions a "search for an absolutely new possibility" (P&P 6).

Lacan's own psychoanalytic ethics remain bounded by language and its aftereffects (the real Real from which its subject suffers). Badiou stipulates to something else. What counts, Badiou says, is

> the possibility of the impossible, which is exposed in every loving encounter, every scientific refoundation, every artistic invention, and every sequence of emancipatory politics, is the sole principle—against the ethics of living well whose real content is the deciding of death—of an ethics of truths. (E 39)

Hence, Badiou's complaint that "psychoanalytic thinking would aim at the *Subject accommodating its real*. . . . For psychoanalysis, the relation to the Real is always in the end *inscribed in a structure*" (P&P 6)—in the very structures Badiou would shake down in the interest of innovative, real Truth. Real Truth, Badiou tells us, "disorganizes" the human animal (E 60); it is an explosive truth that shakes off animal, sexual, humanity in favor of the "joyful or enthusiastic clarity of the seizing [by truth which] becomes a matter of finding out if, and how, I am to continue along the path of vital disorganization" (E 60).

Compare Lacan, for whom "vital disorganization" is the original effect of the introduction of the signifier that divests the "animal" of its organic composition, substitutes for it the logic of language and whose excision of jouissance becomes the cause of the subject. For Badiou, by contrast, it is the event of the Truth (and not the advent of the signifier) that is the cause of the Subject. His vital disorganization is aimed against the symbolic organizations into which (for Lacan) the human subject is required to fit itself once its being is shattered by the signifier: the symbolic orders of kinship, gender, and linguistic systems.[43] When the Lacanian Real returns to disorganize the subject of the signifier, it is not a pretty sight. To Badiou, however, disorganization is its own reward: the Evental Truth.

In another domain—religion—we would call Badiou a "charismatic," preaching the intense experience of a spiritual conversion and a decision to be faithful to the Truth of that experience. His terms are often very close to religious vocabulary (recall Will James's defining the unconscious as "shortcuts in the brain"; hidden forms of a rationality operating so rapidly without conscious awareness that no memory of them remains.) But I would maintain that the real passion animating Badiou, and which, despite its trappings, is not technically religious, is the aesthetic passion: a passion for creation. Only on the aesthetic plane does there exist a space where violence, destruction, the breakdown of logic, and the rejection of all that has gone before are without real and tragic consequences. Only in the artwork is the "signifier permeated with *jouissance*" (S7 53) of the sort Badiou apparently believes is accessed by mathematics alone.

Of course, Badiou would never want to consider his philosophical passion to be aesthetic—even though he is himself an accomplished playwright and published novelist. The Platonic and anti-Heideggerian strain in Badiou would hardly grant the aesthetic the very power over philosophy's thinking being that his colleagues easily concede. And yet, there is something in his relation to the aesthetic that remains as resistive and as ambivalent as his relation to psychoanalysis. Badiou, after all, does make "art" one of his four fundamental conditions of thought, although he does not consider any individual work of art (something done, a part of the *il y a*) to be of any particular consequence for thought. Badiou seems rather more bent on distinguishing his brand of productive-destruction from the simple act of "putting a new signifier into the world" (e.g., an artwork that circulates among subjects like the signifier). He aims, so to speak, well beyond the signifier, and directly at the Event, which becomes for him the bearer of a jouissance beyond the reach of the One," a supplement to mere life—and also its source.

The other name of this supplement remains what Lacan called it: death drive. What distinguishes Badiou from the many denizens of the space of destruction, sadists and artists, however, is that the latter all managed to make a place for a feminine Thing in the field of the Subject's "creationist sublimation" where "She" serves doubly as the Thing and as its opponent, the signifier. Badiou does not want to go it alone in the field of destruction, and he clearly wants the protection the collective we-subject provides. But Woman is not a crucial component of that we-subject. The question is why not? Where has Badiou done with her?

Badiou and Sexuality: "Multiple Subject" against "Woman"?

> So I shall simply say that as far as love is concerned, it can be established that sexual pleasure [*jouissance*] as such is inaccessible to the power of the truth (which is a truth about the two).
> —Alain Badiou, *Ethics*

One might easily have imagined Badiou's we-subject would turn out to permit the recognition of a female component and make a place for it. But, to Badiou, accepting the fact of sexual division is to acquiesce to formal/sexual division by language that only diminishes his Subject. His Subject's real Truth is that it is a "more than one": a "'we'-subject" (WTTC 3), because it is without One, and the logical division of the sexes, he believes, depends on the linguistic One (the phallus). He criticizes the individualism of psychoanalysis as formed around the One. ("The goal of Freud or Lacan is to *think* the singularity of the human subject. Of the human subject confronted on the one side by language, on the other by sexuality," Badiou writes [P&P 5]). But his critique of the singular human subject of psychoanalytic practice is that it is at best, only "half" a Subject, a linguistic-subject produced by the splitting power of language. Which means he must reject the sexual division that (per Lacan) gives this hemi-subject its sexual position.

Badiou critiques psychoanalysis for needlessly limiting the scope of its considerable ability to "reduce the symptom" (P&P 6) for the benefit of a single individual, believing that if psychoanalysis were to focus less on the cure for the nugatory singular human subject, it would find a more universal cure for the subject's painful social/sexual singleness than mere talk. He aims instead at producing a new subject who

> is just the new man, who emerges at the point of lack of self. The individual is then, by his very essence, the nothing that must be dissipated within a we-subject. The affirmative reverse of this sacrificial evidence of the individual is that the "we" that a truth constructs, of which the new man is the support as well as the stake, is itself immortal.[44]

Self-sacrifice? Diderot's definition of virtue comes to mind ("*Qu' est-ce que le vertu? . . . le sacrifice de soi-même*" [What is virtue? . . . one's own sacrifice]). Maybe. But Badiou demands more: the sacrifice of the individual *to* the collective for the sake of its true being (i.e., the truth that the subject is more-than-itself, the "we-Subject"). Badiou insists his is a "thought that is both a-religious and genuinely contemporary with the truths of our time" (*E* 25), and he remains confident that there is no "dark god" in his system to whom this demand to sacrifice one's singularity is made. To him, the sacrifice of the individual simply supports the miraculous transformation of One into the "the multiple 'without-one,'" which is its true "law of being" (*E* 25).

This "law of being" will void all prior numerical hypotheses regarding the definition of human being as singular or capable of coalition with others like and unlike itself. And it necessarily also puts the lie to all prior sexual narratives that regard human sexual union as Love.

In the first case, Badiou's ethics of the possible, his "truth in progress" and the Truth of the multiple-Subject are not supported by an ethics of alterity. Badiou rejects Levinas (and all liberal-ethics') espousal of the notion of an "infinite alterity" in humanity, on the grounds that even alterity is too singularized, a ruse of the One: "Infinite alterity is quite simply *what there is*" (*E* 25). Badiou believes instead that the authentic we-Subject requires recognizing the other as the same as you, and as part of the same, greater whole: he terms it the difficult truth of "*recognizing the Same*" (*E* 25). He is unafraid that his dream of unity is critiqued and demystified in the light of the events of World War II. What safely transforms "nothing" into "the many" for him is simply the very thing that transforms the fearsome Other into the lovable Same: mathematized logic, the overthrow of the reign of the One (God, the Big Other, etc.)

The psychoanalyst could never be confident of such miracles. Nor should the utter absence of sexuality, in Badiou's creative space of destruction, so devoid of a feminine figure (devoid of the Woman who remains there even for Sade!) escape psychoanalytic scrutiny. And yet, theoretically, Badiou is entirely consistent where Woman is concerned. He would consider her absence a result of the rigorous application of his logic of resisting the rule of the One and as proof of the hidden presence of a multiple subject that has nothing to do with alterity and difference, including sexual difference. (In Badiou the unconscious is not sexually delimited and thus neither is the Subject.)[45]

Her specific absence follows inevitably from his decision for mathematized logic and for multiple-being, but it also follows from his deepest mathematical wish: to solve the problem of sex—the problem that Lacan posed as "there is no sexual *relation*."

Indeed, we might think of Badiou as taking the "relation" in sex in a strictly mathematical sense ("relation" mathematically means a 1:1 correspondence). When we do, we find that one of his prime hypotheses is that the lack of relation is quite likely the result of Woman's persisting to exist. Badiou openly wonders, for example, if Woman does not constitute the chief obstacle to overthrowing the rule of the One, to reaching the purity of the Same. He asks:

> Is the Philosophical Idea of the One linked to the fantasy of the Woman? Isn't the main obstacle to the death of God, as moreover Nietzsche thought, to be found on the side of feminine *jouissance*? (P&P 11)[46]

At this point, Badiou and I begin to part company.

I would never say that Badiou is wrong to dis-solve feminine specificity, feminine jouissance, the feminine Thing, any more than I would say that the direction contemporary Lacanian Schools of thought (which often resonate well with Badiou) have followed since Lacan's death is "wrong." Who am I, a mere woman, to question the mathematical-masculist bearing of this thinking, to whose muscular exertion all sexes seem so strongly attracted these days. (Can woman's speech count in Badiou's math?) After all, I myself had the first impression of Lacan that his was a partisan-masculine bent. Fresh from reading Freud as well as Derrida, I had dived into Lacan's *Facteur de la Vérité*, and surfaced from it thinking that here was a very Christian reading of Freud and that Lacan was a Pauline misogynist who seemed to be saying "Boys will be boys" with an indulgent laugh. I very quickly came to realize, however, that my first impression was mistaken and superficial. The more I read Lacan, the more nuanced his treatment of women appeared to be, and the more his astute ability to read Freud and to reanalyze his cases revealed itself. So did his deep understanding of how people are—including women. (I am thinking of his superb revision of Freud's "Little Hans" in *Seminar IV*.[47]) I also quickly came to value Lacan's ability to increase Freud's interpretative powers. Lacan, for all his formalism, for all his topologization has, I would say, added his great knowledge of human relations to Freud's.

Lacan especially, I think, increases our power to understand what Woman signifies. Even more than Freud, Lacan listened for woman to make herself heard, he listened for woman's speech. As I began to hear Lacan speaking up on behalf of the feminine subject, invoking her beyond the limits of the maternal and of the hysterical, I began to hear a Lacan challenged by the hysteric's muteness regarding the other scene (the unconscious), the stage on which her real passions were being played out:

> Analysis is not a matter of discovering in a particular case the differential feature of the theory and in doing so believe that one is explaining why your daughter is silent—for the point at issue is to *get her to speak*.[48]

Such lines as these echoed through me. When I finally was able to read *Seminar VII*, I found a "Ladies' Way" to connect Lacan back to Freud (has there ever really been a more thorough reader of Freud?) and to the great literary figures his writing always brought to my mind.

When I read Lacan on Courtly Love, certain special authors—Rousseau, Stendhal, Duras—came back to me. I did not read Lacan as attacking courtly love poetry and its Lady, as Ford Madox Ford and Denis de Rougemont and Elaine Marks and Slavoj Žižek do. (For Lacan "its central point was an erotics" [S7 145]; one may read how I grasped Lacan in my "Love Outside the Limits of the Law" mentioned at the start of this chapter.) Granted, the Lady of courtly love is the ultimate in creationist sublimation, an overestimated love-object for a poet trying to get his productive engines revving again. Yet, what Lacan brought to my attention as forcefully as his French forebears Rousseau and Stendhal never did, was the perspective of the Lady, a perspective that her poetic sublimation hides and that the foolish poet tries to scribble about without understanding it in the least. This feminine perspective includes her particular, unique sexuality, her enjoyment, her feminine jouissance. Lacan charmingly reads the deferrals and delays that the Lady demands of her poet-lover as providing the masculine subject a way to deal with her Thing-ness (by avoiding her though the poetic detour) and he reads them as her feminine request for foreplay, for slowing down the sexual act, to enable her jouissance. And this feminine jouissance of which Lacan will tell us more in *Seminar XX*, is precisely not the phallic jouissance (of the idiot, the self, the same).

The condition of politics (of the we-Subject beyond political difference), and the condition of Love (of the we-Subject beyond sex) are theoretically underwritten by Badiou's topologized theory. He (and many a woman, too) denounces the rule of the phallogocentric One, a denunciation that topologically leads to her radical deletion. It seems we must now decide about this new version of doing away with Woman, a way which, ironically, starts from beyond the phallus—there where She is so often presumed to dwell. But does Badiou's fraternal we-Subject escape being shaped by the feminine Thing even as it excludes it?

THE REGIME OF THE "WE": OR, FRATERNAL POLITICS AND THE ART OF LOVE

> Any authentic subjectification is collective; . . . any vigorous intellectuality implies the construction of a we . . . a subject is necessarily a historical subject . . . which resonates in its composition, the power of an event.
> —Alain Badiou, "What Do You Think of the Twentieth Century?

> The Immortal that I am capable of being cannot be spurred in me by the effects of communicative sociality, it must be directly seized by fidelity. That is to say: broken, in its multiple-being, by the course of an immanent break, and convoked, finally, with or without knowing it, by the eventual supplement. To enter into the composition of a subject of truth can only be something that happens to you.
> —Alain Badiou, *Ethics*

Badiou's we-Subject is a "new man—anti-predicative, negative and universal."[49] Unlike the subject found at the end of an analysis, sobered by a fleeting glimpse of its own unconscious, the "new man" is a collective Subject, a "multiple-being," a "being 'without one'" (*E* 25): a nonphallic being. Yet, it is no accident that the operative term here is the generic *man*. It is not feminine, but it is a Subject who lives on (and even thrives) in the ruins of its destroyed (phallic) Being; it is a Subject at home in the field of creative-destructive Death Drive. Badiou's reasons for calling on the generic man is both to gesture dismissively toward the individual (an inauthentic one produced by counting/accounting) and especially toward the sexed individual psychoanalysis stubbornly continues to address. To Badiou, the singular subject fractured by logic produces a malignant unconscious rather than a productive void. He looks beyond the reach of the One (outside the limits of the Law of verbal logic) to a new man in a new "scene of representation,"[50] where thinking will no longer be reflection but act, an act made possible by liberating the Subject from the grip of the One who counts. In this other scene, Being acquires the power to "count us from Two," rather than One, and to count us in the "infinite truth of our being," not than in our "infinite alterity," which Badiou rejects as mere animal "seriality" and "ordinary multiplicities" (E 25). A new existential plane, then, where Being counts for "us," where it is on "our" side.

The political aims of Badiou's axiom of multiple-being seem quite straightforward. He slams the dubious piety of those who morally support "cultural differences." His offhand remarks in journalistic venues target the New Philosophers as shallow: "a tourist's fascination for the diversity of morals, customs and beliefs" (E 25). He roundly critiques a modern ethics that privileges "otherness" (Emmanuel Levinas, for example) and "difference" (Jacques Derrida) over what he terms "an intuition of unity." "There are as many differences, say, between a Chinese peasant and a young Norwegian professional as between myself and anybody at all, including myself. As many, but also, then, neither more nor less" (E 26). Breaking with philosophy after Heidegger, Badiou refuses support for the differential predations of the logic of the signifier, including Levinas's "otherwise than being," which posits the ethical relation as a relation to the other,[51] and whose cardinal principle is that what founds a "just state" comes "from just men and women."[52] Since, for Badiou no State is innovative in terms of justice (by definition it is only what *is*), such a notion is invalid. He is interested in politics only where it becomes a condition for innovative thought. Badiou's political critique essentially ends when it has gauged the creativity quotient in any particular politics.

Before Badiou, that is, we might have assumed politics to be a reflection, both practical and theoretical, on concrete events and specific conditions that are rooted in, or model, concrete human relations. Relations of masters to slaves, of workers to owners, men to women, parents to children—the relations shaped by the signifier that Lacan's discourses and his amazing algorithms designate. But, for Badiou, such "relations" are the very conditions to be nullified by mathematized philosophy, partly because they are already so worthless themselves, so nil, and partly because they must be actively voided to make room for real, true (i.e., topological) thought. Relations (correspondences) are not subject matter for topology. Thus, where we might have expected a detailed critique of how ideology and bad governance warp contemporary democracy's human relations, we get nothing but Badiou's unsentimental Platonic invocation to "think the twilight of the democratic Polis" (*MPh* 97). No concrete analysis of how the ideology of the Third Way, how governing from the Center, how "parliamentary-democratic" ideas, and how human rights (all of which Badiou rejects) erode the democratic life they claim to support; Badiou issues only indictments. Any critique we might extrapolate from his denunciation of "counting," remains unconnected to the strange rise of accounting and "bottom line" ideology that is now the First World's weapon of choice for dominating the Rest (think Argentina). Instead, "ethical ideology" is his target, as an apologist for neoimperialism:

> It might well be that ethical ideology, detached from the religious teachings which at least conferred upon it the fullness of a "revealed" identity, is simply the final imperative of a conquering civilization: "Become like me and I will respect your difference." (*E* 25)

Note that Badiou is not pitching his comments at the political level. He avoids targeting specific political practices, attacking instead "ethical ideology's" espousal of "otherness" for its failure to recognize the fragmenting, identitarian politics that tends to trail in its wake. His focus is on thought and its productive ratio. So his critique ends once the conceptual (mathematical) level is reached: the fracturing the we-Subject into "infinite alterities" is harmful because it becomes an endless procession of ones. At times he is as impatient as George W. Bush with parliamentary-democratic governance, the World Court, and organized interests such as "feminism, the environment" (*E* 24), but Badiou is not constitutionally conservative; his exasperation is entirely abstract. He opposes these on theoretical grounds, as established movements, by definition hackneyed and uncreative. He calls such activisms mere "ordinary multiplicities," criticizing all such interest groups and legal innovations in a religious spirit that is without piety and without God.[53] Made, that is, in a spirit of fidelity to the concept of the collective subject rather than to its practical manifestations. (Badiou despises Levinas for being openly religious, and conversely, he detests the philosophers of "human rights" for being "a pious discourse without piety, a spiritual supplement for incompetent governments" [*E* 23]). The authentic Subject, the true we-Subject, in contrast, persists only through its fidelity to its Truth; any dispersal of it into fractionated movements indexes a falsification of the Subject's being.

It is on this virtually spiritual plane that Badiou resonates with the socialisms that fired the imagination of European civilization in the early to mid-twentieth century, and which, like him, often sought to correct the void of human life, to reconnect the splintered parts of its fragmented feudal being, and amend the legacy of its destruction, that is, the riotous freedom of opinion, the turbulence of class conflict, and so forth, that postfeudalism brought. Yet, what does he see coming next?

If Badiou's stance differs from what became the default posture of twentieth-century politics—the politics of conversion—of "winning hearts and minds," or "turning heads around," converting people to communism and capitalism, or rousing them to fascist unanimity, it remains difficult to discern. We know he looks to an impossible being made possible by the conversion experience of the Event. Because it is also an Event that is theoretically bound to evanesce, it is not easy to picture its concrete political outcomes or to specify how they differ from the "religious" and "imperializing" events he denounces. Badiou's writing, that is, lacks clues as to where to draw a line between a void that brings life-altering knowledge of the Same (collective solidarity) and, say, Levinasian otherness. Yet, mathematically, Badiou's evental way is entirely consistent with his method: "the Same is not what is (i.e., the infinite multiplicity of differences) but what *comes to be*,"[54] a "coming-to-be" that is enabled by the simple subtraction of the One. He permits no primal Other to intervene to separate or split the Subject, or merge its multiplicity into a singularity.

What is striking about Badiou's stance is that preventing the One's dominance seems to require no political action, only a change of mind and method. Badiou's thesis is that it can be done formally (topologically)—and formalization is, we must not forget, Badiou's highest criterion of truth-value. Most people still think according to a verbal-symbolic model, rather than according to Badiou's mathematical-imaginary one and will thus not easily grasp how change comes about. His nonmathematical reader may very well find it difficult to fathom his distinction between the subjects of the "unparalleled intensities of existence" he advocates and the subjects of the "ordinary multiplicities" he disdains. Badiou firmly believes, however, that there is a fundamental difference between the Sameness (the imperial "Be like me") to which ethical ideology reduces the Other and his fraternal ideal-yet-real Same, which does not rely on the Other and the One. This difference, of course, only becomes patent if we "do the math." If we think mathematically, we find a Subject doubled without being oppositional, a Subject caused by the unifying Event that realizes Self and Not-Self progressively as the Same; and we would have a Subject not caused by the splitting force of language (Lacan's desiring subject) but one borne up instead by solidarity and effervescent joy.

Phenomenologically, of course, Badiou's distinctions fall flat by comparison with word-based critiques, even those close to his formal perspective. Consider Badiou's fellow (former) Althusserian, Jacques Rancière, who, like Badiou, treasures the concept of the 'Two.' For Rancière, however, it is essentially the "Two of politics" that is his concern. He depicts our flawed contemporary society as a "self-pacified multiplicity."[55] He worries over the political Two's recent eclipse by the modality of "governing from the center," and in highly literary (rather than abstract) terms he describes vividly our current political aversion to opposition and confrontation. If he seems to have the same utopian desire for community as Badiou, it is marked linguistically, not mathematically.

Rancière is no philosopher. Yet, he is an exceptional painter of modern life, and his astute attention to social life as it is permits him to grasp, better than Badiou I think, why modern democracy has so steadily eroded. For example, when he charges that there has been an ideological conversion of "democracy" into an array of artificially carved up marketing niches, Rancière sees the distortion formed and reinforced by the

> banal themes of the pluralist society where commercial competition, sexual permissiveness, world music and cheap charter flights to the Antipodes quite naturally create individuals smitten with equality and tolerant of difference. A world where everyone needs everyone else, where everything is permitted so long as it is on offer as individual pleasure.[56]

To contrast with this, Rancière evokes "a community . . . [with] no material substance . . . borne at each and every moment by someone for someone else—for a potential infinity of others. It occurs but it has no place."[57] The current "state of affairs" is not a natural void for Rancière, that is, it is a corporate concoction, a fictional "fulfillment" that actually blocks democracy's only real promise, which Rancière characterizes this way: "Democracy," he says, is "a wish to speak" and "a wish to hear." It consists of speech addressed to others. Rancière even appears comforted by the ordinary multiplicities required of democracy: "the democratic passion is precisely the possibility of accumulating the choices offered at the crossroads, of being prepared to be torn in all directions at once."[58] This is hardly the unified multiple-subject of which Badiou dreams.

Badiou's concepts superficially parallel Rancière's stirring vision, but they nonetheless augur something else. In Badiou we catch a glimpse of a new political wholeness, a multiple-without-one, a democracy without sovereignty which requires an ebullient solidarity but whose ideological outlines are blurry. Its sole raison d'être is its fostering an "impossible" fraternity: "My comrade is someone who, like me, is only a subject by his belonging to a process of truth that authorizes him to say 'we' " he says; "fraternity is the real itself . . . real manifestation of the new world, and in consequence of the new man" (WTTC 4). Fraternity is a key political and theoretical concept for Badiou, formed by the unreflected experience of a shared Truth. Predictably, the political formations Badiou favors are those of an effervescent camaraderie and a fraternity forged in fugitive political actions (like May 1968).

All the more reason for Badiou to disregard the psychopathologies of everyday life, since everyday life is what hides an essential connectedness between us (fragmented part-subjects) and our higher Self, the Same, the we. The One eclipses this we-subject every day. Only where quotidian life gets voided by the Event does a positive leap into the void open onto an "other scene of representation," completely absent from everyday life, whose nullity is filled out with the ordinary multiplicities of the Subject. The "new scene" is one of the creative/destruction of falsity and the advent of topological truth. Only in this other scene—the True void—is the subject freed from the One, for here, even the dialectic is barred[59] as a ruse of the One disguised as a pseudomultiplicity (the dialectic's triple process).[60] Here, in the field of the unconscious and death drive, the jouissance of multiple-being is realized purely mathematically. And purely imaginarily.[61]

Badiou readily admits that the other scene in which fraternity is represented as flourishing is Imaginary (with a dash of Real-Truth to it). Although Badiou perfectly grasps Lacan's point about the pathologies of the dualized Imaginary, he optimistically rejects all caution. The Imaginary's negative character becomes in Badiou a positive strength once it can take leave of the language that rules the state of things, and enter the Imaginary, which is after all the domain of the possible: here what *is* does not take precedence, and here the impossible is given no quarter.

In classical Lacan, the dualized Imaginary and the supremacy of the Same index an inability to separate the self and the other welded oppositionally to it. The lack of separation results in a violent aggressivity, played out in scenarios of paranoid fantasy. This mirroring relation is broken into only by the Other of Symbolic speech, whose eruption arrests the imagined rivalry and the hatred that locks the self and its specular double in deadly combat. For Badiou the dual is indeed violent, oppositional, and paranoid—but only when—and only because—it is evaluated by the Symbolic Other. Badiou reverses the Imaginary's negative signs simply by setting the Imaginary into the beyond of the signifier—hurling it into a field of destruction that is also a field of creation.

To harness Freud and Lacan for this ideal Imaginary realm beyond the law is a stretch. After all, Freud was suspicious of the psychoanalytic motivations of socialism, and whenever Lacan remarked (largely allusively) on social formations and economic organizations, he tended to find concealed fraternal rivalries or secret sexual enjoyments in them. But Badiou remains devout in his belief that the yield of mathematically localizing the void in the heart of real human, sociopolitical relations is that imaginary fraternity and solidarity will come into its own. And, Badiou believes, so will true Love.

On Love: La Scène du Deux

Love, one of philosophy's "four fundamental conditions," is a centerpiece of Badiou's thought. Badiou will think Love as an other scene—or as he says precisely, as a "new scene of representation." An other scene, a new representation—of what?

Of the sexual relation. The scene's contours follow the ones he imagines for "fraternity," for what fraternity is to ordinary politics Love is to sex: a supplement. Lacan had given love a supplemental function when he said that "love makes up for (*supplée*) the fact that there is no sexual relation." Badiou will describe a purely imaginary, nonparanoid mental space occupiable by the Two, and he will insist that it can be described algorithmically. He will designate love's conceptual space topologically, and in doing so, he will fend off a challenge by the poetic language to dominate love's representation, and make topology the truer path to its *pays du tender* (country of love).

Love is a crucial point in his system, for according to Badiou, it is only ever experienced (existentially) by the systemic breakdown caused by an Event (in this case, the "loving Encounter"). His goal regarding Love is properly described as a desire to reach (if only imaginarily) the scene where love's reality (like politics' real fraternity) is mathematically demonstrable. To arrive, that is, at that other scene of representation, where Being can count from Two, and not from One. In this "love scene," the couple (*le Deux*) becomes a "we" that is not sexually opposite but is instead a multiple being bound by fidelity to the Truth of its Love. Moreover, Sex will no longer be the hidden subject of such a scene—though Badiou admits it will remain a spot of opacity (unnameability). Its darkness, is, however, purely formal: sex is dark because it has relinquished all pretension to participating in the Truth.

Badiou anxiously assures us his other scene will not be simply another escapist utopian romance: his "countries of love" are not formed in opposition to social and symbolic prohibitions. Where certain French thinkers (Rousseau, De Tracy, and Stendhal) saw the laws of thought and the laws of society silently legislating the relations between the sexes (including their rebellions), Badiou believes that instead a scene of representation can exist purely and simply outside the limits of the law—social, linguistic, logical.

Badiou wants Love's other scene to be where the sexual nonrelation gets repaired (just as politics' other scene is where fraternity formally reconciles, as a multiple-being-without-one, the warring classes of modern society) (WTTC 4). Words will not help. For after all, it is the aftermath of words (the introduction of the signifier) that has split the living being in two, dispersing its being between two scenes (conscious and unconscious). Short-circuiting the effects of words will heal sex's "immanent break" (its "*trou local*" Badiou will call it).[62]

Badiou will thus submit the problem of sex to the rigorously descriptive procedures of topology—in order to solve it. *Et voilà*. The results disclose sex's "evental supplementation"—Love (*E* 42): "It is love which makes the truth of which sex is capable, and not the reverse" (SD 178). Like his brief for the Same and for Fraternity, Badiou centers his solution to the problem of sex around a single concept: 'equality.' Equality is not (or is not only) an ideological rallying cry; it is a mathematical solution to be arrived at.[63] And from equality the true Two, the loving couple is destined to be born.

We are thus brought abruptly, theoretically and methodologically, to the significance of Badiou's multiple being when it comes to Love.[64] In his vocabulary, the impasse ("no sexual relation") means that a state of being-sexed exists, it *is*, and therefore it must be surpassed. Sexuality, he says, is "of the order of being" (*SD* 187). Badiou will therefore take Lacan's pithy dictate mathematically: "no sexual relation" = no "1:1" correspondence between the sexes. A void thus exists between the sexes, a void that opens sex to topological exploration and conceptual transformation. And according to Badiou, only an internal void "enables the truth-process as such" (*E* 43). Thus, the broken no sexual relation (sex as immanent break) becomes the perfect foil for demonstrating the "Truth-process" of Love—a truth-process Badiou maintains that no literary or artistic approach can match.[65]

Badiou's truth procedure is crystal clear: by entering the void of sexual difference one can map the topography of the unconscious thought of sexuation. The goal of the expedition is to reach that situation in which Two appears in its Truth without the intervention, mediation, or interference of the One (God) or the "Three" (Society): "Love," he tells us, "is atheistic" (*SD* 190). The truth-procedure of Love requires that sex be vitally disorganized, and, happily, this disruption is familiarly accomplished by the chance Encounter called Love. Love is that Event which suddenly and immediately puts being beyond sexual order: "What love comports of scenic construction of the Two does not go harmoniously with the sexual as such" (*SD* 187).

In a characteristic move, then, Badiou turns the negative, the lack of relation (sex), around to make it into the positive Truth of an absolute relation (Love), which has been concealed by the quotidian absence of sexual relation. The Truth of Badiou's Love? It is that there is no real distinction between self-and-other, and indeed that there is no Other, neither as One nor as Three. It is the same Truth of the Same that gives the lie to the sociosymbolically, differentially organized world. Love permits the couple to leave the voided world behind where its Truth is only obscured by logical, social, theoretical, and rational divisions (especially sexual division)—of which their love is the purest contradiction.

The Neo-romantic (not to mention Neo-Platonic and Pauline) overtones to Badiou's Love are obvious, even though he sternly forces them to pass muster with the rigor of a topological approach. Indeed, in *La Scène du Deux*, Badiou follows precisely the methodological lines he lays down in *L'être et l'événement* as what is required to access the Truth to be encountered in negative space (unconscious thought; the other scene): (1) find the void or flaw in the system; (2) enter it to Encounter its Truth (the Eventmental encounter), and (3) submit this Truth to the test of recognition and faith by the we.

Badiou calls the void in the sexual relation (i.e., nonrelation) its "trou local," but it does not long remain a vacancy. In his hands this "trou" becomes an actively negative object. Lodged in the space of the no sexual relation, it becomes a "non null term which enters into relation with the two sexed positions, and which makes a local hole, or a punctiform relation, in their non-relation" (*SD* 183). The trou local is thus the assertion/insertion of a gap into a nonrelation—a negation of a negation, a situating of a relation where none existed: "Theorem 1: Where there is a lack only an excess can serve as supplementation (or only excess makes up for it: *suppléance*)" (*SD* 178). Love is supplement; love is "eventmental excess" (*SD* 180): "Which means," he tells us, "that it is to the construction of the scene of the Two that one must be attached, in as much as its paradox is that sexual disjunction is simultaneously its matter and its obstacle" (*SD* 180).

La Scène du Deux recapitulates much of Badiou's lengthier study of Love in *Conditions*,[66] but in *La Scène* Badiou dispatches roundly the usual representations of the loving couple—and by usual I mean literary. According to Badiou, in the nihilism of everyday life, Love does not (yet) exist as the Two. Nor does it exist in theory. Technically, this means that Love has not yet found its proper scene of representation—and certainly not in the places one is most likely to look for it, that is, in art, poetic literature, novels, and myths, or the stuff of dreams. Literary love he finds especially wanting. He airily dismisses it—from Mme. de Lafayette to Henry James—because it never arrives at a Two that is not a function of the One (or the Three). Selected literary examples become simple variants on the logical impasse of the no sexual relation to Badiou—all variations on the eclipse of the Two by the One (God) and its henchman Three (society; but wasn't it Emile Durkheim who said "God is just another name for Society"?). Badiou will replace word-dependent representations of love with a comprehensive set of topological variations on the couple Man/Woman to accomplish the proof that the Two really exists. But it only exists where and when it is put into an entirely new situation (created by the blind Event of the Loving Encounter) where it forms an "egalitarian couple" to contrast with and supplement the ordinary, unequal, sexually disjunctive one. Let us turn now to Badiou's scene of the representation of Love rendered strictly topologically, not logically nor aesthetically.[67] His first move is to criticize the narrative "outcomes" of literary romances.

Alluding to works like *La Princesse de Clèves*, Badiou tells us that Art shows us Love as "bound for decadence and dissolution after the encounter." Novelistic art tells us chiefly that love wanes—a conclusion reached to the profit of the One: One-plus-One ends by "dissolv[ing] the Two," and One triumphs (*SD* 179). Poetic art teaches that love subsumes and annuls the sexual nonrelation, but "at the cost, as in *Tristan und Isolde*, of a deadly fusion" (*SD* 179). In this case, the One is "taking revenge" on the Two, and One again triumphs. The modern novel makes sexual renunciation a way of preserving love by rendering it sublime (e.g., *The Ambassadors* by Henry James): "the Two, renouncing the experience of the non-relation, will have been only its proper eclipse, the faded aggrandizement of the One who renounces" (SD 179). Again, One wins. Even in popular fiction, the Two is never shown as "a process, a duration and a construction of a scene" (SD 179). No Scene = no Truth = no Love.

He concludes that the logocentered symbolic system cannot recognize "the possibility of the immanent Two except at the corrosive exteriority of the sexual non-relation" (SD 180) or, more crudely put, the couple that literary art recognizes is still the vulgar couple of sex—a sex produced by the divisive machinations of the signifier. Oddly enough, Badiou leaves out eighteenth-century examples—Rousseau, Diderot, and Richardson, whose imitator l'Abbé Prévost surely made the finest description of the blind love-encounter anywhere. Indeed, I cannot prevent Des Grieux's *foudroyante* (sudden) meeting with Manon Lescaut from popping into my head whenever Badiou speaks of the Evental loving encounter; "*Elle était l'Amour même*" (she was love itself), Des Grieux says, his life revolutionized by a first glimpse of the young whore he will follow, enthralled, to the ends of the earth. And Badiou might have considered Stendhal's *Charterhouse of Parma*, or the couplings in Marguerite Duras—the unforgettable Duras, but Badiou forgot! To have done so would run counter to his aims; nevertheless, they argue against his assertion that the art of the novel fails to paint a true portrait of the couple, nor deliver the true spirit of the Two.

Badiou recently mused, "Is there a relation between sexuation and opinion?"—meaning that a greater degree of discernment than opinion is needed to reach the beyond of sexual difference.[68] Badiou is careful not to permit this beyond called "Love" to be assimilated with fantasies of plenitude or fulfillment such as dominate the representation of the sexed couple in art and culture. No; Love's scene is for Badiou to be triply negative—"an immanent construction of an indeterminate disjunction, which does not pre-exist it" (SD 190). But, of course, as in Hegel and in religion, only from the most negative does the most positive grow: Badiou's Love-space will be that of an "immanent Two," "atheistic," that is, free of the hegemony of the One (God), and free of submission to the Third—to society, to Levinas's preordinate Other, and it will be under no obligation to anything that might be called the demands of social coexistence. What is more, he will prove the viability of this Love-space mathematically.

Badiou takes the first step of transforming Lacan's object a (which for Lacan both shapes and undoes the no sexual -relation) into a mathematical letter u (which represents and also fills in the void of the trou local—the u is the a, but open at the top). Badiou inserts the u into a series of mathemes devised to demonstrate "the various 'relations' that could exist between what language has defined as singularities (Man and Woman)" (SD 181). A language-based relation between singularities is always a power relation, as Nietzsche intuited (SD 181), and it produces only the following combinatories: (1) A relation of equivalence, whose two axioms are transitivity and symmetry; (2) An ordinal relation (First, Second, etc.): two unsubstitutable singularities are placed in a relation of antisymmetry (SD 181); and (3) Or they are reduced to the animal relation in which "all living singularity is related to itself, or to what Sartre called the phenomena of seriality" (SD 181). Badiou remarks:

> The crucial thesis, then, is that the sexed distribution of human animals is not written as a relation, the rapport being precisely concerned as a relation of order. If we name M and W generic WM we will say that as far as sex goes, neither $M \leq W$ nor $W \leq M$, i.e., there is no rapport or sexual compatibility $M \perp W$. (SD 182)

It is only available in

> the VIRTUAL SCENE OF THE TWO—they are constructed in the duration proper to a love, as its non-sexual matter/material, even though identification of this scene, built by subtracting the u, may be in some parts sexually animated. (SD 188)

By dismissing all prior discursive (word-based) models for the sexual relation (they result in an impasse that never solves the sexual relation), Badiou now proves Love virtually by disproving sex.

Lacan and Topological Love?

> Mathematics . . . *entirely empties out* what separates us from the real. Between the real and the mathematical form there is *nothing*.
> —Alain Badiou, "Politics and Philosophy"

For Badiou even if Love is "guided by the dark star of the object" (the sexual object; SD 177) what really forms the Love relation is what is

> in *excess* over it [sex], since it goes straight to what there is of the object that the subject draws its bit of being from, and that, by a reversion contained entirely in the declaration, "I love you," "I love you yourself," and not exclusively the object that you bear and that love comes to sustain—that is its constitutive excess—what there is of the being of the subject and what the

object as cause of desire takes for the singularity of its presentation and the definitive charm of its appearance. (SD 177-78; emphasis added)

For Lacan, Badiou's trou local is the object a, the bearer of fantasy and its obscene (sexual) enjoyment—and it is also the bearer of whatever "aura" the loved one appears to possess. Badiou's "dark star" however functions only partly like the object a: it grants a singular "charm" to what it attaches to, but its secondary function is not sexual and obscene; it is simply topological. It pinpoints mathematically the void of/in sex, but opens on to another scene of representation, not on to the obscene unconscious.

Badiou must however, still account for a common term in the "nonrelation" of the void of sex: and this he will call the u. Badiou posits this (u) as

an element that makes a knot within the space of a non-relation, of the two non-related terms. It is certain that this element is absolutely undetermined, not describable, not composable. It is in fact atomic, in the sense that nothing singularizable enters into its composition. The u is at once "atomic" and "the phantom of an object," something simultaneously in relation with the two positions, but this something—in which one recognizes the phantom of an object—is composed by nothing and cannot be the object of any analytic description. Put otherwise, it is true that there exists a term non-null which enters into relation with the two sexed positions and which make a local hole, or a punctiform relation in that non-relation. (SD 183)

"Non-null." The u that is a zero from the standpoint of the nonrelation becomes the zero from which, topologically we can count Two—starting, that is, from the all-important standpoint of infinity, which is not the All.

We would posit therefore that there is a non-null term at least, which enters into its place in relation with the two sexed positions. We could inscribe this term, presumed local mediator of the global non-relation, under species of the letter (u), which connotes both the ubiquity and the blind usage of it that is seen everywhere. Should one also declare it a unicity? (SD 183)

Hence, the multiple subject of the Two in its infinite truth:

Of this term, one would say that nothing enters into relation with it except the Void. This fundamental axiom indicates that if the sexed positions are such that (u) intersects them both, acting as (u) itself, it remains umcomposed, or indeterminate by the fact that the void itself enters into relation with it. (SD184)

The intersection of the object/non-object u with the Void produces the solution to the (non)equation of the sexed couple, and it is neither a totalization nor a segregation of the sexes. (1) The "complementarities solution" of Aristophanes simply results in the totalization of an All. Or $M \cup W \neq 1$. (2) The "segregative solution"—which deprives Woman of her "indeterminacy" (Badiou's way of stating her equivalence to Man's indeterminacy, their similarly empty conceptuality) and of her relation to Man at the same time, also amounts to the All: "as nothing further atomic knots a woman to a man, there is no masculine *savoir* of the space occupied by a woman. Hence the supposition of a potentially infinite dilation of the feminine, which could, having no atom, be equivalent to the All—$(W - u) \rightarrow (W = 1)$ (SD 185).

The final solution? *Love*. Badiou says it *is* "possible to produce a formal intelligence of love":

> Let us give it its first definition. An amorous encounter is that which attributes eventmentally to the intersection—atomic and unanalyzable—of the two sexed positions a double function. That of the object, where a desire finds its cause, and that of a point from which the two is counted, thereby initiating a shared investigation of the universe. Everything depends, at bottom, on this $u \leq M$ and $u \leq W$ being read in a double fashion: either that one is assembling there the inaugural non-relation of M and W, inasmuch as it affects the non-analyzable u with being only what circulates in the non-relation. The two positions W and M are then only in this misunderstanding over the atom u, cause of their common desire, a misunderstanding that nothing sayable can lift off, since u is unanalyzable. This is the first reading. Or one reads it in the other direction: starting from u, either $(W - u)$ and $(M - u)$, two positions like those the atom u supports by subtracting itself from it. (SD 186-87)[69]

Badiou has succeeded. He has formalized—to an unparalleled degree—the work of the object a in structuring the nonrelation of the sexes and opening the way to the relation that is in excess over them: the supplement called Love.

Something remains amiss in this very clever solution, even though it allows mad love and universal love to be coextensive.

Badiou only looks at the object (the u) in its formal, mathematical sense, as the starting point for a supplementation (Love) that redeems the nihilism or void of a nonrelation (sex). It functions as the (nil) object (of squabble and misprision) between Two who ought to know better. But Badiou also prizes this object as way to grant the Two a *Vita Nuova*, a Love that "subsum[es] the object under the being of the subject." His is thus an idealization (or as he puts it an "ideal of formalisation" [sic]) that he considers to be the only process capable of "constructing the scene of representation where the non-relation becomes a counting, the counting for/from Two" (*SD* 178). By punching a hole within the chasm between the sexes, Badiou's "phantom object" becomes less a passageway than an unconscious knot between the sexes.

The Subject, revealed in this new scene of representation, surges forth, turning the semblance of a void into "Two counted in an immanent way." For Badiou, this "counting" is completely different from the conceptual pairing of half units called "sexual difference": it solves the "problem of a scenic procedure where two is neither fusion nor summation, and where consequently, the Two is in excess over what composed it, without adding a Third to it" (*SD* 178). To confront the abyss of the logical sexual relation is, thus, to go through the "rabbit hole" to emerge on the other side in a space of Love that supports an infinite relation (always already there) between the sexes—or better put, "before" the sexes were logocentrically made into singularities.

What divides Lacan's Love from Badiou's is the considerable difference between the object *a* and the *u*. For Lacan the *(a)* is a remnant of being and non-being (in equal measure); it forms the core or kernel of all subjectivity. It is material and ideal. It incites the drive as the dark star that "guides" love. But Lacan's object *a* is "non-dialectizable," which, to me, means that it is not (as with Badiou's *u*) "subsumable," and cannot therefore be caught in the dialectic that ultimately underlies Badiou's "double function" for love, politics, and so forth. Badiou openly declares his disdain for the dialectic in favor of Maoist contradiction, but whenever he tries valiantly to apply "contradiction" to human affairs (love, politics, etc.), it inevitably takes on a dialectical aura. Lacan's *(a)* never does. The crucial difference thus remains: that Lacan's *(a)* is the kernel of the fantasy of a full enjoyment of one's "being" and this enjoyment is not merely theoretical. It only simulates the Real of *jouissance*, and it is anchored in a body that actively, if unconsciously, disavows *its sexual* enjoyment. Badiou's point of departure, the *u*, on the other hand is a Platonic Real, distorted and imitated by its ordinary manifestation: sex.

His solution is to restart the truth-procedure for Love by beginning with mathematical form, using it to transform what is (the law of ordinary sex) into the impossible of ideally formalized Love. Is it now possible to say what Love is for Alain Badiou? Is it a specific formalization that solves the problem of the irrational persistence of sex? I think it is. Badiou mathematically negates human signifying discourses (de-emphasizing the "reflective" or the "diacritical" function of Lacan's mathemes) in order to reach their Real (Platonic) forms. Lacan begins with social forms (his discursive ties: "Speaking of love, we analysts do nothing else"), aiming less to turn them inside out for the ideals they dissimulate, than to determine how the poetic word promises and delivers the impossible—the possibility of a love outside the limits of the law. It does so by being addressed to the feminine Thing. Lacan's love is, granted, a "creationist sublimation" and is marked by the fact that the masculine responds to the feminine Thing not with violence but with words, only words—poetic words that provisionally traverse the void where words fail between the sexes. But sublimation is not idealization.

Badiou deprives us of this possibility, on wholly mathematical grounds, because he eschews the crutch of poetic narrative. Love "works" only if it is the pure effect of topology, not of words,[70] a topology that takes the everyday no sexual relation and transforms it into a formal relation by negating the negation that sexuation already is. No need, thus, for recourse to speech and its address.

Badiou thinks thus to put love entirely "outside the limits of the law," the law of language and desire: an "amorous process" (yet to be invented) will set us ashore in a new situation where divisive logic and reason will no longer dominate us.

We will not find Woman there. Woman, for Badiou, is not Love's cause, its inspiration, and its limit; she does not give his Love its Law. And so in his system, she ceases to have any reality, for as Lacan told us, "Without the Law the Thing is Dead" (S7 83).[71]

Contemporary Lacanians often readily agree with Badiou's formalization of Love. This is perhaps a function of a hidden wish to solve the Woman problem. But not all who sail these troubled waters will arrive at the same destination, simply because they will have embarked from such different shores. So, yes, between Badiou's reading of (Lacanian) Love and mine there is a crossing: his "love outside the limits of the law" is purely mathematical, and mine is purely literary.

NOTES

1. Loyola University of Chicago cosponsored the conference. My talk was published as "Love Outside the Limits of the Law" in (MacCannell, 1994 and reprinted in my book, *The Hysteric's Guide to the Future Female Subject* (MacCannell, 2000) as Chapter 10.

2. I am especially interested in interpreting certain remarks of his concerning the obstacular function of woman and the feminine. See pages 158–62 and 152–67, as well as notes 21, 49, and 53.

3. Alain Badiou, "The Ethics of Truth," in *Ethics: An Essay on the Understanding of Evil* (London: Verso, 2001).

4. I discuss Badiou's "we-subject" in the section entitled "The Regime of the 'We.'"

5. Badiou's chapter "The Problem of Evil" in *Ethics* (58–71) examines Nazism as a formal error about the truth-process: its adherents, Badiou claims, mistook their State (what *is*) for a full-fledged truth, rather than for a nullity (like any other state). I must ask, however, is there a great yield in reducing the human texture of this horrendous event to a formal analysis?

6. Alain Badiou, "Descartes/Lacan," *Umbr(a)* 1, no. 1 (1992): 16. Translated from *L'être et l'événement*.

7. Badiou describes the "new man" as the focal point of the whole twentieth century: "the new man is a real creation, something which has never existed before, because it emerges from the destruction of historical antagonisms. . . . This conception of the new man—anti-predicative, negative and universal—traverses the century" (ODT 250). Lectures originally delivered at the Collège Internationale de Philosophie (1999). One might compare (and contrast) Jacques Rancière's concept of the 'Athenian *demos*,' characterized by all the negative attributes Badiou mentions. It acts as a political adjunct to a differentiated society, where it alone speaks for the whole.

8. Badiou, "Descartes/Lacan," 15.

9. Badiou, *Ethics* (55). See also his "What Do You Think of the Twentieth Century?" (lecture, University of California–Irvine, April 2002, handout).

10. Badiou poses his critique of contemporary philosophy in terms very like Benjamin's "destructive character who demands, 'Make room!' His 'need for fresh air and open space is stronger than any hatred'" (Walter Benjamin, "The Destructive Character," in *Reflections* (New York: Schoken Books, 1986, 301.) He decries Lacoue-Labarthe's distress that the "architectonics of philosophy" collapsed after Auschwitz, and he is irritated by Jean-François Lyotard's naming philosophy, whose *différend* cannot be shared by two subjects, a space whose "architecture is ruined" (*MPh* 28). For Badiou, the closed destiny they conjure is set up by linking philosophy to poetry's fate, which ends as Adorno said, after Auschwitz. Badiou claims rather that the capital twentieth-century philosophical error was the more or less simple one of desiring to be "realized within time" (*MPh* 135) and to situate itself in actual spaces (States, police, concentration camps). He also claims that its efforts at rectification ("language games, deconstruction, feeble thinking, irremediable heterogeneity" [*MPh* 135]) are the "ruin of Reason." Badiou thus plays the optimist against deconstructionists and postmodernists who condemn philosophy to an exhausted guilt staged in a Sartrean *huis clos* of postwar existential hell in which he himself stifles. Badiou (a proper dramatist) presses for an escape hatch for philosophy, the way a fleeing hero finds a hidden stage door. He thus virtually commands European philosophy to purge its guilt (its misguided philosophical focus on language and the state) whose principal name is "Heidegger." Badiou's "heroic" stance in defense of philosophy does mean, though, that he accepts the Evil in the Holocaust and the War, and that, while he refuses to make them the caesura of philosophy, he nonetheless claims that philosophy cannot really "think Nazism." Is this historical atrocity not really susceptible to philosophical analysis? Lacoue-Labarthe (and others like myself) feel the need for more prolonged philosophical reflection (and practical) analysis. Badiou may be too anxious to cut these (and several other) Gordian knots simply to ensure that philosophy is able to go on.

11. "For destroying rejuvenates in clearing away the traces of our own age; it cheers because everything cleared away means to the destroyer a complete

reduction, indeed eradication of his own condition" (Benjamin, "The Destructive Character," 301).

12. "The linguistic turning is . . . the archi-esthetic recourse to the pacific and enlightened potency of the poem" (L&P 3).

13. Badiou finds support in this from Lacan: "Is the *one* anterior to discontinuity? I do not think so, and everything that I have taught in recent years has tended to exclude this need for a closed *one*. . . . *You will grant me that the* one is that is introduced by the experience of the unconscious is the *one* of the split, of the stroke of the rupture" (Lacan, Seminar XI [1978, 26]). For Lacan the rupture indexes a lost signifier; for Badiou, "Truth" makes the split (by inserting its evental void) and thus what emerges is not the "one," as in Lacan, but the -1. No unconscious division by language, that is.

14. Badiou says "the linguistic turning of contemporary philosophy is ordained finally, in large measure, by a more or less explicit thesis of the identification of logic and mathematics" (L&P 2). He reverses this by mathematizing logic rather than vice versa.

15. "Heidegger and Wittgenstein share the identification of mathematics and logic, within a calculating disposition where thought no longer thinks." Also "I've always said that an event was . . . the breakdown of the count." Badiou will distinguish between what "is counted" and "an intrinsic, uncounted identity" (L&P 3). What he means by "intrinsic identity" is obscure to me; but he seems to want the "uncounted" part of an identity to refer to its Real, which is "impossible to count" (Ethics 134).

16. I am not competent to discuss mathematics in depth. However, from reading Badiou and studying several introductory texts on topology, I believe I can say this much with some assurance.

17. Compare Jacques Lacan, *Le Séminaire: Livre XVII, L'énvers de la psychanalise* (Paris: Éditions du Seuil, 1991, 102–03) on the math/logic problem: mathematics requires the signifier to signify itself ($A = A$, or identification, like God), while the linguistic signifier only signifies a subject for another signifier (S_1 S_2 = gapping, nonidentity). While "*la mathématique représente le savoir du maître en tant que constitué sur d'autre lois que le savoir mythique*" (102), its tautological logic creates propositions that are always "true." Why? To be rid of "*l'instant de la dynamique de la vérité.*" Badiou wants this dynamism. Hereafter Seminar XVII will be indicated by S17 followed by page number.)

18. See Lacan, Seminar XVII, and *Seminar VII: The Ethics of Psychoanalysis*, trans. Dennis Porter (New York: Norton, 1982). (Hereafter Seminar VII will be indicated as S7 followed by page number.

19. Jacques Lacan, *Le Séminaire: Livre XX, Encore* (Paris: Éditions du Seuil, 1975).

20. Lacan says each discourse encounters an "impossibility" (S17 50), for example, the hysteric's discourse: "in order to cure the hysteric of all her symptoms the best way is to satisfy her hysteric's desire—which is for her to posit her desire in

relation to us as an unsatisfied desire" (Jacques Lacan, *Seminar XI: The Four Fundamental Concepts of Psychoanalysis*, trans. Alan Sheridan [New York: Norton, 1973], 12).

21. Lacan, *Seminar XI* (275). Speaking to the fact that the "drama of Nazism" is veiled by the "critique of history," Lacan says that there is no accounting (other than psychoanalytic, perhaps) for its resurgent spirit of sacrifice: "the offering to obscure gods of an object of sacrifice is something to which few subjects can resist succumbing, as if under some monstrous spell. . . . [T]he sacrifice signifies that, in the object of our desires, we try to find evidence for the presence of the desire of this Other that I call here *the dark God*."

22. Badiou acknowledges an "unnamable" portion in us, and he even links it to sexuality (*Ethics* 86). But he does not take the analyst's step of pinpointing its "unnameability" as the common human aversion to knowing the truth about the jouissance that drives us.

23. In the seminar bearing most heavily on his own employment of topology, *Seminar XVII*, Lacan recognizes that there is a truth "without words" ("*sans paroles*"; 11). But, he says, that is only because *discourse*, as an insistent structure (*insistance*) goes beyond words, being a set of fundamental relations that could not be maintained without language. He says that "la relation fondamentale" is "d'un signifiant à un autre signifiant" (of "one signifier to another"):

> Par l'instrument du langage s'instaurent un certain nombre de relations stables, à l'intérieur desquelles peut certes s'inscrire quelque chose qui est bien plus large, va bien plus loin, que les énonciations effectives. Nul besoin de celles-ci pour que notre conduite, nos actes éventuellement s'inscrivent du cadre de certains énoncés primordiaux. S'il n'en était pas ainsi . . . qu'en serait-il de ce qui se retrouve pour nous sous l'aspect du surmoi? (11)

24. Sigmund Freud, "On Constructions in Analysis," in *Le Séminaire: Livre XIII, L'object de la psychanalyse* (unpublished).

25. Ibid.

26. Badiou writes, "How can there exist a knowledge of the truth of the unknown? In psychoanalysis what cannot be known ends up being the knowledge of a truth. Clearly it is because what is not known consciously is known otherwise. Is it not, quite simply, because the unconscious *thinks*? . . . Is this really different to [sic] the philosophical idea according to which being thinks?" (P&P 10). Elsewhere, Badiou speaks of a consistency to truth that he calls "a law of the not-known [*l'insu*] (*Ethics* 46). How does one access knowledge if the content of its truth is precisely what cannot be known? Badiou's answer: through the "mathematization of logic" (L&P 4). According to Badiou, philosophy today is placed "under the condition of an event of fundamental thought: the mathematization of logic" (L&P 4).

27. Citing Lacan's declaration that "Truth can only concern the real," Badiou says, "In fact, for Lacan and for contemporary philosophy, thought is *sepa-*

rated from the real. It has no *direct* access, or relation of knowledge, to this real. Let's say that between thought and the real there is a hole, an abyss, a void. The truth is first of all the effect of a separation, a loss, of a voiding. . . . The entire problem is that of the *localisation* [sic] of the void": "Philosophy localizes the void as the condition of truth on the side of being *qua* being," while "psychoanalysis localizes the void in the Subject." Badiou declares, "It seems that conflict is inevitable. It concerns the triangle: Subject, Truth, Real. The topology is different in philosophy and psychoanalysis" (P&P 8-9).

28. "An evental fidelity is a real break (both thought and practised [sic]) in the specific order within which the event took place. . . . Essentially, a truth is the material course traced, within a situation, by the evental supplementation. It is thus an *immanent break*" (Badiou, *Ethics*, 42).

29. Sigmund Freud, "Notes on the Case of an Obsessional Neurosis," *SE* X (1909; "The Rat Man").

30. Ibid., 166-67.

31. Lacan, *Seminar XI*, 25.

32. Lacan calls "fundamental fantasy" the unconscious space where the subject first took on the role of the One-who-enjoys. Freud calls it the "primal scene." It is the goal of a psychoanalysis to access it, however indirectly. See Jacques Lacan, "The Subversion of the Subject and the Dialectic of Desire," *Écrits* (1977), and Sigmund Freud, "On the History of an Infantile Neurosis," ("The Wolfman"), *SE* XVII.

33. See note 10.

34. Badiou often uses the term *forçage* (forcing growth in the agricultural sense) when he speaks of the "power of truth."

35. Lacan, *Seminar XI*, 33.

36. Ibid., 30-31,

37. In my own view, excessive formalization breeds its own excess; I would even say that the idealization of the excess (the leftover of the idealizing process) is perhaps the most important and dangerous element humanity ever confronts. I have certainly found it at work in all the major political formations of the twentieth century, whose leaders overtly or covertly played upon the allure and the horror of excess/jouissance (see "The Voice of Conscience" in my *Hysteric's Guide*, on Eichmann). Lacan never idealizes excess (object *a*, jouissance); see pages 141-44. For Lacan, unconscious jouissance is unrealized, though its powerful effects are real enough in their consequences. It impacts the very systems that generate it (human minds, human societies, human language, human laws), but it is not a treasure to be exploited.

38. Badiou, *Ethics*, 6-7.

39. Badiou firmly rejects positivist notions of progress (*Ethics*, 84) and the dream of "a true world to come" (*Ethics*, 85). But his entire bent is toward the production of new knowledges. (See my previous discussion of the passage on forcing truth from *Ethics*, 70).

40. Lacan asks: "Is the Law the Thing? Certainly not. . . ." (S7 83).
41. On this point, the reader may consult my article, "Between the Two Fears," *Cardozo Law Review* (forthcoming).
42. "What Lacan still owes to Descartes, the debt whose account must be closed, is the assumption that '*il y a*' was always there" (*Umbr(a)* [1992]: 15; translation from *L'être et l'événement*).
43. Badiou cites Gide, "A very important point here is the hostility towards the family, as the primordial nucleus of egoism, of rooted particularity, of tradition and origin. Gide's cry—'Families, I hate you'—partakes in the apologetics of the new man thus conceived" (ODT 248).
44. Recently, Badiou advocated the sacrifice of the individual, since individuality is the existential nothingness that blocks progression to a new level of being for the subject: "The subject is of the order, not of what is, but of what happens, of the order of the event, and the idea that the individual can be sacrificed to a historical cause which goes beyond him" (WTTC 3).
45. See the epigraph to this section.
46. The death of God is a positive goal of Badiou's.
47. Jacques Lacan, *Le Séminaire: Livre IV, Les formations de l'inconscient* (Paris: Éditions du Seuil, 1998).
48. Lacan, *Seminar XI*, 11; see also S7 111.
49. Badiou's we-subject is founded neither by natural nor traditional historical ties. It is produced by a common history of a collective recognition of its own shared Truth (*Ethics*, 51). The we-subject is more than the simple we of a socialist politics (though Badiou is fond of early Leninism's solidarity effervescence and of the events of May 1968) because, he says, "fraternity" is "the real" of politics. Readers familiar with my *Regime of the Brother* (1991) will recall its critical examination of fraternity from a feminine and democratic point of view. Cf. S7 132: "*dans la société . . . tout ce qui existe est fondé sur la ségrégation, et au premier temps, la fraternité.*"
50. From SD (177-90). All translations from this text are my own.
51. Emmanuel Levinas, *Entre Nous* (1991, 116-17). Levinas founds all political relations on it: "In Marxism . . . there is recognition of the other. . . . Marxism invites humanity to demand what it is my duty to give it" (119).
52. Ibid., 120.
53. Badiou wants to liberate spirit (soul and mind) from institutionalization and organization—a very 1960s orientation but one also resonant with early Christianity. Despite his own adamant atheism, Badiou professes deep affinity with Saint Paul's militancy, and his accent on fidelity to the truth of an Event is also reminiscent of early Christianity.
54. Badiou, "From the Same Truths," in *Ethics*, 27.
55. Jacques Rancière, *Shores* (1995), 22.
56. Ibid.
57. Ibid.

58. Ibid., 80.

59. Badiou, *Ethics*, 25–27.

60. "I call *thinking* the nondialectical or inseparable unity of a theory and a practice" (Psy & Ph 4). In this lecture, he challenges psychoanalysis to extract a "thinking" from the dialectic of theory and practice found necessary in psychoanalysis and which has, up to now, precluded this kind of thought-extraction.

61. He renounces the dialectic in favor of the unifying method of topology, favoring instead Mao's "contradiction" because it preserves the multiaspect required of Truth without the triplicity (a disguised unity) of dialectic.

62. Again, I am extremely wary. European philosophy has infamously encountered these notions before not only in Marx (the classless society) but in the express fascist wish to reconcile workers' and owners' conflicting interests by creating a new man who will overcome the split between mind and body and transcend class antagonisms by thinking unconsciously. Badiou is firmly convinced that Leninist-Maoist communism has nothing to do with fascism, of course, and I am also impatient with the proliferating nonanalytic equations of Nazism and communism. Still, I find Badiou's comments disturbing. Badiou tries to align his multisubject with the subject of Lacanian psychoanalysis, a subject split by language and the "object *a*" remaindered by the introduction of language, but he promotes a subject (which he terms "a rarity"; Badiou, 14) for whom language is an inessential "intrusion of an outside term" (ibid.). For Badiou in "What Is Love?" the "cause of the subject" is the event of its truth, naked but "indiscernible":

> If one would point to a cause of the subject, it is less necessary to return to the truth . . . as to the event. Consequently, the void is no longer the eclipse of the subject [as it is for Lacan, eclipse of the desiring subject]. (ibid., 15)

The truth of the subject's "indiscernible multiple" is only a "finite approximation" (ibid., 14) for Badiou, who does not acknowledge that the unconscious also opens the reality of thought—the free thought that Badiou claims to prize. He thus rejects Lacan's "Cartesian" dualism that finds the cause of the subject in the unconscious:

> What still links Lacan . . . to the Cartesian epoch of science is the thought that it is necessary to hold the subject in the pure void of its subtraction if one wishes that truth be saved." (ibid., 15)

63. The One Badiou rejects is none other than the all-powerful signifier called "the phallus." For Lacan, the symbolic phallus (an effect of the work of language) differentiates the sexes in the unconscious, because symbolic words have no purchase there. Badiou takes literally the (Freudian–Lacanian) notion that words (functions of negation) have no leverage in the other scene. Thus, to transform the unconscious' silent obscurity into a well-lit love scene that, like the

unconscious, remains entirely wordless, Badiou will doubly deny the sway of the signifier and will make sexual difference (the impact of the phallic signifier on the unconscious) simply into a problem to be solved mathematically. He will array his solution to sexuation in a scene of representation that remains fully shielded from the (negating) powers of language, a scene no longer pathological because it is not in dialectical tension with the word. The word's absence permits love to bloom; the topological mapping of this scene will have the value the *carte du tendre* (map of love) had in the seventeenth-century novels Badiou frequently refers to: to unite those divided by sex.

64. Badiou says, "During the century, equality was the strategic aim: politically under the name of communism, scientifically under the name of the axiomatic, artistically under the imperative of the fusion of art and life, sexually as 'mad love'" (WTTC 4).

65. It is easy to imagine that Badiou's is inspired by his teacher (and early political opponent) Gilles Deleuze in divorcing Being from the One it is traditionally equated with. Or that Badiou is moved by a desire to reinstate Parmenides (to whom he sometimes alludes) along with his beloved Plato. But in reality, Badiou reaches his ontological Truth in strictly formal terms, independent of autobiographical and historical narratives and independent of poetic allusion, verbal nuance, or wordplay. He has his reasons.

66. Lacan, too, focuses on the mysterious link of signifier to signifier. But in this link a knowledge lies (a *savoir* [learning] that is neither *connaissance* [knowledge] nor representation), the knowledge of a rapport that "*ne se sait pas*" (does not know itself) (S17 32). For Lacan, the no sexual -relation is neither Real nor representable; it is of the order of an invisible link produced by a "*relation de raison*" (rational relation), that is, by a discourse (ibid.).

67. Badiou, *Conditions* and *La Scène du Deux*.

68. The others are "the events of the matheme, the poem . . . and inventive politics" (MPh 79).

69. Badiou has a very low opinion of opinion. We must therefore conclude that for Badiou, sexuation has nothing in reality to do with the Real, the True Two. Indeed, he calls sex an unnamable element (jouissance), a dark star, an obscurity—that is, a blot—on the Truth of Love. It exerts a drag on the full realization-idealization-formalization of love.

70. Badiou writes:

> Let us say that in one case the *malentendu* [misunderstanding] over the object supports the lack of relation. And that in the other, the excess over the object supports that it not be on it alone that the conjunction depends. In the first case u is the One where the Two gets eclipsed or is indeterminate. In the second case, u is the separate common One from which two gets disposed in the universe. The amorous event is only the chance authorization given to the double reading, that is to the double function of the u. (SD 190)

71. Badiou does admit that sex continues to figure in the human relation of Love, which has not entirely purged itself of its dark stars. He even calls love a "double function" that limps toward its own creation, moving toward the new scene on the far side of sex's destruction: The double function limps (*boite*) and this *boiterie* in the amorous walk that exerts itself remains to be invented. And it is true that *ça marche mal*, that is, it limps. But it is also that it does work (*SD* 187).

EIGHT

Feminine Love and the Pauline Universal

Tracy McNulty

One of the most striking features of Alain Badiou's recent work is its defense of the possibility of a transpositional, universal truth, against the assumption that all truths are particular, position-specific, and therefore formally unpronounceable. In his 1992 essay "Qu'est-ce que l'amour?" (What Is Love?) and his 1997 book *Saint Paul: La fondation de l'universalisme* (Saint Paul: The Foundation of Universalism), Badiou seeks universalism in the most unlikely places: in the divisions of sexual difference and in the personal revelatory experience of the subject who is called by God. There where experience is by definition particular and intransmissible, he seeks the conditions for the pronouncement of a truth that holds for all of humanity.

Despite their different subject matters, these two works pursue almost identical lines of reasoning in defense of the universal. In "What Is Love?" Badiou argues that the positions "man" and "woman" are totally disjointed from one another, defined by irreconcilable, position-specific *savoirs* (sets of knowledge); but humanity is singular, the site of a transpositional truth that treats the disjunction between the two positions without being within it. In *Saint Paul*, he argues that the discourses of "Jew" and "Greek" are symptomatic for Paul of the "worldly proliferation of alterities," in which each position believes that it alone holds the key to salvation; but Pauline universalism consists in an address to all in which universality "must expose itself to all the differences in order to show, in the trial of their sharing, that they can welcome the truth that traverses them."[1] Between these two texts, Badiou establishes an implicit analogy between "man" and "woman" before the declaration of love (WL) and "Jew" and "Greek" before the announcement (SP). In both cases, universality is blocked by an opposition that "splits humanity in two" (SP 45) such that a transpositional truth cannot be recognized. And, in both cases, love is what solves this impasse.

But Badiou defines the love that supports the universal in very precise terms. Love is neither the pursuit of an imaginary object that would procure satisfaction or guarantee unity, nor a shared experience that would undo the disjunction between the sexes or eliminate worldly differences. Instead, love is a "procedure of truth"[2] in which each position, from the vantage point of its particular experience and savoir, welcomes a truth that addresses humanity in its universality. It is thus indispensable to Badiou's nondialectical understanding of the universal, as "the trajectory of a distance with regard to a particularity that subsists" (SP 118). As a procedure of truth, love necessarily originates in a particular experience that marks it with its own savoir. But if the truth it pronounces is not to fall within the disjunction or the opposition it treats, it must not be consumed by the particularity of its point of departure.

More precisely, love involves the transcendence of the object relation that imprisons each position in its particularity. In "What Is Love?" Badiou argues that love cannot be regulated by the object-cause of desire, which condemns man and woman to the insular logics of their respective fantasies and so impedes any pronouncement of the truth of the disjunction. In *Saint Paul*, he suggests that Christian discourse proposes an "absolutely novel relation to its object" (59), by declaring that the object-identifications that cement worldly identity and promise mastery of the universe (law and ritual practice for the Jew; wisdom for the Greek) are indifferent to salvation. One of the most distinctive features of Badiou's thought is the critique of particularity as a kind of rigid uniformity, against the current critical tendency to decry the reduction of the particular by a hegemonic universal. For Badiou, "every particularity is an instance of conformity" (SP 118), rooted in a unary trait that defines identity. Conversely, the universal is *uniting*, but not unary: it traverses particular positions without either absorbing or being absorbed by them.

Simply put, Badiou seeks to define love—and indeed the universal itself—otherwise than in terms of the phallic function: the "universal qualifier" that splits humanity in two according to a logic ruled by the object. In the sexual field, it divides the sexes on either side of a unary trait, *having* or *being* the phallus.[3] But it also governs the quest for the object that would compensate the subject's lack. In the religious domain, it cements the subject's enslavement to the law and to the sinful objects and rites it both prohibits and brings to life as objects of desire. In this sense, the phallic function could never represent the transcendence of particularity because it elevates a unary trait to the status of universal law.

In both essays, feminine love emerges as the necessary support for this nonphallic universalism. In "What Is Love?" Badiou maintains that the feminine position is singularly charged with the relation of love to humanity, and therefore actually sustains the universal totality (273); in *Saint Paul*, he suggests that feminine love supports the sons' universal by mitigating the "crushing symbolic" of the father, with its laws and rituals (46). As he puts it, the upshot of his argument about love is that "the humanity function does not coincide with the phallic function" (WL 273). This point is crucial for understanding how Badiou situates himself with regard to the work of Jacques Lacan. For although Lacan's accounts of ethics and of femininity subtend much of Badiou's analysis, both essays also make significant modifications to his core concepts. In Badiou's words, he adds an "additional rotation" to Lacan's formulae for sexuation. For while Lacan assigns the universal qualifier to the masculine position, and defines woman as "not-all" under the phallic function, Badiou proposes to "return to women . . . the universal qualifier" (WL 273).

In light of Badiou's argument, what should we make of Lacan's thesis that the feminine as such *does not allow for* any universality?[4] This question is all the more pertinent when Badiou's two essays are read side by side: first, because the problem of sexual difference is internal to Paul's account of universalism, and, second, because Paul turns out to embody precisely Badiou's thesis about feminine love. By putting the discourse of feminine love in the mouth of the original proponent of universalism, Badiou radically alters our conceptions of each.

This chapter will examine the stakes of Badiou's appeal to feminine love to contest the phallic function, questioning not only the stakes of feminine love in each essay, but the codependence of their respective arguments. My reading will be guided by the following questions. First, what is the relationship between the feminine love that supports the humanity function and the Christian love that supports the universal by fulfilling and thus eradicating the law? Second, what is at stake in Badiou's contestation of the object relation and the phallic function that supports it? Third, what is the relationship between the sexual difference traversed by a transpositional human truth, and the "worldly alterities" (including both ethnic particularism and sexual difference) traversed by the universal of the resurrection-event? In this analogy, is the disjunction of sexual difference diminished or neutralized? And finally, when Badiou argues that a universal thought "*produces the Same and the Equal*" (SP 117), what are the implications of this claim where the feminine is concerned? To address these questions, I first need to give a brief summary of Badiou's account of feminine love and its relation to the universal.

UNITY OF THE AMOROUS TRUTH:
SEXUATED CONFLICT OF THE TWO SAVOIRS

In "What Is Love?" Badiou seeks to redeem the bad reputation of love in Freudian psychoanalysis by disentangling it from the imaginary stakes of eros, or what he calls the "fusional concept of love" (255). For Badiou, love is not what makes an ecstatic One out of a Two that is taken for granted as a structural given (255). Rather, it is "the advent of the Two as such, the scene of the Two" (263). Only in love is it possible to establish that there are two-sexuated positions, "man" and "woman" (257). This is because love is a procedure of truth that articulates the disjunctive nonrelation between the two positions, rather than supplementing that nonrelation in an imaginary mode: "far from governing the supposed relation between the sexes in a 'natural' way, it is what *makes truth of their non-relation*" (261).

The first stage of Badiou's argument concerns the disjunction between the two sexual positions and its relation to love as a procedure of truth. Badiou begins with four theses. The first is that there are two positions of experience: the position "man" and the position "woman" (Badiou specifies that these are strictly nominalist categories, having no empirical, biological, or social referent). But this twoness can only be established retroactively, through love (257). This is due to the second thesis: the two positions are totally disjointed, such that nothing of the experience of one is shared by the other (257). This is what Badiou calls "disjunction" (258). But neither position has any experience or direct savoir of this state of disjunction. To constitute such a savoir, a third position would be needed. However, Badiou's third thesis is precisely that there is no third position, no *hors-sexe* (outside sex) that might evaluate the situation from without (258). How then can the disjunction be pronounced? Badiou maintains that the situation must be supplemented not by a third structural position, but by a singular event that initiates the amorous procedure, and that he calls the "encounter" (258).

But Badiou's treatment of the love-event concerns not only the disjunction it pronounces, but also the possibility of a truth that would transcend this disjunction. This point introduces his fourth and final thesis, that there is a sole humanity (258). Although the positions "man" and "woman" are totally disjointed from one another in their specific experiences and savoirs, humanity itself does not fall within this disjunction. Humanity is singular in that it cannot be founded by an objective predicative trait (258). Quite simply, it is "what supports generic procedures, or procedures of truth" (259). Badiou identifies four such procedures: science, politics, art, and love. While the sexuated body is the site of a particular savoir, humanity is the "historial body" of truth, "*sustain[ing]* the infinite singularity of the truths inscribed in these types" (259). The thesis that there is a sole humanity means, therefore, that "every truth applies to its *entire* historial body," since "a truth, whatever it may be, is indifferent to any predicative sharing of its support" (259). Thus any truth, as such, is transpositional (260).

But this proposition introduces a dilemma. How can a truth be transpositional if there are at least two positions, man and woman, that are radically disjointed with regard to experience in general (260)? Although we might expect the first three theses to result in the enunciation that all truths are sexuated, Badiou maintains at one and the same time "that the disjunction is radical, that there is no third position, and that nonetheless whatever of the truth emerges [*ce qui advient de vérité*] is generic, withheld from any positional disjunction" (260). Love, he argues, is the site where this paradox is treated. It is an operation that "makes truth [*fait vérité*] of the paradox itself" (261). For this reason, "to love is to think" (261).

The second stage of Badiou's argument concerns the advent of the Two in the encounter, and its nomination in the declaration of love. Badiou demonstrates that is not enough to have two people, a couple, for there to be a scene of the Two. To retain both the disjunction and the fact that there is a truth of it, he argues that we have to start from love as a process, and not from amorous consciousness (263). To say that the disjunction between the two positions is total, that there is no neutral or third position, is to say that the two positions cannot be counted as two (262). For this reason, love has to be distinguished from the couple. The couple "is what, of love, is visible for a third party"; it is "the two *counted* on the basis of a situation in which there are three" (262). For this reason, the two it counts is "an indifferent two, a two entirely external to the Two of the disjunction" (262). Conversely, love as the "scene of the Two" is a work, a process, where the Two is the hypothetical operator of an unpredictable and unstable enquiry [*enquête aléatoire*] (263). The advent of the supposition of a Two is originarily eventmental. The event is the chance supplement to the situation that Badiou calls an "encounter" (263). However, the encounter-event only "happens" in the form of its disappearance or eclipse. It is fixed only by a nomination, and this nomination is the declaration of love. Badiou notes that "I love you" combines two pronouns, *I* and *you*, that are uncombinable as soon as they are referred to the disjunction. The declaration "convokes the unknown [*in-su*] void of the disjunction" (263), producing a scene of the Two as a process where love can inquire after the truth of the situation, a truth that is not itself presented.

The third stage of the argument treats the "advent of the bodies in love" (265), or the material marking of the Two in sexuation. For Badiou, the different sexual traits do not suffice to mark the disjunction or allow for the advent of the bodies, any more than the couple suffices to produce a scene of the Two. He writes: "the differential sexual traits only attest to the disjunction on the condition that there is a declaration of love. If this condition isn't met, *there is no Two*, and the sexual marking is entirely *within* the disjunction, without being able to attest to it" (266). In the sexual field, the distinction between being within the disjunction and attesting to it is manifest in the distinction between desire, as a logic internal to one position, and love as the scene of the Two. The advent of the bodies in love "engages the *mandatory* non-rapport [*dé-rapport*] between desire and love" (265), because "desire is captive to its cause, which is not the body as such, much less the 'other' as subject, but an object that is born by the body, and before which the subject, in the fantasmatic framework, is led to his own disappearance" (265). For Badiou, "every sexual unveiling of the body that is not amorous is strictly masturbatory," since it "deals only with the interiority of a position" (266). Love alone exhibits the sexual as a figure of the Two, by attesting that there are two sexuated bodies, and not one (266). This is why Badiou asserts that "desire is homosexual, regardless of sexuation," while "love is principally heterosexual, however gay it may be" (272). Although love cannot entirely elude the object-cause of desire, it does not have the object of desire as its cause. Instead, it "marks on the bodies, as a materiality, the supposition of the Two it activates" (265). Nonetheless, the bodies can only *mark* the Two, not *present* it: such a presentation would require a third position external to the disjunction, the hors-sexe (266). For Badiou, therefore, the sexuated attestation of the disjunction does not abolish the disjunction: "It is true that there is no sexual relation, because love founds the Two, not the relation of the Ones in the Two" (266).

This point leads to the fourth step in Badiou's argument, that there is "a unity of the amorous truth, a sexuated conflict of the two *savoirs*" (266). Although there is a single truth of love in the situation, Badiou asserts that "the procedure of this oneness operates within the disjunction it gives truth to" (267)—that is, from the perspective of a particular experience or savoir. For this reason, truth has to be rigorously distinguished from savoir. Whereas savoir is internal to the disjunction, "love *produces* a truth of the situation, such that the disjunction is a law for it" (268). However, like the Two of love, this truth is never integrally presented, because it is infinitely composed (268). As a result, the anticipation in savoir of each position remains sexuated: "foreclosed from the truth, the positions return [*font retour*] in *savoir*" (267). Badiou describes the differences between the two *savoirs* in the following terms:

> the position "man" maintains the schism of the Two, the between-two where the void of the disjunction fixes itself. The position "woman" maintains that the Two endures and persists in its errancy. . . . The *savoir* of man orders its judgments according to the *nothing* of the Two, and the *savoir* of woman to the *nothing but* Two . . . The feminine enunciation zeroes in on being as such. Its destination in love is ontological. The masculine enunciation zeroes in on the change in number, the painful violation of the One by the supposition of Two. It is essentially logical. (269)

However, the sexuation of the two savoirs—or the impossibility of one subject occupying both positions—does not mean that the truth itself is sexuated. Rather, "the conflict of the *savoirs* in love reveals that the One of a truth is always exposed both as logical and as ontological" (269).

The fifth and final stage of the argument develops this hypothesis with a meditation on humanity and the feminine position. Badiou maintains that "the position 'woman' is singularly charged with the relation of love to humanity" (270). This is because her position is such that "the subtraction of love afflicts her with inhumanity for herself. Or better, that humanity risks having no value unless the amorous procedure is in place" (270). This, he suggests, is why women excel at the novel, where love deploys humanity in all its other forms: science, politics, and art. For the position 'man', on the other hand, each one of these procedures is able to valorize the humanity function on its own, without taking into account the existence of the others; each type metaphorizes the others (271). The feminine representation of humanity is both *conditional* and *knotted*, which allows for a "more complete perception of inhumanity" (or even, in certain cases, a greater "right to inhumanity"). Conversely, the masculine representation of humanity is at once *symbolic* and *separating*, allowing both for "considerable indifference" and for a "much greater capacity for conclusion" (272).

But where the problem of the universal is concerned, Badiou gives special priority to the position woman. In asserting that the value of the humanity function is dependent, for woman, on the existence of love, he advances that "the position-woman demands for humanity a guarantee of universality" (273). The stakes of this move are to contest the "commonplace" according to which access to the symbolic and to the universal is more immediate for a man (272). On this point Badiou departs from Lacan, for whom "the phallic function is the universal qualifier assigned to the position 'man'," while "the position 'woman' is defined by a combination of the existential and negation, which means that woman is not-all" (273). For Badiou, the problem with this formula is that woman is determined as "not-all" within the logic of the phallic function itself (273). In other words, as the universal qualifier assigned to the masculine position, the phallic function treats the problem of sexual difference from within the disjunction; it treats all of humanity "equally," but from the vantage point of an unequal law. It is uni-positional, rather than transpositional. Hence, the logical consequence of his argument is that "the humanity function does not coincide with the phallic function" (273). Since love, and love alone, makes truth of the disjunction in a way that holds for all humanity (271), the phallic function cannot support the universal. In fact, Badiou argues that with regard to the humanity function, the position woman actually sustains the universal totality, whereas the position man disseminates metaphorically the different unitary compositions of humanity (273). In conclusion, he states that love, in splitting the humanity function from the phallic function, "returns to 'women,' in the full extension of the procedures of truth, the universal qualifier" (273).

WHY LOVE?

Despite its use of the logical language of set theory, "What Is Love?" rides on a number of assumptions that are not justified within the analysis itself. First, why is love privileged as a procedure of truth where the disjunction is concerned? What is at stake in the substitution of love for the phallic function as the universal qualifier? These questions concern Badiou's modifications of Lacan. Although his name is not mentioned until the last page of the essay, Lacan's work underlies much of Badiou's argument, from his formulation of the disjunction or nonrelation between the sexes to his account of sexuated savoir as foreclosed from truth. In particular, Badiou's insistence that love must not be limited to the pursuit of an imaginary object of desire draws on Lacan's account of ethics, as the assumption of a "desire without object." But whereas Badiou locates the transcendence of the object-cause of desire in the "declaration of love," in which the subject invokes the void of the disjunction in the address to another person ("*I* love *you*"), Lacan links it to the traversal of the fantasy of castration, in which the subject is obliged to encounter his own lack (or the absence of any object that might anchor the drives) in the absence of any Other to whom he could address himself.[5]

In short, Badiou modifies Lacan's account of ethics by favoring the "declaration of love" as a nomination of the void, instead of castration. This is not just a question of nomenclature, though, because it highlights the ambiguous relationship between love and castration in Badiou's thought. In some respects, his understanding of love as the pronouncement of a disjunction seems to imply castration, since there is a loss of the object and an acknowledgment, in speech, of the impossibility of the sexual relation. In this regard, one might draw the conclusion that what is universal is castration itself, which is localized in the declaration that names the void between the "I" and the "you." But in other respects, Badiou's account of love—and feminine love in particular—seems to exclude any notion of castration, since it supports humanity as the site of a "universal totality." Although castration is universal where humanity is concerned, it could not be said to support humanity as the site of a universal totality. The same could be said of Badiou's account of sexual difference. The fact that there are two positions, and thus two savoirs that are not shared, does not necessarily imply castration: it could simply imply something additional, a surplus of knowledge with regard to the natural being. In Badiou's account of the "material marking" of the bodies through love, it is almost as though the two sexes are simply within the brute oppositions of natural sexuality until the declaration comes along to name the void of the disjunction, thereby creating a scene of the Two that did not exist before. Conversely, Lacan emphasizes that the one of nature was lost with the advent of language, and that the address and the disjunction into which it falls are symptoms of this loss.

This shift in emphasis is important, because it minimizes the dimension of sexual difference as a split in the universal: a split that is brought about by language itself, and not simply an aftereffect of the phallic function. As Juliet Flower MacCannell puts it, "The Law of Sexual Difference (though not of its inequality) is . . . a split in the form of the universal, as two different positions the subject (as distinct from the ego) may take toward its castration by language."[6] Badiou takes the disjunction between the positions man and woman as his starting point. But this disjunction does not come from nowhere. Lacan states that "the subject . . . thinks as a consequence of the fact that a structure, that of language—the word implies it—carves up his body, a structure that has nothing to do with anatomy."[7] The nonrelation between the sexes results from this castration or "carving up," the loss of the natural aims of the organism through the human being's confrontation with the void at the heart of the address. If for Lacan "there is no sexual relation," it is not because women and men are categorically different entities, but because they cease to be natural complements when the logic of eroticism displaces the natural aims of the organism.

The phallic function represents one response to the carving up of the body, the quest for an imaginary object that would supplement the sexual nonrelation by providing a provisional aim for the drives. Badiou's account of the "homosexuality of desire" seems to allude to what Lacan, in a play on words, calls *l'hommosexuel*: the "man-sexuality" of the one who stands under the banner of the phallic function, and who is thus unable to approach woman, because "what he approaches is the cause of his desire, the object *a*."[8] Although Badiou acknowledges that love cannot be regulated by the object-cause of desire, he does not underscore the castration implied in the absence or impossibility of this object. Lacan is more blunt. He states that "there is no chance for a man to have *jouissance* of a woman's body, otherwise stated, for him to make love, without castration; in other words, without something that says no to the phallic function."[9] The castration needed to "make love" is the castration implied in having to pass through the desire of the Other, or language: that is, to address a woman, and therefore lose her as an object.

Lacan and Badiou both see the phallic function as an impediment to love. But Lacan is categorical in stating that nothing except castration can "say no" to the phallic function. For Badiou, however, it seems that woman's love (and the "humanity function" it supports) can "say no" to the phallic function without castration. If the love that supports the universal totality is a feminine love, does this mean that it does not have to submit to castration? At the end of the essay, Badiou seeks to undo the pejorative connotations of woman's designation as not-all by proposing that love, in splitting the humanity function from the phallic function, "returns the universal qualifier to women." But why "returns"? This suggests that it was once in the possession of women, but was lost or wrested away. What then is the nature of this universal qualifier, and how was it lost? And what are the stakes (for women, for men, for "humanity") of its restitution, and the (re)instatement of woman as the site of the "all"? How does the feminine allow for the totalization of the universal, or the assertion of the "oneness" of humanity?

To address these questions, we need to turn to *Saint Paul*. This is because the link between women and universalism that Badiou hypothesizes in "What Is Love?" actually finds its "proof" in Badiou's reading of Paul, where the characteristics he associates with feminine love are generalized as features of Christian discourse. Like the "position-woman," Christianity is "singularly charged with the relation of love to humanity," and aspires to remove the obstacles to universalism posed by the particular discourses of Jew and Greek and their restrictive logics of identification. Moreover, the feminine position that "humanity risks having no value if the amorous procedure is not in place" actually finds an eloquent spokesperson in Paul himself: "if I speak in the tongues of men and of angels, but have not love, I am a noisy gong or a clanging cymbal. And if I have prophetic powers, and understand all mysteries and all knowledge, and if I have all faith, so as to remove mountains, but have not love, I am nothing. If I give away all I have, and if I deliver my body to be burned, but have not love, I gain nothing" (1 Cor. 13:1–3). These parallels are surprising, since Paul's letters really have very little to do with sexual difference (and femininity in particular), but are concerned primarily with the "new man's" liberation from the mortifying effects of the law.

But although the contexts of these two essays are very different, there are important parallels between Badiou's portrayal of feminine love as sustaining the universal totality and his appreciation of Paul's attempts to overcome the death introduced into human life by the law. When these arguments are read side by side, we can see that in both cases there is a real ambiguity about the work that love is supposed to do: not only with regard to the phallic function or the law, but with respect to castration. What light does *Saint Paul* shed on the meaning of "feminine love" in Badiou's thought, and its function with regard to the universal totality? Is the feminine position fundamentally a Christian one for Badiou? Or, at the very least, already read through the lens of Pauline universalism? To address these questions, I will first briefly summarize Badiou's argument.

WORLDLY ALTERITY AND THE TRANSCENDENT UNIVERSAL

In *Saint Paul*, Badiou underscores the novelty of Paul's discourse in relation to the positions of Jew and Greek, which he understands not as ethnic designations but as the two dominant discourses of subjectivity with which Paul has to contend in his invention of Christianity. He argues that the persistence of the Jewish and

Greek discourses blocks the universality of the announcement, because each discourse supposes the persistence of the other (45). Badiou's treatment of Jew and Greek before the announcement is thus exactly analogous to his account of the nonrelation between man and woman before the declaration of love. In both cases, universality is blocked by an opposition that splits humanity in two, such that a transpositional truth cannot be recognized. Moreover, this analogy is internal to Paul's discourse, structuring the celebrated declaration that Badiou reads as the key tenet of Pauline universalism: "there is neither Jew nor Greek, there is neither slave nor free, there is neither male nor female; for you are all one person in Christ Jesus" (Gal. 3:28-29). In this formulation, ethnic particularism, sexual difference, and social inequality are grouped together as distinctions to be abolished. But Badiou's reading is concerned primarily with the newness of Paul's discourse with regard to the positions of Jew and Greek, which is more central to his understanding of Pauline universalism than his treatment of man and woman.

For Badiou, the Jewish and Greek discourses are both instances of "particularity," since they are centered around obedience to worldly objects that function as unary traits of identification. In Jewish discourse, the object is election, the exceptional alliance between God and his people; observance of the law is what cements it (60). In Greek discourse, the object is the finite cosmic totality as the domain of thought (60). The positions of Jew and Greek are therefore analogous to what Badiou calls the "homosexuality of desire" in "What Is Love?" In each case, obedience to the object promotes the insular logic of particularity and impedes transcendence. Moreover, the opposition between desire and love is once again central, since it is fundamental to Paul's critique of Jewish law as condemning the subject to a transgressive desire for the object it proscribes.

The corollary of this particularism is that each discourse supposes that the key to salvation can be found in the universe: through "direct mastery of the situation," in the case of Greek wisdom, or through "mastery of the literal tradition and the deciphering of signs," in the case of Jewish prophecy (45). Conversely, Paul's discourse ties salvation to the event wherein the subject is called forth as a subject: "by the grace of God I am who I am (1 Cor. 15:10)" (18). Badiou notes that after the conversion event of Damascus, Paul turns away from "any authority other than that of the Voice that personally called him to become a subject" (19). The authority of the Voice is opposed to Greek wisdom and Jewish signs, embodying a "demonstration of the spirit" that forgoes any appeal to the letter or to rational argumentation: "For Jews demand signs and Greeks desire wisdom, but we proclaim Christ crucified, a scandal for the Jews and folly for the Gentiles" (1 Cor. 1:22-23).

The counterpart of Paul's denunciation of the Jews' enslavement to the law—and to the sinful objects and rites it both prohibits and brings to life as objects of desire—is the affirmation of a love born of the resurrection event, which Badiou reads as a liberation of the subject from the repetition-compulsion of desire, and thus from subservience to worldly objects and ritual practice (83). He argues that Christian discourse implies an "absolutely novel relation to its object" (59), because it must be an "indifferent traversal of worldly differences, avoiding the casuistry of customs" (107). The most important manifestation of this indifference is the overcoming of the law in its particularity. To the "multiplicity of legal prescriptions, whose objects fuel the mortifying autonomy of desire," Paul opposes "a sole maxim, affirmative and not tied to an object, that would not solicit the infinity of desire with the transgression of the interdiction" (94). For Badiou, "love" (or what was long translated as *caritas* or "charity") is Paul's name for the universal address of the truth whose process the Christian sustains, and that he makes into a nonliteral law (92). However, Paul does not imply that the Christian discourse is entirely without law. If "Christ is the end of the law" (Rom. 10:4), it is only because "love is the fulfillment of the law (Rom. 13:10)" (92). Love implies the "existence of a trans-literal law, a law of the spirit" that supersedes the authority of all particular laws (91). For the New Man, therefore, love is the "law of his break with the law" (94).

For Badiou, this break is intimately tied to the status of Christianity as a filial discourse. He argues that the Greek and Jewish discourses, in their particularity, are both "discourses of the father," because they cement communities together in a form of obedience. Conversely, Christianity is the "discourse of the son," and thus the only discourse capable of addressing humanity in its universality (45). This is because the discourse of the son is detached from all particularism, liberated from the object-identifications that regulate worldly adherences. But for Badiou, the universal it inaugurates is defined not only by the production of equality, but by the subsuming of the Other as such:

> Thought is universal only when it addresses itself to all the others, and in this address installs itself as power. But as soon as all are counted according to the universal, including the solitary militant, the result is the subsuming of the Other by the Same. Paul shows in detail how a universal thought, departing from the worldly proliferation of alterities (the Jew, the Greek, women, men, slaves, free men, etc.), *produces* the Same and the Equal (there is neither Jew nor Greek, etc.). (117)

However, Badiou specifies that this production of the Same does not amount to a dialectical negation of the particular:

> Paul, as I have insisted, is not a dialectician. The universal is not the negation of particularity. It is the trajectory of a distance with regard to a partic-

ularity that subsists. Every particularity is an instance of conformity, a conformism. Paul attempts to sustain a non-conformity against what is always making us conform.... As Paul so superbly puts it: "Do not conform to the present age, but be transformed by the renewal of your thought (Rom. 12:2)." (118)

Nonetheless, it seems that for Badiou there is no alterity, indeed no Other, that is not already "particular," and therefore "conformist." Under the heading of "particularity," therefore, he groups not only the objects and identificatory traits that distinguish one position from another and define its mode of mastering the universe, but difference or alterity as such. Conversely, he does not view the filial and fraternal bent of Christian discourse as incompatible with its universalism, even where woman is concerned. The status of sexual difference in these formulations is therefore very ambiguous. In "What Is Love?" Badiou argued that the particular *savoir* of each sexuated position is internal to that position, and therefore unable to assume the status of a transpositional truth. But here he makes a much bolder—and, I think, more questionable—claim, in maintaining that difference as such (the disjunction of sexual difference, the Other) is internal to the logic of particularity, and that there is no "real" of difference, no absolutely Other.

Indeed, Badiou maintains that Christian love allows not only for the overcoming of interiority, but for a rupturing of the boundary between self and Other:

> Under the law, the subject, decentered by the automatic life of desire, occupied the place of death, and sin (or unconscious desire) lived an autonomous life in him. But when the subject is pulled away from death by the resurrection, he participates in a new life whose name is Christ. The resurrection of Christ is also *our* resurrection, shattering the death wherein the subject, under the law, was exiled in the closed form of the Self: "If I live, it is no longer me who lives, but Christ who lives in me (Gal. 2:20)." (SP 91)

Whereas the "declaration of love" named the void of the disjunction between man and woman, and the absence of any third position that might evaluate or resolve that disjunction from without, here Christian love dissolves all "worldly" oppositions, including sexual difference, by appealing to a third term that transcends the opposition and allows it to be overcome. The "closed form of the Self" is ruptured not by the advent of an Other it fails to assimilate (the "indigestible other" of Levinas's thought, for example), but by the Same. In this sense, love does not so much interrupt or question the subject's integrity as complete a subject whose closedness is its lack. In Badiou's words, it "gives the faithful subject its consistency" (92). Indeed, the "address to all" that conditions Pauline universalism is for

Badiou nothing more than a generalization of the "self-love" born of the resurrection event: "only the event authorizes the subject to be something other than a dead Self, impossible to love. The new law is thus the deployment of the power of self-love made possible by subjectivation (conviction), directed toward others and destined to all" (95).

THE CRUSHING SYMBOLIC OF THE FATHERS: THE ANTILAW OF LOVE

The fifth step of Badiou's argument in "What Is Love?"—the thesis that feminine love supports the universal totality—does not seem to have a counterpart in *Saint Paul*, even though many of the positions Badiou attributes to women, especially with regard to love, are enunciated by Paul and generalized as features of Christian discourse. But despite the absence of any real meditation on the feminine position as such in this text, the question of feminine love once again plays a central, if easily missed, role. It comes up in an unlikely place, at the heart of his argument that Christianity is the discourse of the son, whose claim to universality inheres in its liberation from the discourse of the father and his law. This argument appears immediately following Badiou's detailed summary of Pier Paolo Pasolini's *San Paolo*, a screenplay based on the life of the apostle that was never filmed. In Pasolini's treatment, Paul's mission is transposed to the twentieth century, and takes on radical Marxist overtones. Badiou, in his commentary, suggests that Pasolini is uniquely poised to appreciate Paul's message, because he understands that only a militant fraternalism can make way for the universal.[10] However, this fraternalism in turn depends on an appeal to maternal love. In Badiou's words,

> The Greek discourse and the Jewish discourse are both discourses *of the Father*. . . . The only discourse that has a chance to be universal, detached from all particularity, is one that presents itself *as a discourse of the Son*.
>
> The figure of the son obviously impassioned Freud, just as it underlies Pasolini's identification with the apostle. For the first, with regard to the Jewish monotheism for which Moses is the decentered founding figure (the Egyptian as the Other of the origin), Christianity poses the question of the sons' relation to the Law, against the background of the symbolic murder of the father. For the second, the power of thought internal to homosexual desire is oriented toward the advent of an egalitarian humanity, where the fraternal pact annuls the crushing symbolic of the father, incarnated in institutions (the Church, or the communist party), in favor of the mother's love. (46)

This is a seemingly incongruous remark, because the question of maternal love, although important to Pasolini's work as a whole, does not actually appear in his screenplay treatment, and has no apparent analogue either in Paul's writings or in Freud's account of the sons' symbolic murder. So where does this "mother" come from, and what is the function of her love where the universal is concerned?

To unpack this dense passage, we need to situate it within Badiou's larger argument. What is at stake in each example is the role of love in the son's contestation of the father's law. In Paul's invention of Christianity, the sons accomplish the "symbolic murder" of the father by annulling his law and putting the gospel of love in its place. For Pasolini, the fraternal pact—guided by "homosexual desire"—annuls the father's "crushing symbolic" and replaces it with maternal love. The passage establishes an implicit analogy between the Pauline polemic against the law and the mother's love, since both defy the inequality of the father's symbolic with the promise of an "egalitarian humanity." In "What Is Love?" we saw that Badiou's thesis was that feminine love alone can support the universal totality, because the phallic function does not coincide with the humanity function. But here Badiou introduces something new. Feminine love contests not only the supremacy of the phallic function, but the crushing symbolic itself. It represents the possibility of an undivided, "egalitarian" One. But why, in the context of his reading of Paul, does Badiou once again make a point of coding this love "feminine"? And what does it tell us about the stakes of the "symbolic murder of the father" in Paul's discourse?

The logical conclusion I draw from Badiou's argument is that love—and "feminine love" in particular—does not simply follow after the symbolic murder of the father, it accomplishes it. Of course, the passage above does not say anything of the sort. It speaks of the symbolic murder of the father as preparing the way for the son's universal, which, in a second movement, will in turn be predicated on love. However, the allusion to Freud complicates this picture by introducing a highly compacted, alternate genealogy of Paul's innovation, which points to the interdependence of "symbolic murder" and "love." Let me begin by examining this relationship, and then try to account for its "feminization."

In *Moses and Monotheism*, Freud's thesis is that Paul correctly diagnoses the Jews' devotion to the law as guilty penance for an original crime, for which they have been punished with death. Although Paul does not realize it himself, this crime was the primeval murder of the father, who was later deified. For Freud, the Jews' lingering guilt over the repressed primal murder is the source of their enthusiasm for Mosaic monotheism, which both exalted the primeval father and set forth an ethical doctrine that "formed their character for good," by encouraging them to abandon their magical practices and "progress in spirituality and sublimations."[11] But the crime itself was not remembered; in its place remained only the fantasy of expiation. Through Paul, Freud argues, this fantasy found expression in the gospel of salvation, which proclaimed that a Son of God, innocent of all sin, had sacrificed himself and thereby assumed the guilt of the world. The redeemer had to be a son, because the sin had been the murder of the father. But Freud reasons that this redeemer could not have been innocent, as the gospel maintained:

> That the Redeemer sacrificed himself as an innocent man was an obviously tendentious distortion, difficult to reconcile with logical thinking. How could a man who was innocent assume the guilt of the murderer by allowing himself to be killed? In historical reality there was no such contradiction. The "redeemer" could be no one else but he who was most guilty, the leader of the brother horde who had overpowered the Father. Whether there had been such a chief rebel and leader must, in my opinion, remain uncertain. It is quite possible, but we must also consider that each member of the brother horde certainly had the wish to do the deed by himself and thus to create for himself a unique position as a substitute for the identification with the father which he had to give up when he was submerged in the community. If there was no such leader, then Christ was the heir of an unfulfilled wish-phantasy; if there was such a leader, then Christ was his successor and his reincarnation.[12]

But Freud notes that although this religious innovation was meant to appease the Father Deity, it actually resulted in his being dethroned and cast aside. This is because in Paul's gospel, the father now took second place to the son, who stood in his stead just as the sons of the primal horde had longed to do. Hence "Paul, by developing the Jewish religion further, became its destroyer."[13]

In essence, Freud identifies three distinct moments in the evolution of Christianity. First, the Jews murder the primal father, but repress the memory of this crime. They then reinstate the father's law as a revered substitute, effectively bringing him back to (symbolic) life. Finally, the Christians acknowledge and expiate the primeval crime, but in the process murder the father "symbolically": that is, they kill off the symbolic residue of the father, the law that secured his exalted position in the Jewish faith. In this way, Christianity both reenacts and completes the totemic murder, by bringing about the final victory of the sons' rebellion: this time without the guilty internalization of the father's law. To push this interpretation a bit further, I would say that Paul's genius is having perceived the parricidal potential of Christ, who, in dying for the expiation of this crime, would actually succeed in killing the father once and for all. Implicit in Paul's gospel of salvation, therefore, is another rallying cry, very much in the spirit of Sade's later call to arms: "Jews, yet another effort . . . if you want to be parricides!"[14]

The symbolic murder of the father in Pauline Christianity is a second-order murder, a destruction of the father's law itself: and thus not merely a symbolic murder, but a *murder of the symbolic*. In these formulations, I am adding a further twist to Freud's reading, by introducing something that his reading does not address directly, but that Badiou appreciates fully. Paul does not so much say that we *are* guilty, as that the law *makes us guilty*: "for the law brings wrath, but where there is no law there is no transgression" (Rom. 4:15). If there is no law, there is no crime, for "sin is not counted where there is no law" (Rom. 5:13). This is the ambiguity of Paul's meditation on "death to the law" in the epistle to the Romans: initially, death comes through the law, which enslaves me to sin; but when I die *to* the law, I liberate myself from its injunctions. Like Nietzsche before him, Badiou understands that for Paul, Christ is first and foremost "the destroyer of the Law."[15] But he differs from Nietzsche in upholding Paul's claim not only that "Christ is the end of the law" (Rom. 10:4), but that "love is the fulfillment of the law" (Rom. 13:10). For the Christian, love alone can "murder" the symbolic, since—as Badiou puts it—love is the "law of his break with the law" (94). But to understand what is at stake in Badiou's account of love, and especially maternal love, we have to understand what is being gotten rid of in the crushing symbolic it eradicates.

For Badiou, as we have seen, the discourse of the father is the site of particularity, the discourse of obedience to a unary trait or object that he sees as impeding universalism. In this respect, the father's law is precisely analogous to the object-cause of desire in "What Is Love?"—the imaginary object that love must transcend if it is to found the conditions for the universal. The same analogy is, of course, central to the discourse of Paul, whose polemic against the law zeroes in on the commandments themselves in their relation to the object-cause of desire. For Paul, the law is a force of death insofar as it prohibits (and thereby incites longing for) the object of desire, which causes me to sin, and therefore to die:

> I should not have known what it is to covet if the law had not said "You shall not covet." But sin, finding opportunity in the commandment, wrought in me all kinds of covetousness. Apart from the law sin lies dead. I was once alive apart from the law, but when the commandment came, sin revived and I died; the very commandment which promised life proved to be death to me. For sin, finding opportunity in the commandment, deceived me and by it killed me. (Rom. 7:7-11)

But as this example suggests, Badiou also borrows from Paul a highly compacted understanding of the law. On the one hand, it denotes the symbolic incarnated by institutions (and thus the logic of particularity ruled by the unary trait or object), while on the other hand, it is the bearer of "death," the mortal breach introduced into human life by the inadequation of the flesh to the word.[16] In psychoanalytic terms, Paul conflates the "father's law"—the Oedipal interdiction or "thou shalt not"—with castration itself, the alienation of being by language. But although the father's law represents castration within a particular context (or, to use Badiou's expression, in the mode of particularity), it does not actually introduce castration into human life, any more than its eradication relieves it. This is why Lacan will say of the Ten Commandments that "whether or not we obey them, we still cannot help hearing them—in their indestructible character they prove to be the *very laws of speech*."[17]

In arguing for the illegitimacy of the law by underscoring its particularity, Badiou, like Paul, gets rid of more than just the father's law, with its object-bound logic of obedience. He also implies that the universal rule of castration might be vanquished along with the particular law of prohibition. When love "fulfills" the law, it not only frees the subject from the sinful allure of the object, but eliminates death as such: in "dying to the law," the Christian also "dies to death." In Badiou's words, the message of Paul's gospel is that "we *can* overcome our impotence, and rediscover what the law has separated us from" (93).

The appeal to love supports this fantasy by upholding an exception to the general law of castration: a "law *beyond* the law," as Badiou puts it (92). It is not surprising, then, that this love should be coded "feminine," even "maternal": if the sons appeal to the mother's love to support their fantasy of a universal totality purged of the symbolic and its crushing effects, is it not because she appears to be the one exception to castration, the only one who enjoys fully? This gesture recalls Sade's attempt to demonstrate the illegitimacy of patriarchal law by appealing to another avatar of maternal love, the reign of an all-permissive Mother Nature. He too attempts to reduce castration to the particularity of the father's law, whose authority he undercuts by demonstrating its inability to "castrate the mother," to put a limit to jouissance.

Importantly, then, this freedom from the law and its divisive effects depends on an identification with a principle behind the law that both fulfills it and renders it obsolete. Elsewhere I have argued that Paul's discourse distinguishes not only between the law and love, but between the illegitimate authority of the signifier and the true authority of the Voice: the disembodied Voice that interpellates Paul on the road to Damascus, but also the inner voice of the Christian liberated from the law, the voice of freedom.[18] In this argument, I follow Juliet Flower MacCannell's distinction between the jouissance of the Other as *voice* and the Other as *speech*. She notes that for Lacan, speech is defined classically as the field of the symbolic pact, the social contract that divides us from each other as mutual aggressors. But the voice, in its materiality, is already the object *a*, the "embodiment of a principle behind the law of speech."[19] It took shape in Lacan's discourse as one of the four fundamental objects *a* (gaze, voice, breast, feces) around which the partial drives circulate. Its earliest manifestation is the maternal voice the infant hears in the womb, whose murmurings are not yet interrupted and differentiated by the paternal signifier that institutes the function of speech. MacCannell notes that while speech, as the field of the signifier, works to limit the jouissance of the Other by erecting barriers against it, the Voice as object *a* is a bearer of the jouissance that insists within the fantasy.

For Lacan, the function of the signifier is to maintain a distance with regard to the object-cause of desire, or what he calls "*das Ding*" (the Thing): "the distance between the subject and *das Ding* is precisely the condition of speech."[20] But the paternal function or *nom-du-père* (name-of-the-father) that institutes speech does not work simply to interdict—and thereby incite desire for—the impossible object of desire (the mother of the Oedipal scenario), but to put a stop to the jouissance that the child first encounters in the body of the mother. In this sense, castration applies first and foremost not to the subject, but to the Other. To eliminate the law in its spoken particularity is also, therefore, to give free rein to the jouissance of this uncastrated Other. In Paul's case, the authority that is lacking in the symbolic Other or law assumes consistency in the Voice that, without ever issuing any specific directives or imperatives, nonetheless commands his total obedience. Perhaps this is what Lacan had in mind when he said that "Christianity ended up inventing a God who enjoys,"[21] a God of jouissance.

MacCannell describes the jouissance of the Other as the "imaginary invasion of the One,"[22] a suggestive formula where Paul's relationship to Judaism is concerned. In his influential study of Moses, Martin Buber suggests that the defining characteristic of early Judaism is its break with the worship of nature, symbolized by the gap introduced into the solar and lunar cycles of day and month by the commandment to honor the Sabbath.[23] This suggests that the "father's symbolic" is not merely the set of inegalitarian laws that cement the discourse of particularity, but the signifier that introduces a lack—and thus a space for desire and for sublimation—into the undifferentiated Oneness constitutive of the natural world. Conversely, the closing of the "wound" introduced by the signifier or law not only allows for the universal address of Paul's discourse, but potentially gives rise to a Oneness that forecloses in advance the place of the subject. Freud notes that while Mosaic monotheism encouraged sublimation by weaning the Jewish people of magic and mysticism, the victory of Christianity not only represented a "cultural regression" compared to Judaism, but allowed for a reversion to magic, polytheism, and the cult of the mother goddess that "proved a great hindrance to the spiritual development of two following millennia."[24] Of course, this regression is not easily attributed to Paul, whose account of the spiritual implications of monotheism is quite rigorous. But it does suggest that Paul's overturning of the law potentially allows for the renewed insistence of this imaginary Oneness in and beyond the One of universalism.

MacCannell notes that for Lacan, the object a is what "founds our notions of the 'atom,' the 'constant' of energy, and the 'One' of God." She muses that "it is no accident that [he] likens this object to entities with the capacity to overwhelm us if they are not contained—the atomic particle, energy, the Deity."[25] This point invites a reexamination of the logic of Badiou's "What Is Love?" essay, in which, as I noted earlier, the "declaration of love" takes the place of what Lacan calls the traversal of the fantasy of castration. For Lacan, castration implies the assumption of a "desire without object" that affirms the subject (and the Other) in its lack. In this respect, it always involves a mutual castration: of the subject, and of the jouissance of the Other. But for Badiou, love—and especially "maternal love"—not only frees the sons from the object-economies of the father's law, but also becomes a new kind of object: one that not only "gives the faithful subject its consistency" (92), but gives consistency to the One of the universal totality.

UNIVERSALISM AND EQUALITY: ONE FOR ALL

What is the fate of femininity—or the "position-woman"—in the filial discourse of Christianity? In Badiou's allusion to Pasolini, the complicity between the mother and son does not engage the feminine position as such: it is simply a matter of what "the mother's love" means for the son in his battle against the father's law. In this scenario, woman is reduced to embodying the "all," the forbidden Good behind the law. Indeed, the most immediate consequence of the elevation of feminine love to the status of support for the universal totality seems to be the neutralization or even elimination of the feminine as such, which disappears under this filial and fraternal egalitarianism. Is it a coincidence that the egalitarian humanity Badiou envisions as an alternative to the crushing symbolic of the father is the project of the fraternal pact, supported by "homosexual desire"? If a homosexual desire is one from which the desire of the Other is excluded, we might wonder whether this egalitarianism comes at the cost of women as such (the Other) being eliminated in becoming a figure of love. Paul, according to Badiou, sees the two positions of Jew and Greek as impeding the universal, because the existence of one supposes the existence of the other. Does this then mean that the existence of Christian love does not suppose an other position, and that this very exclusion of the Other is what constitutes its universality?

These questions problematize the equality that Badiou sees as the aim of Paul's discourse. It is true—as Badiou notes in "What Is Love?"—that woman loses out in the particular version of the symbolic that the phallic function sustains. However, she often does not fare much better in the "egalitarian" logics that have claimed to replace it. In Pasolini's dream of an egalitarian humanity, she supports the dream of "equality" only at the cost of embodying or giving consistency to a "sole humanity" figured as beyond the law of castration. And although Paul's version of the universal gives a place to "real" women, equality still comes at the cost of giving voice to the feminine in its specificity.

In Paul's famous words to the Galatians, ethnic particularism (Jew and Greek), social inequity (slave and freeman), and sexual difference (man and woman) are grouped together as distinctions to be abolished by Christ. But in this grouping, the disjunctive nature of the nonrelation of man and woman seems to be diminished—both in Paul's thought and in Badiou's reading—by analogy to the discursive and epistemological oppositions of Jew and Greek, and the economic or political inequality of slave and freeman, in relation to which the discourses of man and woman become nothing more than instances of particularity. The same could be said of Badiou's treatment of the theme of sexual difference, in his analysis of Paul's notoriously conservative pronouncements concerning women. Suggesting that we cannot expect Paul to say about women things that are to our taste today, Badiou asserts that the real question is whether, with regard to his age, Paul was more progressive or more reactionary as concerns the status of women (111). Paul's progressive invention, according to Badiou, is to derive a universalizing equality from the reversibility of an unequal rule (111). Thus, while he recognizes the husband's authority over his wife's body, he also gives the wife authority over her husband's body (1 Cor. 7:4). In so doing, says Badiou, he shows that "the necessity of traversing and attesting the difference of the sexes, in order for it to become undifferentiated in the universality of the declaration, results in symmetrical constraints, and not in unilateral constraints" (112). But is the reversing of the phallic function tantamount to an acknowledgment of the feminine position? Does this reversibility not remain within the logic of the phallic function, in which woman gains the attribute of the universal only through negation? To the extent that Badiou's argument retains the disjunctive nature of sexual difference, it does so in a way that is mediated by the (in)equality of the phallic function. At one point, Badiou actually argues for the persistence of sexual difference in Paul's account of the universal by noting his respect for the different grooming requirements of men and women—if a woman must not shave her head, it is because long hair is "a woman's glory" (112)! But as this example shows, there is really only a superficial retention of difference (gender, not sexual difference), operating against the background of a phallicized indifference.[26]

THE FEMININE, OR "EACH AND EVERY" FOR NOT-ALL

What does it mean for a woman to be "not-all under the phallic function"? Very schematically, "all under the phallic function" means wholly inscribed within the signifying function that limits jouissance, and wholly within the object economy that compensates for castration by proposing partial objects that give consistency to the One, while impeding the advent of what Badiou calls "the scene of the Two." Conversely, "not-all under the phallic function" means not wholly inscribed within the signifier that limits jouissance (and thus subject to an excess that the signifier is unable to limit), and not wholly within the economy of the object: "for ~~the~~ woman, something other than the object *a* is involved in the attempt to supplement the sexual relation that doesn't exist."[27]

Badiou opposes the *All*, the universal address, to the object-logic of particularity. But as the preceding analysis makes clear, this is a false opposition. Within the logic of the phallic function, the object is inseparable from the One it guarantees. Conversely, not-all under the phallic function means neither within the economy of the object, nor linked to the totality of the One. The result is that the feminine position proposes an alternate logic of particularity, one not centered around the object. MacCannell notes that the structure of feminine logic is

> distinguished from that of the masculine by virtue of an alternative and virtually incompatible (contrary and contradictory) way of relating to language (or to "castration"). In this distinction, the number "one" plays a large role, essentially because "masculine logic" is formed around the opposition All versus (an exceptional) One; whereas "feminine logic" is formed on the basis of opposing Each and Every to Not-all.[28]

Feminine logic sustains an "each and every" born of the fact that there is no object to constitute the One. This is why, for Lacan, the feminine does not admit any universality: "If [any speaking being] inscribes itself on the side of woman, it will not allow for any universality, but will be this not-all, insofar as it has the choice of positing itself in Φx [the phallic function] or of not being there."[29]

For Lacan, as I noted earlier, a man cannot enter love except through castration. But what about woman? Of course she has to face castration too, but the particular modality in which she confronts it does not come into Badiou's essay. Whereas a man turns to the object to supplement the nonrelation between the sexes, woman is involved in the quest for an imaginary Other whose love would give her what she seeks on the level of the signifier. It is the recognition of the absence of this Other that constitutes her particular relation to castration. For Lacan, therefore, castration implies both the lack of an object for desire and the absence of the Other of the address: it puts a limit to the phallic function and its attempt to circumvent castration through the pursuit of an imaginary object, but also to seduction, or the attempt to construct an Other in whose gaze the subject would come into being as a unified ego.[30] Badiou is attentive to the first, but not necessarily to the second. In fact, it seems important that woman's way of supplementing the sexual nonrelation—or of denying castration—be retained, and made the support for a universal totality.

Lacan says that feminine jouissance reveals "one face of the Other, the God-face."[31] It is what emerges in the gaze of Dante's Beatrice: "her whom he, Dante, cannot satisfy, because from her, he can have only this look, only this object, but of whom he tells us that God fulfills her utterly."[32] But this also suggests that in her imagined communion—this Other—woman allows for "the identification of the Other with the One."[33]

MacCannell suggests that within the logic of masculinity, the jouissance of the Other as an "imaginary invasion of the One" is embodied most vividly by the uncastrated father of the primal horde. But although the "One of the god" that takes shape in feminine jouissance may represent an attractive alternative to it where man is concerned, MacCannell follows Lacan in insisting that woman cannot occupy the place assigned to her by this masculine fantasy:

> Lacan . . . positions woman (or at least Dante's woman) opposite both the *père jouissant* figure, and also opposite a One which shades toward the god the poet imagines as "fulfilling" her. This One of the god is potentially as monstrous, potentially as brutal as the primal father which was made salient by Freud in *Totem and Taboo* as the (retroactive myth of) the remainder of the logic of masculinity.[34]

Although we glimpse it in her experience, woman cannot just surrender to the "God-face of the Other" or lose herself in this jouissance. For MacCannell, woman "must do double battle": "against the *Jouissance* of the Other, *the* One—against her invasion by the brute—and against her invasion by the divine. She is always tempted by these Imaginary Others. She seeks love from the Other. But she finds only the One. She must refuse its proffered 'love.' She must resist demanding recognition (love) from this One. She must insist. To ex-sist?"[35] Her case should serve as a cautionary tale where Paul is concerned. If, as Lacan suggests, the great innovation of Christianity was its invention of "a God who enjoys," then its "love"—and the One it promises—must be greeted with suspicion. She, like man, must recognize that "the *jouissance* of the Other . . . is not the sign of love."[36]

Lacan says that "in being not-all, [woman] has, with regard to the *jouissance* of the phallic function, a supplementary jouissance."[37] The jouissance that attests to the God-face of the Other is one expression of it. But although it may give consistency to the One, the "other jouissance" of the feminine does not inevitably lead to the jouissance of the Other. This is because what it opposes to phallic jouissance is the satisfaction of speech. Lacan defines the other jouissance as "what is satisfied at the level of the unconscious, insofar as something is said there and is not said there . . . a *jouissance* supported by language."[38] This jouissance derives not from the imaginary dimension of the signifier, or "meaning," but from the vagaries and vicissitudes of the sign that exceeds it. Its satisfaction is "not understanding, not a diving at meaning, but a flying over it as low as possible without the meaning gumming up this virtue, thus enjoying the deciphering."[39] As a result, writes MacCannell, the other jouissance is "not tied down by the one, nor therefore to the signifier that is its counterpart—the minus-one of the phallus. [Lacan] says it is 'not something that can be ciphered [given a number] but only deciphered.'"[40] The feminine must therefore be situated "not on the side of *sense, meaning, the elementary particle, the phallus the One*, but of the *not-all, the sign*, what cannot be ciphered, but only de-ciphered."[41]

THE LAUGHTER OF ISRAEL

This not-all is very much in evidence in the narratives of the Hebrew Bible, in the feminized attitude toward the sign that will come to define Israel's attitude toward God. Long before the "laughter of the saints" that Lacan discusses as an expression of feminine jouissance, there was the laughter of Sarah, the laughter at the origin of the Hebrew lineage. I am referring to the episode that precedes the miraculous birth of Isaac to Abraham and Sarah, who, at more than ninety years old apiece, have long since given up hoping for a child. When Sarah hears the angels' promise that she will have a son, she bursts out laughing, saying, "After I am grown old shall I have pleasure, my lord being old also?" (Gen. 18:12). Sarah's famous laughter, and the doubt to which it bears witness, are not without a certain pleasure. Her enjoyment inheres not only in the untimely "pleasure" she is promised—sexual pleasure or the pleasure of maternity—but the negative mode in which this very possibility is considered: the laughter that mistrusts the signifier, that deforms the word, that insists upon its inadequation to the promise.

Sarah's doubting laughter will serve as an important model for Israel, whose name means "the one who strives with God" (and not, as Badiou's reading of Paul would suggest, the one who obeys God). Emmanuel Levinas has shown how the struggle with the angel that results in the naming of Israel (Gen. 32) shapes not only Sarah's subsequent history with God and her neighbors, but a hermeneutic strategy and a relation to the letter that are defined by struggle and doubt.[42] For the Israelites marked by this struggle, the covenant implies a relationship more complex than either obedience or simple faith. This special relation to the word challenges Badiou's contention that the key figure of the Jewish discourse is the prophet, the interpreter of signs. In fact, the history of Israel is itself marked by a constant struggle between two very different positions: a feminine errancy that is not-all under the phallic function, on the one hand, and a more rigid adherence to the covenant's discourse of consolidated personhood and to traits of group identity on the other hand. In the prophetic books, Israel's "feminine" errancy is repudiated to prepare the way for a new kingdom of faith, identification with the "oneness" of personhood.[43] But in this respect, Paul's discourse is not so much opposed to the discourse of Jewish prophecy as an extension of it.

For this reason, I would dispute Badiou's interpretation of the line "the Jews seek signs, the Greeks seek wisdom." In the mouth of the inventor of figural reading, I do not think this phrase pegs the Jews as "masters of the literal tradition," as Badiou would have it, but as incompetent or overtimid readers of signs. Paul's words have a different intonation to my ear, more akin to Pablo Picasso's "I do not seek, I find." In his reading of the Hebrew Bible, Paul will eliminate altogether the searching, ambivalence, and doubt that define both the Jewish tradition of exegesis and its founding figures. In his interpretation of the Abraham saga, Paul eliminates all mention of the doubting laughter that defines Sarah and Abraham alike, casting husband and wife as figures of "simple faith" who are unwavering in their trust of the divine promise.[44]

Now, this laughter has been interpreted in many ways. But it would be difficult, I think, to read it as an expression of simple faith. Certainly, God does not read it that way. Immediately following Sarah's outburst, he says to Abraham, "Why did Sarah laugh, and say, 'Shall I indeed bear a child, now that I am old? Is anything too wonderful for the LORD?'" At these words, it is written that "Sarah denied, saying 'I did not laugh,' for she was afraid." To which God replies, "Oh yes, you did laugh" (Gen. 18:13-14). God clearly reads the laughter as a sign of doubt or disbelief. But importantly, he does not punish it. His rebuke of Sarah is more comical than truly stern, anticipating the patience and even fondness with which he will later entertain Abraham's doubts when he questions the soundness of making the righteous few of Sodom and Gomorrah perish with the sinners. So why, for Paul, must this doubting laughter be foreclosed?

I think it is because it introduces the possibility that the Voice itself might be castrated, that in having to pass through the signifier it must necessarily lose something of his power. For this reason, Sarah's quiet—and unintentional—insurrection is to me richer and more suggestive than the militancy of Badiou's fraternal pact. The God she engages is not a monstrous specter of terrifying might, but an Other whose manifestation is marked by a lack, the failure that presides over the transmission of the signifier and provokes laughter. When Badiou characterizes the Jewish discourse as one of obedience to signs and enslavement to objects, he misses the specifically feminine dimension of Israel's discourse and its complex relationship to the divine word that brings the nation into being as the object of God's love.

Importantly, it is Sarah's laughing pleasure that will be her legacy to Jewish discourse, and not the maternal love that for Badiou sustains the desire of the fraternal pact by lending consistency to the One. In Paul's typological reading, Sarah gives birth to the "Jerusalem above," the Christian brotherhood liberated by the promise. But in the text of the Hebrew Bible, her doubt leaves behind a residue that persists in and beyond this interpretation as a kind of laughing commentary on it. I am referring to Isaac himself, the child of the promise, whose name means "he laughs." His name is a poetic remainder of Sarah's *jouissance*, one that exceeds both the covenant sealed by his birth and the transcendent meaning Paul extracts from the text.

NOTES

1. *SP* 113. All translations are my own.
2. QQA 267. All translations are my own.
3. See Jacques Lacan, "The Signification of the Phallus," in *Écrits: A Selection*, trans. Alan Sheridan (London: Tavistock, 1977).
4. Jacques Lacan, *On Feminine Sexuality: The Limits of Love and Knowledge, 1972–1973*, ed. Jacques-Alain Miller, trans. Bruce Fink (New York: Norton, 1998), 80, emphasis added.
5. For a detailed account of castration in relation to the absence of the Other, see Willy Apollon, "L'événement ou l'avènement de l'Autre," *L'Universel, perspectives psychanalytiques* (Québec: GIFRIC, 1997), 51–91.
6. Juliet Flower MacCannell, "*Jouissance* between the Clinic and the Academy: The Analyst and Woman," *Qui Parle* 9, no. 2 (1996): 117.
7. Jacques Lacan, *Television*, trans. Denis Hollier, Rosalind Krauss, and Annette Michelson (New York: Norton, 1990), 6.
8. Lacan, *On Feminine Sexuality*, 72.
9. Ibid., 71–72.
10. In this and other essays, Badiou also celebrates "militant fraternalism" as an indispensable ingredient of any universal thought. See in particular his *Abrégé de métapolitique* (Paris: Editions du seuil, 1998).
11. Sigmund Freud, *Moses and Monotheism*, trans. Katherine Jones (New York: Vintage Books, 1967), 109.
12. Ibid., 110–11.
13. Ibid., 111.
14. I am referring to the title of Sade's revolutionary tract "Français, encore un effort si vous voulez être républicains," which calls for the eradication not only of the monarchy, but of the symbolic as such (*The Complete Justine: Philosophy in the Bedroom and Other Writings* [New York: Grove Press, 1965]).
15. Friedrich Nietzsche, aphorism 68 of *Daybreak*, trans. R. J. Hollingdale (Cambridge: Cambridge University Press, 1982). There are, of course, important

differences between their respective readings, since where Nietzsche sees the machinations of *ressentiment* and self-interest, Badiou sees inspired militancy.

16. "We know that the law is spiritual; but I am carnal, sold under sin. I do not understand my own actions. But I do not do what I want, but I do the very thing I hate. Now if I do what I do not want, I agree that the law is good. So then it is no longer I that do it, but sin which dwells within me. For I know that nothing good dwells within me, that is, in my flesh. I can will what is right, but I cannot do it" (Rom. 7:14-18).

17. Jacques Lacan, *The Ethics of Psychoanalysis, 1959–1960*, ed. Jacques-Alain Miller, trans. Dennis Porter (New York: Norton, 1992), 174; emphasis added.

18. "Wrestling with the Angel," in *Saint Paul and Modernity*, ed. Lowell Gallagher and Kenneth Reinhard (Stanford, CA: Stanford University Press, forthcoming).

19. Juliet Flower MacCannell, "Fascism and the Voice of Conscience," in *The Hysteric's Guide to the Future Female Subject* (Minneapolis: Minnesota University Press, 2000), 129.

20. Jacques Lacan, *The Seminar Book VII: The Ethics of Psychoanalysis*, ed. Jacques-Alain Miller, trans. Dennis Porter (New York: Norton, 1992), 69.

21. Lacan, *On Feminine Sexuality*, 76; translation modified.

22. MacCannell, "Jouissance between the Clinic and the Academy," 115.

23. Martin Buber, *Moses* (New York: Harper & Row, 1958).

24. Freud, *Moses and Monotheism*, 112.

25. MacCannell, "Jouissance between the Clinic and the Academy," 110-11; MacCannell is glossing a passage from Lacan's *Television*, 22.

26. In my view, Paul's own account of sexual difference is less "progressive" than Badiou's, but ultimately richer. It maintains that the wound of sexual difference is not healed by the Christ-event, but persists even afterward as a fundamental feature of human life. In Paul's diatribe against the Corinthians who have fallen under the sway of gnostic evangelizers (who pretend that sexual difference has been surmounted such that man, like the angels, has acceded to an asexual state), he refutes the idea (very contemporary, really) that we all contain within us a "feminine" and a "masculine" side. Thus, any treatment of sexual difference in Paul needs to consider not merely the contradictions—or even the misogyny—of his direct ritual pronouncements concerning women (1 Cor. 7:8-11), but what is actually more surprising given the universalizing statement of Galatians: the insistence, against the Corinthians, of the real of sexual difference. Perhaps this is the crux of Lacan's somewhat cryptic allusion to Paul as the one who announced as a truth that there is no sexual relation, by demonstrating "that it was the consequence of the Message that the men are at one pole and the women at the other" (*Feminine Sexuality*, 12; translation modified).

27. Ibid., 63; translation modified.

28. MacCannell, "Jouissance between the Clinic and the Academy," 116.

29. Lacan, *On Feminine Sexuality*, 80; translation modified.

30. On this point, see Lacan, "The Mirror Stage as Formative of the Function of the 'I'," in *Écrits: A Selection*, trans. Alan Sheridan (London: Tavistock, 1977), 1–7.

31. Lacan, *On Feminine Sexuality*, 77.

32. Lacan, *Television*, 23.

33. Ibid.

34. MacCannell, "Jouissance between the Clinic and the Academy," 120.

35. Ibid., 119.

36. The expression is Lacan's (*On Feminine Sexuality*, 4).

37. Ibid., 51; translation modified.

38. Lacan, *Television*, 22.

39. MacCannell, "Jouissance between the Clinic and the Academy," 116 (MacCannell is citing Lacan's *Television*, 18–19).

40. Ibid., 119.

41. Lacan, *Television*, 24.

42. Emmanuel Levinas, "The Pact," in *The Lévinas Reader*, ed. Sean Hand (Oxford, UK: Blackwell, 1989), 211–26. Originally published in *L'Au-delà du verset* (Paris: Minuit, 1982), 82–106.

43. I have analyzed this relationship at length in "Israel as Host(ess): Hospitality in the Bible and Beyond," *Jouvert: A Journal of Postcolonial Studies* (fall 1998). Available: http://www.social.chass.ncsu.edu/jouvert/index.htm.

44. In Romans, Paul expunges all mention of Abraham's own doubting laughter from his summary of Genesis 17. When the patriarch receives the divine promise, Paul writes that

> He *did not weaken in faith* when he considered his own body, which was already as good as dead (for he was about a hundred years old), or when he considered the barrenness of Sarah's womb. *No distrust made him waver* concerning the promise of God, but he grew strong in his faith as he gave glory to God, being *fully convinced* that God was able to do what he had promised. That is why his faith was "reckoned to him as righteousness." (Rom. 4:19–22; emphasis added)

In the long figural reading that structures chapters 2–4, Sarah is nothing more than a symbol of a liberated Christianity, having no specific character traits.

PART FOUR

POLITICS AND ETHICS

NINE

On the Ethics of Alain Badiou

Simon Critchley

I have two questions in this chapter: What is ethical experience for Badiou? What can be said of the subject who has this experience in his work? But first I need to explain what I mean by ethical experience and how such experience implies a conception of the subject.

Let me begin by trying to pick out the formal structure of ethical experience or what with Dieter Henrich we can call the "grammar of the concept of moral insight."[1] Ethical experience begins with the experience of a demand to which I give my approval. *Approval* and *demand*: that is, there can be no sense of the good—however that is filled out at the level of content, and I am just understanding it formally and emptily—without an act of approval or affirmation. That is, my moral statement that "x is good or bad" is of a different order to the veridical, epistemological claim that "I am now seated in a chair." This is because the moral statement implies an approval of the fact that x is good, whereas I can be quite indifferent to the chair I am sitting on. If I say, for example, that it would be good for parrots to receive the right to vote in elections, then my saying this implies that I approve of this development. Practical reason is in this way distinct from theoretical reason. In Badiou's terms, the order of the event (*l'événement*) is distinct from the order of being (*l'être*).

However, if the good only comes into view through approval, it is not good by virtue of approval. Namely, that the approval is an approval of something, that is, of a demand that demands approval. Ethical *noesis* (intuitional object) requires a *noema* (ideal content). In my example, my approval of parrots receiving the right to vote is related to the fact that—at least in my moral imagination—parrots make a certain demand, namely, the demand for political representation. Ethical experience is, first and foremost, the approval of a demand, one that demands approval. Ethical experience has to be circular, although hopefully only virtuously so.

Leaving parrots to one side, in the history of philosophy (and also in the history of what Badiou calls antiphilosophy, namely, religion), this formal demand is filled out with various contents: the Good beyond Being in Plato, faith in the resurrected Christ in Paul and Augustine, the fact of reason or the experience of respect for the moral law in Kant, the certitude of practical faith as the goal of subjective striving (*Streben*) in Fichte, the abyssal intuition of freedom in Schelling, the creature's feeling of absolute dependency on a creator in Schleiermacher, pity for the suffering of one's fellow human beings in Rousseau or for all creatures in Schopenhauer, eternal return in Nietzsche, the idea in the Kantian sense for Husserl, the call of conscience in Heidegger, the claim of the nonidentical in Adorno, or whatever.[2] All questions of normativity and value, whether universalistic (as in Kant in the categorical imperative, and his latter-day heirs such as Rawls and Habermas) or relativistic (as in Wittgenstein on rule following and his latter-day heirs such as Rorty), follow from such an experience. Without some experience of a demand—that is, without some experience of a relation to the otherness of a demand of some sort—to which I am prepared to bind myself, to commit myself, the business of morality would not get started. There would be no motivation to the good, the good would not have the power to move the will to act. Kant calls that which would produce the power to act, the motivational power to be disposed to the good, "the philosopher's stone." So, what is essential to ethical experience is that the subject of the demand assents to that demand, agrees to finding it good, binds itself to that good, and shapes its subjectivity in relation to that good. A demand meets with an approval. The subject who approves shapes itself in accordance with that demand. All questions of value begin here.

Let me take this a little further. If we stay with the example of Kant, then this dimension of ethical experience or moral insight—the capacity of being motivated to the good—resolves itself, in a rather complex fashion, in the seemingly contradictory notion of the fact of reason. That is, there is a *Faktum* (fact) that places a demand on the subject and to which the subject assents. There is a demand of the good to which the subject assents, and this demand has an immediate apodictic certainty that is analogous to the binding power of an empirical fact (*Tatsache*). The difference between the apodicticity of a fact of reason as distinct from an empirical fact is that the demand of the former is only evident insofar as the subject approves it. It is, if you like (and Kant would not), the fiction of a fact constituted through an act of approval. However things may stand with the doctrine of the fact of reason, Dieter Henrich argues, rightly I think, that the entire rational universality of the categorical imperative and Kantian moral theory follows from this experience of moral insight. The philosopher's stone would consist precisely in the link between the motivational power of the fact of reason and the rational universality of the categorical imperative. Now, because Kant's entire moral theory is based on the principle of autonomy, the fact of reason has to correspond to the will of the subject. The fact of reason is a fact, it is the otherness of a demand, but it has to correspond to the subject's autonomy. Hence, for Kant, the ethical subject has to be a priori equal to the demand that is placed on it.

It is arguably this structure that Heidegger repeats in his analysis of conscience in *Being and Time*, where conscience is constituted in the experience of a demand or appeal that seems to come from outside Dasein, but which is really only Dasein calling to itself. Heidegger writes, "In conscience Dasein calls itself."[3] In this sense, the grammar of moral insight in Heidegger, at least in the analysis of authenticity, would be an existential deepening of Kantian autonomy. Heidegger recognizes as a "positive necessity" the Faktum that has to be presupposed in any analysis of Dasein. The Kantian fact of reason here becomes the ontic-existentiell testimony, attestation, or witnessing (*Zeugnis*) of conscience that is relativistically translated into the key notion of the "situation."[4]

We can see already, from this little sketch of Kant and Heidegger, that the claim about ethical experience being constituted in a demand that I approve is also a claim about the nature of the self or subject. The response to the question of ethical experience also entails a response to the question of the subject of that experience. The self is something that shapes itself through its relation to whatever is determined as its good, whether that is the law of Moses, the resurrected Christ, the suffering other, the intuition of freedom, the call of conscience, the nonidentical, or whatever. That is, if the demand of the good requires the approval of that demand, then that approval is given by a self. The good is good insofar as the self approves of it. An ethical subject can be defined as a self relating itself approvingly to the demand of the good. For me, the ethical subject is the name for the way the self relates itself bindingly to the good.

This claim about the entailment between ethical experience and the subject can be buttressed by claiming not simply—and rather neutrally—that the demand of the good requires approval by a self in order to be experienced as a demand, but by asserting that this demand of the good founds the self, or is the fundamental organizing principle of the subject's articulation. Namely, that what we think of as a self is fundamentally an ethical subject, a self that is constituted in a certain relation to a good. This is perhaps best proved negatively through the experience of failure, betrayal, or evil. Namely, as Badiou notes, that if I act in such a way that I know to be evil, then I am acting in a manner destructive of the self that I am, or that I have chosen to be. I have failed myself or betrayed myself. Once again, such a claim is quite formal and does not presuppose specific content for the good. For example, my good could be permanent revolution, perpetual peace, or pedophilia. The point here is that the ethical subject is constituted through a certain relation to a demand that is determined as good and that this can be felt most acutely when I fail to act in accordance with that demand or when I deliberately transgress it and betray myself. This is why Plato is perfectly consequent when he claims that vice is destructive of self. Anyone, who has tried—and failed—to cure themselves of some sort of addiction, whether cigarettes, alchohol, permanent revolution, or whatever, will understand what is meant here. The subject that I have chosen to be enters in to conflict with the self that I am, producing a divided experience of self as self-failure and the concomitant overwhelming affect of guilt. Guilt is the affect that produces a certain splitting or division in the subject, which is something that Saint Paul understood rather well: "For the good that I would I do not: but the evil which I would not, that I do" (Rom. 7:19).

THREE APPLICATIONS OF THE STRUCTURE OF ETHICAL EXPERIENCE: LEVINAS, LACAN, AND BADIOU

Leaving Kant and Heidegger to one side, can this formal structure of ethical experience be used to illuminate other moral theories? I think it can. Before turning in detail to Badiou, let me make some remarks on Levinas and Lacan, and attempt a small rapprochement between them. For Levinas, the core of ethical experience is, indeed, the demand of a Faktum, but it is not a *Faktum der Vernunft*, a fact of reason, as much as a *Faktum des Anderen*, a fact of the other. In *Totality and Infinity* at least, the name for this fact is the "face of the other." Now Levinas's difference from Kant (or Heidegger for that matter) is that ethical experience turns around the alterity of a demand that does not correspond to the subject's autonomy, but which places that autonomy in question, at least at the ethical level (although autonomy can be said to come back at the level of justice, politics, and everything that Levinas gathers under the heading of "the third party"). What Levinas tries to articulate in his work is the experience of a demand to which the subject assents ("tu ne tueras point"), but that heteronomously determines the ethical subject. The ethical subject in Levinas is constituted through a relation, an act of approval, to the demand of the good to which it is fundamentally inadequate. The Levinasian ethical subject chooses to relate itself to something that exceeds its relational capacity. This is what Levinas calls "le rapport sans rapport," the relation without relation, the antidialectical core of Levinas's work that fails to respect the principle of noncontradiction, that is, how can there be a relation between beings that remain absolute within that relation? Logically speaking there cannot, and yet it is precisely such a relation between persons that Levinas wants to describe as ethical.

This dimension of ethical experience can be explored in relation to the theme of trauma in Levinas's *Otherwise Than Being or Beyond Essence*. What is a trauma? The source of trauma is a heteronomous event that comes from outside the self (for example, a terrorist explosion or an earthquake), but which lives on in the subject after the fact in, say, traumatic neurosis. Levinas constructs what he calls an "ethical language," composed of several rather strange and hyperbolical terms: *persecution, obsession, substitution, hostage,* and *trauma.* Focusing on the notion of trauma allows one to bring out the links between Levinas and the psychoanalytic dimensions of ethical experience, studiously refused by Levinas himself. But for Levinas, ethics is the dimension of a traumatic demand, something that comes from outside the subject, but that leaves its imprint, trace, or mark within the subject. My heterodox but, I think, justified claim in relation to Levinas is that the condition of possibility for ethics, that is, for the ethical relation to the other, is found in a certain picture of the subject, that is, it is because of a disposition of the subject that relatedness to the other is possible. This is why I privilege Levinas's later work, *Otherwise Than Being,* over his earlier work, *Totality and Infinity,* for it is here that ethics is worked out as a theory of the subject, conceived as the other within the same, and not simply in terms of the relation to the other.

So, the grammar of moral insight in Levinas is that ethical responsibility begins with a subject approving of an impossible demand, or a demand that it could never meet. This makes responsibility infinite and splits open the subject through an experience of heteronomy. I decide to be a subject that I know I cannot be, I give myself up to a demand that makes an imprint on *me* without my ever being fully able to understand *it* (you can perhaps already see the psychoanalytic implications of such a claim). In other words, for Levinas, ethics is not ontology, which simply means that the ethical relation to the other that lives on as an imprint within the subject is not a relation of comprehension, of totality. So, the notion of ethical experience that I am trying to elicit in Levinas produces a certain picture of the subject as fundamentally split, between itself and a demand that it cannot meet, but which is that by virtue of which it becomes a subject.

Once this psychoanalytically reconceived account of the Levinasian ethical subject is in place, it can be shown that there is a rather interesting homology between it and Lacan, that is, that there is a common formal structure to ethical experience in both of them, although they obviously differ at the level of content, not to mention their rather different evaluations of the importance of Freud. But let's ask: what is the basic claim of Lacan's *L'éthique de la psychanalyse?* Lacan's thesis is that the ethical as such is articulated in relation to the order of the real, which is variously and obscurely glossed as "that which resists, the impossible, that which always come back to the same place, the limit of all symbolization, etc. etc." Indeed, this thesis is finessed in the following, crucial way: namely, that the ethical, which affirms itself in opposition to pleasure is articulated in relation to the real insofar as the latter can be the guarantor of what Lacan calls, following a certain idiosyncratic and radical reading of Freud, "*das Ding,*" "*la Chose*" (the

Thing). The main example of das Ding in the ethics seminar is the Freudian figure of the *Nebenmensch*, the fellow human being, and I think what we might call a "Nebenmensch complex" is at work in both Levinas and Lacan, that is, there is a Thing at the heart of the subject that defines the subject in terms of an "interior exteriority," as it were, what Lacan calls something "strange or foreign to me that is at the heart of me."

However, more generally, what is interesting is how well the ethics of psychoanalysis fits into the structure of ethical experience and the subject that I have tried to describe. One might say that psychoanalytic experience begins with recognition of the demand of the unconscious, the impingement of unconscious desire. In the analytic situation, that is, if the analysand has agreed to the interpretation of the symptom, the Faktum of this desire provokes an act of approval of the part of the subject. That is, the ethical subject decides henceforth to relate itself approvingly to the demand of its unconscious desire. This demand produces what I see as the categorical imperative of Lacan's ethics seminar, namely, "do not give way on its desire" (*ne pas céder sur son désir*). That is, do not cease to approve of the demand that is unconscious desire. For Lacan, as much as for Kant, it is this act of approval that founds the subject, where he claims that "tout le cheminement du sujet," the entire itinerary of the subject, articulates itself around the Thing that shadows the subject. This is why Lacan can claim that Freudian psychoanalysis, as much as Kant's critical philosophy, subscribes to the primacy of practical reason. The difference between Lacan and Kant is that between the heternomous and autonomous determinations of the ethical subject. I will come back to Lacan shortly, but my psychoanalytic question to Badiou is whether his ethical theory loses sight of this dimension of the Thing, that is, whether his privileging of love over law risks reducing the traumatic demand to the real to the symbolic order.[5]

Turning to Badiou, the structure of ethical experience I have described can be applied to his wonderful reading of Saint Paul. What interests Badiou in Paul is the connection between the subject and the event. More precisely, Badiou's question is: what law can structure a subject deprived of all identity in relation to an event "of which the only 'proof' is rightly that a subject declares it" (*dont la seule "preuve" est justement qu'un sujet le déclare*)? This event is the resurrection of Christ, something that can only have the status of a fable for Badiou. What interests Badiou, and I will come back to this in details, is the notion of an event that is not empirically demonstrable in the order of being. The event demands an act of belief that Paul rightly compares to folly. That is, the event is a Faktum that is analogous but irreducible to an empirical Tatsache. Now, the structure of ethical experience in Badiou's reading of Paul can be formalized into the following four moments:

1. There is the universality of the demand of the good, or what Badiou calls the "*adresse,*" which is what Paul calls "grace" (*charis*).
2. The charisma of the subject consists in the declaration of this grace in an act of faith, or what Badiou prefers to call "conviction" (*la conviction*). Thus, faith is the arising or coming forth of the subject (*surgir du sujet*), a subjective certitude that approves of the demand that is placed on it.
3. If faith is *le surgir du sujet*, then love (*agape*) is the practical labor of the subject (*labeur du sujet*) that has bound itself to its good in faith. The practical maxim of love is "love your neighbour as yourself." That is, if the human being is justified by faith, then she or he is redeemed by love. Love is what gives consistency to an ethical subject, which allows it to persevere with what Badiou elsewhere calls a process of truth (*un processus de vérité*).
4. Love binds itself to justice on the basis of hope (*espérance, elpis*). The hope is that justice will be done and the subjective maxim that this requirement of justice produces is, as elsewhere in Badiou, "Continuez!". That is, continue to love your neighbor as yourself. That is, we might define *hope* as political love.

In terms of the account of ethical experience given above, it is the first two moments of this structure that are essential. Ethical experience begins with the experience of a demand or address, which is the event of grace, and the subject defines itself by approving of this event in a declaration of faith. Thus—and this is essential—*the Christian subject does not preexist the event that it declares*. Subject and event come into being at the same time. As I have already shown, in ethical experience, the subject defines itself by binding itself approvingly to the demand that the good makes on it. For Badiou, it is this feature of Paulinian Christianity, its singular universality based on the Faktum of an event irreducible to an empirical Tatsache, that provides an exemplary figure for contemporary political militancy.

THE PLACE OF ETHICS IN BADIOU'S SYSTEM

With this in mind, I would now like to turn to the more detailed account of ethical experience presented in *L'Éthique: Essai sur la conscience du Mal*. The eighty pages of *L'Éthique* fall, very roughly, into two parts: (1) a refreshingly direct presentation and critique of the so-called return to ethics in contemporary French philosophy; and (2) an exposition of Badiou's ethical theory in relation to the problem of evil. Consequent upon this division of the argument, the intention of *L'Éthique* is twofold: (1) to show how the contemporary inflation of ethics in French philosophy is a symptom of a more general nihilism; and (2) to provide a quite other meaning to ethics, by relating it not to abstractions, such as Man, God, or the Other, but to concrete situations. That is, for Badiou, what is ethical is the production of durable maxims for singular and determinate processes, what he calls "processes of truth."

The subtext of the opening chapter is a countercritique of the "return to ethics" in the critique of *la pensée '68* found in the work of Luc Ferry and Alain Renaut, but also "les nouveaux philosophes," Bernard Henri-Levy and André Glucksmann. Badiou rightly understands the critique of *la pensée '68*, and its defense of human rights, democracy, and individualism, as a reactionary response to the foundering of revolutionary Marxism in France. Badiou defends the antihumanism of Foucault, Althusser, and Lacan because it was complicit with the critique of (and rebellion against) the established order, whereas the critique of *la pensée '68*, with its defense of ethics, of the individual, and human rights, is simply, for him, at the service of official Western ideology. For Badiou, with some justification, the contemporary return to ethics is essentially a return to Kant and to a Kantian conception of the subject of the moral law as universal and context-free and not situationally bound. Reading Kantianism a little too straightforwardly as an ethical formalism, Badiou basically runs a Hegelian–Marxist critique against this position by claiming that a neo-Kantian ethics is incapable of thinking the singularity of situations, that is, of being orientated to praxis. Beneath the de-contextualized pallor of contemporary neo-Kantianism, Badiou detects in its ethical universalism an implicit apologia for Western ideology insofar as all human beings are judged according to the same standards, Western standards. Badiou also tags on the more Nietzschean thesis to this critique of Kantianism insofar as the traditional notion of ethics turns human beings into victims. It is an ethics of *ressentiment*, of blaming the other and self-blame (in the auto-laceration of conscience), of reactive rather than active forces in Deleuze's sense.

Against the neo-Kantianism implicit in the contemporary return to ethics, Badiou poses three theses:

1. The human being identifies itself, in the Freudian sense (i.e., we are always already intersubjectively situated), through an affirmative thinking—by action rather than reaction—by "verités singulières" (singular truths), that is, truths that arise from and apply to singular situations.

2. It is from this affirmative, processual character of the human, and its ethics of truths, that one is to determine, and determine positively, the Good. Namely, that evil is derived from this good by privation and not vice versa, which is a view that Badiou attributes to Kant. Badiou reads Kantian ethics, with Hegel, as a form of ethical stoicism in an evil world devoid of value.

3. Badiou writes, "All humanity enroots itself in the identification in thought of singular situations" (*E* 18); that is, there is no ethics in general, there is only an ethics of processes whereby one deals with possible courses of action that arise in a specific situation.

So much for the contemporary return to ethics in French philosophy insofar as it is based on the figure of "man" or the Same. The question posed in the second chapter of *L'Éthique* is whether the contemporary ethics of the Other, habitually derived from Levinas, disrupts this critique. Unsurprisingly perhaps, Badiou's response is negative, and it must be said that the critique of Levinas is rather violent and certainly contestable. However, he does make a good point in claiming that in order for the relation between the Same and the Other to escape from the narcissistic and aggressive logic of identification described by Lacan in the Mirror Stage, there is a requirement that the alterity of the Other be supported by an alterity or exteriority that transcends finite human alterity. This alterity is that of the *tout-autre*, namely, God. This move enables Badiou to make his coup de grâce (although he is not the first to make it), namely, that ethics as first philosophy is dependent upon an axiom derived from religion. Thus, Levinas's claim that ethics is first philosophy subordinates philosophy to theology. This is not wrong, but I just think there are other ways of reading Levinas—for example *my* way—where I try to read Levinas through the categories of psychoanalysis. But let's suppose that Badiou is right, that "l'éthique pour Levinas est une catégorie du discours pieux" (ethics is a category of pious discourse), then would not Levinas simply be another in that long line of *anti-philosophes*, such as Saint Paul, Luther, Pascal, Rousseau, Kierkegaard, and Nietzsche, some of whom he elsewhere praises? On this point, let me attempt a small criticism in terms of the four conditions of philosophy for Badiou (art, mathematics, politics, and love).

For Badiou, quite simply, there is no God. This is also to say that "l'Un n'est pas" (the One is not) (*E* 25). Hence, multiplicity is the general law of being, what Badiou means by *être*. Every situation is a multiplicity composed of an infinity of elements. Given this facticity of the multiple, the order of the event as the realm of the subject distinct from being is characterized by a return to the Same (*le Même*). For Badiou, the Same is not what is simply given—*être*—but rather *ce qui ad-vient*, that which comes to itself in relation to the facticity and alterity of multiplicity. What Badiou sees as the "*être immortel*" (immortal being) of each singularity is its capacity for the true, that is, to become this Same that constructs itself, that ad-venes to itself, through the processual character of Sameness (*Mêmeté*). A subject is not something that I *am*, it is something that I *become*, that comes to itself in a process of becoming. Thus, for Badiou, there is only an ethics of truths, that is, an ethics of processes of truths, of the labor that allows truths to "*advient au monde*," to ad-vene to the world. Thus, ethics in general does not have any validity, it is always an ethics in relation to a specific situation under particular conditions. Thus, although Badiou's ethical theory is highly formalistic, it only takes on flesh in relation to specific and by definition variable situational conditions. That which is ethical, then, corresponds to what Badiou adjudges as the four sole conditions for philosophy: politics, love, mathematics, poetry.

This brings me back to the question of religion. If it is granted that religion, at least for Saint Paul but perhaps also for Levinas, is antiphilosophical, then I do not see why it cannot be a condition for ethical action. Obviously for Paul, Pascal, and others, such as Luther and Kierkegaard, religion plays *precisely* this role and it is privileged *because* it is antiphilosophical. In this sense, at the very least, one would have to admit that in addition to the four conditions of philosophy that can be conditions for ethical action, one needs to add a fifth, namely, religion. Yet, one might want to go further and claim that precisely because of the exemplary way in which the logic of the event plays itself out in relation to Paul, namely, that Paul's notion of the grace shows most clearly the subjectivity of the event, religion is perhaps the paradigm of ethical action, a paradigm upon which the other four conditions should be modeled.[6]

In terms of my account of ethical experience, Badiou's ethics is an entirely formal theory, a grammar of ethical experience, and not a specific determination of the good. However, what is motivating this formalism is a theory of the subject that has strong normative connotations—located in Badiou's Beckettian formula: "*il faut continuer*"—although the specific content given to the good is subject-relative. As I have shown, every account of ethical experience has at its base a demand on the self to which the self assents. The ethical subject is the name for this structure. Ethics, for Badiou, cannot be premised upon any pregiven account of the subject because the subject is not something that one is, it is something that one becomes. One can only speak of the subject as a subject in becoming or a becoming-subject. As Nietzsche, the shadowy twin to Saint Paul, would say, "*Werde was du bist!*" (Become what you are!).

For Badiou, we are simply the sort of animals who are claimed by circumstances to become a subject. What are those circumstances? For Badiou, they are the circumstances of a truth. What are they? These circumstances cannot be what there is (*ce qu'il y a*). What there is for Badiou is the factical-being-multiple of the world, a plurality irreducible to any theological principle, henology, or even postontotheological *singulare tantum*. Thus, the circumstances of the being-multiple of the world do not, for Badiou, place a claim or demand on the subject. A subject—which is that which becomes—demands something more, it demands that something happens that supplements its insertion into that which is. Badiou calls this supplement an "event," hence, the distinction between *l'être et l'événement*. Thus, the event is what calls a subject into being, into the creation of a truth, whereas being is that which simply is the order of *episteme* (knowledge) in Plato, which is to be explained by mathematics. As Badiou states in the initial thesis of *L'être et l'événement*, "l'ontologie s'accomplisse historiquement comme mathématique" (ontology is accomplished historically as mathematics) (*EE* 9-10; *CTOT* 189).

Let's just note en passant that this founding dualism of being and the event might raise certain philosophical worries. First, simply because it is a dualism and, hence, in Heidegger's terms, splits the phenomenon of being-in-the-world. Second, insofar as it does split the phenomenon, Badiou's theory might bear a certain family resemblance to other dualisms, for example, that of the Sartrean dualism of *en soi* (in itself) and *pour soi* (for itself) by which Badiou confesses he was attracted by in his youth at the beginning of his little book on Beckett, "j'étais un parfait sartrien" (I was a perfect Sartrean). Third, the dualism of being and event risks reproducing the Kantian or early Wittgensteinian distinction of pure and practical reason, between the ontological order of knowledge, explicable through logical form, and the ethical order of truth, an ethical order which, like that of Kant and perhaps more particularly Fichte, is based on an infinite *Streben*: "Continuer!"

THE LOGIC OF THE EVENT IN BADIOU— VIRTUOUSLY OR VICIOUSLY CIRCULAR?

Thus, Badiou's theory of ethical experience and the subject of that experience turns entirely on his account of the event. I would now like to bring out the logic of this event, a circular logic, although hopefully only virtuously circular. On this basis, certain critical questions can be raised.

From the standpoint of being, the event is, one might say, "invisible" (I cannot think of a better word, but this is not satisfactory). That is, there is only an event for the subject who assents to the event, who declares it, and who defines their subjectivity in terms of a fidelity to the event. The event is the event only *for* the subject who pledges themselves to the event. But—and this is important—this is not to say that the event is the *act* of the subject, or that the event is the subject's *invention*. Rather, the event is an event *for* a subject who carries out the act that *binds* their subjectivity to that event, who defines their subjectivity through a fidelity to the event.

Thus, the event is only visible to the subject who decides to pledge their subjectivity to that event. For example, the event of Christ's resurrection is just not visible as such to the nonbeliever, who sees only an empty tomb. This is not to say that Christ's resurrection did not take place—we have all read enough Pascal to keep a rather selfishly open mind on such matters—but that it only becomes an event for the subject who pledges themselves to the event, for the subject who has *pistis*, the conviction of faith. In a similar way, the event of the French Revolution does not appear as a revolution to the opponent of the revolution, say the supporter of the ancien régime. For the latter, the revolution is only visible as chaos and disorder. The "event" of the French Revolution is not the same event for Edmund Burke as for Thomas Paine. Analogously, multinational global capitalism looks like chaos to its insurrectionary opponent, whereas it looks like order to the capitalist. To put this into a formula: the event is not the mere act of a subject, but it only becomes an event through a subjective act.

On the question of the "reality" of the event, thinking of Saint Paul's faith in the event of Christ's resurrection, Badiou emphasizes that the only "proof" of the event is the subject who declares it. What interests Badiou is a notion of an event that is not empirically demonstrable in the order of being. As Erasmus—another antiphilosopher—emphasizes in his *Enconium Moriae*, if Christ's crucifixion and resurrection was an act of folly, then such madness is all the more true of the Christian who decides to make the leap of faith. The only "evidence" for Paul's leap of faith is the presence of grace, which is hardly a strong empirical guarantee.

Of course, there are events *and* events, and Badiou's choice of Paul as a paradigm for the event is all the more compelling because his act of faith is so strange to the modern atheist. For example, I can imagine pledging myself more easily to the event "French Revolution" than I can to the event "Christ's Resurrection." But that, of course, is to miss the point. The choice of Paul is intended to show the extreme subject-dependency of the event, that is, that the event is not reducible to the act of a subject, but that the event is only visible as such to the subject who acts in such a way as to pledge themselves to the event. Thinking of Wallace Stevens's "The Idea of Order at Key West," an event is an idea of order, it is something that we impose on the world, the grid through which and in terms of which we see it. But the event is also what makes the world a world *for us*, that is to say, a meaningful world: "She was the single artificer of the world / In which she sang. And when she sang, the sea, / Whatever self it had, became the self / That was her song, for she was the maker. Then we, / As we beheld her striding there alone, / Knew that there never was a world for her / Except the one she sang and, singing, made."

HOW TO DISTINGUISH A TRUE FROM A FALSE EVENT— THE QUESTION OF HEGEMONY

In other words, the eventhood of the event is the consequence of a decision. For Badiou, a subject is the always local occurrence of a process of truth, and the subject binds itself to a process of truth, an event, on the basis of a decision. Now, I have a couple of questions on this notion of decision. But let me try to formalize my argument to recapitulate what I have said so far and to make one further step:

1. First, the logic of the event, as I have tried to describe it, is very close to the description of ethical experience discussed previously, that is, that an event is a demand made *on* the subject, *of* which the subject approves, and *to* which it decides to bind itself. Thus, the logic of the event corresponds to the structure of ethical experience.

2. The consequence of this argument is that every event is an ethical event. That is, every exception to the order of being belongs to the domain of practical rather than theoretical reason.

3. In this sense, the circularity of the logic of the event is not a problem, it is just the way it is, the very nature of practical reason. The event, like ethical experience, is virtuously and not viciously circular.

4. But if that is the case, then my question is very simple: how can one speak of the event as an event of truth, or a process of truth? Let me try to explain myself.

If the event is the consequence of a decision, namely the decision to define one's subjectivity in terms of a fidelity to the event, then this event is true only in the sense that it is true *for* a subject that has taken this decision (True = true for a subject). Now, if that argument is valid, then how and in virtue of what is one to distinguish a true event from a false event? That is, I do not see how—on the basis of Badiou's criteria—we could ever distinguish a true event from a false event. The only realm of superior evidence to which such questions can be referred is the order of being, which is a priori excluded from discussions of the event. As Badiou admits in his "Dictionary" at the end of *L'être et l'événement*, "il n'y a donc pas de contraire de vrai" (there is therefore no contrary to the true) (*EE* 561). Now, if there is no way of distinguishing truth from falsity at the level of the event, then might we not be better advised to stop talking about truth in this domain?

One inference from this argumentation—let's call it the "pragmatist inference"—would be the following. We might imagine the pragmatist saying, "Sure, we cannot distinguish between a true and a false event. True just means true for a subject who decides in favor of this event. False just means that the subject decides not to define itself in terms of such an event, and perhaps to define what is true for it in terms of explicit opposition to such a perceived falsehood."

Now, if one accepts this pragmatist inference, that is, if true just means true for the subject, then why not go on to conclude that every event is the consequence of what Gramsci or Laclau would call a "hegemonic articulation"? That is, why not conclude that every event is the consequence of a decision to relate oneself to the situation in a certain way, and that every decision is a hegemonic act.

Therefore, otherwise stated, my question is how and in virtue of what is one to distinguish between truth and hegemonic articulation in Badiou's theory of the event? Isn't Badiou's talk of truth in ethical and political matters simply, as Wittgenstein would say, a way of talking, and doesn't it risk obscuring the real question in ethics and politics, which is that of power.

THE HEROISM OF THE DECISION IN BADIOU

Allow me a final series of questions on the decision. If the eventhood of the event is the consequence of a decision, then how might that decision be characterized? Is a decision something taken by a subject? Badiou, it seems to me, would happily say Yes. But if that is the case, then doesn't the notion of decision have to presuppose some conception of the subject defined in terms of an active, virile will, as it does, say, in Carl Schmitt? That is, doesn't Badiou's concept of the decision have to presuppose some notion of an autarkic will? Obviously, if this criticism is justified, then it would have significant political consequences, particularly as the very concept of the political (*le politique*) depends on how we understand the voluntaristic power of decision.

Against this, and I am thinking of Derrida's reading of Schmitt in *Politics of Friendship*, can one, might one, should one, not try to rethink the concept of decision, and hence the concept of the political in terms of a passive or unconscious decision, what we might call the "decision of the other in me"? That is, rather than thinking of the decision taken by the subject, might we not do better to think of the subject taken by the decision? In this sense, the decision is an event with regard to which I am passive, the decision taken by the other in me, a decision based not on a sheer autarkic act of will, or even a *Faktum der Vernunft* as much as what one might call a *Faktum des Anderen*.[7]

LOVE AND LAW—BADIOU AND PSYCHOANALYSIS

Such a position on the decision would seem to be entailed by the very logic of Badiou's position. There is, I think, the risk of a certain heroism of the decision in Badiou's work, a heroism enshrined in the central maxim of his ethics: Continuez! Yet, I also think that this heroism can be avoided by another understanding of Badiou that can be seen by considering his relation to Lacanian psychoanalysis.

In *L'Éthique*, Badiou provides a formal definition of an ethics of truths: the ethical is defined as the free submission to a principle that decides to continue with a process of truth. In relation to psychoanalysis, we might say that the ethics of the psychoanalytic situation consists in the decision to continue in the process of the transferential interpretative situation under the normative constraint of a desire that is not to be given way on. More generally, the ethical is that which gives consistency to the presence of someone (*un quelqu'un*—the specific, punctual individual that pledges itself to a process of subjectivization) in the composition of the subject that effectuates the process of truth. This ethical consistency on the part of someone is a fidelity to a process of subjectivization that is in excess of that someone. That is, it is a process of subjectivization that passes through the specific, punctual individual, but which the latter cannot exhaust or fully know. Thus, the someone is ethically committed to a process of subjectivization that exceeds its knowledge, that *existe à son insu*, and is, to this extent, unconscious.

But if this is the case, then the subject has to commit itself to a process of truth that is in part unconscious. That is, the subject has to commit itself to a decision that has already been taken within me, *à mon insu*, as it were. This takes us back to Lacan's ethics of psychoanalysis. Badiou reads Lacan's ethical imperative from *Seminar VII*, "do not give way on its desire," as "do not give way on that of oneself one does not know." For Badiou, the someone who embarks upon a path of subjectivization is seized by a process of truth that cannot be cognitively or reflectively exhausted. Thus, the someone has to be faithful to a fidelity that it cannot understand, which is one way of understanding the analytic pact of transference in psychoanalysis, namely, to give oneself over to a process of interpretation of which one does not know the outcome.

Badiou claims, with some justification, that this is an ethics of the real insofar as the real is of the order of the *rencontre* (encounter) for Lacan, it is that which we cannot know, what resists symbolization, where *das Ding* addresses and claims the subject without the subject being able to address and claim it. Of course, as Lacan shows in *The Ethics of Psychoanalysis*, the prime figure for *das Ding* in Freud is the fellow human being, der Nebenmensch; that is, in my language, the ethical relation to the other person is a relation to the Real.

In this sense, the heroism of the decision in Badiou can be avoided by showing that ethical decisions always confront elements of the Real that are irreducible to the conscious will. Thus, the decision is taken with regard to the other within me, the *Faktum* of unconscious desire. However, there is also a problem in Badiou's understanding of Lacanian psychoanalysis that I alluded to when I said that his ethical theory risks losing sight of the dimension of the Thing. Badiou claims that his theory is an ethics of the real insofar as the real is of the order of the rencontre for Lacan, it is what we cannot know, that which resists symbolization, where *das Ding* addresses and claims the subject without the subject being able to address and claim it. This is the structure of *der Komplex der Nebenmechen* (the fellow human being complex) installed at the heart of the Lacanian and Levinasian ethical subject as its Law.

Now, although Badiou describes his theory as an ethics of the real, my question is: isn't this traumatic dimension of the Thing as the Law that divides the subject overcome in Badiou through his emphasis on love? This is revealed particularly clearly in his reading of Saint Paul, where Badiou writes in his seventh theorem, "Le processus subjective d'une vérité est une seule et même chose que l'amour de cette vérité" (The subjective process of a truth is the sole and same thing as the love of that truth) (*SP* 97). That is, the way in which a subject relates itself to the event is through an act of love that overcomes the dimension of Law, which is always identified with death, "le premier des noms de la mort, c'est: Loi" (the first of the names of death is the Law) (*SP* 78). In this sense, Badiou's moral theory would be structurally Christian, whereas Lacan and Levinas would be structurally Judaic insofar as their conception of ethics is based around a dimension of Law that cannot be overcome through the work of Love.

Let me put the same criticism another way. On the one hand, Badiou would seem to grant that there has to be a dimension of what he calls the unnameable (*l'innomable*) in all ethical action, "le Bien n'est le Bien qu'autant qu'il ne prétend rendre le monde bon" (the Good is only Good insofar as it does not claim to make the world good) (*E* 75). In this sense, the subject always confronts elements of the real, aspects of the situation that remain inaccessible to it. Yet, on the other hand, how is this claim consistent with the emphasis on love, which would seem to entail the overcoming of the law of the Real in an act of almost mystical identification with the *événement*? That is, in Lacanian terms, isn't there a risk of a reduction of the order of the Real to the Symbolic through Badiou's emphasis on love? This is revealed most clearly perhaps in Badiou's seeming hostility to the death drive as the basic law of the unconscious in Freud and Lacan.[8] Two things are revealed here: (1) the *structural Judaism* of psychoanalysis is confirmed through its preoccupation with the unsurpassable character of the death drive, the Law, and the Real, a fact that would simply confirm my attempted rapprochement between Levinas and Lacan; and (2) the *structurally Christian* character of Badiou's work is revealed in what is perhaps its most attractive feature, namely, its persistant and restless affirmation of life and its refusal of the tragic pathos of Lacanian psychoanalysis in the name of courage and energy. In this sense, Lacan would be closer to Levinas than to Badiou. But maybe for precisely this reason Lacan, Levinas, and everybody else should try to be closer to Badiou. Let me try to explain myself by turning to the question of comedy.

BECKETT AS HEROIC COMIC ANTIHERO OF BADIOU'S WORK—AGAINST TRAGEDY

I would like to return to the question of heroism and wager a final series of questions on the figure whom I would choose to see as the real hero of Badiou's work, not Saint Paul but Sam Beckett. Let me begin with a quotation from Badiou's "Thèses sur le théâtre":

> I do not believe that the principal questions of our epoch are horror, suffering, destiny or despair. We are saturated with them and the fragmentation of these terms into theatrical ideas is incessant. . . . Our question is that affirmative courage, of local energy. To seize hold of a point and to maintain it. Our question is therefore less that of the conditions for a modern tragedy than those for a modern comedy. Beckett understood this, whose theatre, correctly performed, is hilarious. (PMI 117–18)

It is true, Beckett understood this very well; but have we really understood Beckett? Let me take a small sideways step to try to explain myself. Ethics, for Badiou, is that which governs our lives as subjects, what gives them consistency, and its only maxim is "Continuer!" Submission to this ethical principle involves a certain asceticism, a certain renunciation, but this is only at the service of our desire, which sometimes seems close to Spinoza's notion of *conatus essendi* (to persevere in being). As is well known, and in fidelity to a largely German tradition that stretches back from Heidegger to Hegel and Hölderlin, Lacan's prime example of someone who acts in accordance with their desire and who continues is Antigone. She exemplifies the position of being "*entre deux morts*" (between two deaths), which, for Lacan, best describes the situation of human finitude. Antigone is the heroine of Lacanian psychoanalysis—that is, she is possessed by that transgressive *atè* or madness that enables her to stand out against the conformism of the state, where all ethical action is reduced to what Lacan calls "*le service des biens*" (the service of goods), and achieve an authentic relation to finitude.

Now, I have problems with Antigone, not so much with her personage, but with its exemplarity. I have elsewhere attempted to criticize Lacan for employing tragedy as his paradigm of sublimation, arguing that the reading of *Antigone* in *Seminar VII* makes psychoanalysis the inheritor of a tragic paradigm that stretches back to Schelling's Identity Philosophy.[9] I criticize this paradigm for making finitude too heroic, where the tragic heroine achieves a certain purification of desire in the experience of being-towards-death. Inspired by Lacoue-Labarthe's anti-Heideggerian reading of Hölderlin's translation of the *Antigone*, I call this the "tragic-heroic paradigm."[10] I argue simply that a quite different picture of finitude emerges if we focus on the phenomena of the comic and humor. The picture of finitude that I want to recommend is not accessible in the form of tragic affirmation, but rather comic acknowledgment, the acknowledgment of the ubiquity of the finite, but also its ungraspability. My approval of the demand of finitude is not equal to that demand, but makes that demand even more demanding. To put this in a formula, I think that humor is a form of minimal sublimation that corresponds to the structure of depression in the Freudian sense, but which is not at all depressing. On the contrary, Freud concludes his essay on humor by claiming that humor—dark, sardonic, wicked humor—is "liberating and elevating." "Look!" he concludes, "'Here is the world, which seems so dangerous! It is nothing but a game for children—just worth making a jest about.'"[11] Ethical subjectivity is comic rather than tragic.

To return to Badiou, what perhaps most interests me in his work is the link between affirmative ethical courage and comedy as the form of aesthetic sublimation that would best exemplify this ethical stance. *This* is what Beckett understood so well and it is why his tragicomedy—which is how he describes *Godot*—uses the strategy of humor, hilarity, and *drôlerie* ("funnyness") to attain an ethical stance of courage and love of humanity. As Badiou rightly writes, "Beckett has to be played in the most intense drôlerie . . . and it is only then that the true destination of the comic comes into view: not a symbol, not a disguised metaphysics, still less a derision, but a powerful love for human obstinacy, for an insatiable desire" (*B* 74–75). Thus, for Badiou, it is the strange cast of characters who populate Beckett's fiction and theater that best exemplify the maxim "Continuer!": "I must go on, I can't go on, I will go on."

I could not agree more. And yet, I have a question on this interpretation of Beckett. For Badiou, Beckett practices a form of "*ascèse méthodique*," a methodical asceticism that reduces all ethical considerations to the bare maxim: "Continuez!" (*B* 19). The problem I have here is that this makes Beckett sound like a stoic. Now, although there are obviously strongly stoical elements of discipline, denial, rigor, and exactitude in his work, I do not think that Beckett is only a stoic. That is, Beckett does not just say "il faut continuer" (one must go on), but also "je ne peux pas continuer" (I cannot go on) and what is perhaps the most characteristic feature of Beckett's writing is not just the decision to continue, but also the acknowledgment that I cannot continue. That is to say, Beckett's prose is characterized by an aporetic rhythm of continuity and discontinuity, of being able to go on and not being able to go on. This aporetic rhythm is the very movement of Beckett's writing, what he calls a "syntax of weakness," a self-undoing language that cannot go on and cannot but go on, that continues *in* its failure, and continues *as* that failure. For example, "Live and invent. I have tried, Invent. It is not the word. Neither is live. No matter. I have tried."[12] Or a longer example:

> What am I to do, what shall I do, what should I do, in my situation, how proceed? By aporia pure and simple? Or by affirmations and negations invalidated as uttered, or sooner or later. Generally speaking. There must be other shifts. Otherwise it would be quite hopeless. But it is quite hopeless.

I should mention without going any further that I say aporia without knowing what it means. Can one be ephectic otherwise than unawares? I don't know.[13]

But this syntax of weakness is at its most explosive when it becomes a comic syntax. For example, Clov to Hamm in *Endgame*, "Do you believe in the life to come?"; Hamm to Clov, "Mine was always that. Got him that time."[14] Or again, as I began with talk of parrots, here is Molloy on Lousse's parrot:

Fuck the son of a bitch, fuck the son of a bitch. He must have belonged to an American sailor, before he belonged to Lousse. Pets often change masters. He didn't say much else. No, I'm wrong, he also said, Putain de merde! He must have belonged to a French sailor before he belonged to the American sailor. Putain de merde! Unless he had hit on it alone, it wouldn't surprise me. Lousse tried to make him say, Pretty Polly! I think it was too late. He listened, his head on one side, pondered, then said, Fuck the son of a bitch. It was clear he was doing his best.[15]

Beckett's work is characterized by a syntax of weakness, a comic syntax that continues and then decides not to continue, simply to realize that it cannot not continue and that it must continue. It is this experience, like that of Vladimir and Estragon trying and failing to hang themselves in *Godot*, that is so comically tragic, or tragically comic. But if that is the case, then there are two conflicting norms in Beckett's work: on the one hand, there is Continuez! and, on the other hand, "*Ratage!*" (Fail!). The logic of Beckett's work follows the aporetic rhythm of these two imperatives, between the demand to continue and the acknowledgment that all continuation is failure. The courage to continue does not simply derive from a stoical act of ascetic will, from some Spinozist *conatus essendi* or Fichtean *Streben*, but rather from the continual experience of failure: "Try again, fail again, fail better."

Let me try one last time. There seems to be a residual heroism at work in Badiou, the heroism of resistance and militant activism: Saint Paul, Jean Cavaillès, or Georges Canguilhem. But this does not seem to be Beckett's world, filled as it is with antiheroic personages, a gallery of moribunds who seem riveted to the spot, unable to move: Murphy, Molloy, Malone, Mahood, Watt, and Worm. But is such blatant inactivity another form of resistance? Might not Beckett's heroes best exemplify what it would mean to be, in Badiou's allusion to Mallarmé, "militants of restrained action" (les militants de l'action restreinte) (*AMP* 118)? Now, I would quite like to be a militant of restrained action, particularly as it does not sound too demanding, but what is it exactly?

The question of heroism is urgent because the stakes are not just ethical, they are political. As Badiou admits at the beginning and end of his *Abrégé de métapolitique*, true politics is rare, the last good example being 1968 (17, 167). Now perhaps this is true, but nevertheless what I suspect in Badiou is the seduction of a great politics, the event that would, in Nietzsche's words, break history in two. Now, perhaps the epoch of great politics, like the epoch of great art for Heidegger and Hegel, is over. Perhaps. And perhaps that is a good thing. Perhaps we have had enough of the virile, Promethean politics of the will, the empty longing for total revolution. In my view, to be seduced by great politics is to risk nostalgically blinding oneself to the struggles of the present. As such, the seduction risks being politically disempowering. What we have to *hope* for, in Paul's sense of the word, is the knowledge that it is, in Beckett's words, all quite hopeless. But such hopelessness is not resignation and could provide a bridge to another model of politics, what I would see as a micropolitics of continual interruption, interruptions both internal to civil society and internationally at a transstate level. Such interruptions would be movements of dissensual emancipatory praxis that work against the consensual horizon of the state. Perhaps we just have to content ourselves with smaller actions and smaller victories, an everyday and heroically antiheroic militancy. That is, we have to learn to expect much more from much less. To my mind, such a politics is not approached through the figure of the tragic hero—lofty, solitary, derelict, and *unheimlich* (uncanny)—but rather through what Badiou calls "humoristic pragmatism" of Beckett. As Malone quips in what I would like to imagine as an ironic response to Saint Paul, "For why be discouraged, one of the thieves was saved, that is a generous percentage."[16]

NOTES

1. Dieter Henrich, "The Concept of Moral Insight and Kant's Doctrine of the Fact of Reason," in *The Unity of Reason* (Cambridge, MA: Harvard University Press, 1994), 55–87. I would like to thank Alain Badiou, Barbara Cassin, Charles Ramond, Sandra Laugier, and other participants at a conference on Badiou held in Bordeaux in October 1999 for their critical responses to a French version of this chapter. I would like to thank Jay Bernstein for first alerting me to the rich potential of Henrich's argument for contemporary moral theory and Peter Osborne for an acute critical reading of the first draft of this chapter.

2. The philosopher who does not really fit in this list is Hegel, who rejects the Kantian version of moral insight in the strongest terms as that "cold duty, the last undigested log in our stomach, a revelation given to reason" (quoted in Henrich, *The Unity of Reason*, 69). However, one might say that the notion of moral insight in Hegel is the awareness of freedom as the self-consciousness of Spirit in its

historical development, something to be learned by consciousness by recapitulating the experiences described in the *Phenomenology of Spirit*. In other words, moral insight would be identical with the achievement of rational self-determination.

3. Martin Heidegger, *Being and Time*, trans. John Macquarrie and Edward Robinson (Oxford, UK: Blackwell, 1962). German pagination p. 275.

4. Ibid., 310

5. A very similar line of criticism of Badiou can be found in Slavoj Žižek's *The Ticklish Subject* (London: Verso, 1999), see chapter 3 "The Politics of Truth, or, Alain Badiou as a Reader of Saint Paul" (127-70).

6. For a useful critique of Badiou on this question of religion, see Jean-Jacques Lecercle, "Cantor, Lacan, Mao, Beckett, *même combat*: The Philosophy of Alain Badiou," *Radical Philosophy* 93 (1999): 6-13.

7. I have argued for such a view in detail in the final chapter of my *Ethics-Politics-Subjectivity* (London: Verso, 1999). See also my "Remarks on Derrida and Habermas," *Constellations* 7, no. 4 (2000): 455-65.

8. A more detailed version of this line of criticism can be found in Žižek, *The Ticklish Subject*, 145-67.

9. The most succinct version of this argument can be found in my "Comedy and Finitude: Displacing the Tragic-Heroic Paradigm in Philosophy and Psychoanalysis," *Constellations* 6, no. 1 (1999): 108-22.

10. Philippe Lacoue-Labarthe, *Metaphrasis* (Paris: Presses Universitaires de France, 1997).

11. Sigmund Freud, "Humour," trans. J. Riviere, in *Standard Edition*, vol. 21 (London: Hogarth Press, 1961), 166.

12. Samuel Beckett, *The Trilogy* (London: Picador, 1979), 179.

13. Ibid., 267.

14. Samuel Beckett, *Endgame* (London: Faber, 1958), 35.

15. Beckett, *The Trilogy*, 179.

16. Ibid., 233.

TEN

Can Change Be Thought?
A Dialogue with Alain Badiou

Bruno Bosteels

THE ROAD TO DAMASCUS

BRUNO BOSTEELS: I would like to begin by situating your work in the context of May '68 in France. In *Theory of Contradiction*, you say that the events of that year mark, both in philosophical terms and in every other regard, your road to Damascus. This statement seems almost to be a direct anticipation by some thirty years of your recent book, *Saint Paul: The Foundation of Universalism*, as if to suggest that all this time was needed in order to come to grips with the effects of the student movement and the encounter between students and workers. What has always impressed me, in this regard, is the force of continuity between your thought and the events of May '68 and its aftermath. There are few philosophers who have been able to continue in that line of thinking without falling into either melancholy or resentment. How do you see this situation today? Could we not say that your two most important books to date, *Theory of the Subject* and *Being and Event*, even if we put aside for a moment the profound change that occurred between them, are in some way the answer after the fact to this event that struck you on your road to Damascus?

ALAIN BADIOU: Indeed, I think that, to use my own terminology, my fidelity to what happened in that period is unshakable but it is also profound, because a large part of my philosophy in reality is an attempt fully to come to terms, including from my own experience, with what has happened there and then, while at the same time explaining the reasons for remaining loyal to those events. I am always surprised, in fact, by the many cases of disloyalty, backlash, and abandonment. I cannot see any justification for this, other than a certain form of historicism, namely, the argument that, ultimately, you should always keep up with the times at all cost, and since times are changing and, as is only normal, the counterrevolution comes after the revolution, so then, to be modern means always that you should somehow fall in line with the sequence of events of your time.

I am surprised to see, for instance, that today everything that does not amount to surrender pure and simple to generalized capitalism, let us call it thus, is considered to be archaic or old-fashioned, as though in a way there existed no other definition of what it means to be modern than, quite simply, to be at all times caught in the dominant forms of the moment. I ask myself if behind all this there does not lurk still a difficult settling of accounts with historicism, and with the conviction that you must always be in tune with what I would call the average of our time, and that, otherwise, you are marginalized, lagging behind, or archaic.

For me, I would add that this loyalty to the sequence initiated by May '68 has never posed any real difficulties, except for the fact that this has become rare nowadays—and, of course, that is the real problem. Subjectively, not only does this loyalty not present any problem, but I continue to think that the complete elucidation of what took place there, together with the invention of ways of remaining loyal to those events, is the real task of contemporary thinking. I, for one, cannot see any other task. That being said, I also would not like to make a virtue, or an heroic exception, out of this fidelity. For me, in any case, it is probably abandonment that would be difficult, and not loyalty.

THE MOTIF OF THE END

B.B.: On several occasions in your work, particularly in *Abridged Metapolitics* but already in *Theory of the Subject*, you have addressed a particular way of responding, or of failing to respond, to the events of '68. One case in point would be the New Philosopher who—according to your thesis in "What Is a Thermidorean?"—can be defined as someone who makes it impossible even to think of this sequence of events. Today, however, I see only little interest in replying to the New Philosophers. More daunting is the challenge put forth by other thinkers, some of them being among the most subtle and lucid interpreters in the tradition of Heidegger and Derrida. I am thinking for example of Philippe Lacoue-Labarthe and Jean-Luc Nancy, who from a rather melancholy point of view, including in the psychoanalytical sense of the term, attempt to transform this very impossibility and retreat of the revolution, of sovereignty, or, even more generally, of all politics as hitherto conceived, into the argument for a new beginning, or a retreatment, of the political as such. In your case, even though there are evidently breaks and reformulations in your work, I see no reticence, and thus almost no melancholy, no desire to explain the past as if it were an effect of youthful fervor, a misguided dream, or even the expression of an unfounded hope in another order beyond the law of capital and market administration. To anticipate a bit, what is your position with regard to this other tendency, which clearly is not that of the New Philosophers, being more akin to the critique of metaphysics in the wake of Heidegger?

A.B.: I see what you mean. I should say, by the way, that for quite a long time now I have been traveling in friendship along the sides of Philippe Lacoue-Labarthe and Jean-Luc Nancy. I hold them in the greatest esteem and love them very much. We met in the early eighties, precisely at a time which for me, no doubt, was the period of maximum isolation, because the New Philosophy had been installed, everybody had rallied more or less to the Socialist Left and to Mitterrand, and, truth be told, if you consider my own politico-philosophical position, precisely at the time of *Theory of the Subject*, you will find that it went completely against the grain and was worked out in absolute isolation. I really should thank Lacoue-Labarthe and Nancy for not having participated in this isolation, and for having invited me to the political seminar that they directed at the time in Rue d'Ulm. Therefore, I absolutely distinguish what you call their "tendency" from that of denegation pure and simple. At the same time, it is true that we do not share the same subjectivity and, as a result, we do not think in the same terms about those events, because they nonetheless confirm a certain paradigm of the end which, I think, comes from the crossing between their Heideggerianism, after all, and their evaluation of the twentieth century. This authorizes them, by the way, to present themselves, truthfully I believe, as left-Heideggerians. I mean, in an allusion to Hegel, we could speak of "young" Heideggerians, in comparison to the "old" Heideggerians: Heideggerians of the Left.

Nevertheless, the motif of the end is there, and something in the thesis of the retreat of the political, which is their own nostalgic thesis, is in tune with, or can be fully understood only from within, the space of the closure of metaphysics. I am convinced that this is indeed one of the modalities of the closure of metaphysics. In terms of their account of the twentieth century, this means that they accept to say that what has been blindly attempted in the past century is now effectively closed, and this statement will then converge with, or will be tied to, a much vaster historical framework of which the question of politics is only one modality among others. Hence, probably also the need, in their vocabulary, to desublimate politics, to consent to a politics without the sublime. This can also be phrased as follows: to pass from the poem into prose, or to conceive of the poem itself as prose. I understand this politically too: to conceive of the poem as prose means, really, that the heroic form of politics is effectively finished and over with, and that we should seek out or reopen another figure for the labor of thought that is politics. For this reason, I think, they need to pass through the end, or the figure of the end, in order to reopen the question of the political or of politics, in a modality that I am afraid remains by and large prophetic. I am afraid that this is no less but also no more than the promise of the return of the gods as in Heidegger. I am afraid that whenever a notion of the end has this kind of historical importance or density, the announcement of the resurrection remains always at bottom the natural regime of thought. Thinking, then, remains installed in a certain linkage between the lack and the announcement from which it can find no escape.

My own position is different. I am convinced that at all times the politics of emancipation have been essential, that in any case there has not been, properly speaking, one unique experience in the twentieth century but a diversity of experiences which surely presented certain common traits but which were nevertheless essentially multiple and heterogeneous, and that these sequences are saturated. The questions posed by this saturation are extremely complex, but not more so than at other times. I mean, at bottom, what were the questions posed to the thinkers and militants from the beginning of the nineteenth century by the fact that the sequence of the French Revolution was in all evidence closed? These questions are somehow replayed today. Besides, the various tendencies that we can discern today already existed, metaphorically or analogically speaking, at that time. The nostalgic-melancholy tendency can easily be found among writers of the early nineteenth century, and so can the prophetic-idealist tendency as well. And then Marx proposes an entirely different angle, because if you consider things in terms of the effect of capital and so on, you are elsewhere, somewhere else absolutely than where the French Revolution was.

In this regard, my loyalty cannot be any less clear: I can perfectly well admit that a whole series of internal features of politics from the past century, let us say of revolutionary politics and its avatars, is saturated, and, at the same time, admit that we still have considerable difficulties, both in thought and in practice, to go beyond this saturation. A large part of the current disposition in this matter is purely experimental, trying out new possibilities neither in the eschatological sense of the end or the retreat of the political, nor in the sense of a renunciation, that is only another figure of the end, namely, the end of illusions.

The ambiguity of the motif of the end comes from the fact that this question can receive two possible treatments. When an end is declared, whether it is the end of metaphysics, the end of politics, or eventually the end of philosophy itself, two approaches are possible. The first is to say: it was only an illusion, and we have been awakened, our eyes have been opened, and we have ceased being duped. And then the second treatment is: it was much more than an illusion, it was an historical disposition, something of the nature of a figure, but this figure has perished, and we should move one to another. With regard to this motif of the end, in other words, you basically have a critical figure, that of disillusion, and then a prophetic one, which consists in passing from one figure to another. Both, in my eyes, render politics practically impossible; the first because, after all, it amounts to the acceptance of the established order. This has been true ever since the modern Bildungsroman, as can be seen in *Les illusions perdues* by Balzac: when all illusions are lost, this means that one is finally part of the world as it is, and thus the world will be administered, but there will be no politics as I understand it. Nor will there be in the second treatment, though, because in this case what replaces politics is the announcement of the conditions of possibility of its resurrection, while politics itself is paralyzed.

I really believe that the motif of the end is politically intractable. It is of course true that things come to an end, but then a sufficiently elaborated ontology of multiplicity is needed in order to be able to admit that what comes to an end is always only *one* figure among others of the politics of emancipation, and that the latter has always existed in such multiplicity.

IN THE SHADOW OF MAO

B.B.: In order to understand how your current work responds to, or avoids both these positions, particularly with regard to the motif of the end, I would like to go back in time once again, to the period right before and after May '68. Philosophically speaking, this moment is dominated by the famous debates regarding structure and history, or structure and subject, let us say: Althusser against Sartre, or Lacan against Debord and the Situationists. Once we admit that it is at this time that the question of the event as such begins to be formulated, particularly from the point of view of politics, your work appears to sit astride between these two positions, by articulating the later philosophy of Sartre with that of Althusser, or by reformulating Lacanian psychoanalysis in terms of the Marxist doctrine, in *Theory of the Subject*. I would argue that it is in this in-between of the traditions of Sartre and Althusser that you make it possible to think of the event *in* a situation. The articulation of these two apparently heterogeneous traditions, though, in large part becomes possible only thanks to the input of Maoism. More so than in the trends of post-Marxism, as is the case for other members of your generation, could your work not be resituated in the line of post-Maoism?

A.B.: Yes, absolutely.

B.B.: Now, in this debate regarding the site of the event between history and structure, how do you see the place of your own work, particularly at the time of your texts on Maoism, from *Theory of Contradiction* all the way to *Theory of the Subject*?

A.B.: I would like to say first of all that your question seems to me absolutely pertinent, because for a long time now I thought that I had had the chance, in a sense, of being just a little bit older than the rest of my generation, if I can use this slightly absurd expression [laughs]. If I think of those who have been Althusserians, Lacanians, and Maoists—which was the normal itinerary for the militant intelligentsia from 1968 to 1972—they were all a bit younger than me. So what did this mean? It meant that, in a way, they had not had the time to be Sartreans. They had not really been Sartreans, and they also had not known any political situation in which they would have had to think in the categories proper to Sartre. As for me, I had known a very powerful political situation, the Algerian war, and I believe that it makes a big difference to have known this situation, in which progressive positions could be taken up from within the philosophical categories that were Sartre's own. These were the categories of commitment, of anticolonialism, and the kind of Sartrean thesis that held that colonialism is a system, which can be found in his texts of that period.

I found in Sartre's theory of practical freedom, and particularly in the subjectivized Marxism that he was already trying to produce, something with which to engage myself politically, in spite of everything, in the situation. This did not keep me from taking my distance from Sartre, nor from participating in that generation of mine which indeed started to take a major interest in the question of the structure. But in the end, I entered in this debate from the point of view of Sartre, whereas for most others in my generation this question of the structure has been their immediate philosophical education, so that they really entered the debate *against* Sartre and not *from* Sartre. And in general, one should say, against phenomenology.

So there was a small temporal discrepancy, which in effect put me in a position in between, I think we could put it that way. This meant that, against all odds, I have always been concerned in a privileged way by the question of how something could still be called "subject" within the most rigorous conditions possible of the investigation of structures. This question had an echo for me of an even older question, which I had posed at the time when I was fully Sartrean, namely, the question of how to make Sartre compatible with the intelligibility of mathematics. Of course, this is not at all a Sartrean question, but at bottom I had always been a secret Platonist for love of mathematics and their regime of intelligibility. I remember very clearly having raised the question, having formed the project of one day constructing something like a Sartrean thought of mathematics, or of science in general, which Sartre had left aside for the most part. This particular circumstance explains why I nevertheless have always been interested in the question of structural formalism while sustaining a category of the subject.

This meant that in the end I was more Lacanian than Althusserian, even though I was close to Althusser. But I have never been a member of the group of Althusserians from the first generation. I was always an Althusserian free agent, always a bit marginal. Besides, I was not a member of the Communist Party:

politically and philosophically, there was always something that did not quite fit. Althusserians, by the way, always reproached me for continuing to be a Sartrean after all. That debate was always present. Maoism has tied all this together.

Maoism has played an absolutely essential role. I mean the flamboyant kind of Maoism, from the period of the Cultural Revolution: Maoism presenting itself as an alternative to revisionism, that is to say, after all, as an alternative to the fate of the USSR, and in the final instance, but this is now completely obscured even though it is most important, as an alternative to Stalinism. This was a conscious effort on the part of Mao. Everything then becomes very complicated because at one point the Chinese seem to have defended Stalin against Krutschev, while the truth of the matter is that, particularly at the time of the Cultural Revolution, Mao thought of himself as attempting or proposing an alternative to the path in the construction of socialism on which Stalin had taken Leninism. So why was this so important? Because in Maoism, a very special place seemed to have been reserved for the question of subjectivity in politics—for a properly political subjectivity. In other words, there is the novelty of a break with the theory according to which consciousness is never anything more than consciousness of the objective conditions. Of course, Maoism also inherited much of the analyses of Marx, of Leninism, and the categories of the situation, of knowing the situation, and so on, are very important, but clearly there is a movement—how should we put this?—that tends toward the subjective heroism of thought and of the capacity for thinking, which struck an entirely new tone and which has tied me to the events of '68, opening up a space from where to read those events, and thus constituting the road to Damascus that we discussed a moment ago.

Maoism, in the end, has been the proof for me that in the actual space of effective politics, and not just in political philosophy, a close knot could be tied between the most uncompromising formalism and the most radical subjectivism. That was the whole point. In Maoism, I found something that made it possible for there to be no antinomy between whatever mathematics is capable of transmitting in terms of formal and structural transparency, on the one hand, and on the other, the protocols by which a subject is constituted. These two questions were no longer incompatible. And I would add that I remain very sensitive in this regard, even though this also goes completely against the grain but that's fine with me, to the Chinese political style. This is something that always struck me, namely, its extraordinary formulaic quality, in an almost mathematical sense of the word.

B.B.: The capacity to present mathemes, as it were?

A.B.: Exactly, to present the matheme of the situation, using sentences that possess at the same time an absolute transparency and an exceptional complexity or density, because they take charge of the situation in its entirety. This formulaic political style, which you very legitimately connect with the matheme, and which I myself have always connected with the matheme in the Lacanian sense of the word, has also contributed to the fact that Maoism has been for me a considerable school from the point of view of my personal history, in politics but also in philosophy. Moreover, and to conclude this point, it was also manifest that for Mao and for the Chinese there existed a system of statements regarding the respective places of philosophy, politics, and economy, which completely upset the traditional disposition of these grand registers. That is absolutely obvious, and it is not by chance that at the heart of Mao's work you find *Five Philosophical Essays*. It is not simply out of coquetry that they are called this way, but the disposition of philosophy with regard to politics in my eyes is not at all the same for Mao and in Stalinism, nor even for Mao and for Lenin.

B.B.: Isn't it for this same reason that Maoism constitutes a crucial point of reference for Althusser in his theory of overdetermination, as the inner limit of structuralism?

A.B.: Exactly. I think that Althusser has found the Maoist theory of contradiction at the exact moment when he was trying, with considerable difficulties I should add, to determine the point where the structure is in excess over itself, that's right, the point which he sought for in the Leninist theory of the weakest link, in the question of overdetermination, and, finally, in the theory of the principal aspect of the contradiction according to Mao. All this means pinning down the structural point that is also at the same time the point of breakdown of the structure.

B.B.: Maoism, in sum, enables a certain combination, or no longer finds an incompatibility, between an extremely rigorous, almost mathematical form of structuralism and a kind of subjectivism that would no longer be humanist in the strict sense of Sartre?

A.B.: Yes, yes.

B.B.: It is at this very point where we find ourselves in the company of another great tradition of contemporary thought, for example, in the work of Ernesto Laclau—whose trajectory in Argentina and later in Great Britain, is to some extent parallel to yours. To use your later terminology, this tradition concentrates on the void, on the point of excess, or on what you also call the "outsite" of the structure, on the one hand, and, on the other, on a subject which would no longer be the humanistic subject of plenitude but a subject that is "split" from within. It is at the point of articulation between the two that you, as a Sartrean–Althusserian–Lacanian, can propose a thought of the event combined with a rigorous analysis of the situation.

A.B.: Yes, definitely, that is absolutely evident. There are many of us who finally have worked with different means in that breach in our heritage. And I think that it was indispensable for me to do so, in the conditions that were specifically ours, by going through the experience of Maoism. Besides, but here we are moving a bit in another direction, this is a question about which I am quite passionate at the moment. I mean, when I am listening to you, my question is: What of all this can be effectively transmitted? At bottom, what is the internal link between the traversing of the Maoist experience in all its dimensions and the arrangement of thought, the matrix or the kernel of which we have just recalled? And is this link of such a nature as to enable us truly and persuasively to isolate it, in the way I have attempted to do, starting in *Being and Event*, so as to reconstruct all the elements while separating them from their political genealogy? In a way, we can say that *Theory of the Subject* is a book in which the essential elements are already absolutely present while remaining in close proximity to their genealogy. That is why I have often said that this book is rather more like Hegel's *Phenomenology of Spirit* than like his *Logic*. It is rather something that remains caught in the movement itself of the figures, very close to the experience of Maoism; it integrates this experience and thinks through the philosophical disposition in close proximity to its genealogy. Afterwards, in *Being and Event*, I have attempted a separation, but sometimes I wonder whether this is justified, I mean: In the end, should a true transmission not also be capable of transmitting this genealogy and this experience themselves?

Transmitting an experience is always of a slightly different order than transmitting the formal arrangement in which this experience is reflected or thought out. That is a question that intrigues me in terms of my job as a teacher. After all, I would very much like that all this were transmitted to the young people. We must corrupt the youth; after all, that is the job of the philosopher [*laughter*]. I wouldn't mind corrupting the youth, who are in dire need of a bit of corruption, or are completely corrupted but in the wrong sense. And I observe, since that is a bit the topic of our conversation, that they end up demanding the transmission not only of the intellectual or theoretical or philosophical framework but also of that which enabled us to think in such a way, and not otherwise, in the first place. Thus, we find ourselves again talking about the sixties, not only in the architecture of their thought but as a site, to use my own vocabulary: as an evental site. What has this site been? I am currently looking for protocols of transmission that would enable us to think that too. That is why, in my lectures at the Collège International de Philosophie, I began to talk about the twentieth century and about the figures of the present, and so on.

This is not a question of history, or of historical facts. It is a matter of transmitting the experimental adherences of the very concept itself, and how the concept is a result, in the sense of being a result of experiences. All this goes to confirm absolutely your thesis according to which Maoism has been decisive in this context.

DEVIATIONS LEFT AND RIGHT: TOWARD RADICAL PHILOSOPHY?

B.B.: For this reason I always insist that your early Maoist works, *Of Ideology* or *Theory of Contradiction*, should not be forgotten. Besides, I am convinced that even *Being and Event* should be read with the concepts of *Theory of the Subject* in mind, rather than only the other way around and precisely because the articulation with the historical situation, as in the case of the aftermath of May '68, can then be mapped out dialectically. What is more, in the way in which this sequence of events is later reinterpreted, we can already perceive the beginnings of a backlash, which you describe in detail in *Theory of the Subject*. In fact, you distinguish two types of backlash. On the one hand, there are those who would say that the event is absolutely pure, untainted by the situation, so that ultimately nothing really new takes place in terms of the consequences of the event for the situation itself; on the other, there are those who would deny that an event even occurred to begin with, so that all that really takes place is the placement of pure being as such. These two extremes, in a sense, could also serve to define the reception of your work as a whole. The two perspectives, which your philosophy aims to articulate by avoiding precisely their extremism, could still be said to correspond to pure subjectivism and pure structuralism. In Maoist terms, we might call these the two types of deviation, respectively, on the Left and on the Right: adventurism and opportunism, or anarchism and determinism, the delirium of spontaneity and the necessary laws of history. In the context of contemporary philosophy, finally, this same alternative seems to repeat itself between, on the one hand, a prophetic, or messianic, philosophy of the event, which remains absolutely outside the situation, and, on the other, the purely structural analysis of what is objectively given, which remains on the level of what you label the state of the situation. In this last case, the analysis can even pinpoint the void or the excess of the structure over itself, but finally does nothing more than recognize that inner limit itself. The event, then, would merely consist in an instantaneous apparition of the void as such, to be recognized by the political philosopher, without actually processing the consequences of any fidelity to the event.

In this context, the question of the void and the point of excess seem to me to be essential. For this reason, I would add, the pivot of your work could very well be said to be the concepts, first, of the "outsite," in *Theory of the Subject*, and later, of the "evental site," in *Being and Event*. These concepts alone keep us from losing sight of the specificity of the event, while at the same time avoiding the two extreme interpretations, which would reaffirm either that "nothing will have taken place but the place," or else that what has taken place is a force or an event so pure, or so sovereign, reminiscent of the "beautiful soul," so as to have no connection whatsoever to the situation in which it finds its place.

A.B.: Yes, absolutely, I agree with your interpretation. This is indeed the battle that is raging quietly on the question of the event. Let us say that everything in philosophy that is somewhat progressive and that does not inherit a completely rotten view of politics somehow hovers around the notion of the event. We can all agree on that. However, there are considerable divergences within the space of this agreement. And I believe that you have perfectly mapped out the terrain. Thus, on the one hand, the event will itself be conflated with something that in fact pertains to its structural condition of possibility. It is not at all the same thing to say that there is a site of an event and to say that there is an event. It is not at all the same thing to say that every situation contains a point of excess, a blank space, a blind spot, or an unpresented point, and to say that this already amounts to the event's effectuation properly speaking. In that case, the event becomes structuralized, having been revealed to be the intimate point of breakage of the situation, that is, in fact, something like its being, or its real. But then there is no politics, no fidelity, only a kind of blockage. All this in the end produces conceptions that in terms of politics are inevitably pessimist, in a Lacanian sense. On the other hand, indeed, the event can appear in its pure form, which we can find in Christian Jambet, who directly gives it a theological framework, but also in the work of many others. In this case, the event ultimately seems to be transhistorical.

B.B.: Without horizon, the event is being itself?

A.B.: At that moment, the event is being, absolutely, but being in its specific historicality that is finally inappropriate for being in the situation. I think that this is the right way of marking out the field. And it is true that my effort has always been one of articulation, in the sense that one can at the same time push to the end the properly structural theory of lack and excess, as well as their dialectical correlation in the renewed sense of the dialectic as used in *Theory of the Subject*, and consider the arrival of the event, which evidently would not be readable without such structural formalism, but which can neither be reduced to it nor is indifferent to it. And it is from there that everything will be exploited in the system of consequences. That is indeed my position, absolutely. Of course, one could say that it is still a measure of my original fidelity to the events of '68, because my position sustains that there are always consequences. Especially because I think that the regime of consequences is intrinsically infinite. Thus, there are always consequences, we are not reduced to waiting until the promise is kept, which is, after all, the prophetic position, nor obliged to say that there is nothing left, and to make do with this nothing. Subjectively, that is the alternative to which I do not want to limit myself. That's for sure.

LACK OR DESTRUCTION: BREAKING DOWN THE RULE OF ORDER

B.B.: I think that, for this very same reason, even before *Being and Event*, where you polemicize mostly with the ontologies of presence, that is, ultimately, with Heidegger, it is in *Theory of the Subject* that the passage from lack to destruction, in your polemic with Lacan, is really pivotal, even if later on you seem to want to abandon, or correct, the concept of destruction. In any case, it is the torsion by which something passes through at the site of the event.

A.B.: The concept of torsion is fundamental.

B.B.: To avoid conflating the site of the event, or the void of the situation, with the event itself, a passage is needed through the impasse. It is not enough to recognize the impasse of the structure, but it is also necessary, in a sense, to pass through it.

A.B.: I come back to this question of lack and destruction in subsequent elaborations. In *Theory of the Subject*, I was strictly Mallarméan: "Destruction was my Beatrice," and the passage from lack to destruction is the exemplary torsion. I am more reserved on this topic in *Being and Event*, because in some way I think that there is something in "destruction," even in the signifier itself, that is a bit one-sided, in relation to the properly creative dimension of that which occurs or arrives. I now plan completely to rework this matter, since what I am doing right now is once again closer to *Theory of the Subject* than to *Being and Event*. In some regards, it is once again more dialectically worked out. I think that I will end up by saying that in any case, there has to be a *déréglement*, a deregulation, or a breakdown of the rules.

B.B.: In an active sense?

A.B.: That's it. One cannot pretend simply to recognize the place of the void, let us keep this name for the moment. It is absolutely indispensable that there be a breaking of the rule, because otherwise there is nothing more than a recognition. But recognition is equivalent to misrecognition, in my eyes it has no virtue in and of itself. So then, there has to be a breakdown of the rule, that is to say, there must be something that, including in the order of appearing itself, in the way in which the situation is simply given, no longer remains within the bounds of the analysis, not even in terms of its immanent excess, something that no longer is of the same order as before. You call this traversing the impasse, I totally agree with the formulation. In any case, I would say deregulation of the excess itself, and not just identification of its position or of its law. In fact, the consequences are always those of a breakdown of the rule, they are not the consequences of the structural position of the excess. They are the results of the upsetting and breaking down of the rule. If we suppose, as I do in *Being and Event*, that there is something supernumerary, then we must understand how this is not simply supernumerary but an intrinsic factor in the deregulation of the previous situation as given.

Hence, I will combine supernumerary and destruction, instead of opposing them as I did in *Being and Event*. I will say: Let us not underestimate the fact that there is something that appears as such and that in a way was not there before, so that there is a supplementation, or a creation, a positive dimension, and that remains the point around which everything hangs together. But, at the same time, we would not understand what is at issue, if we did not see that this supernumerary element has a completely deregulating function in the regime of appearance of the situation itself and, thus, in a certain sense, it does destroy something after all, namely, it destroys a regime of existence, if I can say so, which was previously given. Indeed, something that was not entirely present in *Being and Event*, and that I will now redeploy, finally going back to my oldest sources, is the real distinction between being and existence. In fact, I will combine a certain generic stability of being, an uncovering of being, with something that nevertheless profoundly changes the regime of existence. Finally, and to wrap up this discussion which is extremely important politically speaking, but also very abstract, I believe that I will assert that there is supplementation of being and destruction of existence whenever an event occurs.

EVENT OR ENCOUNTER:
ALTHUSSER'S POSTHUMOUS WRITINGS

B.B.: I have one other question about the genealogy of your work, which concerns your relation to Althusser. In your analyses, you mostly concentrate on those canonical texts by Althusser in which he speaks of history as a process with neither subject nor end. However, I am thinking more now of Althusser's posthumous texts, published in the two volumes of *Écrits: Philosophiques et politiques*. Here, Althusser seems to extend his analysis of the structure of overdetermination by trying to pinpoint the weakest link for the events of May '68, for example, even though he is ultimately unable to recognize the subjective forces capable of shaking up the structure at this very point. My question refers to Althusser's subsequent attempt, perhaps in answer to his earlier blindness, to reconstitute what he calls a "subterranean" tradition, namely, the tradition of a materialism of the encounter, or of the aleatory, which seems to be his quest for a philosophy of the event, now called the encounter.

A.B.: Yes, absolutely.

B.B.: At that point, though, we are speaking of the early eighties, could we not say that the master finally has become the disciple to one of his own disciples? What is your relation to this part in the final, posthumous work of Althusser?

A.B.: Listen, I have the impression that what you say tells the essence. I believe that in his final research Althusser realized, first of all, that an ontological framework was needed, and that materialism finally could not simply be an epistemological category, that it was necessary to go further than that, and, in the end, he saw that this ontology needed to include the aleatory, in what he then called an aleatory materialism. Like everyone else, he went to look for this on the side of atoms, *clinamen* [swerve], Lucretius, etc. That's unavoidable, besides, in *Theory of the Subject*, that is also very much present. For my part, I think that Althusser indeed remains our contemporary, because he saw very clearly that something of the order of the event, of chance, of the aleatory, had to be inscribed and understood ontologically in the framework of intelligibility that finally led to revolutionary politics itself. At the same time, I believe that he did not say his final word on the issue. All that remains a transitional clue and it would have been necessary to see how in the final analysis, having grasped, reworked, and redeployed this, he would have rearticulated it to the ensemble of his previous framings. I have the feeling that he did not submit his intuitions in this regard to the ultimate test, that he had neither the time nor perhaps the desire or the subjective possibility of doing so. This goes to show to what extent Althusser remained a fundamental contemporary for us, even after I attacked him most vigorously for political reasons.

RADICALS AND DOGMATISTS: REPLYING TO THE CRITICS

B.B.: Let's turn now to the question of radical philosophy that I anticipated a moment ago. Often continuing in the vein of Althusserianism and Lacanianism, various authors have criticized your work, in the name of philosophical radicalism, for being dogmatic, or absolutist, in the way you would oppose being and event, or the situation and an unbounded beyond that would be so pure and so transcendent as to seem almost religious. It might be possible, however, to answer this charge of dogmatism from within your very own categories. First, we might say that in several of these readings, the event is conflated with the site of its possibility. Second, and more important, we might also say that the two deviations which you discuss in your work from the seventies and early eighties, let us call them "anarchism" or "voluntarism," on the one hand, and, on the other, "structuralism" or "determinism," strangely enough are being articulated, I wouldn't say in a dialectical synthesis, but rather by virtue of their inherent antinomical character. I am thinking, in particular, of the work of Ernesto Laclau and Slavoj Žižek. From the point of the structure, or the state of the situation, they may very well pinpoint the void, or the term of excess and/or lack in the Lacanian sense, a term which, as a vanishing cause, sustains the entire symbolical or social order, even while being itself in retreat—and here there would be an interesting parallel with Heidegger.

A.B.: Yes, totally.

B.B.: But this term, or this multiple, also allows the critic to adopt an ever-more radical point of view, from which any concrete event or specific fidelity to the event will inevitably appear to be either naïve or dogmatic, or both at once—not unlike the sense in which Maoism was accused of being a strange mixture of anarchic voluntarism and ferocious totalitarianism. What I found in your work, however, is precisely a set of concepts and categories that allowed me to understand the logic of such radical arguments. Finally, this logic seems to remain on the level of the state, or of structural representation. Or rather, insofar as it is a matter of the void or gap that sustains this totality, we should perhaps speak of poststructural representation. Thus, we have the often-repeated argument about the subject divided by the gap in the structure. In the end, the void circulates a bit everywhere, mainly between subject and structure, but this circulating void, whether as the real or as the kernel of antagonism and so on, can then be turned back against any trajectory, however precarious, of fidelity with regard to an event. Today, radical philosophy seems to amount to some strange and paradoxical kind of structural, or poststructural, anarchism: an ideal combination of adventurism that allows one to be radical, and of a structuralism that allows one to be rigorous.

A.B. [*laughing very hard*]: Yes, absolutely. You describe the situation very well. And in this regard I would like to insist that, even in the title *Being and Event*, the "and" is fundamental.

B.B.: The disjunction?

A.B.: It is not the opposition between the event and the situation that interests me first and foremost. That is not the focus of my interest. Besides, from this point of view, I have always complained about being read in a way that is askew, or about being read only for the first chapters and then nobody reads the core of the proposal. Because, in my eyes, the principal contribution of my work does not consist in opposing the situation to the event. In a certain sense, that is something that everybody does these days. The principal contribution consists in posing the following question: what can be deduced, or inferred, from there from the point of view of the situation itself? Ultimately, it is the situation that interests me.

I don't think that we can grasp completely what a trajectory of truth is in a situation without the hypothesis of the absolute, or radical, arrival of an event. Okay. But in the end, what interests me is the situational unfolding of the event, and not the transcendence or the entrenchment of the event itself. Thus, in my eyes, the fundamental categories are those of *genericity* and of *forcing*. Genericity can be understood as the trajectory of aleatory consequences, which are all suspended from whatever the trace of the event is in the situation; and forcing consists in the equally extremely complex and hypothetical way in which truths, including political truths, influence and displace the general system of our encyclopedias, and thus, of knowledge.

In the end, therefore, I would like to be evaluated or judged on this part of my project, because in my opinion that is where the heart of the matter lies as well as its novelty, even as far as the attempt is concerned to illuminate the militant dimension of a procedure of truth. However, I am very surprised to see that, in general, for reasons due to their own interests, the commentators jump on the event to qualify it as transcendence, and then they tackle the category of truth as being inadequate, or as dogmatizing the figure of intimate excess. But I do not see how it can be dogmatized, given that we are in a register of consequences.

Truth, for me, is not the name of the event, even though that is how it is often interpreted. Truth is what unfolds as a system of consequences, secured by an unheard-of figure of the subject as consequence of the rupture of the event. It is so little dogmatic that it is rather always declared in the figure of an aleatory wager, which is kept up without having anything dogmatic about it, and without any guarantees from the event's transcendence in and of itself.

Thus, finally, what I try to develop is a series of conceptions that adopt neither a statelike or structuralized figure of immanent excess, nor a figure that would remit the event to some ineffective archetypal promise. Really, in the end, I have only one question: what is the new in a situation? My unique philosophical question, I would say, is the following: can we think that there is something new in the situation, not outside the situation nor the new somewhere else, but can we really think through novelty and treat it in the situation? The system of philosophical answers that I elaborate, whatever its complexity may be, is subordinated to that question and to no other. Even when there is event, structure, formalism, mathematics, multiplicity, and so on, this is exclusively destined, in my eyes, to think through the new in terms of the situation. But, of course, to think the new in situation, we also have to think the situation, and thus we have to think what is repetition, what is the old, what is not new, and after that we have to think the new.

At least in this regard I remain more profoundly Hegelian. That is, I am convinced that the new can only be thought as process. There certainly is novelty in the event's upsurge, but this novelty is always evanescent. That is not where we can pinpoint the new in its materiality. But that is precisely the point that interests me: the materiality of the new.

THE SOVEREIGN EVENT?

B.B.: In a way, you have already started answering some of the charges of dogmatism or absolutism that are frequently leveled against your work. I would like to tease out more specifically the reasons behind these charges. The first reason, which you have just answered, concerns the rigid oppositions such as between being and event. In your work, however, the point is not simply to oppose them, but to know what happens between the two in terms of transformation, disordering, or forcing. Thus, with regard to all the other oppositions as well—opinion and truth, history and politics, the animal and the immortal in us, interests and eternity—it is always a question of studying how these oppositions themselves are subject to a torsion?

A.B.: Absolutely.

B.B.: A second motif behind the allegation of dogmatism holds that the event is presented as absolutely sovereign, in the sense of being self-referential. The event would refer to nothing outside itself. It is a multiple with the property of belonging to itself. To this reading, we should first of all reply that the event is clearly not only a self-referential multiple.

A.B.: Not at all, precisely.

B.B.: In that case we would indeed be in the trap of an absolute purity.

A.B.: The event is self-referential and, in addition, it is nothing else than the set of elements of its site. Here, the same principle applies: If you isolate self-referential and a set of elements of the site, you cannot adequately think through what I propose as the event's figure. Because as multiple, the event's figure mobilizes the elements of the site, delivering them from the axiom of foundation. Subtracted from this axiom, and thus unfounded, the multiple of the elements of the site is going to act in a peculiar manner, namely, by immanentizing its own multiplicity. But you cannot isolate the material singularity of the event as such, since the event is tied to the situation by way of its site, and the theory of the site is fairly complex. It was Deleuze who, very early on, even before our correspondence, at the time when *Being and Event* was about to appear, told me that the heart of my philosophy was the theory of the site of the event. It was this theory, he told me, that explained why one is not in immanence, which he regretted a lot, but neither is one in transcendence. The site is that which would diagonally cross the opposition of immanence and transcendence.

B.B.: Deleuze also offered another reading, perhaps prior to your correspondence, in *What Is Philosophy?* This other reading, which signals a third reason for our debate, concerns the position of philosophy itself in relation to its conditions. Here, too, it is often said that in your work, philosophy appears to occupy a position that is transcendent to its conditions. However, in response to this last objection, the opposite could also be said, since for you philosophy produces no truths of its own, being rather always under condition, and thus by no means is philosophy put on a pedestal.

A.B.: Not at all. In this aspect, too, I think that I am fairly Hegelian. In certain regards, philosophy would rather have a tendency always to arrive too late. Ultimately, the owl of Minerva only takes off when night falls. I understand this fairly well, even though obviously not for the same reasons as Hegel. I understand that the major problem for the philosopher is to arrive early enough. I really believe this is the case. This is why philosophers must constantly engage with the experiences of their time, have an ear for what happens, and especially listen to the antiphilosopher, because the antiphilosopher is always busy saying to him, "But what you, the philosopher, are talking about no longer exists, or it doesn't really exist, and then there is this, which you don't talk about and which is essential," and so on. That is a real convocation to one's time. It is, truly, a race against time. Indeed, I am convinced that the procedures of truth do not wait for philosophy. Thus, to speak of transcendence when it is really a matter of designating as quickly as possible whatever is proceeding, of saying "yes, that is where it proceeds," frankly I think that is an unfair trial, unfair because it often dissimulates its very opposite, that is, the refusal to place philosophy really under the system of its conditions. In fact, I am surprised to see in this regard how the majority of philosophers of our time are content with very little. That is, after all, they isolate very few things in our actual experience that they would consider sufficient to assure the contemporariness of philosophy.

REDEFINING HISTORY: THE LEGACY OF MICHEL FOUCAULT

B.B.: Someone who seems to have had the intention to think his time is certainly Michel Foucault. In one of the earliest interviews with Foucault, an interview in which you participated along with Georges Canguilhem, you already try to define philosophy as the thought of one's time—what you would later describe as providing a space of compossibility for the conditions of truth. In *Abridged Metapolitics*, you recognize in Foucault someone who, despite seeking to think through the singularity of his time, finally would have lost sight of the event itself, having reduced it to sheer history in the heterogeneous articulation of knowledge and power, the discursive and the nondiscursive. My question concerns the topics of history and historicism, which you mentioned before. In your earlier work, in *Theory of the Subject*, for instance, you oppose structure and history by privileging the latter without wanting to ignore the former; in *Being and Event*, similarly, you oppose nature and history. In more recent texts such as *Abridged Metapolitics*, though, you seem to follow the position of your friend and colleague Sylvain Lazarus by rejecting time as a category to think through politics, just as you seem rather forcefully to reject history. If we think of the work of Foucault, however, could we not say that his lifelong effort has also been to reflect upon the conditions of art, of literature, of science, particularly the threshold of the human sciences in most of his writings, and then, in *History of Sexuality*, we might say that he talks of love, and finally, of the question of politics, which is also patent in his active militantism. Even if Foucault's terms would seem to fall on the side of those categories which, in *Saint Paul*, you oppose to the conditions of truth properly speaking, that is, even if he prefers knowledge over truth, sexuality over love, and so on, should we not recognize in him this gigantic effort to reflect upon the events of our time in what he called an "ontology of actuality," or a "critical ontology of the present"? Even this expression itself has lost nothing of its provocative power. Indeed, if we were to follow the dominant line of ontological inquiry in the wake of Heidegger, how could we even think of such a project as an "ontology of actuality"? From the point of view of the destruction of the metaphysics of presence, this would seem to be sheer nonsense. And yet, this project is in line with your own attempt to find an alternative ontological path to the tradition of Heidegger. Should we not consider Foucault, then, as someone who has similarly recast the ontological situation, by mapping out his time according to the four conditions of truth?

A.B.: What you suggest about Foucault is very illuminating and seems quite right. In Foucault, besides, I have always felt, rather than understood, this liveliness or this tension for making thought contemporary with its time. You could sense this in his very character. When he died, I wrote that for me he had always been like a streetwalker: someone whom you could perfectly well imagine as a man of the archives and the libraries, but in reality he was very much the opposite, he only did all that in order to walk in the city. I think that's true. But what always struck me in him is the way in which he almost systematically took one step to the side in comparison to what I considered to be the conditioning center of philosophy. I don't know how to say this, except by suggesting that, in effect, instead of love, you have sexuality. That would be the major case. But, to be more detailed, consider for example Foucault's eighteenth century: that seems to be almost the negative of my view. If someone asks me about the eighteenth century, I would say Rousseau, about whom he says almost nothing; I would say the set of developments in mathematics up until and including Gauss; I would say the emergence of revolutionary critical theory and the putting down of religion. But he would say something else entirely. It almost seems as if, in some way, the discursive truth of a time comes at the price of stripping this time of its generic procedures. Finally, the situation for him draws out an *episteme* insofar as one first of all subtracts that which made an exception to it.

Come to think of it, as I am listening to you, that is what I would call history. It is the attempt to write the history of everything, to grasp a situation outside the belaboring of this situation by the generic procedures properly speaking. That is only normal, because history must treat of time without eternity, at least that is one way of putting it. When I reject history, or when I polemicize against history, that is what I am opposed to. I am not against the relation to our past, even less so against the presence of the past, because, on the contrary, I think that the past can convoke you with an enormous liveliness as present. But I am against this figure that apprehends situations in their time by first subtracting any hypothesis concerning the way in which this time has been treated by something other than itself, that is, ultimately, by subtracting the procedures of truth of which this time occasionally has been the site. It is in this sense that I would say that there is a certain complacency toward history on the part of Foucault. Not in the sense in which he would have opposed history to what after him you call an ontology of actuality. Thus, I have always understood that the full comprehension of the epistemes ultimately was meant for him to provide a thought of the singularity of the present. I really believe so. But the understanding of history, which is methodical, at bottom consists in deposing the singularity of a time in a subtraction of its genericity, while I would proceed the other way around, I would pick up a given time from the point of its genericity.

CONDITIONS FOR PHILOSOPHY

B.B.: Moving on to a fourth possible objection, I sometimes have the impression that there is, if not exactly a problem, then at least a complementary risk in your way of reading the actuality of our time. Let us take the condition of art or literature, for instance, your readings of Mallarmé or Beckett. As a literary critic, I get the impression that the events you study are converted, and I don't know if this is inevitable, into theoreticians of the event itself. Thus, when I read your analysis of Beckett, I find a very subtle and at the same time systematic account of the trajectory of the event itself. Likewise, with Mallarmé. In these readings, I find Mallarmé or Beckett, not so much as events in the field of the literature of their time, but rather as thinkers in their own right of the eventmentality of the event itself.

A.B.: Yes, you are right in making me this reproach, which obviously entails a rather large amount of philosophical appropriation of the condition. If one were to make the objection that I submit the condition to the conditioned, it is rather in the way you've just done so that one should proceed, instead of in terms of transcendence. Because it is evident that, first of all, the selection of examples is oriented for me by the fact that the conceptual means that are needed strategically in order to allow for philosophical compossibility push me to choose certain writers or authors in whom precisely there is already present something like an internal disposition toward the event and its consequences. Besides, I would add that the writers whom I discuss in terms of philosophy are not necessarily the ones I prefer.

If, on the other hand, I were to remain, so to speak, in my literary innocence, that is, receiving the eventmental imprint of a writer from within the question of writing itself, from within literature, then my choices would be entirely different, because it is true that the eventmental mode of existence of a writer in the very field of literature is not exactly the same as his or her existence as a conditional figure for a determinate philosophical framework. Thus, I think that literary events are indeed operative for philosophy, but when philosophy puts them as conditions for its own development, it nonetheless proceeds through operations of selection, change, or transformation. These operations are not exactly falsifications but they are, after all, displacements. The most intense subjective feeling I have about this is that there are artists, even whole artistic fields such as painting, or specific artists for whom I have a strong appreciation and who have contributed to my intimate education, if I can say so, in a decisive manner, but about whom I have never said a word in my philosophy. This is because we have to take very seriously the fact that what operates as a condition for a certain philosophical disposition is indeed the eventmental value of literature, but not at all in and of itself, and because we are not obliged in philosophy to speak about everything.

We are not in a relation to the totality; we stand rather in a relation to whatever has come, or to that which we have allowed to arrive in a position of condition. Of course, at any given moment, this condition can be thought dialectically, or interactively, as we would say today. Thus, there can be no doubt that Mallarmé, above all, but also Beckett have been instructive for me on the question of the event, but if, in return, I do justice to this instruction from within philosophy, it is evident that I will make them out to be, more so than they actually are, theoreticians of themselves—which they are, by the way, more so than others, and that is the reason why they have functioned as a condition for my philosophy. So, yes, the network of interactions is very complicated, but I don't think that, in the end, it is a transcendent subsumption, but rather a practical interaction—which, it is true, I don't perform just about anything whatsoever.

ON THE QUESTION OF CULTURE

B.B.: Still in relation to the conditions of philosophy, I would like to raise another question, which might signal a fifth and final motif in the debate. I am referring no longer to the subsumption of the conditions by philosophy, but rather to the purity of the conditions themselves and to the eventual relations between them. In *Saint Paul*, you clearly distinguish "true" art and "mere" culture, just as you oppose love and sexuality, politics and administration, truth and knowledge. Similarly, in *Conditions*, you write against the confusion between various of these conditions: "Politics itself is a-cultural, as is all thought and all truth. Comical, purely comical, is the theme of a cultural politics, as is that of political culture." I found this rather surprising, coming from someone who has been so profoundly marked by the sequence of the so-called Cultural Revolution! I am thinking of your works written under the influence of this particular sequence, leading up to the major synthesis in *Theory of the Subject*. Even if, in this last text, you write, "there only is a political subject, which explains why the subject is rare and sequential," you nonetheless offer many analyses of the other conditions as well: not only love, or science and mathematics, but also the poetry of Mallarmé. The four conditions are already fully present. Why, then, this need not only to preserve their purity but also to avoid their interaction? Furthermore, in response to your recent text on "The Age of the Poets," Lacoue-Labarthe also points out that the real problem, even in your own terms, is not so much to de-suture philosophy from poetry alone, but rather the far more complicated problem of undoing the political resuturing of the suture of philosophy and art, that is, undoing the "aestheticization of politics" already denounced by Walter Benjamin—whose general argument Lacoue-Labarthe and Nancy adopt in *The Nazi Myth*. In this context, it does seem necessary indeed to de-suture the conditions of philosophy. However, if we go back to the sequence of the Cultural Revolution, or to the events of May '68 and so much that went on in the sixties, is it not equally important to understand the peculiar articulation of art, politics, love, and science? Can we really understand this era if we separate and purify these conditions? I know that you are working on this very question, by studying the possible "networks" between various procedures of truth. And I believe that Deleuze and Guattari—in *What Is Philosophy?*—are faced with the same problem. Thus, after distinguishing art, science, and philosophy, they too end by discussing the issue of what they call the possible "interferences" between them.

A.B.: Yes, it is evident that we must conceive of a theory of the network of conditions and, thus, we must come back to the question of culture, which in *Saint Paul* had an essentially polemical function. I did not want to enter a culturalist approach for this series of questions, because then everything necessarily gets lost completely. But that does not mean that we could in effect maintain a doctrine of the absolute purity of the conditions with regard to one another.

The point is simply to know what exactly is a crossing, or a linkage, between various truth-procedures. The privileged field of exercise for this type of question, indeed, has always been that of art and politics. The attempts to do the same for science and politics have been more adventurous, even though I always found that it was extremely interesting to see, for example, if it made sense to oppose proletarian science and bourgeois science. Such attempts were extremely radical and they go back a long time. Already I am thinking of the intervention made at the trial of Lavoisier: "The Republic has no need for scientists." This is not exactly the issue of culture, but it does point to the crossover between science and politics. And then there is also the question of the expert: how the expert must first be a communist and only then an expert, or how one should be expert *and* communist. These questions in the end are fundamental. Of course, in philosophy, one always proceeds first by separation, but now I am indeed convinced that we have to study the knots or networks. By doing so, you have to realize that we enter a complex investigation about the historicity of the situation, because in fact, the linkages are the ways in which the historicity of a situation causes the active truth-procedures to follow trajectories that will no longer remain entirely independent from one another.

We need a theory of what I call the "networking" or the "tying together" of truth-procedures. Eventually, I see no reason why this could not be called "culture," provided that we completely reconstruct a formalized concept of culture. Indeed, we can consider culture to be the network of various forcings, that is, at a given moment in time, the manner in which the encyclopedic knowledge of the situation is modified under the constraints of various operations of forcing, which depend on procedures that are different from one another. There is indeed the tying together of various procedures, but on the other hand, there is also the fact that knowledge is changed under the blind or unperceived pressure of these truth-procedures. Thus, I will have to pick up this question of the binding, or knotting, both on the level of forcing and on the level of the procedures themselves. This might signal my path toward a reconstruction of the concept of culture. However, we must proceed with caution in this matter, because the history of philosophy shows that, just as the moments of separation can be radical and foundational, so too are the moments of binding always traps for the imaginary and for historicism.

Let us take the example of Kant. Nobody has divided more radically, but beginning with the *Critique of Judgment*, we realize that he is obsessed with tying together everything that previously had been divided. Besides, this is the principal interest of most contemporary Kantians: not so much the divisions, but rather questions such as the reflective judgment, the harmony of faculties, the resonance among things. I have the impression that this puts us immediately on a terrain that is infinitely less stable and more complex, but that is exactly where we have to go.

B.B.: You also asked me once about the status of cultural studies in the United States. Following the explanations you have just given, this is perhaps how we might define a valid project for cultural studies, provided that we pass through a reflection on what constitutes an event: to study the interactions among the conditions of art, politics, and so on. This is not where cultural studies is at for the moment, because they may seem to present more of a mixture instead of a rigorous articulation, mostly between art and politics, or between art, politics, and sexuality. The great model, of course, is most often Foucault, who has always been the thinker of such links.

A.B.: Of course, absolutely, that was entirely his purpose. What is more, I am convinced that in order to think through the linkages or interferences among the various conditions, I will be once more coming in close proximity to Foucault. You are right in saying that he is the great thinker of such linkages. For him, that was the principal motif. An episteme, for example, is a knot, or an interweaving.

RETURN TO THE VOID

B.B.: I have one last question, which concerns the place of the void in your latest work. In the conclusion to your *Ethics*, you distinguish the event from its doubles, or its simulacra: terror, betrayal, and disaster. I have the impression, though, that in order to be able to sustain the truth of the events, without conceding anything to the temptation of their simulacra, you have recourse to an axiomatic argument that is once more based on respect for, or recognition of, the void that would be inherent in everything that happens in the aftermath of an event. I wonder whether this does not put us back in a doctrine of lack, and ultimately, in a state-like prescription, even negatively formulated, of the being of the event, which would be tied to the permanence of a gap, or a void, which one cannot fill nor substantialize without falling into Evil. Do you foresee other perspectives to distinguish an event that is true, not to say authentic, from its doubles?

A.B.: Sure. The answer in *Ethics* is insufficient even in my own eyes. It is always possible to object to it that we are thus sent back to a kind of arch-conscience, or to some faculty of discernment between the pure void and the filled void. In the end, then, we are still in the theory according to which there is an arch-perception of Evil. I expect to respond to this question in a different way in my upcoming work. This will require some considerable detours, which in fact are caught up in the revision that I am currently undertaking of the theory of the event, on the one hand, and, on the other, of the theory of the subject. I am now coming back to a theory of the subject that arranges for a plurality of figures, as in *Theory of the Subject*, whereas in *Being and Event*, I went back in a sense to a unique figure of the subject. The quadrupolar construction (courage, anxiety, superego, and justice) in *Theory of the Subject* allowed for a broader configuration, and I am going to return to this theory of configurations in my forthcoming *Logics of Worlds*. From within this theory, I should be able to treat in a completely different way the question regarding the distinction between the event and its simulacrum.

Bibliography

WORKS BY ALAIN BADIOU

Le Concept de modèle: Introduction á une épistémologie matérialiste des mathématiques. Paris: Maspero, 1972.
Théorie de la contradiction. Paris: Maspero, 1975.
De l'Idéologie. Paris: Maspero, 1976.
Théorie du sujet. Paris: Éditions du Seuil, 1982.
Peut-on penser la politique? Paris: Seuil, 1985.
L'être et l'événement. Paris: Éditions du Seuil, 1988). *Being and Event*, trans. Oliver Feltham. London: Continuum Press, forthcoming 2005.
Manifeste pour la philosophie. Paris: Éditions du Seuil, 1989). *Manifesto for Philosophy*, trans. Norman Madarasz. Albany: State University of New York Press, 1999.
Le Nombre et les nombres. Paris: Éditions du Seuil, 1990.
Rhapsodie pour le théâtre. Paris: Le Spectateur français, 1990.
D' un désastre obscur (Droit, Etat, Politique). Paris: L'Aube, 1991.
Conditions. Paris: Éditions du Seuil, 1992.
L'Éthique: Essai sur la conscience du Mal. Paris: Hatier, 1983). *Ethics: An Essay on the Understanding of Evil*, trans. Peter Hallward. London: Verso, 2001.
Beckett: L'increvable désir. Paris: Hachette, 1995. *On Beckett*, trans. Alberto Toscano and Nina Power. London: Clinamen Press, 2004.
Gilles Deleuze: "La clameur de l'être". Paris: Hachette, 1997). *Deleuze: The Clamor of Being*, trans. Louise Burchill. Minneapolis: Minnesota University Press, 2000.
Saint Paul: La fondation de l'universalisme. Paris: PUF, 1997. *Saint Paul: The Foundation of Universalism*, trans. Ray Brassier. Stanford, CA: Stanford University Press, 2003.
Abrégé de métapolitique. Paris: Éditions du Seuil, 1998.
Court traité d'ontologie transitoire. Paris: Éditions du Seuil, 1998. *Briefings on Existence: A Transitory Ontology*, trans. Norman Madarasz. Albany: State University of New York Press, 2004.

Petit manuel d'inesthétique. Paris: Éditions du Seuil, 1998. *Handbook of Inaesthetic*, trans. Alberto Toscano. Stanford, CA: Stanford University Press, 2004.
Matrix: Machine Philosophique. Paris: Ellipses, 2003.
Circonstances, 1. Paris: Ligne et Manifeste, 2003.
Circonstances, 2. Paris: Ligne et Manifeste, 2004.
Infinite Thought: Truth and the Return to Philosophy, ed. Justin Clemens and Oliver Feltham. London: Continuum, 2004.
Alain Badiou: Theoretical Writings. London: Continuum Press, 2004.
Le siècle. Paris: Editions du Seuil, forthcoming 2005.

SHORTER WORKS BY ALAIN BADIOU

"Marque et manqué: À propos du zéro." *Cahiers pour l'analyse* 10 (1969): 150–73.
"Custos, quid noctis?" (on Lyotard's *Le différend*). Critique 450, no. 851 (1984): 63.
"Six propriétés de la vérité." *Ornicar?* 32 (1985): 39–67 and 33 (1985): 120–49.
"Dix-neuf réponses à beaucoup plus d'objections." *Cahiers du Collège International de Philosophie* 8 (1989): 247–68.
"On a Finally Objectless Subject" (1989). In *Who Comes after the Subject?* ed. Eduardo Cadava, 24–32. London: Routledge, 1991.
"L'Entretien de Bruxelles." *Les Temps Modernes* 526 (1990): 1–26.
"Gilles Deleuze, The Fold, Leibniz and the Baroque" (1990). In *Gilles Deleuze: The Theater of Philosophy*, ed. Constantin Boundas and Dorothea Olkowski, 51–69. New York: Columbia University Press, 1994.
"Le Lieux de la vérité." *Art Press spécial*, hors série no. 13 (1992): 113–18.
"L'Âge de Poètes." In *La Politique des poètes: Pourquoi des poètes en temps de détresse*, ed. Jacques Rancière, ed. Paris: Bibliothéque du Collége International de Philosophie, Rue Descartes, 1992.
"Que pense le poème?" In *L'art est-il une connaissance?* Paris: Le Monde Editions, 1993.
"Nous pouvons rédeployer la philosophie." *Le Monde*, 31 Aug. 1993, 2.
"Philosophie et poésie au point de l' innomable." *Po&sie* 64 (1993): 88–96.
"Being by Numbers." *Artforum* 33, no. 2 (1994): 84–87, 118, 123–24.
"Silence, solipsisme, sainteté: L'antiphilosophie de Wittgenstein." *BARCA! Poésie, Politique, Psychanalyse* 3 (1994): 13–53.
"Paul le Saint." *Artpress* 235 (May 1998): 53–58.
"Penser le surgissement de l'événement." *Cahiers du Cinéma*, numéro spécial (May 1998).
"Politics and Philosophy." *Angelaki* 3, no. 3 (1998): 113–33.
"Les langues de Wittgenstein." *Rue Descartes* 26 (Dec. 1999), 107–16.
"La Scène du Deux." In *De l'Amour, sous la direction de l'École de la Cause Freudienne*, 177–90. Paris: Champs Flammarion, 1999.
"Considerations sur l'état actuel du cinéma." In *L'Art du cinéma* 24 (Mar 1999): 1–16.

"Huit thèses sur l'universel." In *Universel, singulier, sujet*, ed. Jelica Sumic, 11–20. Paris: Kimé, 2000.
"Un, Multiple, Multiplicité(s)." *Multitudes* 1 (Mar. 2000): 195–211.
"La poésie en condition de philosophie." *Europe* 849–50 (Jan. 2000): 121–31.

WORKS ON ALAIN BADIOU

Aguilar, Tristan. "Badiou et la Non-Philosophie: Un parallele." In *La Non-Philosophie des contemporains*, ed. François Laruelle, 37–46. Paris: Kime, 1995.
Alliez, Eric. "Que la vérité soit." In *De l'Impossibilité de la phénoménologie: Sur la philosophie française contemporaine*, 81–87. Paris: Vrin, 1995.
———. "Badiou/Deleuze." *Futur antérieur* 43 (1998): 49–54.
———. "Badiou/Deleuze (II)." *Multitudes* 1 (2000): 192–94.
———. "Badiou: La grâce de l'universel." *Multitudes* 6 (2001): 26–34.
Barker, Jason. *Alain Badiou: A Critical Introduction*. London: Pluto, 2002.
Bensaid, Daniel. "Alain Badiou et le miracle de l'événement." In *Resistances: Essai de taupologie générale*, 143–70. Paris: Fayard, 2001.
Bosteels, Bruno. "Por una falta de política: Tests sobre la filosofía de la democracia radical." *Acontecimiento: Revista para pensar la política* 17 (1999): 63–89.
———. "Travesías del fantasma; Pequeña metapoética del '68 en México.'" *Metapolítica: Revista Trimestral de Teoría y Ciencia de la Política* 12 (1999): 733–68.
———. "Alain Badiou's Theory of the Subject, Part 1: The Re-commencement of Dialectical Materialism" *Pli (Warwick Journal of Philosophy)* 12 (2002): 200–29.
———. "Alain Badiou's Theory of the Subject, Part II." Pli (Warwick Journal of Philosophy) 13 (2002): 173-208.
———. "Vérité et forçage: Badiou avec Heidegger et Lacan." In *Badiou: Penser le multiple*, ed. Charles Ramond, 259–93. Paris: L'Harmattan, 2002.
Brassier, Ray. "Stellar Void or Cosmic Animal? Badiou and Deleuze." *Pli (Warwick Journal of Philosophy)* 10 (2000): 200–17.
Burchill, Louise. "Translator's Preface: Portraiture in Philosophy, or Shifting Perspective." In *Alain Badiou, Deleuze: The Clamor of Being*, vii–xxiii. Minneapolis: University of Minnesota Press, 1999.
Châtelet, Gilles. Rev. of Le Nombre et les nombres. In *Annuaire philosophique 1989–1990*, 117–33. Paris: Éditions du Seuil, 1991.
Clemens, Justin. "Platonic Meditations: The Work of Alain Badiou." *Pli (Warwick Journal of Philosophy)* 11 (2001): 200–29.
Clucas, Stephen. "Poem, Theorem." *Parallax* 7-A (2001): 48–65.
Critchley, Simon. "Demanding Approval: On the Ethics of Alain Badiou." *Radical Philosophy* 100 (2000): 16–27.

Desanti, Jean-Toussaint. "Quelques remarques à propos de l'ontologie intrinsèque d'Alain Badiou." *Les Temps modernes* 526 (May 1990): 61-71.
Dews, Peter. "Uncategorical Imperatives: Adorno, Badiou, and the Ethical Turn." *Radical Philosophy* 111 (Jan. 2002): 33-37.
Fink, Bruce. "Alain Badiou." In *Umbr(a)* 1 (1996): 11-12.
Gil, José. "Quatre méchantes notes sur un livre méchant." Rev. of Badiou, *Deleuze: Futur antérieur* 43 (1998): 71-84.
Gillespie, Sam. "Hegel Unsutured (An Addendum to Badiou)." *Umbr(a)* 1 (1996): 57-69.
——. "Neighborhood of Infinity: On Badiou's Deleuze: The Clamor of Being." *Umbr(a)* (2001): 91-106.
——. "To Place the Void: Badiou on Spinoza." *Angelaki* 6:3 (Dec. 2001): 63-67.
——. Rev. of Alain Badiou, Ethics. *Pli (Warwick Journal of Philosophy)* 12 (2002): 256-65.
Hallward, Peter. "Generic Sovereignty: The Philosophy of Alain Badiou." *Angelaki* 3, no. 3 (1998): 87-111.
——. "Ethics without Others: A Reply to Simon Critchley." *Radical Philosophy* 102 (July 2000): 27-31.
——. Translator's introduction to Badiou. *Ethics*, vii-li.
——. *Badiou: A Subject to Truth*. Minneapolis: University of Minnesota Press, 2003.
Hyldgaard, Kirsten. "Truth and Knowledge in Heidegger, Lacan, and Badiou." *Umbr(a)* (2001):79-90.
Ichida,Yoshihiko. "Sur quelques vides ontologiques" (on Badiou and Negri). *Multitudes* 9 (May 2002): 49-65.
Jambet, Christian. "Alain Badiou: L'être et l'événement." In *Annuaire philosophique 1987-1988*, 141-83. Paris: Éditions du Seuil, 1989.
Kouvélakis, Eustache. "La Politique dans ses limites, ou les paradoxes d'Alain Badiou." *Actuel Marx* 28 (2000): 39-54.
Lacoue-Labarthe, Philippe. Untitled discussion of *L'être et l'événement*. *Cahiers du College International de Philosophie* 8 (1989): 201-10.
——. "Poésie, philosophie, politique." In *La Politique des poètes: Pourquoi des poètes en temps de détresse?* ed. Jacques Rancière, 39-63. Paris: Albin Michel, 1992.
Laerke, Mogens. "The Voice and the Name: Spinoza in the Badioudian Critique of Deleuze." *Pli (Warwick Journal of Philosophy)* 8 (1999): 86-99.
Lecercle, Jean-Jacques. "Cantor, Lacan, Mao, Beckett, *même combat*: The Philosophy of Alain Badiou." *Radical Philosophy* 93 (Jan. 1999): 6-13.
Lyotard, Jean-François. Untitled discussion of *L'être et l' événement*. *Cahiers du College International de Philosophie* 8 (1989): 227-46.
Madarasz, Norman. Translator's introduction to *Manifesto for Philosophy*, by Alain Badiou. Albany: State University of New York Press, 1999.

Ophir, Adi, and Ariella Azoulay, "The Contraction of Being: Deleuze after Badiou." *Umbr(a)* (2001): 107-20.
Pesson, Rene. Rev. of *Manifesto pour la philosophie*. In *Annuaire philosophique 1988-1989*, 243-51. Paris: Éditions du Seuil, 1989.
Ramond, Charles, ed. *Alain Badiou: Penser le multiple*. Paris: L'Harmattan, 2002.
Rancière, Jacques. Untitled discussion of *L'être et l'événement*. *Cahiers du College International de Philosophie* 8 (1989): 211-26.
Riera, Gabriel. "Don du Poème: Alain Badiou after the 'Age of Poets,'" *(a): The Journal of Culture and the Unconscious* 1 (Mar./Apr. 2000): 10-33.
Simont, Juliette. "Le Pur et l'impur (sur deux questions de l'histoire de la philosophie dans *L'être et l'événement*)." *Les Temps modernes* 526 (May 1990): 27-60.
Terray, Emmanuel. "La Politique dans *L'être et l'événement*." *Les Temps modernes* 526 (May 1990): 72-78.
Toscano, Alberto. "To Have Done with the End of Philosophy" (Rev. of Badiou's *Manifesto* and *Deleuze*). *Pli (Warwick Journal of Phihsophy)* 9 (2000): 220-39.
Toscano, Alberto, and Ray Brassier, eds. Introduction to *Badiou: Theoretical Writings*. London: Continuum, 2004.
Verstraeten, Pierre. "Philosophies de l'événement: Badiou et quelques autres." *Les Temps modernes* 529-30 (Aug. 1990): 241-94.
Villani, Arnaud. "La Metaphysique de Deleuze. *Futur antérieur* 43 (1998): 55-70.
Wahl, François. "Le Soustractif." Preface to *Conditions*, by Alain Badiou, 9-54. Paris: Éditions du Seuil, 1992.
i ek, Slavoj. "The Politics of Truth, or, Alain Badiou as a Reader of St. Paul." In *The Ticklish Subject*, 127-70. London: Verso, 1999.
——. "Political Subjectivization and its Vicissitudes." In *The Ticklish Subject*, 171-43. London: Verso, 1999.

Contributors

Bruno Bosteels is assistant professor of Spanish at Cornell University. He is currently preparing a book manuscript, *Badiou and Politics*, and is the author of several articles on modern Latin American literature and culture, contemporary European philosophy, and modern political theory.

Ray Brassier is a graduate student in the Philosophy Department at Warwick University. He is the translator of *Saint Paul: The Foundation of Universalism* (Stanford University Press, 2003) and *Theoretical Writings* (Continuum, 2004).

Joan Copjec is professor of English at State University of New York–Buffalo and director of the Center for the Study of Psychoanalysis and Culture. Her work includes *Shades of Noir: A Reader* (Verso, 2003), *Imagine There's No Woman: Ethics and Sublimation* (Cambridge University Press, 2002), *Giving Grounds: The Politics of Propinquity* (Verso, 1999), *Read My Desire: Lacan against the Historicist* (MIT Press, 1994), and *Radical Evil* (Verso, 1993). She was the editor of *Supposing the Subject* (Verso, 1994), *Shades of Noir* (Verso, 1993), and *Lacan's Television* (Norton, 1990).

Simon Critchley is professor of philosophy at the New School, and directeur de programme at the Collège International de Philosophie, Paris. He is the author of *Ethics-Politics-Subjectivity: Essays on Derrida, Levinas and Contemporary French Thought* (Verso, 1999), *Very Little ... Almost Nothing: Death, Philosophy, Literature* (Routledge, 1997), and *The Ethics of Deconstruction* (Blackwell, 1992). He coedited *Re-reading Levinas, Deconstructive Subjectivities* (State University of New York Press, 1996), *Emmanuel Levinas: Basical Philosophical Writings* (Indiana University Press, 1996), *A Companion to Continental Philosophy* (Blackwell, 1999) and *On Humour* (Routledge, 2002).

Miguel de Beistegui is lecturer in philosophy at the University of Warwick. He is the author of *Truth and Genesis: Philosophy as Differential Ontology* (Indiana University Press, 2004), *Being Asunder: Philosophy as Differential Ontology* (Indiana University Press, 2003), *Thinking with Heidegger: Dystopias II* (Indiana Unviersity Press, 2002), and *Heidegger and the Political: Dystopias* (Routledge, 1998). He coedited *Philosophy and Tragedy* (Routledge, 2000).

Marilyn Gaddis Rose is distinguished service professor of comparative literature at State University of New York–Binghamton and director of the Center for Research in Translation. Her selected publications include *Translation and Literary Criticism* (St. Jerome Publishing, 1997) and *Katharine Tynan* (Bucknell University Press, 1974). Her translations include *Volupte: The Sensual Man* by Sainte-Beuve (State University of New York Press, 1995), *Adrienne Mesurat* by Julian Green (Holmes & Meier, 1991), *Lui: A View of Him* by Louise Colet (University of Georgia, 1986), *Axel* by Villiers de l'Isle-Adam (Dolmen, 1970; Soho, 1986 reissue), and *Eve of the Future Eden* by Villiers de l'Isle-Adam (Coronado Press, 1981). She has also published articles on W. B. Yeats and Jack B. Yeats, Samuel Beckett, Julian Green, and others and is the founding editor of the ATA Series and Translation Perspectives. She is editor of the SUNY series, Women Writers in Translation.

Juliet Flower MacCannell is emeritus professor of English and comparative literature at the University of California-Irvine. She has published *An Hysteric's Guide for the Future Female Subject* (University of Minnesota Press, 2000), *The Regime of the Brother: After the Patriarchy* (Routledge, 1991), *Figuring Lacan: Criticism and the Cultural Unconscious* (Routledge and University of Nebraska, 1986), *The Other Perpspective on Gender and Culture* (Columbia University Press, 1990), and *The Time of the Sign: A Semiotic Interpretation of Modern Culture* (Indiana University Press, 1982). She has also authored on subjects ranging from Rousseau to racism, from comparative literature to postcolonial theory, violence, and the psychoanalytic structure of love and perversion. She is the director of the California Psychoanalytic Circle and editor of *(a) journal of culture and the unconscious*.

Pierre Macherey is professor of philosophy at the Université de Lille. He has published *Histoires de dinosaure: faire de la philosophie 1965–1997* (PUF, 1999), *Introduction à l'éthique de Spinoza: Première partie, La nature des choses* (PUF, 1995), *In a Materialist Way: Selected Essays* (Verso, 1998), *A quoi pense la littérature?: exercices de philosophie littéraire* (PUF, 1990; translated as *The Object of Literature* [Cambridge University Press, 1995]), *Avec Spinoza: études sur la doctrine et l'histoire du spinozisme* (PUF, 1992), *Comte: La philosophie et les sciences* (PUF, 1989), *Hegel ou Spinoza* (Maspero, 1979), and *Pour une théorie de la production littéraire* (Maspero, 1966; translated as *A Theory of Literary Production* [Routledge, 1978]). He coedited *Hegel et la société* (PUF, 1984), and *L'Anomalie sauvage: puissance et pouvoir chez Spinoza* (PUF, 1982).

Norman Madarasz is docteur de philosophie from the Université de Paris. He is editor and translator of Alain Badiou's *Briefings on Existences: A Transitory Ontology* (State University of New York Press, 2004) and his *Manifesto for Philosophy* (State University of New York Press, 1999). His research has dealt with the idea of fabric and networks, and contemporary French philosophy broadly understood, as well as with the philosophies of Apel, Habermas, and Searle. Employed as a communications consultant in Rio de Janeiro, he writes political and economic analysis on North–South relations in the Americas for *Counterpunch* and other publications

Tracy McNulty is assistant professor of romance studies at Cornell University. She has published essays on Jacques Lacan and on the Hebrew Bible and is completing a book on hospitality, *The Hostess, My Neighbor*. She is editing and translating a collection of Pierre Klossowski's texts, with Eleanor Kaufman, for the University of Minnesota Press.

Jean-Michel Rabaté is professor of English at the University of Pennsylvania. He has published *Language, Sexuality and Ideology in the Cantos* (State University of New York Press, 1986), *James Joyce: Authorized Reader* (Johns Hopkins University Press, 1991), *Joyce upon the Void* (Macmillan, 1991), *Beckett avant Beckett* (Presses de la ENS, 1984), *La beauté amère* (PUF, 1986), *Ghosts of Modernity* (University Press of Florida, 1996), *Joyce and the Politics of Egoism* (Cambridge University Press, 2001), *Jacques Lacan and Literature* (Palgrave, 2001), and *The Future of Theory* (Blackwell, 2002). He has also edited several collections of essays including *Writing the Image after Roland Barthes* (University of Pennsylvania Press, 1997), *L'éthique du don: Jacques Derrida et la pensée du don* (Métalié, 1992), *Jacques Lacan in America* (Other Press, 2000), and *The Cambridge Companion to Jacques Lacan* (Cambridge Universitiy Press, 2003).

Gabriel Riera is assistant professor of comparative literature at Princeton University. He has published essays on twentieth-century literature, philosophy and psychoanalysis, Heidegger, and Lacan. He is the author of *Intrigues of the Other: Ethics and Literary Writing in Levinas and Blanchot* and *Littoral of the Letter and Desire* (*Affects and Percepts in Juan José Saer*).

Index

actual
  versus virtual, 54-56
  See also Deleuze, Gilles
Adorno, Theodor, 100
Althusser, Louis, 1, 2, 242, 249-50
  and interpellation, 12
Anglo-saxon philosophy, 25
Antigone, 119-20, 231
Aristotle, 24, 32-33, 62, 70
art, 25, 61-62
  See also conditions of philosophy
atomism, atoms, 250
  See also void
axioms of set theory, 10
  extensionality, 36
  foundation, 37, 40
  infinity, 3
  void (empty set axiom), 3, 36

Balibar, Étienne, 1
Barthes, Roland, 107
Being, 31-35
  and difference, 56
  and non-being, 3
  and presentation, 7-8
  as being, 33
  as pure multiplicity, 45, 49, 3, 224
  univocity of, 34, 53
  See also ontology
belonging, 10, 62
  See also inclusion; set theory

Beckett, Samuel, 83, 85-111, 224, 230-34, 257-58
  and *Watt* 91-107
Bell, Joseph, 28, 37, 42 n4-5, n11, n13, n15-18, n22.
Benjamin, Walter, 140, 177 n10, 258
Bersani, Leo, 128-29
Blanchot, Maurice, 73-74, 82
Brecht, Bertold, 62
Buber, Martin, 203

Canguilhem, George, 2, 255
Cantor, Georg, 27, 46, 68
  See also continuum hypothesis
category theory, 26-31
  and object and relation, 29
Cavaillès, Jean, 2
Célan, Paul, 70, 83
Char, René, 73
Christ's Resurrection, 4, 225
Cohen, Paul, 41
Communist Party, 243
Communist Manifesto, 65
compossibility, 2, 69, 82-83
conditions of philosophy, 2, 13, 257-58
continuum hypothesis (CH), 41
  See also Cantor, Georg; one
cultural relativism, 2
Cultural Revolution (in China), 243
culture, 258-60

David-Ménard, Monique, 104
decision, 7-8, 33, 41, 226-28
   See also intervention
deconstruction, 5
Déguy, Michel, 73
Deleuze, Gilles, 28, 50-51, 53-58, 65, 106, 253
   Difference and Repetition, 58n2
   Logic of Sense, 58n3
   What is Philosophy?, 254, 258
Derrida, Jacques, 65, 163, 228
Desanti, Jean-Toussaint, 13-14, 27, 35, 37, 42n3, n12
Déscartes, René, 1, 2
Diderot, Denis, 159, 171
difference, 48, 56-57
   See also ontological difference, 49
Duras, Margarite, 171

end of philosophy, 4-7, 64-68, 70, 85n9, 239-41
episteme, 14, 15
   See also Althusser, Louis; Foucault, Michel
epistemology, 2
eternal return
   and Deleuze, 9
   and Heidegger, 8-9
ethics, 130-48, 168nl, 215-35
   and event, 3
   and experience, 215
   and fidelity, 229
   and the poem, 79-84
   and truth, 223-24
   Kant's conception, 99-103, 222
   of alterity, 159-60
   Sade's conception, 99, 103-7
   See also psychoanalysis and ethics
event, 2, 3, 8-11, 64, 149, 225-26, 246-47
   and history, 152-53, 255-56
   and its site, 11
   and self-referentiality, 253
   and truth, 4
   as paradoxical supplement, 91-94, 249
   as what subtracts itself from being, 4, 10, 48

   Deleuze's definition of, 9, 11, 48
   Heidegger's definition of, 48
   Maldiney's definition of, 9
   Romano's definition of, 9
   naming of, 4, 10-11
   randomness of, 50, 252
   undecidability of, 6
   See also Beckett, Samuel
excess, 4

fidelity, 3-4, 12, 229
finitude, 83-84
forcing, 3, 252
   of knowledge
   See also truth
Foucault, Michel, 125, 255-56
Frege, Gottlob, 1, 13, 30, 65
French Révolution of 1789, 4, 8, 226
Freud, Sigmund, 119, 124-25
   and *Group Psychology*, 120-22, 133-34
   and the "Rat Man," 98, 148-49
   and *Moses and Monotheism*, 199-200
   and repression, 125-27, 130-31
   and "Three Essays," 128
   and the unconscious, 144, 148, 151-53

Generic(ity), 2, 13, 252
Good, 230
Gramsci, Antonio, 227

Hegel, G. W. F., 62, 110, 120, 234 n2, 245, 254
hegemony, 226-28
Heidegger, Martin, 45-47, 50-52, 62, 65, 67, 140, 217, 225
Henrich, Dieter, 215, 216, 217, 234 n1
Hölderlin, Friedrich, 51-52, 231
Hyppolite, Jean, 2

inclusion, 10, 62
   See also inclusion; set theory
inesthetics, 61-85, 109
   as different from aesthetics, 61-64
   as different for Heidegger's ontology of art, 62

infinite, the, 3, 31-35
  and the appearing
  and set theory, 32
intervention, 12
  See also decision

Jambet, Christian, 247
James, Henry, 128, 171
James, William, 150
Joyce, James, 123

Kafka, Franz, 93-94
Kant, Immanuel, 32, 100-1, 130, 132-33, 216, 260
Klossowski, Pierre, 97, 103-4
knowledge
  as language of the situation, 3-4
  See also language; opinions; psychoanalysis

Lacan, Jacques, 2, 62, 96, 106, 119
  and death drive, 154-55
  and ethics, 96, 119-20, 156-57, 219-20, 229
  and feminine sexuality, 120-21, 123
  and *jouissance*, 103-7, 206-7
  and the letter, 146-47
  and love, 124, 131
  and *objet petit a*, 142-43, 175, 202-3
  and phallic function, 175, 193, 205
  and the Real, 153
  and sexual relation, 160
  and *suppléance*, 123, 170
  and the Thing, 156
  and truth, 142
  and woman, 160-62, 206
  See also psychoanalysis
Laclau, Ernesto, 227, 244
Lacoue-Labarthe, Philippe, 83, 85n11, 258
language, 24
  See also knowledge; opinions
Lautmann, Albert, 2
law
  moral law, 104
  and desire, 104

and Judaism, 195-96, 203
  and limits, 170-75, 202
  See also Rousseau, Jean-Jacques
Lawvere, W., 40, 43 n20
Lazarus, Sylvain, 255
Leibniz, Gottfried Wilhelm, 69, 89-94
Leiris, Michel, 111
Leninism, 242
Levinas, Emmanuel, 160, 163-64, 181 n51, 208, 218-19, 223
linguistic turn, 6-7, 51
love, 119, 160, 167-76
  and declaration of, 192
  and Freud, 120-22
  and Badiou's conception, 168-69, 186-89
  and literature, 170
  feminine love, 185-210
  See also conditions of philosophy; psychoanalysis
Lucretius, 1, 38, 250
Luther, Martin, 30
Lyotard, Jean-François, 7

MacCanell, Juliet, 134 n5, 135 n13, 193, 202, 203, 204, 206, 207, 208
Macherey, Pierre, 1, 3
McLarty, 37, 39, 42n7, 16
Mallarmé, Stéphane, 2, 82-83, 109-15, 257
Mao Tse Tung, 244
Maoism, 19n1, 182 n62, 241, 243-46
Marquis, J-P, 39, 42 n8, 43 n19
Marx, Karl, 240
Marxism, 1, 65, 222, 241
mathematics
  and logics, 1, 37-38
  and philosophy, 37-42
  as ontology, 7-8, 47
  as science of being qua being, 24
matheme(s), 64, 66, 244
  and transmission, 245-46
May 1968, 222, 237, 248
militancy, 64-65, 234
metaphysics 24,
  and Aristotle, 24
  and Heidegger's fundamental critique, 24

and overcoming, 45
and Romantic conceptions, 24
multiple
   and belonging and inclusion, 3
   and counting as one, 27
multiplicity, 3

Nancy, Jean-Luc, 19 n2, 239, 258
Nazism, 96, 100, 176n5
New philosophers, 5, 163, 222, 238
Nietzsche, Friedrich, 77, 201
numbers, 25, 48–49

October Revolution, 4
one, the
   "is not," 5–7, 27
   See also multiple; Plato
ontology, 3, 24
   as mathematics, 24, 32
   as transitory, 26
   See also Heidegger, Martin
ontological difference, 49, 58
opinions, 183 n69
   See also language; knowledge

Parmenides, 6
   See Plato
Pasolini, Pier Paolo, 198, 204
Peano, Giuseppe, 25, 42n1
Pessoa, Fernando, 83
philosophy, 69–70
   and its possibility, 68
   See also conditions of philosophy; suture
Picasso, Pablo 209
Plato, 32, 46, 62, 70, 76
   and return to, 6–7, 67–68
   and simulacrum, 32
   and simulacrum in Deleuze, 28
Platonism, 32, 34–35, 45–46
   and overturning of, 45–46
poem, 6, 52–53, 67, 71, 110–15
   and Heidegger's conception, 73–75
   and language, 81
   and naming of the event, 82
   and philosophical use, 72, 76
   and suture, 68–70

poets, age of, 6–7, 69, 71, 79
   and the withdrawal of God, 6, 52, 83
   See also conditions of philosophy
politics, 162–67
   See also conditions of philosophy
postmodernism, 4, 75
post-marxism, 2, 241
psychoanalysis, 1
   and Badiou, 143–47, 157–58
   See also Freud, Sigmund; Lacan, Jacques

Rancière, Jacques, 1, 26, 165–66
reduction 23–24
relation(s), 34–36, 160, 163
   See also axioms of set theory; ontology; set theory
religion, 52
   and death of God, 52
rhetoric, 64–67, 76–78
   and metaphor, 79–80
romanticism, 63
Rousseau, Jean-Jacques, 77, 161, 168, 171
Russell, Bertrand, 30

sacrifice, 159
Sade, 94–97, 100–1, 103, 156, 202, 210 n14
Saint Paul, 12, 185–86, 194–98, 220–21
   and the law, 201
same, the 57
   See also difference
Sarah, 208–10
Sartre, Jean-Paul, 1, 132, 242
set(s), 29
   and set theory, 3, 25, 26
   and philosophy of mathematics, 26
   See also axioms of set theory
Shaw, George Bernard, 121
singularity, 223
   of humanity, 185
site, 250–51
   See also event
situation, 3, 8, 252
   and state of a, 3, 8
   and the new of a, 252–53
   See also counting as one; set theory

socialism, 164
Sollers, Philippe, 107
Sophists, 5, 65-67
Spinoza, Baruch, 34
Stendhal, 161, 168, 171
structuralism, 1
subject, 158-59, 162, 248
  and Deleuze's conception of, 12
  and process of subjectivization, 4, 12
  See also fidelity
Surrealism, 65
suture, 5, 13, 68
  See also poem

time, 3
topology, 140-41, 142-50, 173-74
topos, 38, 40-41
truth, 1, 2, 138-41, 252
  and conditions of philosophy, 77-78
  and forcing of knowledge, 4, 252
Two, the
  as amorous encounter, 167-76, 188
  versus the One, 189

universal, 186
  against particularism(s), 205
  and the position "woman," 186
void, 3, 147, 151, 247, 260-61
  and sexual relation, 170
  as proper name of being, 27
  See also axioms of set theory; set theory
von Hofmannsthal, Hugo 99
von Neumann's formalization, 27

Watt, James, 101
Wittgenstein, Ludwig, 7, 13, 25, 67, 141

Zermelo, Ernst, and Fraenkel, Abraham, 27
Zermelo-Fraenkel Axiom of Choice (ZF), 27, 30, 39
i ek, Slavoj, 161, 251
Zola, Emile, 65

www.ingramcontent.com/pod-product-compliance
Lightning Source LLC
Chambersburg PA
CBHW020641230426
43665CB00008B/271